Looking Out/Looking In

Looking Out/Looking In
INTERPERSONAL COMMUNICATION

Fifth Edition

Ronald B. Adler
Santa Barbara City College

Neil Towne
Grossmont College

Holt, Rinehart and Winston
New York   Chicago   San Francisco   Philadelphia   Montreal   Toronto
London   Sydney   Tokyo   Mexico City   Rio de Janeiro   Madrid

Cover: Door photographs selected from a collection taken for "Door Posters of Famous Cities," published and distributed by Door Center Publishing, Skillman, NJ 08558.

Library of Congress Cataloging-in-Publication Data

Adler, Ronald B. (Ronald Brian), date.
  Looking out/looking in.
  Includes bibliographies and index.
  1. Interpersonal communication. I. Towne, Neil,
date. II. Title.
BF637.C45A34   1987   158′.2   86-14855

ISBN 0-03-007693-5

CBS COLLEGE PUBLISHING
Holt, Rinehart and Winston
The Dryden Press
Saunders College Publishing

Credits

ii *"Peanuts"* by Charles Schulz. © 1970 United Media. Used by permission.

Chapter 1

5 "The Silencing" Copyright 1973, by Newsweek, Inc. All Rights Reserved. Reprinted by Permission. **7** From *Encounters with Others* by Don E. Hamachek. Copyright © 1982 by CBS College Publishing. Reprinted by permission of Holt, Rinehart and Winston. CBS College Publishing. **8** "Talk for Sale" Copyright 1973, by Newsweek Inc. All Rights Reserved. Reprinted by Permission. **10** "Notice Me" from *The Voice of the Hive* by Ric Masten. Reprinted by permission of Publisher, Sunflower Ink, Palo Colorado Road, Carmel, CA 93923. **23** Graphic: "Stages in Learning Communication Skills" from *Student Workbook: Increasing Awareness and Communication Skills* by Daniel Wackman, Sherod Miller, Elam Nunnally. (1976) Inter-personal Communication Programs, 300 Clifton Ave., Minneapolis, MN 55403.

Chapter 2

29—30 From *Person to Person* by Barry Stevens. © 1967 Real People Press. Used by Permission. **32** "Ziggy" by Tom Wilson. Copyright 1973, Universal Press Syndicate. Reprinted by Permission. All Rights Reserved. **33** Drawing by Chon Day. Copyright © 1971 Saturday Review Magazine Co. Used by permission of Chon Day. **34** Drawing by Jules Feiffer. Copyright © 1977, Universal Press Syndicate. Reprinted with Permission. All Rights Reserved. **39** "Premier Artiste" by Lenni Shender Goldstein. Used with permission of poet. **41—42** "Cipher in the Snow" by Jean Mizer from *Today's Education,* November 1964. Used by permission of Jean Todhunter Mizer and *Today's Education.* **45** "Love and the Cabbie" by Art Buchwald. Reprinted by permission of the author and the Los Angeles Times Syndicate. **46** "Miss Peach" by Mell Lazarus. Used by permission of Mell Lazarus and News America Syndicate. **48** From *The Psychology of Romantic Love* by Nathaniel Branden. By permission of Bantam Books, Inc. Copyright © 1980 by Nathaniel Branden, Ph.D. All rights reserved. **51** Poetry by Leonard Nimoy. Reprinted by permission of International Creative Management, Inc. Copyright © 1978 by Leonard Nimoy. **52** "Broom-Hilda" by Russell Myers. Reprinted by permission: Tribune Media Services. **55** Column by Ellen Goodman. Copyright © 1977 The Boston Globe Newspaper Company. Reprinted with permission. **57** From *Crazy Talk, Stupid Talk* by Neil Postman. Copyright © 1976 Dell Publishing Co., Inc. Used by permission. **63** From *The Velveteen Rabbit* by Margery Williams. Reprinted courtesy of Doubleday & Company.

(Credits continue following Index.)

The field of Interpersonal communication is growing up, and *Looking Out/ Looking In* has grown with it. A side-by-side comparison of this edition with the 1975 first edition reveals the distance the discipline has covered. Thanks to the efforts of scores of researchers in communication and other social sciences, students have a better chance than ever of communicating effectively with the important people in their lives.

Despite these changes, *Looking Out/Looking In* still contains the features that students and professors have appreciated over the years: the assumption that awareness of one's present ways of communicating and exposure to alternatives can lead to change; the strong emphasis on experiential learning through exercises and other activities; the presentation of ideas through a wide variety of readings, quotations, cartoons, photos, and poetry; and a writing style that strives to explain ideas simply without being simplistic.

Notwithstanding these familiar features, this fifth edition of *Looking Out/ Looking In* contains some important changes. Most noticeably, the book is now divided into three sections: "Looking In" focuses on the internal, mostly cognitive activities that shape our communication. "Looking Out" examines the linguistic and nonverbal elements of the communication process, as well as the important topic of listening. "Looking at Relationships" discusses the dynamics of relational communication.

Since the academic calendar has not expanded to accommodate the changes in the field, the overall length of *Looking Out/Looking In* has remained roughly the same. Nonetheless, a new Chapter Nine, "Improving Interpersonal Relationships," pulls together the material on communication climate and defensiveness that was previously sprinkled throughout the book. This chapter adds to the book's clarity without increasing its length.

Every chapter has been revised to improve understanding and broaden the book's scope. For example, Chapter One now contains information on communication competence in answer to the question "What Makes an Effective Communicator?" Chapter Five offers new material on powerful and powerless language. Chapter Eight discusses the dimensions of interpersonal relationships and relational stages; it also provides a more complete and less ideological look at the subject of self-disclosure. Chapter Ten contains an expanded section on assertive communication, including material on the clear message format that formerly resided in the first chapter. This new location shows better how clear messages use the principles discussed throughout the book.

All these changes shouldn't dismay instructors who have used *Looking Out/ Looking In* in the past. As always, after Chapter One the material can be covered in any order. In addition, a revised *Instructor's Manual* offers suggestions on schedules, assignments, and student evaluation. A new *Activities Manual* provides additional activities and exercises to broaden understanding and sharpen communication skills, and a *Computerized Test Bank* containing the same test items to be found in the *Instructor's Manual* is now available for use with the fifth edition.

The changes that have made *Looking Out/Looking In* a better book haven't occurred in a vacuum. We owe a large debt to the following reviewers whose

suggestions were so helpful: David E. Axon, Johnson Community College; Ruth
F. Eisenberg, Pace University; Vernon Gantt, Murray State University; M. Nicholas
Gilroy, Bronx Community College; Virginia Katz, University of Minnesota at
Duluth; Nancy Lampen, Monroe Community College; Jim Mammarella, San
Antonio College; Gerard F. McDade, Community College of Philadelphia; Patsy
Meisel, Mankato State University; Ramona Parrish, Virginia Western Community
College; Wesley L. Robertson, Jefferson College; and Katherine M. Stannard,
Framingham State College.

We also owe a great deal to the team of professionals at Holt, Rinehart and
Winston who have been models of both talent and good communication: Lucy
Rosendahl, Lester A. Sheinis, Nancy Myers, and Louis Scardino. And as always,
we reserve a special thank-you for our designer, Janet Bollow, whose talents
have contributed so much to the effectiveness of *Looking Out/Looking In*.

RBA
NT

Because this is a book about interpersonal communication, it seems important to begin by introducing ourselves, the authors. The word *we* you'll be reading in the following pages isn't just an editorial device: It refers to us, Ron Adler and Neil Towne. We both live in California, where we spend our professional lives teaching interpersonal communication. We love our work: It helps us grow, helps our students get along better, and it's fun. In fact, we often think we get as many rewards from our students as they do from us. Although we share many things in common, there are differences, too.

Ron, the younger by fifteen years, lives in Santa Barbara with his wife, Sherri, and their two daughters, Robin and Rebecca, aged thirteen and ten. Ron enjoys being a husband and a father most of the time, although he longs for more quiet moments than he can find.

Ron enjoys trees, views, old houses, traveling, food, and the company of good friends. Running and cycling help keep his body and mind healthy. Sherri describes Ron as a family man who is organized, conscientious, ambitious, and a worrier. In addition to helping to create *Looking Out/Looking In,* Ron has written three other books by himself and has coauthored three more. Besides teaching and writing, Ron helps professionals and businesspeople improve their communication.

Neil has trouble believing he has taught more than a quarter century, has lived more than twice that long, and still has all his hair (gray though it may be). Despite his twenty-six years of teaching, Neil has no intention of retiring. He enjoys his work as much as ever. Recently Neil was honored by his colleagues for "commitment to excellence in the classroom, campus, and community." Knowing that his peers appreciate him as a teacher and as a person is very meaningful to Neil.

Neil's other great love is his family. Bobbi, his wife, is his best friend and number one fan. Presently she divides her time between homemaking and counseling individuals, couples, families, and school children with emotional problems. Bobbi and Neil have developed a communication course for couples, which they teach at a local college.

The Towne family includes four sons, two daughters, a son-in-law, and most recently Bobbi's mentally retarded sister, Aunt Janet. Along with the regular household members, a guest or two is usually at home with the Townes: Petra, an AFS exchange student from West Germany, children home for the weekends, visiting relatives, and friends. Life is usually busy at home: softball, applying for college, guitar playing, keeping the Baja Bug running, homework, exercising, sharing laughs and hurts, choir practice, feeding friends, remodeling the kitchen, and leaving Dad alone to struggle at his book-writing chores.

With growing families, new students and projects each semester, Ron and Neil are never without the chance to practice interpersonal skills. The challenges are great, and so are the rewards. At this time in their lives, neither Ron nor Neil would have it any other way.

Our attempt to write in a personal way is deliberate. We think of our relationship with you as a meeting of real individuals and not as a treatise by faceless authors addressed to nameless readers. We assume that in many ways,

Right now I can only hypnotize you, persuade you, make you believe that I'm right. You don't know. I'm just preaching something. You wouldn't learn from my words. Learning is discovery. There is no other means of effective learning. You can tell the child a thousand times, "The stove is hot." It doesn't help. The child has to discover it for himself. And I hope I can assist you in learning, in discovering something about yourself.

Fritz Perls,
Gestalt Therapy Verbatim

you are like the people we have taught in our own classes. So as you read on, realize we are thinking of you.

Our goal in creating *Looking Out/Looking In* is to provide a tool that will help you improve your ability to communicate with the important people in your life. In other words, our emphasis is practical rather than theoretical. Since this may be the only time you study communication in a concentrated way, we believe strongly that the book needs to do more than "talk about" the subject. We hope it will actually help you find more satisfying ways to behave. If at the end of the course you have learned only to list the rules for good listening, identify defensive behaviors, or recite definitions of communication, we'll have failed to meet our goal. The kind of results we are aiming for include relationships that run more smoothly, friendships that become more meaningful, and a newfound ability to speak up effectively when you want to.

To promote these goals, we have filled *Looking Out/Looking In* with exercises and other activities, which you'll find printed in colored type. These activities fall into two categories. Some are designed to help you recognize more clearly your present styles of communicating, so that you can explore just how well they work for you. A second type of activity is aimed at showing you alternatives to those already existing styles. These are, alternatives that research and experience have showed work well for most people, and we are convinced they will work for you . . . if you are willing to put in the energy to learn them.

Contents

Part Three   Looking at Relationships   265

Chapter Eight

Chapter Nine

Chapter Ten

Looking Out/Looking In

Part One

Looking In

Chapter One

As his name was called, James J. Pelosi, the 452nd West Point cadet of the class of '73, drew in his breath and went to the podium—steeling himself for one last moment of humiliation. The slender, bespectacled young man accepted his diploma, then turned to face the rows of starched white hats and—so he expected—a chorus of boos. Instead, there was only silence. But when he returned to his classmates, the newly fledged lieutenant was treated to something new—a round of handshakes. "It was just as if I were a person again," he said. Thus ended one of the strangest and most brutal episodes in the long history of the corps.

Nineteen months ago, the Long Island cadet was hauled up before the West Point Honor Committee and charged with cheating on an engineering exam. In spite of conflicting testimony given at his trial and his own determined plea of innocence, the third-year cadet, one of the most respected in his company and himself a candidate for the Honor Committee, was convicted. Pelosi's case was thrown out by the Academy superintendent after his military lawyer proved there had been undue influence over the proceeding by the Honor Committee adviser, but that wasn't the end of it. The Academy honor code reserves a special fate for those thought by the majority to be guilty even when there is insufficient evidence to convict. It is called Silencing.

Pelosi's fellow cadets voted to support the Honor Committee sentence. And so for most of his third and all of his fourth year at West Point, Pelosi was ostracized. He was transferred by the Academy to what one friend called a "straight-strict" company—"one of the toughest in the corps." He ate alone each day at a table for ten; he lived by himself in a room meant for two or three; he endured insult and occasional brickbats tossed in his direction; he saw his mail mutilated and his locker vandalized. And hardly anyone, even a close friend who wept when he heard the Silencing decision, would talk to him in public. Under those conditions, most cadets resign. But even though he lost 26 pounds, Pelosi hung tough. "When you're right," he said later, "you have to prove yourself . . . I told myself I didn't care."

And in the end, James Pelosi survived—one of only a handful of Academy cadets in history to graduate after Silencing. He may even be the last, since six other cadets are now in the process of suing the Academy over its honor system. Now that he is out, and even though he faces the possibility of Silencing by some West Point graduates for the rest of his life if he stays in the Army, Lieutenant Pelosi is almost dispassionate in his criticism of the Academy and his fellow cadets. About as far as he will go is to say that "Silencing should be abolished. It . . . says cadets are above the law. This attitude of superiority bothers me." As for his own state of mind during the ordeal, he told NEWSWEEK's Deborah Beers last week: "I've taken a psychology course and I know what isolation does to animals. No one at the Academy asks how it affects a person. Doesn't that seem strange?"

Newsweek Magazine

Perhaps you played this game as a child. The group chooses a victim—either as punishment for committing a real or imagined offense, or just for "fun." Then for a period of time, that victim is given the silent treatment. No one speaks to him or her, and no one responds to anything the victim says or does.

If you were the subject of this silent treatment, you probably experienced a range of emotions. At first you might have felt—or at least acted—indifferent. "Who cares?" you might have boasted. "I don't need you!" But after a while the strain of being treated as a nonperson probably began to grow. If the game went on long enough, it's likely you found yourself either retreating into a state of depression or lashing out with hostility: partly to show your anger and partly to get a response from the others.

Just like young schoolchildren, the West Point cadets described in "The Silencing" understood the importance of communication. They knew that the company of others is one of the most basic human needs and that lack of contact is among the cruelest punishments a person can suffer. Besides being emotionally painful, the lack of contact and companionship is so serious that it can affect life itself.

Research demonstrating the importance of communication has existed for centuries. Fredrick II, emperor of Germany from 1196 to 1250, was probably the first social scientist to prove the point systematically. A medieval historian described one of his significant, if inhumane, experiments:

> . . . He bade foster mothers and nurses to suckle the children, to bathe and wash them, but in no way to prattle with them, for he wanted to learn whether they would speak the Hebrew language, which was the oldest, or Greek, or Latin, or Arabic, or perhaps the language of their parents, of whom they had been born. But he labored in vain because all the children died. For they could not live without the petting and joyful faces and loving words of their foster mothers.[1]

Fortunately, contemporary researchers have found less dramatic ways to illustrate the importance of communication. In one study of isolation, subjects were paid to remain alone in a locked room. Of the five subjects, one lasted for eight days. Three held out for two days, one commenting, "Never again." The fifth subject lasted only two hours.[2]

The need for contact and companionship is just as strong outside the laboratory, as individuals who have led solitary lives by choice or necessity have discovered. W. Carl Jackson, an adventurer who sailed across the Atlantic Ocean alone in fifty-one days summarized the feelings common to most loners:

> I found the loneliness of the second month almost excruciating. I always thought of myself as self-sufficient, but I found life without people had no meaning. I had a definite need for somebody to talk to, someone real, alive, and breathing.[3]

Why We Communicate

You might object to stories like this, claiming that solitude would be a welcome relief from the irritations of everyday life. It's true that all of us need solitude, often more than we get. On the other hand, each of us has a point beyond which we do not *want* to be alone. Beyond this point solitude changes from a pleasurable to a painful condition. In other words, we all need people. We all need to communicate.

> *Whether the consequence of a mental attitude or a living condition, loneliness affects millions, usually for the worse. Death certificates read heart attack, cancer, or suicide; but coroners are missing the point. With no one to love or to love us, we tend to smoke, drink, brood, or simply cry ourselves into earlier graves.*
>
> Don E. Hamachek,
> *Encounters with Others*

Physical Needs   Communication is so important that its presence or absence affects physical health. In fact, evidence suggests that an absence of satisfying communication can even jeopardize life itself. Medical researchers have identified a wide range of medical hazards that result from a lack of close relationships. For instance,

1. Socially isolated people are two to three times more likely to die prematurely than are those with strong social ties. The type of relationship doesn't seem to matter: Marriages, friendship, religious and community ties all seem to increase longevity.[4]
2. Divorced men (before age seventy) die from heart disease, cancer, and strokes at double the rate of married men. Three times as many die from hypertension; five times as many commit suicide; seven times as many die from cirrhosis of the liver; and ten times as many die from tuberculosis.[5]
3. The rate of all types of cancer is as much as five times higher for divorced men and women, compared to their single counterparts.[6]

TALK FOR SALE

Even talk isn't cheap any more. In the San Francisco suburb of Kensington, talk is going for $8 an hour in a sadly modern kind of coffee-house called "Conversation." The café offers a troupe of twenty "conversationalists" for hire at $5 for the first 30 minutes and $3 for each additional half hour, along with fourteen soundproofed booths to chat in. The owners, Dick Braunlich and his wife, Chris, opened Conversation last month. They insist that they are not dispensing therapy, but simply providing the customer with "a nice person to talk to." Says Chris Braunlich: "Most of our patrons want to discuss their philosophy of life. They don't need a psychiatrist."

Indeed, even the hint of therapy is discouraged. When more than 100 applications for the conversationalist job came in, those who stressed guidance and counseling—even those with degrees in psychology—were turned down. "We hired those we felt were good, warm people," says Dick Braunlich. Engel Devendorf, 57, one of the café's more popular professional talkers, recalls a blond divorcée who, striken with terminal loneliness, wandered in after dropping her children off at a movie matinee. "She was new to California and didn't know anyone here," he says. "She didn't stop talking from the moment she came in." There are many other places—such as churches—where lonely people can find companionship. But, as Chris Braunlich points out, "people think if you're not paying, you're not getting anything."

NEWSWEEK MAGAZINE

4. Poor communication can contribute to coronary disease. One Swedish study examined thirty-two pairs of identical twins. One sibling in each pair had heart disease, whereas the other was healthy. The researchers found that the obesity, smoking habits, and cholesterol levels of the healthy and sick twins did not differ significantly. Among the significant differences, however, were "poor childhood and adult interpersonal relationships": the ability to resolve conflicts and the degree of emotional support given by others.[7]

5. The likelihood of death increases when a close relative dies. In one Welsh village, citizens who had lost a close relative died within one year at a rate more than five times greater than those who had not suffered from a relative's death.[8]

Research like this demonstrates the importance of satisfying personal relationships. Remember: Not everyone needs the same amount of contact, and the quality of communication is almost certainly as important as the quantity. The important point here is that personal communication is essential for our well-being. In other words, "people who need people" aren't "the luckiest people in the world" . . . they're the *only* people!

Identity Needs   Communication does more than enable us to survive. It is the way—indeed, the *only* way we learn who we are. As Chapter Two explains, our sense of identity comes from the way we interact with other people. Are we smart or stupid, attractive or ugly, skillful or inept? The answers to these questions don't come from looking in the mirror. We decide who we are based on how others react to us.

Deprived of communication with others, we would have no sense of identity. In his book *Bridges, Not Walls,* John Stewart dramatically illustrates this fact by citing the case of the famous "Wild Boy of Aveyron," who spent his early childhood without any apparent human contact. The boy was discovered in January 1800 while digging for vegetables in a French village garden. He showed no behaviors one would expect in a social human. The boy could not speak but uttered only weird cries. More significant than this absence of social skills was his lack of any identity as a human being. As author Roger Shattuck put it, "The boy had no human sense of being in the world. He had no sense of himself as a person related to other persons."[9] Only after the influence of a loving "mother" did the boy begin to behave—and we can imagine, think of himself as a human.

Like the boy of Aveyron, each of us enters the world with little or no sense of identity. We gain an idea of who we are from the way others define us. As Chapter Two explains, the messages we receive in early childhood are the strongest, but the influence of others continues throughout life.

Social Needs   Besides helping define who we are, communication is the way we relate socially with others. Psychologist William Schutz describes three types of social needs we strive to fulfill by communicating.[10] The first is **inclusion,** the need to feel a sense of belonging to some personal relationship. Inclusion needs are sometimes satisfied by informal alliances: the friends who study together, a group of runners, or neighbors who help one another with yard work. In other cases, we get a sense of belonging from formal relationships: everything from religious congregations to a job to marriage.

A second type of social need is the desire for **control**—the desire to influence others, to feel some sense of power over one's own life. Some types of control are obvious, such as that of the boss or team captain, whose directions make things happen. Much control, however, is more subtle and is often wielded by people without any position of authority. Experts in child development suggest that children who insist on staying up past their bedtime or having a treat in the supermarket may be less concerned with the issue at hand than with knowing that they have at least some ability to make things happen. Likewise, a couple's apparently foolish arguments over trivial matters such as what movie to watch or what to eat for dinner may be more concerned with control than with the topic being discussed. Chapter Eight discusses these kinds of relational needs in detail.

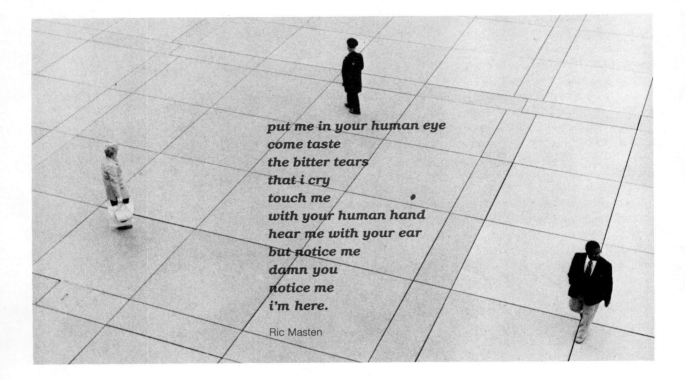

put me in your human eye
come taste
the bitter tears
that i cry
touch me
with your human hand
hear me with your ear
but notice me
damn you
notice me
i'm here.

Ric Masten

The third social need is **affection,** which can be defined more broadly as *respect.* We all need to know that we matter to others, for our self-esteem is created and nourished by the regard others hold for us. Without the affection and respect of others, mere inclusion holds little satisfaction. Even the power to influence other people is little comfort if they don't feel some regard for us.

Practical Needs We shouldn't overlook the everyday, important functions communication serves. Communication is the tool that lets us tell the hair stylist to take just a little off the sides, the doctor where it hurts, and the plumber that the broken pipe needs attention *now!* Communication is the means of learning important information in school. It is the method you use to convince a prospective employer that you're the best candidate for a job, and it is the way to persuade the boss you deserve a raise. The list of common but critical jobs performed by communicating goes on and on, and it's worth noticing that the inability to express yourself clearly and effectively in every one of these examples can prevent you from achieving your goal.

Psychologist Abraham Maslow suggested that human needs such as the preceding fall into five categories, each of which must be satisfied before we concern ourselves with the following ones.[11] As you read on, think about the ways in which communication is often necessary to satisfy each need. The most basic of these needs are *physical:* sufficient air, water, food, and rest and the ability to reproduce as a species. The second of Maslow's needs involve *safety:* protection from threats to our well-being. Beyond physical and safety concerns are the *social* needs we have mentioned already. Even beyond these, Maslow suggests that each of us has **self-esteem** needs: the desire to believe that we are worthwhile, valuable people. The final category of needs described by Maslow involves **self-actualization:** the desire to develop our potential to the maximum, to become the best person we can be.

The Process of Communication

So far we've been talking about communication as if the actions described by this word were perfectly clear. We've found, however, that most people aren't aware of all that goes on whenever two people share ideas. Before going further we want to show you exactly what does happen when one person expresses a thought or feeling to another. By doing so we can introduce you to a common working vocabulary that will be useful as you read on, at the same time previewing some of the activities we'll cover in later chapters.

A Communication Model   Since we need to begin somewhere, let's start with a **sender,** the person (or group) who creates a message. If you think about it for a moment, you'll realize that most ideas you have don't come to you already put into words. Rather, they're more like mental images, often consisting of un-verbalized feelings (anger, excitement, and the like), intentions (wants, desires, needs), or even mental pictures (such as how you want a job to look when it is finished). We can represent your mental image like this:

Since people aren't mind readers, you have to translate this mental image into symbols (usually words) that others can understand. No doubt you can recall times when you actually shuffled through a mental list of words to pick exactly the right ones to explain an idea. This process, called **encoding,** goes on every time we speak. Chapter Four will deal in some detail with the problems and skills of being an effective encoder.

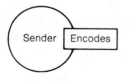

Once you've encoded an idea, the next step is to send it. We call this step the **message** phase of our model. There are a number of ways by which you can send a message. For instance, you might consider expressing yourself in a letter or over the telephone. In this sense writing and speaking words are two of the **channels** through which we send our messages. In addition to these channels we transfer our thoughts and feelings by touch, posture, gestures, distance, clothing, and many other ways as described in Chapter Five. The important thing to realize now is that there are a number of such channels.

People don't get along because they fear each other.
People fear each other because they don't know each other.
They don't know each other because they have not properly communicated with each other.

Martin Luther King, Jr.

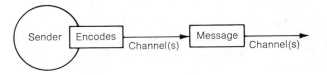

When your message reaches another person, much the same process we described earlier occurs in reverse. The **receiver** must make some sense out of the symbols you've sent by **decoding** them back into feelings, intentions, or thoughts that mean something.

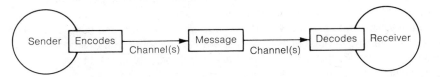

A **linear communication model** characterizes communication as a one-way activity in which information flows from sender to receiver. In a linear model, communication seems like something that an active sender "does" to a passive receiver. A linear model suggests that messages exist in a sender and that conveying meaning is the sender's role alone. As some scholars metaphorically suggest, a linear model implies th. .t communication is like giving or getting an inoculation: Ideas and feelings are prepared in some form of message and then injected in a straight line into a receiver. Although some types of messages (print and broadcast media, for example) appear to flow in a one-way manner, a linear model is not a complete or accurate representation of any type of communication, especially the interpersonal variety. What's missing? The model we've just examined ignores the fact that receivers *react* to messages.

Consider, for instance, the significance of a friend's yawn as you describe your vacation exploits. Imagine the blush you might see as a listener's response to one of your raunchier jokes. Nonverbal behaviors like these show that most communication—especially in interpersonal situations—is two way. The discernible response of a receiver to a sender's message is called **feedback.** Not all feedback is nonverbal, of course. Sometimes it is oral, as when you ask questions to clarify a speaker's remarks. In other cases it can be written, as when you demonstrate your knowledge of this material to your instructor on an examination. When we add the element of feedback, we have a description of communication as an **interactive communication model.** A sender formulates and transmits a message to a receiver, who, in turn, formulates and sends a response. An interactive, "Ping-Pong" model looks like this:

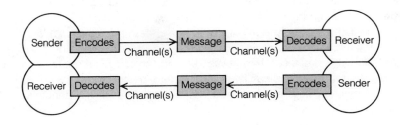

The interactive model suggests that after a period of interaction the mental images of the sender and receiver ought to match. If this happens, we can say that an act of successful communication has occurred. However, as you know from your own experience, things often go wrong somewhere between the sender and the receiver. For instance,

> Your constructive suggestion is taken as criticism.
> Your carefully phrased question is misunderstood.
> Your friendly joke is taken as an insult.
> Your hinted request is missed entirely.

And so it often goes. Why do such misunderstandings occur? To answer this question, we need to add more details to our model. We recognize that without several more crucial elements our model would not represent the world.

First, it's important to recognize that communication always takes place in an environment. By this term we do not mean simply a physical location but also the personal history that each person brings to a conversation. The problem here is that each of us has a different environment because of our differing backgrounds. Although we certainly have some experiences in common, we also see each situation in a unique way. For instance, consider how two individuals' environments would differ if

> A were well rested and B were exhausted;
> A were rich and B were poor;
> A were rushed and B had nowhere special to go;
> A had lived a long, eventful life and B were young and inexperienced; or
> A were passionately concerned with the subject and B were indifferent to it.

Obviously this list could go on and on. The problem of differing environments is critical to effective communication. Even now, though, you can see from just these few items that the world is a different place for sender and receiver. We can represent this idea with a revised model:

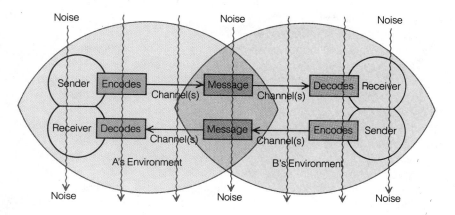

Notice that we've overlapped the environments of A and B. This overlapping represents those things that our communicators have in common. This point is important because it is through our shared knowledge and experiences that we are able to communicate. For example, you are able at least partially to understand the messages we are writing on these pages because we share the same language, however imprecise it often may be.

Different environments aren't the only cause of ineffective communication. Social scientists use the term **noise** to label other forces that interfere with the process and point out that it can occur in every stage.

There are three types of noise that can block communication—external, physiological, and psychological. **External noise** includes those factors outside the receiver that make it difficult to hear, as well as many other kinds of distractions. For instance, too much cigarette smoke in a crowded room might make it hard for you to pay attention to another person, and sitting in the rear of an auditorium might make a speaker's remarks unclear. External noise can disrupt communication almost anywhere in our model—in the sender, channel, message, or receiver. **Physiological noise** involves biological factors in the receiver that interfere with accurate reception: hearing loss, illness, and so on.

Psychological noise refers to forces within a communicator that interfere with the ability to express or understand a message accurately. For instance, an outdoors person might exaggerate the size and number of the fish he caught in order to convince himself and others of his talents. In the same way, a student might become so upset upon learning that she failed a test that she would be unable (perhaps unwilling is a better word) to understand clearly where she went wrong. Psychological noise is such an important communication problem that we have devoted much of Chapter Nine to investigating its most common form, defensiveness.

.   Even with the addition of these new elements our model isn't completely satisfactory. Notice that the preceding discussion portrays communication as a static activity. It suggests that there are discrete "acts" of communication that begin and end in identifiable places and that a sender's message "causes" some "effect" in a receiver. Furthermore, it suggests that at any given moment a person is either sending or receiving.

In fact, none of these characterizations are valid for interpersonal communication. The activity of communicating is usually not interactive but transactional. A **transactional communication model** differs from the more simplistic ones we've already discussed in several ways.

First, a transactional model reveals that communicators usually send and receive messages simultaneously, so that the images of sender and receiver should not be separated as if a person were doing only one or the other, but rather, superimposed and redefined as "participants."[12] At a given moment we are capable of receiving, decoding, and responding to another person's behavior, while at the same time that other person is receiving and responding to ours. Consider, for example, what might occur when you and a housemate negotiate household chores. As soon as you begin to hear (receive) the words sent by your partner, "I want to talk about cleaning the bathroom..." you grimace and clench your jaw (sending a nonverbal message of your own while receiving the verbal one). This reaction causes your partner to interrupt himself, defensively sending a new message: "Now wait a minute...."

Besides illustrating the simultaneous nature of face-to-face interaction, this example shows that it's difficult to isolate a single discrete "act" of communication from the events that precede and follow it. Your partner's comment about cleaning the bathroom (and the way it was presented) probably grew from exchanges you had in the past. Likewise, the way you'll act toward one another in the future depends on the outcome of this conversation. By now you can see that a transactional model of communication should be more like a motion picture film than a gallery of still photographs. Although the following figure does a fair job of picturing the phenomenon we call communication, an animated version, in which the environments, communicators, and messages constantly changed, would be an even better way of capturing the process. You can also see that communication is not something that people do *to* one another but a process in which they create a relationship by interacting *with* each other.

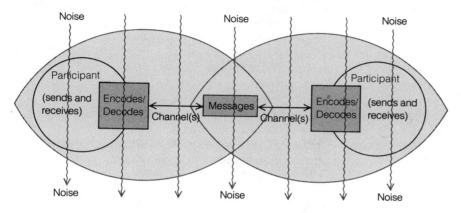

Before moving on to examine the special nature of communication in interpersonal contexts, let's summarize our definition. **Communication** is a *continuous, irreversible, transactive process* involving *participants* who occupy different but overlapping *environments* and are *simultaneously senders and receivers of messages,* many of which are distorted by external, physiological, and psychological *noise.*

Make Your Own Model

Check your understanding of the communication model by applying it to your own life.

1. In a group of three, share two important messages you intend to express within the next week.

2. For each message, describe
   a. The idea you want to send and the various ways you could encode it.
   b. Channels by which you could send it.
   c. Problems your receiver might have in decoding it.
   d. Possible differences between your environment and that of the receiver, and how those differences might make it difficult to understand your full message.
   e. Likely sources of physical, physiological, and psychological noise that might make it difficult for you to phrase your message clearly or for your receiver to understand it.
   f. Ways you can make sure your receiver uses feedback to verify an accurate understanding of the message.

Interpersonal Communication Defined   Now that you have a better
understanding of the overall process of communication, it's time to look at what
makes some types uniquely interpersonal.

One way to define interpersonal communication is by looking at the number
of people involved and how much access they have to one another. In this sense
a salesclerk and a customer or a police officer ticketing a speeding driver would
be examples of interpersonal acts (two-person, face-to-face meetings), whereas
a teacher and class or authors such as us and readers like you would not be.

You can probably sense that there's something wrong with this definition. The
kind of exchanges that often go on between salespeople and their customers or
bureaucrats and the public hardly seem interpersonal . . . or personal in any
sense of the word. In fact, after transactions like this we commonly remark, "I
might as well have been talking to a machine." And conversely, some "public"
kinds of communication seem quite personal. Teachers, religious ministers, and
entertainers often establish a personal relationship with their audiences, and we
certainly hope this book has at least some personal flavor.

If context doesn't make communication interpersonal, what does? When we
talk about interpersonal communication in this book, we're referring to the *quality*
of interaction between individuals.[13] In **interpersonal communication** we treat
others as individuals, whereas in **impersonal communication** we treat them as
objects. This definition doesn't mean that all impersonal communication is cruel
or that you need to establish a warm relationship with every person you meet.
The fact to remember here is that not all two-person interaction is interpersonal.

Several characteristics distinguish interpersonal relationships from impersonal
ones. First, in less personal relationships we tend to classify the other person by
using *labels*. We fit others into neat pigeonholes: "Anglo," "woman," "professor,"
"preppie," and so on. Such labels may be accurate as far as they go, but they
hardly describe everything that is important about the other person. On the other
hand, it's almost impossible to use one or two labels to describe someone you
know well. "She's not *just* a police officer," you want to say. Or "Sure, he's against
abortions, but there's more. . . ."

A second element in interpersonal relationships is the degree to which
communicators rely on *standardized rules* to guide their interactions. When we
meet someone for the first time, we know how to behave because of the
established social rules we have been taught. We shake hands, speak politely,
and rely on socially accepted subjects: "How are you?" "What do you do?"
"Lousy weather we've been having." The rules governing our interaction have
little to do with us or the people with whom we interact; we are not responding to
each other as individuals.

As we continue to interact, however, we sometimes gain more information
about each other, and we use that information as the basis for our communicating. As we share experiences, the rules that govern our behavior will be less
determined by cultural rules and more determined by the unique features of our
own relationship. This doesn't mean that we abandon rules altogether but rather
that we often create our *own* conventions, ones that are appropriate for us. For
example, one pair of friends might develop a procedure for dealing with conflicts
by expressing their disagreements as soon as they arise, whereas another could
tacitly agree to withhold a series of gripes, then clear the air periodically.
Although we could digress here and speculate about which procedure is more

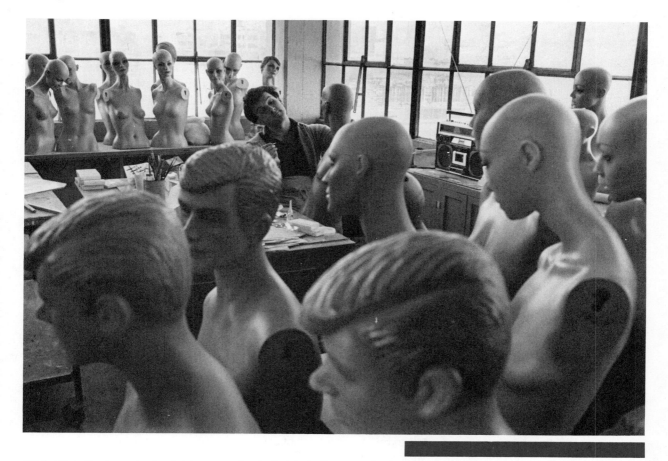

productive, the important point to recognize is that in both cases the individuals created their own rules.

A third characteristic that distinguishes interpersonal relationships from impersonal ones involves the *amount of information* the communicators have about each other. When we meet people for the first time, we have little information about them, usually no more than what we are told by others and the assumptions we make from observing what they wear and how they handle their bodies. As we talk, we gain more information in a variety of areas. The first topics we talk about are usually nonthreatening, nonintimate ones. If we continue talking, however, we may decide to discuss relatively few impersonal things. We may decide to increase the number of topics we talk about and choose to be more revealing of ourselves in doing so.

As we learn more about each other and as our information becomes more intimate, the degree to which we share an interpersonal relationship increases. This new degree of intimacy and sharing can occur almost immediately or else may grow slowly over a long period of time. In either case, we can say that the relationship becomes more interpersonal as the amount of self-disclosure increases. We'll have a great deal to say about this subject in Chapter Eight.

If we accept the characteristics of individual regard, creation of unique rules, and sharing of personal information as criteria for a developmentally interpersonal relationship, several implications follow. First, many one-to-one relationships never reach an interpersonal state. This is not surprising in itself since establishing a close relationship takes time and effort. In fact, such relationships are not always desirable or appropriate. Some people, however, fool themselves into thinking that they have close interpersonal friendships when in fact their associations are interpersonal only in a situational context.

Another implication that follows from looking at interpersonal communication in developmental terms is that the ability to communicate interpersonally is a skill people possess in varying degrees. For example, some communicators are adept at recognizing nonverbal messages, listening effectively, acting supportively, and resolving conflicts in satisfying ways, whereas others have no ability or no idea how to do so. The skills you will learn by studying the material in this book can help you become a more skillful communicator.

Use the preceding definition to think about your own relationships. Make a list of several people who are "close" to you: family members, a person with whom you live, friends, co-workers, and so on.

Where would you place each of these relationships on a spectrum with "interpersonal" at one end and "impersonal" at the other? Realize that "interpersonalness" isn't an either-or matter; many relationships are partially personal and partly impersonal.

Use the information you just read to develop your answers:

> Do you treat the people on your list as individuals, or do you pigeonhole and stereotype them?

> Have you developed your own rules and customs, or do you rely on standardized customs?

> Have you shared important personal information, or have you kept it to yourself?

Now ask yourself the most important question: How satisfied are you with the answers from your list?

Communication Principles and Misconceptions

Before we look at some of the qualities that contribute to effective interpersonal relationships, we need to take a final look at what communication is and what it isn't and examine what it can and can't accomplish.

Communication Principles   It's possible to draw several important conclusions about communication from what you have already learned in this chapter.

Communication Can Be Intentional or Unintentional   People usually plan their words carefully before they ask the boss for a raise or offer a constructive criticism. Not all communication is so deliberate, however. Sooner or later we all carelessly make a comment that would have gone better unsaid. Perhaps you lose your temper and blurt out a remark that you later regret, or maybe your private remarks are overheard by a bystander. In addition to these slips of the tongue, we unintentionally send many nonverbal messages. You might not be aware of your sour expression, impatient shifting, or sign of boredom, but others see them regardless.

It's Impossible Not to Communicate   These facial expressions, movements, and other nonverbal behaviors mean that although we can stop talking, we can't stop communicating. Chapter Six introduces the multitude of ways we send messages without saying a word: through posture, gesture, distance, body orientation, and clothing, among others. For instance, does a friend's silence reflect anger, contentment, or fatigue? Whether or not these sorts of messages are understood, they do communicate constantly.

All Messages Have a Content and a Relational Dimension   Virtually every verbal statement has a *content* dimension, the information it explicitly conveys: "Please pass the salt," "Not now, I'm tired," "You forgot to buy a quart of milk." In addition to this sort of obvious content, all messages also have a *relational* dimension. This relational component expresses how you feel about the other person: like or dislike, control or subordination, comfort or anxiety, and so on. For instance, consider how many different relational messages you could communicate by simply saying "Thanks a lot" in different ways.

   Sometimes the content of a message is all that matters. You may not care how the directory assistance operator feels about you as long as you get the phone number you're seeking, for example. In truly interpersonal contexts, however, the relational dimension of a message is often more important than the content under discussion.

   This explains why some apparently insignificant incidents seem so important to us. Failure to return a phone call or offer to help out on a simple task can take on meaning beyond their immediate context, signaling a change in the relationship.

Communication Is Irreversible   We sometimes wish that we could back up in time, erasing words or acts and replacing them with better alternatives.

Unfortunately, such reversal is impossible. There are occasions when further explanation can clear up another's confusion or when an apology can mollify another's hurt feelings; but in other cases no amount of explanation can erase the impression you have created. Despite the warnings judges issue in jury trials, it's impossible to "unreceive" a message. Words said and deeds done are irretrievable.

Communication Is Unrepeatable   Because communication is an ongoing process, it is impossible to repeat the same event. The friendly smile that worked so well when meeting a stranger last week might not succeed with the person you encounter tomorrow: It might feel stale and artificial to you the second time around, or it might be wrong for the new person or occasion. Even with the same person, it's impossible to re-create an event. Why? Because neither you nor the other *is* the same person. You've both lived longer. The behavior isn't original. Your feelings about one another may have changed. You need not constantly invent new ways to act around familiar people, but you should realize that the "same" words and behavior *are* different each time they are spoken or performed. Chapter Eight will alert you to the stages through which a relationship progresses.

Communication Misconceptions   It's just as important to know what communication is not as to understand what it is.[14] Avoiding the following misconceptions can save you a great deal of personal trouble.

Meanings Are in People, Not Words   The biggest mistake we can make is to assume that *saying* something is the same thing as *communicating* it. To use the terminology of our communication model, there's no guarantee that a receiver will decode a message in a way that matches the sender's intention. (If you doubt this proposition, list all the times you've been misunderstood in the past week.) Chapter Three outlines the many reasons why people can interpret a statement differently from the way you intended it, and Chapter Five describes the most common types of verbal misunderstandings and suggests ways to minimize them. Chapter Seven introduces listening skills that help ensure that the way you receive messages matches the ideas a speaker is trying to convey.

More Communication Is Not Always Better   Whereas not communicating enough can cause problems, there are also situations when too *much* talking is a mistake. Sometimes excessive communication is simply unproductive, as when two people "talk a problem to death," going over the same ground again and again without making progress. There are other times when talking too much actually aggravates a problem. We've all had the experience of "talking ourselves into a hole"—making a bad situation worse by pursuing it too far. As one communication book puts it, "More and more negative communication merely leads to more and more negative results."[15]

There are even times when *no* communication is the best course. Any good salesperson will testify that it's often best to stop talking and let the customer think about the product, and when two people are angry and hurt, they may say things they don't mean and will later regret. In such cases it's probably best to spend time cooling off, thinking about what to say and how to say it. Chapter Four will help you decide when and how to share feelings.

Communication Will Not Solve All Problems   Sometimes even the best-planned, best-timed communication won't solve a problem. Imagine, for example, that you ask an instructor to explain why you received a poor grade on a project you believe deserved top marks. The professor clearly outlines the reasons why you received the low grade and sticks to that position after listening thoughtfully to your protests. Has communication solved the problem? Hardly.

Sometimes clear communication is even the *cause* of problems. Suppose, for example, that a friend asks you for an honest opinion of the $200 outfit he has just bought. Your clear and sincere answer, "I think it makes you look fat," might do more harm than good. Deciding when and how to self-disclose isn't always easy. See Chapter Eight for suggestions.

Communication Is Not a Natural Ability   Most people assume that communication is an aptitude that people develop without the need for training—rather like breathing. Although almost everyone does manage to function passibly without much formal communication training, most people operate at a level of effectiveness far below their potential. However, learning and practicing the skills introduced in this book can help virtually every reader become a better communicator.

What Makes an Effective Communicator?

It's easy to recognize good communicators, and even easier to spot poor ones. But what are the characteristics that distinguish effective communicators from their less successful counterparts? Answering this question has been one of the leading challenges for researchers in recent years.[16] Despite the many questions that still exist about what constitutes communication competence, most experts would agree that at least four elements characterize effective communicators.

A Wide Range of Behaviors   Effective communicators are able to choose their actions from a wide range of behaviors. To understand the importance of having a large communication repertoire, imagine that someone you know repeatedly tells jokes—perhaps racist or sexist ones—that you find offensive. You could respond to these jokes in a number of ways:

> You could decide to say nothing, figuring that the risks of bringing the subject up would be greater than the benefits.
>
> You could ask a third party to say something to the joke teller about the offensiveness of the stories.
>
> You could hint at your discomfort, hoping that your friend would get the point.
>
> You could joke about your friend's insensitivity, counting on humor to soften the blow of your criticism.
>
> You could express your discomfort in a straightforward way, asking your companion to stop telling the offensive stories, at least around you.
>
> You could even demand that the other person stop.

With this choice of responses at your disposal (and you can probably think of others as well), you could pick the one that had the best chance of success. But if you were able to use only one or two of these responses when raising a delicate issue—always keeping quiet or always hinting, for example—your chances of success would be much smaller. Indeed, many poor communicators are easy to spot by their limited range of responses. Some are chronic jokers. Others are always belligerent. Still others are quiet in almost every situation. Like a piano player who only knows one tune or a chef who can only prepare a few dishes, these people are forced to rely on a small range of responses again and again, whether or not they are successful.

Ability to Choose the Most Appropriate Behavior   Simply possessing a large array of communication skills isn't a guarantee of effectiveness. It's also necessary to know which of these behaviors will work best in a particular situation. Choosing the best way to send a message is rather like choosing a gift: What is appropriate for one person won't suit another one at all. This ability to choose the best approach is essential, since a response that works well in one setting would flop miserably in another one.

Although it's impossible to say precisely how to act in every situation, there are at least three factors to consider when you are deciding which response to choose:

Context   The time and place will almost always influence how you act. Asking your boss for a raise or your lover for a kiss might produce good results if the time is right, but the identical request might backfire if your timing is poor. Likewise, the joke that would be ideal at a bachelor party would probably flop at a funeral.

Your Goal   The way you should communicate depends on the results you are seeking. Inviting a new neighbor over for a cup of coffee or dinner could be just the right approach if you want to encourage a friendship; but if you want to maintain your privacy it might be wiser to be polite but cool. Likewise, your goal will determine your approach in situations in which you want to help another person. As you will learn in Chapter Seven, there are times when offering advice is just what is needed. But when you want to help others develop the ability to solve problems on their own, it's better to withhold your own ideas and function as a sounding board to let them consider alternatives and choose their solutions.

The Other Person   Your knowledge of the other party should also shape the approach you take. If you're dealing with someone who is very sensitive or insecure, your response might be supportive and cautious. With an old and trusted friend you might be blunt. In fact, understanding the other person is so important that researchers have labeled empathy the most important aspect of communication competence.[17] For this reason a major part of Chapter Three is devoted to developing your ability to empathize.

The social niche of the other party will often influence how you communicate. For instance, you would probably act differently toward an eighty-year-old person than you would with a teenager. You would probably behave differently toward the president of your institution than you would toward a classmate, even in identical circumstances. Likewise, there are times when it's appropriate to treat a man differently than a woman, even in this age of gender equity.

Skill at Performing Behaviors   Once you have chosen the most appropriate way to communicate, it's still necessary to perform the necessary skills effectively. There is a big difference between knowing *about* a skill and being able to put it into practice. Simply being aware of alternatives isn't much help unless you can skillfully put these alternatives to work.

Just reading about communication skills in the following chapters won't guarantee that you can start using them flawlessly. Like any other skills—playing a musical instrument or learning a sport, for example—the road to competence in communication is not a short one. As you learn and practice the communication skills in the following pages, you can expect to pass through several stages.[18]

Beginning Awareness   The first step in learning any new skill is a beginning awareness. This is the point at which you first learn that there is a new and better way of behaving. If you play tennis, for example, awareness might grow when you learn about a new way of serving that can improve your power and accuracy. In the area of communication, *Looking Out/Looking In* should bring this sort of awareness to you.

Awkwardness   Just as you were clumsy when you first tried to ride a bicycle or drive a car, your initial attempts at communicating in new ways may also be awkward. This doesn't mean that there's anything wrong with these methods but rather that you need more experience with them. After all, if it's reasonable to expect difficulty learning other skills, you ought to expect the same fumbling with the concepts in this book. As Ringo Starr put it when talking about music, "If you want to play the blues, you gotta pay your dues. . . . It don't come easy."

Skillfulness   If you are willing to keep working at overcoming the awkwardness of your initial attempts, you will arrive at the third learning stage, which is one of skillfulness. At this point you'll be able to handle yourself well although you will still need to think about what you're doing. In learning a new language, this is the time when you're able to speak grammatically and use the correct words although you still need to think hard to express yourself well. As an interpersonal communicator, you can expect the stage of skillfulness to be marked by a great deal of thinking and planning and also by good results.

Integration   Finally, after a period of time in the skillful phase, you'll find yourself at the final level of integration. This occurs when you're able to perform well without thinking about it. The behavior becomes automatic, a part of you. Integrated speakers of a foreign language converse without translating mentally from their native tongue. Integrated cyclists ride skillfully and comfortably, almost as if the bike were an extension of each cyclist's own body. And integrated communicators express themselves in skillful ways, not as a self-conscious act but because that is who they have become.

It's important to keep these stages in mind as you try out the ideas in this book. Prepare yourself for the inevitable awkwardness, knowing that if you're

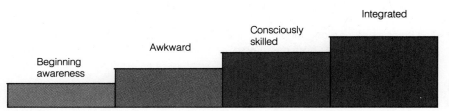

Stages in learning communication skills

willing to keep practicing the new skills, you will become more and more comfortable and successful with them. Realize that the effort is worth it, for once you have learned new methods of communicating, you'll be rewarded with far more satisfying relationships.

Commitment to the Relationship   One feature that distinguishes effective communication in almost any context is commitment. In other words, people who seem to care about the relationship communicate better than those who don't.[19] This concern shows up in several kinds of commitment:

Commitment to the Other Person   This concern for the other party shows up in a variety of ways: a desire to spend time with the other person instead of rushing, willingness to listen carefully instead of doing all the talking, the use of language that makes sense to the other person, and openness to change after hearing the other person's ideas.

Commitment to the Message   Effective communicators also care about what they have to say. They appear sincere, seem to know what they are talking about, and demonstrate through words and deeds that their ideas matter. Phony communication is a turnoff. So are wishy-washy positions and uninformed, ignorant statements.

A Desire for Mutual Benefit   The best communication leaves both parties as winners, each gaining from an exchange. In contrast, when communicators appear to be self-centered or manipulative, the relationship suffers. In fact, Chapter Ten shows how both parties can wind up losers when they care only about their own welfare.

A Desire to Interact and to Continue the Relationship   Communication is most effective when people care about one another. This doesn't mean it's necessary for gas station attendants and telephone operators to establish a deep relationship with every customer. Even these sorts of business transactions, however, are more satisfying when the implicit message is "I sincerely want to help you and hope you'll be a satisfied customer."

How do you measure up as a competent communicator? Competence isn't a trait that people either possess or lack. Rather, it's a state that we achieve more or less frequently. A realistic goal, then, is not to become perfect but to boost the percentage of time when you communicate in ways outlined in this section.

Check Your Competence

Other people are the best judges of your competence as a communicator. You can find out how they rate you by following these steps:

1. Choose one or more people who are important to you. To see how your competence varies from one type of relationship to another, you might choose one friend, one family member, one fellow student or worker.

2. Ask each person you choose to rate you according to each of the qualities described in the preceding section:

a. Your range of communication behaviors.
b. Your skill at choosing the most appropriate way of communicating for the situation at hand.
c. Your commitment to the people with whom you communicate and to your messages.

3. Based on your findings, rate your competence as a communicator by listing your strengths and shortcomings. For each shortcoming, describe how you could communicate differently to gain a higher rating.

More Readings

DeVito, Joseph. *Communication Concepts and Processes,* 3d ed. Englewood Cliffs, N.J.: Prentice-Hall, 1981.
   The first section of DeVito's anthology, entitled "Preliminaries," contains six useful selections that provide a good overview to communication principles and challenges.

Knapp, Mark L. *Interpersonal Communication and Human Relationships.* Boston: Allyn and Bacon, 1984.
   Part V, "Toward More Effective Communication," provides a more detailed treatment of communication competence. Knapp summarizes much of the wide-ranging research and theorizing on this subject, as well as citing sources for readers who want to explore the subject further.

Littlejohn, Stephen W. *Theories of Human Communication,* 2d ed. Belmont, Calif.: Wadsworth, 1983.
   This thorough book surveys the status of theories and research in human communication. The sections on interpersonal communication (Chapters 9–11) expand on several topics introduced in Looking Out/Looking In, *including perception, self-disclosure, interpersonal attraction, and conflict.*

Lynch, James J. *The Broken Heart: The Medical Consequences of Loneliness.* New York: Basic Books, 1977.
   Lynch is director of the Psychosomatic Clinics at the University of Maryland's School of Medicine. He documents the strong link between poor physical health and inadequate interpersonal relationships.

Miller, Sherod, Elam Nunnally, and Daniel B. Wackman. *Alive and Aware: How to Improve Your Relationships Through Better Communication.* Minneapolis, Minn.: Interpersonal Communication Programs, 1975.
   This book provides a detailed description of the elements of a clear message. Though it doesn't include the consequence step described in Looking Out/Looking In, *it is a valuable second step in learning this important set of skills.*

Rubin, Zick. "Seeking a Cure for Loneliness." *Psychology Today* 13:4 (October 1979).
   This article describes recent research on loneliness as reported at the first national research conference on the subject.

Stewart, John. "Interpersonal Communication: A Meeting between Persons." In *Bridges, Not Walls: A Book about Interpersonal Communication,* 4th ed. New York: Random House, 1986.
   This introductory essay in Stewart's excellent reader elaborates on the differences between interpersonal and impersonal communication. In addition, it comments on the basic needs that communication fills.

Chapter Two

The Self-Concept: Key to Communication

In the beginning, I was one person, knowing nothing but my own experience.

Then I was told things, and I became two people: the little girl who said how terrible it was that the boys had a fire going in the lot next door where they were roasting apples (which was what the woman said)—and the little girl who, when the boys were called by their mothers to go to the store, ran out and tended the fire and the apples because she loved doing it.

So then there were two of I. One I always doing something that the other I disapproved of. Or other I said what I disapproved of. All this argument in me so much.

In the beginning was I, and I was good.

Then came in other I. Outside authority. This was confusing. And then other I became very confused because there were so many different outside authorities.

Sit nicely. Leave the room to blow your nose. Don't do that, that's silly. Why, the poor child doesn't even know how to pick a bone! Flush the toilet at night because if you don't it makes it harder to clean. DON'T FLUSH THE TOILET AT NIGHT—you wake people up! Always be nice to people. Even if you don't like them, you mustn't hurt their feelings. Be frank and honest. If you don't tell people what you think of them, that's cowardly. Butter knives. It is important to use butter knives.

Butter knives? What foolishness! Speak nicely. Sissy! Kipling is wonderful! Ugh! Kipling (turning away).

The most important thing is to have a career. The most important thing is to get married. The hell with everyone. Be nice to everyone. The most important thing is sex. The most important thing is to have everyone like you. The most important thing is to be sophisticated and say what you don't mean and don't let anyone know what you feel. The most important thing is a black seal coat and china and silver. The most important thing is to be clean. The most important thing is to always pay your debts. The most important thing is not to be taken in by anyone else. The most important thing is to love your parents. The most important thing is to work. The most important thing is to be independent. The most important thing is to speak correct English. The most important thing is to go to the right plays and read the right books. The most important thing is to do what others say. And others say all these things.

All the time, I is saying, live with life. That is what is important.

But when I lives with life, other I says no, that's bad. All the different other I's say this. It's dangerous. It isn't practical. You'll come to a bad end. Of course . . . everyone felt that way once, the way you do, but *you'll learn.*

Out of all the other I's some are chosen as a pattern that is me. But there are all the other possibilities of patterns within what all the others say which come into me and become other I which is not myself,

and sometimes these take over. Then who am I?

I does not bother about who am I. I is, and is happy being. But when I is happy being, other I says get to work, do something worthwhile! I is happy doing dishes. "You're weird!" I is happy being with people saying nothing. Other I says talk. Talk, talk, talk. I gets lost.

I know that things are to be played with, not possessed. I likes putting things together, lightly. Taking things apart, lightly. "You'll never have anything!" Making things of things in a way that the things themselves take part in, putting themselves together with surprise and delight to I. "There's no money in that!"

I is human. If someone needs, I gives. "You can't do that! You'll never have anything for yourself! We'll have to support you!"

I loves. I loves in a way that other I does not know. I loves. "That's too warm for friends!" "That's too cool for lovers!" "Don't feel so bad, he's just a friend. It's not as though you loved him." "How can you let him go? I thought you loved him?" So cool the warm for friends and hot up the love for lovers, and I gets lost.

So both I's have a house and a husband and children and all that, but both I's are confused because other I says, "You see? You're lucky," while I goes on crying. "What are you crying about? Why are you so ungrateful?" I doesn't know gratitude or ingratitude, and cannot argue. I goes on crying. Other I pushes it out, says, "I am happy! I am very lucky to have such a fine family and a nice house and good neighbors and lots of friends who want me to do this, do that." I is not reason-able either. I goes on crying.

Other I gets tired, and goes on smiling because that is the thing to do. Smile, and you will be rewarded. Like the seal who gets tossed a piece of fish. Be nice to everyone and you will be rewarded. People will be nice to you, and you can be happy with that. You know they like you. Like a dog who gets patted on the head for good behavior. Tell

funny stories. Be gay. Smile, smile, smile.... I is crying.... "Don't be sorry for yourself! Go out and do things for people!" "Go out and be with people!" I is still crying, but now, that is not heard and felt so much.

Suddenly: "What am I doing?" "Am I to go through life playing the clown?" "What am I doing, going to parties that I do not enjoy?" "What am I doing, being with people who bore me?" "Why am I so hollow and the hollowness filled with empti-ness?" A shell. How has this shell grown around me? Why am I proud of my children and unhappy about their lives which are not good enough? Why am I disappointed? Why do I feel so much waste?

I comes through, a little. In moments. And gets pushed back by other I.

I refuses to play the clown any more. Which I is that? "She used to be fun, but now she thinks too much about herself." I lets friends drop away. Which I is that? "She's being too much by herself. That's bad. She's losing her mind." Which mind?

Barry Stevens,
Person to Person

To be nobody-but-yourself in a world which is doing its best, night and day, to make you everybody-else means to fight the hardest battle which any human being can fight, and never stop fighting.

e. e. cummings

Who are you? Take a moment now to answer this question.

How did you define yourself? As a student? A man or woman? By your age? Your religion? Your occupation? Of course, there are many ways of identifying yourself.

Take a few more moments, and list as many ways as you can to identify who you are. You'll need this list later on in this chapter, so be sure to complete it now. Try to include all the characteristics that describe you:

Your moods or feelings
Your appearance and physical condition
Your social traits
Talents you possess or lack
Your intellectual capacity
Your strong beliefs
Your social roles

Self-Concept Defined

Now take a look at what you've written. You'll probably see that the words you've chosen represent a profile of what you view as your most important characteristics. In other words, if you were required to describe the "real you," this list ought to be a good summary.

What you've done in developing this list is to give a partial description of your self-concept: the relatively stable set of perceptions you hold of yourself. If you imagine a special mirror that not only reflected your physical features but also allowed you to view other aspects of yourself—emotional states, talents, likes, dislikes, values, roles, and so on—the reflection you'd see would be your self-concept.*

You probably recognize that the self-concept list you recorded earlier is only a partial one. To make the description complete, you'd have to keep adding items until your list ran into hundreds of words.

Take a moment now to demonstrate the many parts of your self-concept by simply responding to the question "Who am I?" over and over again. Add these responses to the list you started earlier.

Of course, not every item on your self-concept list is equally important. For example, the most significant part of one person's self-concept might consist of social roles, and for another it might be physical appearance, health, friendships, accomplishments, or skills.

You can discover how much you value each part of your self-concept by rank-ordering the items on the list you've compiled. Try it now: Place 1 next to the most fundamental thing about you, 2 next to the second most important term, and continue on in this manner until you've completed your list.

* You might object to the idea of a single self-concept, insisting that the image you hold of yourself changes frequently, as Alice suggested to the caterpillar in the quote on page 53. You might see yourself as looking good one day and ugly the next, for example. Although this kind of variation does exist, it's useful to think about the self-concept as a single entity that is roughly consistent over at least a short period of time.

This self-concept you've just described is extremely important. To see just how fundamental it is, try the following exercise.

Take Away

1. Look over the list of words you've just used to describe yourself. If you haven't already done so, pick the ten items that describe the most fundamental aspects of who you are. Be sure you've organized these items so that the most fundamental one is in first place and the one that is least central to your identity is number 10, arranging the words or phrases in between in their proper order.

2. Now find a comfortable spot where you can think without being interrupted. You can complete this exercise in a group with the leader giving instructions, or you can do it alone by reading the directions yourself when necessary.

3. Close your eyes and get a mental picture of yourself. Besides visualizing your appearance, you should also include in your image your less observable features: your disposition, your hopes, your concerns . . . of course including all the items you described in step 1.

4. Keep this picture in mind, but now imagine what would happen if the tenth item on your list disappeared from your makeup. How would you be different? Does the idea of giving up that item leave you feeling better or worse? How hard was it to let go of that item?

5. Now, without taking back the item you just abandoned, give up the ninth item on your list, and see what difference this makes to you. After pausing to experience your thoughts and feelings, give up each succeeding item on your list one by one.

6. After you've abandoned the number-one feature of who you are, take a few minutes to regather the parts of yourself that you abandoned, and then read on.

For·most people this exercise dramatically illustrates just how fundamental the concept of self is. Even when the item being abandoned is an unpleasant one, it's often hard to give it up. And when they are asked to let go of their most central feelings or thoughts, most people balk. "I wouldn't be *me* without that" they insist. Of course, this proves our point: The concept of self is perhaps our most fundamental possession. Knowing who we are is essential, for without a self-concept it would be impossible to relate to the world.

How the Self-Concept Develops

Most researchers agree that we are not born with a self-concept. An infant lying in a crib has no notion of self, no notion—even if the ability to speak were miraculously made available—of how to answer the question "Who am I?" Consider what it would be like to have no idea of your characteristic moods, physical appearance, social traits, talents, intellectual capacity, beliefs, or important roles. If you can imagine this experience—*blankness*—you can start to understand how the world appears to someone with no sense of self. Of

Copyright 1973 Universal Press Syndicate.

course, you have to take it one step further and *not know* you do not have any notion of self.

Soon after birth the infant begins to differentiate among the stimuli in the environment: familiar and unfamiliar faces, the sounds that mean food, the noises that frighten, the cat who jumps in the crib, the sister who tickles—each becomes a separate part of the world. Recognition of distinctions in the environment probably precedes recognition of the self.

At about six or seven months the child begins to recognize "self" as distinct from surroundings. If you've ever watched children at this age you've probably marveled at how they can stare with great fascination at a foot, hand, and other body parts that float into view, almost as if they were strange objects belonging to someone else. Then the connection is made, almost as if the child were realizing "The hand is *me*," "The foot is *me*." These first revelations form the child's earliest concept of self. At this early stage, the self-concept is almost exclusively physical, involving the child's basic realization of existing and of possessing certain body parts over which some control is exerted. This limited self-concept barely resembles the more fully developed self-concepts older children hold.

Along with this budding sense of identity, certain behaviors develop that suggest infants are born with some social characteristics. Psychologist Jerome Kagan reports that 10 percent of all children seem to be born with a biological disposition toward shyness.[1] Babies who stop playing when a stranger enters the room, for example, are more likely than others to be reticent and introverted

"Guess who Miss Price picked to play poison ivy in the class play."

FEIFFER

I AM A CRITIC.

I AM NOT A BOOK, ART, THEATRE, FILM, MUSIC OR DANCE CRITIC.

I AM A BERNARD CRITIC.

A RESIDENT CRITIC WORKING INSIDE THE HEAD OF A BERNARD.

HE WAKES UP, I TELL HIM, "YOU'RE LATE." AT THE OFFICE I TELL HIM, "YOU'RE BEHIND." AT DINNER PARTIES I TELL HIM, "YOU'RE BORING."

WHEN HE FALLS IN LOVE I TELL HIM, "YOU'RE NOT GOOD ENOUGH."

ON OCCASION HE CAN'T TAKE ANY MORE REVIEWS AND ORDERS ME OUT OF HIS HEAD.

SO I RIP OFF MY MASK AND SAY, "IS THAT THE WAY TO TALK TO YOUR MOTHER?"

as adolescents. Likewise, Kagan found that another 10 percent of infants seem to be born with especially sociable dispositions. Research with twins also suggests that personality may be at least partially biologically determined.[2] Biologically identical twins are much more similar in sociability than are fraternal twins. These similarities are apparent not only in infancy but also when the twins have grown to adulthood and have had different experiences.

Although children may behave more or less sociably, they don't automatically view themselves in a way that reflects their actual communication behavior. In fact, the opposite is closer to the truth: The self-concept is extremely subjective, being almost totally a product of interaction with others. You can begin to get a sense of how your self-concept has developed by trying the following exercise. Be sure to complete it before reading on.

Uppers and Downers

1. Either by yourself or with a partner, recall someone you know or once knew who was an "upper"—who helped enhance your self-esteem by acting in a way that made you feel accepted, competent, worthwhile, important, appreciated, or loved.

   This person needn't have played a crucial role in your life as long as the role was positive. Often your self-concept is shaped by many tiny nudges as well as by a few giant events. A family member with whom you've spent most of your life can be an upper, but so can the stranger on the street who spontaneously smiles and strikes up a friendly conversation.

2. Now recall a "downer" from your life—someone who acted in a large or small way to reduce your self-esteem. As with uppers, downer messages aren't always intentional. The acquaintance who forgets your name after you've been introduced or the friend who yawns while you're describing an important problem can diminish your feelings of self-worth.

3. Now that you've thought about how others shape your self-concept, recall a time when you were an upper to someone else—when you deliberately or unintentionally boosted another's self-esteem. Don't merely settle for an instance in which you were nice: Look for a time when your actions left another person feeling valued, loved, needed, and so on. You may have to ask the help of others to answer this question.

4. Finally, recall a recent instance in which you were a downer for someone else. What did you do to diminish another's self-esteem? Were you aware of the effect of your behavior at the time?

   Your answer might show that some events we intend as uppers have the effect of downers. For example, you might joke with a friend in what you meant as a friendly gesture, only to discover that your remarks are received as criticism.

After completing the Uppers and Downers exercise (you *did* complete it, didn't you?), you should begin to see that your self-concept is shaped by those around you. This process of shaping occurs in two ways.

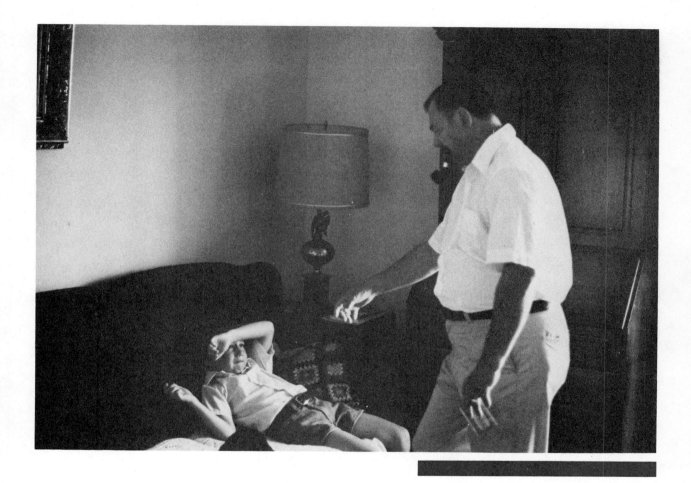

Reflected Appraisal: The Looking-Glass Self

As early as 1912, psychologist Charles Cooley used the image of a mirror to identify the process of **reflected appraisal:** the fact that each of us develops a self-concept that matches the way we believe others see us.[3] In other words, we are likely to feel less valuable, lovable, and capable to the degree that others have communicated downer signals; and we will probably feel good about ourselves to the extent that others seem to feel good about us. The validity of the principle of reflected appraisal will become clear when you realize that the self-concept you described in the list at the beginning of this chapter is a product of the positive and negative messages you have received throughout your life.

To illustrate this point further, let's start at the beginning. Newborn children aren't born with any sense of identity: They learn to judge themselves only through the way others treat them. At first the evaluations aren't linguistic. Nonetheless, even the earliest days of life are full of messages that constitute the first uppers and downers that start to shape the child's self-concept. The amount of time parents allow their baby to cry before attending to its needs nonverbally communicates over a period of time how important it is to them. Their method of

handling the child also speaks volumes: Do they affectionately toy with it, or do they treat it like so much baggage, changing diapers, feeding and bathing it in a brusque, businesslike manner? Does the tone of voice with which they speak express love and enjoyment or disappointment and irritation?

Of course, most of these messages are not intentional ones. It is rare when a parent will deliberately try to tell a child it's not lovable; but whether they're intentional or not doesn't matter—nonverbal statements play a big role in shaping a youngster's feelings of being "OK" or "not OK."

As the child learns to speak and understand language, verbal messages also contribute to a developing self-concept. Every day a child is bombarded with scores of messages about him- or herself. Some of these are uppers:

> "You're so cute!"
> "I love you."
> "What a big girl!"
> "It's fun to play with you."

whereas other messages are downers:

> "Can't you do anything right?"
> "What's the matter with you?"
> "You're a bad boy!"
> "Leave me alone. You're driving me crazy!"

As we've said, the evaluations others make of us are the mirror by which we know ourselves; and since children are trusting souls who have no other way of viewing themselves, they accept at face value both the positive and negative evaluations of the apparently all-knowing and all-powerful adults around them.

These same principles in the formation of the self-concept continue in later life, especially when messages come from what sociologists term a **significant other**—a person whose opinions we especially value. A look at the uppers and downers you described in the previous exercise (as well as others you can remember) will show that the evaluations of a few especially important people can have long-range effects. A teacher from long ago, a special friend or relative, or perhaps a barely known acquaintance whom you respected can all leave an imprint on how you view yourself. To see the importance of significant others, ask yourself how you arrived at your opinion of yourself as a student . . . as a person attractive to the opposite sex . . . as a competent worker . . . and you'll see that these self-evaluations were probably influenced by the way others regarded you.

The figure on this page illustrates how the self-concept both causes much of our communication behavior and is affected by it. We can begin to examine the process by considering the self-concept you bring to an event.[4] Suppose, for example, that one element of your self-concept is "nervous with authority figures." That image probably came from the evaluations of significant others in the past—perhaps teachers or former employers. If you view yourself as nervous with authority figures like these, you'll probably behave in nervous ways when you encounter them in the future—say in a teacher-student conference or a job interview. That nervous behavior is likely to influence how others respond to you—probably in ways that reinforce the self-concept you brought to the event. Finally, the responses of others will affect the way you perceive future events: other job interviews, meetings with professors, and so on. This cycle illustrates the chicken-and-egg nature of the self-concept, which is both shaped by significant others in the past and which influences the way significant others will view you in the future.

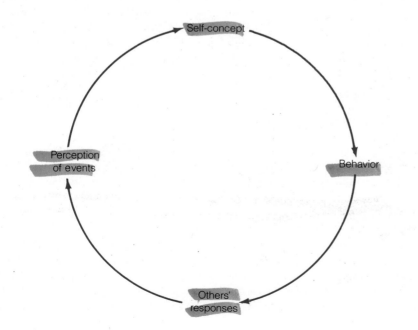

The self-concept and communication: a cyclic process

We are not only our brother's keeper; in countless large and small ways, we are our brother's maker.

Bonaro Overstreet

Social Comparison   So far we have looked at the way others' messages shape your self-concept. In addition to these messages, each of us forms our self-image by the process of **social comparison**: evaluating ourselves in terms of how we compare with others.

Two types of social comparison need highlighting. In the first, we decide whether we are *superior or inferior* by comparing ourselves to others. Are we attractive or ugly? A success or failure? Intelligent or stupid? It depends on whom we measure ourselves against.

You might feel just ordinary or inferior in terms of talent, friendships, or attractiveness if you compare yourself with an inappropriate reference group. You'll probably never be as beautiful as a Hollywood star, as agile as a professional athlete, or as wealthy as a millionaire. When you consider the matter logically, these facts don't mean you're worthless. Nonetheless, many people judge themselves against unreasonable standards and suffer accordingly. You'll read more about how to avoid placing perfectionistic demands on yourself in Chapter Three.

In addition to feelings of superiority and inferiority, social comparison provides a way to decide if we are the *same as or different from* others. A child who is interested in ballet and who lives in a setting where such preferences are regarded as weird will start to accept this label if there is no support from others. Likewise, adults who want to improve the quality of their relationships but are surrounded by friends and family who don't recognize or acknowledge the importance of these matters will think of themselves as oddballs. Thus, it's easy to recognize that the **reference groups** against which we compare ourselves play an important role in shaping our view of ourselves.

Using reference groups to determine whether we are different from others can get tricky because those others don't always reveal how they really think and feel. Many students in interpersonal communication classes, for example, discover that others share occasional feelings of social uncertainty that they thought were unusual. Thus, it's important to remember that people don't always *act* the way they *feel* and that you may not be as different as you think. Chapter Eight discusses self-disclosure and offers some guidelines on how to get beyond the kind of mask-wearing and game-playing that often prevents people from recognizing some of their similarities.

You might argue that not every part of one's self-concept is shaped by others, insisting there are certain objective facts that are recognizable by self-observation. After all, nobody needs to tell a person that he is taller than others, speaks with an accent, has acne, and so on. These facts are obvious.

Though it's true that some features of the self are immediately apparent, the *significance* we attach to them—the rank we assign them in the hierarchy of our list and the interpretation we give them—depends greatly on the opinions of others. After all, there are many of your features that are readily observable, yet you don't find them important at all because nobody has regarded them as significant.

Recently we heard a woman in her eighties describing her youth. "When I was a girl," she declared, "we didn't worry about weight. Some people were skinny and others were plump, and we pretty much accepted the bodies God gave us." In those days it was unlikely that weight would have found its way onto the self-concept list you constructed because it wasn't considered significant.

Compare this attitude with what you find today: It's seldom that you pick up a popular magazine or visit a bookstore without reading about the latest diet fads, and television ads are filled with scenes of slender, happy people. As a result, you'll rarely find a person (especially female) who doesn't complain about the need to "lose a few pounds." Obviously, the reason for such concern has more to do with the attention paid to slimness these days than with any increase in the number of people in the population who are overweight. Furthermore, the interpretation of characteristics such as weight depends on the way people important to us regard them. We generally see fat as undesirable because others tell us it is. In a society where obesity is the ideal (and there are such societies), a person who regards herself as extremely heavy would be a beauty. In the same way, the fact that one is single or married, solitary or sociable, aggressive or passive takes on meaning depending on the interpretation society attaches to those traits. Thus, the importance of a given characteristic in your self-concept has as much to do with the significance you and others attach to it as with the existence of the characteristic.

By now you might be thinking, "Adler and Towne are telling me it's not my fault that I've always been shy or unconfident. Since I developed a picture of myself as a result of the way others have treated me, I can't help being what I am." Though it's true that to a great extent you are a product of your environment, to believe you are forever doomed to a poor self-concept would be a big mistake. Having held a poor self-image in the past is no reason for continuing to do so in the future. You *can* change your attitudes and behaviors, as you'll shortly read. So don't despair, and most of all don't use the fact that others have shaped your self-concept as an excuse for self-pity or for acting helpless. Now that you know the effect overly negative evaluations have had on you in the past, you'll be in a better position to revise your perception of yourself more favorably in the future.

Premier Artiste

Watch me perform!
I walk a tightrope of unique
  design.
I teeter, falter, recover
  and bow.
    You applaud.
I run forward, backward,
  hesitate
  and bow.
    You applaud.
If you don't applaud
  I'll Fall.
Cheer me! Hurray me!
Or you push me
Down.

Lenni Shender Goldstein

CIPHER IN THE SNOW

It started with tragedy on a biting cold February morning. I was driving behind the Milford Corners bus as I did most snowy mornings on my way to school. It veered and stopped short at the hotel, which it had no business doing, and I was annoyed as I had to come to an unexpected stop. A boy lurched out of the bus, reeled, stumbled, and collapsed on the snowbank at the curb. The bus driver and I reached him at the same moment. His thin, hollow face was white even against the snow.

"He's dead," the driver whispered.

It didn't register for a minute. I glanced quickly at the scared young faces staring down at us from the school bus. "A doctor! Quick! I'll phone from the hotel...."

"No use, I tell you he's dead." The driver looked down at the boy's still form. "He never even said he felt bad," he muttered. "Just tapped me on the shoulder and said, real quiet, 'I'm sorry. I have to get off at the hotel.' That's all. Polite and apologizing like."

At school, the giggling, shuffling morning noise quieted as the news went down the halls. I passed a huddle of girls. "Who was it? Who dropped dead on the way to school?" I heard one of them half-whisper.

"Don't know his name; some kid from Milford Corners" was the reply.

It was like that in the faculty room and the principal's office. "I'd appreciate your going out to tell the parents," the principal told me.

"They haven't a phone and, anyway, somebody from school should go there in person. I'll cover your classes."

"Why me?" I asked. "Wouldn't it be better if you did it?"

"I didn't know the boy," the principal admitted levelly. "And, in last year's sophomore personalities column I note that you were listed as his favorite teacher."

I drove through the snow and cold down the bad canyon road to the Evans place and thought about the boy, Cliff Evans. His favorite teacher! I thought. He hasn't spoken two words to me in two years! I could see him in my mind's eye all right, sitting back there in the last seat in my afternoon literature class. He came in the room by himself and left by himself. "Cliff Evans," I muttered to myself, "a boy who never talked." I thought a minute. "A boy who never smiled. I never saw him smile once."

The big ranch kitchen was clean and warm. I blurted out my news somehow. Mrs. Evans reached blindly toward a chair. "He never said anything about bein' ailing."

His stepfather snorted. "He ain't said nothin' about anything since I moved in here."

Mrs. Evans pushed a pan to the back of the stove and began to untie her apron. "Now hold on," her husband snapped. "I got to have breakfast before I go to town. Nothin' we can do now anyway. If Cliff hadn't been so dumb, he'd have told us he didn't feel good."

After school I sat in the office and stared blankly at the records spread out before me. I was to close the file and write the obituary for the school paper. The almost bare sheets mocked the effort. Cliff Evans, white, never legally adopted by stepfather, five young half-brothers and sisters. These meager strands of information and the list of D grades were all the records had to offer.

Cliff Evans had silently come in the school door in the mornings and gone out the school door in the evenings, and that was all. He had never belonged to a club. He had never played on a team. He had never held an office. As far as I could tell he had never done one happy, noisy kid thing. He had never been anybody at all.

How do you go about making a boy into a zero? The grade-school records showed me. The first and second grade teachers' annotations read "sweet, shy child," "timid but eager." Then the third grade note had opened the attack. Some teacher had written in a good, firm hand, "Cliff won't talk. Uncooperative. Slow learner." The other academic sheep had followed with "dull"; "slow-witted"; "low I.Q." They became correct. The boy's I.Q. score in the ninth grade was listed as 83. But his I.Q. in the third grade had been 106. The score didn't go under 100 until the seventh grade. Even shy, timid, sweet children have resilience. It takes time to break them.

I stomped to the typewriter and wrote a savage report pointing out what education had done to Cliff Evans. I slapped a copy on the principal's desk and another in the sad, dog-eared file. I banged the typewriter and slammed the file and crashed the door shut, but I didn't feel much better. A little boy kept walking after me, a little boy with a peaked, pale face; a skinny body in faded jeans; and big eyes that had looked and searched for a long time and then had become veiled.

I could guess how many times he'd been chosen last to play sides in a game, how many whispered child conversations had excluded him, how many times he hadn't been asked. I could see and hear the faces and voices that said over and over, "You're a nothing, Cliff Evans."

A child is a believing creature. Cliff undoubtedly believed them. Suddenly it seemed clear to me: When finally there was nothing left at all for Cliff Evans, he collapsed on a snowbank and went away. The doctor might list "heart failure" as the cause of death, but that wouldn't change my mind.

We couldn't find ten students in the school who had known Cliff well enough to attend the funeral as his friends. So the student body officers and a committee from the junior class went as a group to the church, being politely sad. I attended the services with them, and sat through it with a lump of cold lead in my chest and a big resolve growing through me.

I've never forgotten Cliff Evans nor that resolve. He has been my challenge year after year, class after class. I look for veiled eyes or bodies scrouged into a seat in an alien world. "Look, kids," I say silently, "I may not do anything else for you this year, but not one of you is going to come out of here a nobody. I'll work or fight to the bitter end doing battle with society and the school board, but I won't have one of you coming out of here thinking himself a zero."

Most of the time—not always, but most of the time—I've succeeded.

Jean Mizer

Children Learn
What They Live

If a child lives with criticism
  he learns to condemn.
If a child lives with hostility
  he learns to fight.
If a child lives with ridicule
  he learns to be shy.
If a child lives with shame
  he learns to feel guilty.
If a child lives with tolerance
  he learns to be patient.
If a child lives with
  encouragement
  he learns confidence.
If a child lives with praise
  he learns to appreciate.
If a child lives with fairness
  he learns justice.
If a child lives with security
  he learns to have faith.
If a child lives with approval
  he learns to like himself.
If a child lives with
  acceptance and
  friendship
  he learns to find love
  in the world.

Dorothy Law Nolte

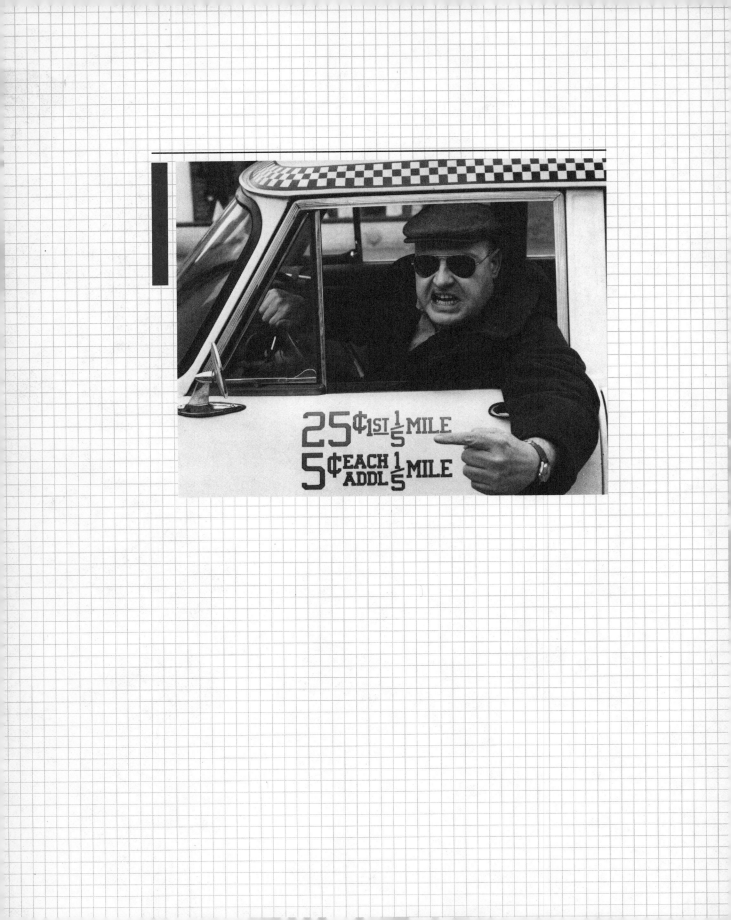

I was in New York the other day and rode with a friend in a taxi. When we got out my friend said to the driver, "Thank you for the ride. You did a superb job of driving."

The taxi driver was stunned for a second. Then he said:

"Are you a wise guy or something?"

"No, my dear man, and I'm not putting you on. I admire the way you keep cool in heavy traffic."

"Yeh," the driver said and drove off.

"What was that all about?" I asked.

"I am trying to bring love back to New York," he said. "I believe it's the only thing that can save the city."

"How can one man save New York?"

"It's not one man. I believe I have made the taxi driver's day. Suppose he has twenty fares. He's going to be nice to those twenty fares because someone was nice to him. Those fares in turn will be kinder to their employees or shopkeepers or waiters or even their own families. Eventually the goodwill could spread to at least 1,000 people. Now that isn't bad, is it?"

"But you're depending on that taxi driver to pass your goodwill to others."

"I'm not depending on it," my friend said. "I'm aware that the system isn't foolproof so I might deal with 10 different people today. If, out of 10, I can make three happy, then eventually I can indirectly influence the attitudes of 3,000 more."

"It sounds good on paper," I admitted, "but I'm not sure it works in practice."

"Nothing is lost if it doesn't. I didn't take any of my time to tell that man he was doing a good job. He neither received a larger tip nor a smaller tip. If it fell on deaf ears, so what? Tomorrow there will be another taxi driver whom I can try to make happy."

"You're some kind of a nut," I said.

"That shows you how cynical you have become. I have made a study of this. The thing that seems to be lacking, besides money of course, for our postal employees, is that no one tells people who work for the post office what a good job they're doing."

"But they're not doing a good job."

"They're not doing a good job because they feel no one cares if they do or not. Why shouldn't someone say a kind word to them?"

We were walking past a structure in the process of being built and passed five workmen eating their lunch. My friend stopped. "That's a magnificent job you men have done. It must be difficult and dangerous work."

The five men eyed my friend suspiciously.

"When will it be finished?"

"June," a man grunted.

"Ah. That really is impressive. You must all be very proud."

We walked away. I said to him, "I haven't seen anyone like you since 'The Man from La Mancha.'"

"When those men digest my words, they will feel better for it. Somehow the city will benefit from their happiness."

"But you can't do this all alone!" I protested. "You're just one man."

"The most important thing is not to get discouraged. Making people in the city become kind again is not an easy job, but if I can enlist other people in my campaign . . ."

"You just winked at a very plain looking woman," I said.

"Yes, I know," he replied. "And if she's a schoolteacher, her class will be in for a fantastic day."

Art Buchwald

Characteristics of the Self-Concept

Now that you have a better idea of how your self-concept has developed, we can take a closer look at some of its characteristics.

The Self-Concept Is Not Objective   Many people view themselves much more harshly than the objective facts suggest. You may have known people, for instance, who insist that they are unattractive or incompetent in spite of your honest insistence to the contrary. In fact, you have probably had feelings of excessively negative self-evaluation yourself. Recall a time when you woke up with a case of the "uglies," convinced that you looked terrible. Remember how on such days you were unwilling to accept even the most sincere compliments from others, having already decided how wretched you were. Whereas many of us fall into the trap of being overly critical only occasionally, others constantly have an unrealistically negative self-concept.

What are the reasons for such excessively negative self-evaluations? One source is *obsolete information*. A string of past failures in school or social relations can linger to haunt a communicator long after they have occurred, even though such events don't predict failure in the future. Similarly, we've known slender students who still think of themselves as fat and clear-complexioned people who still behave as if they were acne-ridden.

Distorted feedback can also create a self-image that is worse than that of a more objective observer. Overly critical parents is one of the most common causes of a negative self-image. In other cases the remarks of cruel friends, uncaring teachers, excessively demanding employers, or even memorable strangers can have a lasting effect. As you read earlier, the impact of significant others and reference groups in forming a self-concept can be great.

A third cause for an unrealistically negative self-concept is the *myth of perfection,* which is common in our society. From the time most of us learn to understand language we are exposed to models who appear to be perfect. Children's stories and advertisements imply that the way to be a hero, the way to be liked and admired, is to show no flaws. Unfortunately, many parents perpetuate the myth of perfection by refusing to admit that they are ever mistaken or unfair. Children, of course, accept this perfectionist façade for a long time, not being in any position to dispute the wisdom of such powerful beings. And from the behavior of the adults around them comes a clear message: "A well-adjusted, successful person has no faults." Thus, children learn that in order to gain acceptance, it's necessary to pretend to "have it all together," even though they know this isn't the case. Given this naive belief that everyone else is perfect and the knowledge that one isn't, it's easy to see how one's self-concept would suffer.

Courtesy of Mell Lazarus and News America Syndicate.

Don't misunderstand: It's not wrong to aim at perfection as an *ideal*. We're only suggesting that achieving this state is usually not possible, and to expect that you should do so is a sure ticket to an inaccurate and unnecessarily low self-concept.

A final reason people often sell themselves short is also connected to *social expectations*. Curiously the perfectionistic society to which we belong rewards those people who downplay the strengths we demand they possess (or pretend to possess). We term these people "modest" and find their behavior agreeable. On the other hand, we consider those who honestly appreciate their strengths to be "braggarts" or "egotists," confusing them with the people who boast about accomplishments they do not possess. This convention leads most of us to talk freely about our shortcomings while downplaying our accomplishments. It's all right to proclaim that you're miserable if you have failed to do well on a project, but it's considered boastful to express your pride at a job well done. It's fine to remark that you feel unattractive but egocentric to say that you think you look good.

After a while we begin to believe the types of statements we repeatedly make. The disparaging remarks are viewed as modesty and become part of our self-concept, and the strengths and accomplishments go unmentioned and are thus forgotten. And in the end we see ourselves as much worse than we are.

To contrast this kind of distortion, try the following exercise. It will give you a chance to suspend the rules we've just discussed by letting you appreciate yourself publicly for a change.

I am not what I think I am.
I am not what you think I am.
I am what I think you think I am.

Aaron Bleiberg and Harry Leubling

Group Bragging

1. This exercise can be done either alone or with a group. If you are with others, sit in a circle so that everyone can see one another.

2. Each person should share three brags about oneself. These brags needn't feature areas in which you are an expert, and they don't have to be concerned with momentous feats. On the contrary, it's perfectly acceptable to brag about some part of yourself that leaves you feeling pleased or proud. For instance, you might brag about the fact that instead of procrastinating you completed a school assignment before the last minute, that you spoke up to a friend even though you were afraid of disapproval, that you bake a fantastic chocolate cake, or that you frequently drive hitchhikers to their destinations although it's out of your way.

3. If you're at a loss for brags, ask yourself
   a. What are some ways in which you've grown in the past year? How are you more skillful, wise, or a better person than you were previously?
   b. Why do certain friends or family members care about you? What features do you possess that make them appreciate you?

4. After you've finished, consider the experience. Did you have a hard time thinking of things to brag about? Would it have been easier to list the things that are *wrong* with you? If so, is this because you are truly a wretched person or because you are in the habit of stressing your defects and ignoring your strengths? Consider the impact of such a habit on your self-concept, and ask yourself whether it wouldn't be wiser to strike a better balance distinguishing between your strengths and shortcomings.

> *It has become something of a cliché to observe that if we do not love ourselves, we cannot love anyone else. This is true enough, but it is only part of the picture. If we do not love ourselves, it is almost impossible to believe fully that we <u>are loved</u> by someone else. It is almost impossible to accept love. It is almost impossible to receive love. No matter what our partner does to show that he or she cares, we do not experience the devotion as convincing because we do not feel loveable to ourselves.*
>
> Nathaniel Branden,
> *The Psychology of Romantic Love*

Not all inaccurate self-concepts are overly negative. Sometimes the images people hold of themselves are more favorable than the objective facts or the opinions of others warrant. You might know someone, for instance, who sees himself as a witty joketeller when others can barely tolerate his attempts at humor. Another person might view herself as highly intelligent although one or more instructors see her academic work as substandard. Or perhaps you consider yourself an excellent worker, in contrast to the employer who wants to fire you.

There are several reasons why some people have a self-concept that others would regard as being unrealistically favorable. First, a self-estimation might be based on *obsolete information*. Perhaps your jokes used to be well received or your grades were high or your work was superior, and now the facts have changed. As you'll soon read, people are reluctant to give up a familiar self-image; this principle makes especially good sense when it's possible to avoid the unpleasant truth of the present by staying in the more desirable past.

A self-concept might also be excessively favorable because of *distorted feedback* from others. A boss may think of himself as an excellent manager because his assistants lave him with false praise in order to keep their jobs. A child's inflated ego may be based on the praise of doting parents.

A third reason for holding what appears to be an unrealistically high self-concept has to do with the *expectations of a society that demands too much of its members*. Much of the conditioning we receive in our early years implies that anything less than perfection is unsatisfactory, so that admitting one's mistakes is often seen as a sign of weakness. Instructors who fail to admit they don't know everything about a subject are afraid they will lose face with their colleagues and students. Couples whose relationships are beset by occasional problems don't want to admit that they have failed to achieve the "ideal" relationship they've seen portrayed in fiction. Parents who don't want to say, "I'm sorry, I made a mistake" to their children are afraid they'll lose the children's respect. Once you accept such an irrational idea—that to be less than perfect is a character defect—admitting your frailties becomes difficult, as if you were admitting you were a failure—and failure is not an element of most peoples' self-concept. Rather than label themselves failures, many people engage in self-deception, insisting to themselves and to others that their behavior is more admirable than the circumstances indicate. We'll have more to say about the reasons behind such behavior and its consequences when we discuss defensiveness in Chapter Nine.

Self-love, my liege, is not so vile a sin as self-neglecting.

Shakespeare,
King Henry V

The Self-Concept Is Multidimensional   It is an oversimplification to talk about "the" self-concept as if each of us possesses only one. There are at least three selves involved at any moment when we communicate.

The Private "Me"   The **perceived self** is the person you believe yourself to be in moments of candor. The perceived self contains many elements: beliefs about your social skills, appearance, intelligence, talents, flaws, and so on. As we've already seen, this perceived self may not be an accurate image, but it is tremendously powerful because it embodies the way you *believe* you are.

The Ideal "Me"   Whereas the perceived self reflects the kind of person you *think* you are, the **desired self** is a picture of the person you *wish* you were. Some

I celebrate myself and sing myself.

Walt Whitman

elements in the desired self match the perceived self. You may, for instance, already be satisfied with the kind of student or friend you are. In other areas, however, your desired self may differ radically from your perceived self.

The Public "Me"   The **presenting self** is the face you try to show others. The presenting self sometimes matches the perceived self. For instance, you might confess to the belief that you behaved admirably or made a fool of yourself last Saturday night. In other cases you present yourself publicly in ways that more closely match the desired self, as when you know you behaved poorly but try to

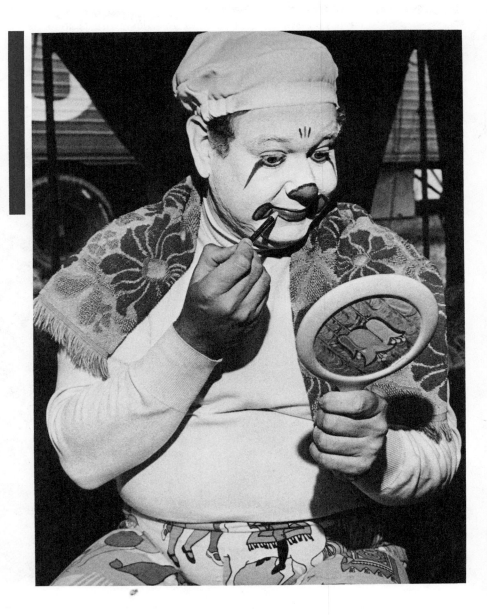

pass your behavior off as justified or even virtuous ("I didn't file an income tax return because I wanted to make a statement about the unconstitutional activities of the IRS!"). There are also causes in which the image you present to others falls somewhere between the perceived and ideal selves, as when you say, "Well, maybe I did act a *little* unfairly. . . ."

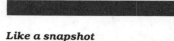

Like a snapshot
  You develop
Unlike a snapshot . . .
  You never stop

Leonard Nimoy

The Self-Concept Affects Communication   The way we feel about ourselves has a direct bearing on how we behave with others. A variety of research highlights differences such as these:[5]

Persons with High Self-Esteem	Persons with Low Self-Esteem
1. Likely to think well of others.	1. Likely to disapprove of others.
2. Expect to be accepted by others.	2. Expect to be rejected by others.
3. Evaluate their own performance more favorably than people with low self-esteem.	3. Evaluate their own performance less favorably than people with high self-esteem.
4. Perform well when being watched: not afraid of others' reactions.	4. Perform poorly when being watched: sensitive to possible negative reaction.
5. Work harder for people who demand high standards of performance.	5. Work harder for undemanding, less critical people.
6. Inclined to feel comfortable with others they view as superior in some way.	6. Feel threatened by people they view as superior in some way.
7. Able to defend themselves against negative comments of others.	7. Have difficulty defending themselves against others' negative comments: more easily influenced.

These differences make sense when you realize that people who don't like themselves are likely to believe that others won't like them either. Realistically or not, they imagine that others are constantly viewing them critically, and they accept these imagined or real criticisms as more proof that they are indeed unlikable, incompetent people. To use the well-known terminology of psychiatrist Eric Berne, they adopt an "I'm not OK—you're OK" orientation of life.

A Healthy Self-Concept Is Flexible   People change. From moment to moment we aren't the same. We wake up in the morning in a jovial mood and turn grumpy before lunch. We find ourselves fascinated in a conversational topic one moment, then suddenly lose interest. One moment's anger often gives way to forgiveness the next. Health turns to illness and back to health. Alertness becomes fatigue, hunger becomes satiation, and confusion becomes clarity.

We also change from situation to situation. We might be relaxed conversationalists with people we know but at a loss for words with strangers. We might be patient when explaining things on the job and have no tolerance for such things at home. We might be wizards at solving mathematical problems but have a terribly difficult time putting our thoughts into words. Despite this variation,

many people do believe—usually mistakenly—that they have stable person-alities. In one study, researchers found that there was little behavioral difference between people who defined themselves as "shy" and those who chose the label "not shy." In other words, both groups acknowledged reacting to some social situations with pounding heart, butterflies in the stomach, and blushing. Labeling made a significant difference: Whereas some subjects said "I *am* shy," their more confident counterparts—who behaved in exactly the same manner—instead chose to say "I sometimes *act* shy."

It's not hard to see that this second way of thinking leads to a much more satisfying—and in most cases a more realistic—self-appraisal. We'll have a great deal more to say about thinking and emotions in Chapter Four.

Over longer stretches of time we also change. We grow older, learn new facts, adopt new attitudes and philosophies, set and reach new goals, and find that others change their way of thinking and acting toward us.

Since we change in these and many other ways, to keep a realistic picture of ourselves we must also change our self-concept. Thus, an accurate self-portrait of the type described on page 31 would probably not be the same as it would have been a year or a few months ago or even the way it would have been yesterday. This doesn't mean that you will change radically from day to day. There are certainly fundamental characteristics of your personality that will stay the same for years, perhaps for a lifetime. It is likely, however, that in other important ways you are changing—physically, intellectually, emotionally, and spiritually.

The Self-Concept Resists Change   In spite of the fact that we change and that a realistic self-concept should reflect this, the tendency to resist revision of our self-perception is strong. When confronted with facts that contradict the mental picture we hold of ourselves, the tendency is to dispute the facts and cling to the outmoded self-perception.

It's understandable why we're reluctant to revise a previously favorable self-concept. As we write these words, we recall how some professional athletes doggedly insist that they can be of value to the team when they are clearly past their prime. It must be tremendously difficult to give up the life of excitement, recognition, and financial rewards that comes with such a talent. Faced with such a tremendous loss, the athlete might well try to play one more season, insisting that the old skills are still there. In the same way a student who did well in earlier years but now has failed to study might be unwilling to admit that the label "good scholar" no longer applies; and a previously industrious worker, pointing to past commendations in a personnel file and insisting that she is a top-notch employee, might resent a supervisor's mentioning increased absences and low productivity. (Remember that the people in these and other examples aren't *lying* when they insist that they're doing well in spite of the facts to the contrary; they honestly believe that the old truths still hold precisely because their self-concepts have been so resistant to change.)

Curiously, the tendency to cling to an outmoded self-perception also holds when the new image would be more favorable than the old one. We recall a former student whom almost anyone would have regarded as beautiful, with physical features attractive enough to appear in any glamour magazine. In spite of her appearance, in a class exercise this woman characterized herself as "ordinary" and "unattractive." When questioned by her classmates, she described how as a child her teeth were extremely crooked and how she had worn braces for several years in her teens to correct this problem. During this time she was often kidded by her friends, who never let her forget her "metal mouth," as she put it. Even though the braces had been off for two years, our student reported that she still saw herself as ugly and brushed aside our compliments by insisting that we were just saying these things to be nice—she knew how she *really* looked.

Examples like this show one problem that occurs when we resist changing an inaccurate self-concept. Our student denied herself a much happier life by clinging to an obsolete picture of herself. In the same way some communicators insist that they are less talented or worthy of friendship than others would suggest, thus creating their own miserable world when it needn't exist. These unfortunate souls probably resist changing because they aren't willing to go through the disorientation that comes from redefining themselves, correctly anticipating that it *is* an effort to think of oneself in a new way. Whatever their reasons, it's sad to see people in such an unnecessary state.

A second problem arising from the persistence of an inaccurate self-concept is self-delusion and lack of growth. If you hold an unrealistically favorable picture of yourself, you won't see the real need for change that may exist. Instead of learning new talents, working to change a relationship, or improving your physical condition, you'll stay with the familiar and comfortable delusion that everything is all right. As time goes by, this delusion becomes more and more difficult to maintain, leading to a third type of problem: defensiveness.

To understand this problem, you need to remember that communicators who are presented with information that contradicts their self-perception have two choices: They can either accept the new data and change their perception accordingly, or they can keep their original viewpoint and in some way refute the new information. Since most communicators are reluctant to downgrade a favorable image of themselves, their tendency is to opt for refutation, either by discounting the information and rationalizing it away or by counterattacking the person who transmitted it. The problem of defensiveness is so great that we will examine it in Chapter Nine.

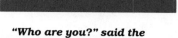

"Who are you?" said the caterpillar.

This was not an encouraging opening for a conversation. Alice replied rather shyly, "I hardly know, sir, just at present—at least I knew who I was when I got up this morning, but I think I must have changed several times since then."

Lewis Carroll,
Alice's Adventures in Wonderland

HATE YOURSELF? IT MAY NOT BE THE REAL YOU

Call it gossip, call it character analysis, call it what you will, the demand for private information about public people is running full throttle. We want to know who they *really* are. We want to know what they're *really* like.

We want the warts, and nothing but the warts.

We have come to associate character revelations with Digging Up the Dirt, and we are currently convinced that only the dirt is real. In short, we think the worst of ourselves. We think the worst *is* ourself.

This rampant pessimism comes up in all kinds of little ways. It came up one night when I visited a friend in a state of terminal grubbiness—matched only by the condition of her apartment. She put one hand on her hair rollers, pointed to the laundry with the other hand and grimaced, "Well, now you've seen the Real Me." This woman, who relines her kitchen drawers twice a year, was sure that she had revealed the secret inner soul of a slob.

But why is it that we are all so sure the *real me* is the one with the dirty hair, the one in dire need of a tube of Clearasil, the one screaming at the children, the one harboring thoughts of dismembering the driver behind us?

Why isn't the *real me* the one who remembers birthdays, keeps the scale within the limits of self-hate and plays "Go Fish" with the kids? Doesn't that count? Why are we so convinced that anything good about us is a civilized shell hiding the *real me*?

The *real me* problem is horribly destructive. If one assumes that the truth about ourselves is too bad to be false, then of course we have to hide it from others. They in turn can't truly love us because they don't know the real us. The unlovable real us.

Our belief in the bad comes from religion on the right and Freud on the left—original sin and original id. Between psychology and theology we've had a double-whammy that's convinced us that way down deep there in the old subconscious or whatever, we are a mass of grasping, greedy, destructive, angry and rather appalling characteristics.

Abraham Maslow, who was one of the few psychologists to try and help us out of this pessimistic view, once observed that not only do we associate our nature with animal nature, but with the worst of the animals.

"Western civilization has generally believed that the animal in us was a bad animal, and that our most primitive impulses are evil, greedy, selfish and hostile," he said, adding that we have chosen to identify with "wolves, tigers, pigs, vultures, or snakes, rather than with at least milder animals like the elephants or chimpanzees."

Maslow was one of those who tried to convince us that the *real me* is no more angry than loving, selfish than generous. He also tried to show us that people are motivated not just by neurotic needs, impulses, and fears, but also out of a positive desire to grow, and out of a sense of fun and pleasure.

But we are not yet convinced. The common street-wisdom of the day is that the most successful of us are "compensating" for some lack, and that the happiest-seeming of us are really "repressing" some unhappiness.

Now, I hate to sound like Little Mary Sunshine, and I am not advocating that we accept everyone at face value. We've been plagued by masked men. But maybe we can get off the hook by letting others off it. The things we hate about ourselves, from the roll around the stomach to the bad temper, aren't more real than the things we like about ourselves. The good isn't a fake. Even if we have to dig for it.

Ellen Goodman

The Self-Fulfilling Prophecy and Communication

The self-concept is such a powerful force on the personality that it not only determines how you see yourself in the present but also can actually influence your future behavior and that of others. Such occurrences come about through a phenomenon called the self-fulfilling prophecy.

A **self-fulfilling prophecy** occurs when a person's expectations of an event makes the outcome more likely to occur than would otherwise have been true. Self-fulfilling prophecies occur all the time although you might never have given them that label. For example, think of some instances you may have known.

> You expected to become nervous and botch a job interview and later did so.

> You anticipated having a good (or terrible) time at a social affair and found your expectations being met.

> A teacher or boss explained a new task to you, saying that you probably wouldn't do well at first. You did not do well.

> A friend described someone you were about to meet, saying that you wouldn't like the person. The prediction turned out to be correct—you didn't like the new acquaintance.

In each of these cases there is a good chance that the event occurred because it was predicted to occur. You needn't have botched the interview, the party might have been boring only because you helped make it so, you might have done better on the job if your boss hadn't spoken up, and you might have liked the new acquaintance if your friend hadn't given you preconceptions. In other words, what helped make each event occur was the expectation of it.

Types of Self-Fulfilling Prophecies   There are two types of self-fulfilling prophecies. *Self-imposed* prophecies occur when your own expectations influence your behavior. In sports you've probably "psyched" yourself into playing either better or worse than usual, so that the only explanation for your unusual performance was your attitude. Similarly, you've probably faced an audience at one time or another with a fearful attitude and forgotten your remarks, not because you were unprepared, but because you said to yourself, "I know I'll blow it."

Certainly you've had the experience of waking up in a cross mood and saying to yourself, "This will be a 'bad day.' " Once you made such a decision, you may have acted in ways that made it come true. If you approached a class expecting to be bored, you most probably did lose interest, owing partly to a lack of attention on your part. If you avoided the company of others because you expected they had nothing to offer, your suspicions would have been confirmed—nothing exciting or new did happen to you. On the other hand, if you approached the same day with the idea that it could be a good one, this expectation probably would have been met also. Smile at people, and they'll probably smile back. Enter a class determined to learn something, and you probably will—even if it's how not to instruct students! Approach many people with the idea that some of them will be good to know, and you'll most likely make some new friends. In these cases and ones like them, your attitude has a great deal to do with how you see yourself and how others will see you.

> *... there is a joke which goes right to the heart of this matter. It is about a man whose tire goes flat on a dark and lonely country road. When he discovers that he doesn't have a jack, he recalls seeing a farm house about a mile back. And so he starts to walk there in the hopes of borrowing one. While he is walking, he talks to himself about his situation: "Wow, I'm really stranded here. The guy will probably want a few dollars to lend me his jack. Why should he do it for nothing? Everyone wants to make a few bucks. A few bucks! If I don't get the jack, I'll never get out of here. He'll realize that, and probably want fifteen dollars, maybe twenty-five dollars. Twenty-five dollars? This guy's really got me by the old cashews. He'll ask fifty dollars, for sure—maybe a hundred."*
>
> *Well, he goes on in this way until he reaches the farm house. He knocks at the door. An elderly farmer answers and with a cheerful smile asks, "Is there something I can do for you, young man?" "Do for me? Do for me?" says the man, "I'll tell you what you can do, you can take your goddamn jack and shove it!"*
>
> *... If, as in this case, you predict that you will not be lent a jack in a spirit of gracious cooperation, you prepare yourself for the confrontation in such a way that you guarantee the jack will not be lent in a spirit of gracious cooperation. Your prediction is transformed into a fact, which then becomes the reality.*
>
> Neil Postman
> *Crazy Talk, Stupid Talk*

A second category of self-fulfilling prophecies is imposed by one person on another, so that the expectations of one person govern another's actions. The classic example was demonstrated by Robert Rosenthal and Lenore Jacobson in a study they described in their book *Pygmalion in the Classroom:*[6] The experimenters told teachers that 20 percent of the children in a certain elementary school showed unusual potential for intellectual growth. The names of these 20 percent were drawn by means of a table of random numbers, which is to say that the names were drawn out of a hat. Eight months later these unusual or "magic" children showed significantly greater gains in IQ than did the remaining children, who had not been singled out for the teachers' attention. The change in the teachers' expectations regarding the intellectual performance of these allegedly "special" children had led to an actual change in the intellectual performance of these randomly selected children. In other words, the children did better, not because they were any more intelligent than their classmates, but because they learned that their teachers—significant others—believed they could.

To put this phenomenon in context with the self-concept, we can say that when a teacher communicates to a child the message "I think you're bright," the child accepts that evaluation and changes her self-concept to include it. Unfortunately, we can assume that the same principle holds for students whose teachers send the message "I think you're stupid."

This type of self-fulfilling prophecy has been shown to be a powerful force for shaping the self-concept and thus the behavior of people in a wide range of

There is an old joke about a man who was asked if he could play a violin and answered, "I don't know. I've never tried." This is psychologically a very wise reply. Those who have never tried to play a violin really do not know whether they can or not. Those who say too early in life and too firmly, "No, I'm not at all musical," shut themselves off prematurely from whole areas of life that might have proved rewarding. In each of us there are unknown possibilities, undiscovered potentialities— and one big advantage of having an open self-concept rather than a rigid one is that we shall continue to expose ourselves to new experiences and therefore we shall continue to discover more and more about ourselves as we grow older.

S. I. Hayakawa

settings outside the schools. In medicine patients who unknowingly use placebos—substances such as injections of sterile water or doses of sugar pills that have no curative value—often respond just as favorably to treatment as those who actually received a drug. The patients believe they have taken a substance that will help them feel better, and this belief actually brings about a "cure." In psychotherapy Rosenthal and Jacobson describe several studies suggesting that patients who believe they will benefit from treatment do so regardless of the type of treatment they receive. In the same vein, when a doctor believes a patient will improve, the patient may do so precisely because of this expectation, whereas another person for whom the physician has little hope often fails to recover. Apparently the patient's self-concept as sick or well—as shaped by the doctor—plays an important role in determining the actual state of health.

Influence of Self-Fulfilling Prophecies

The influence of self-fulfilling prophecies on communication can be strong, acting either to improve or harm relationships. If, for instance, you assume that another person is unlikable, then you'll probably act in ways that communicate your feelings. In such a case, the other person's behavior will probably match your expectations: We usually don't go out of our way to be nice to people who aren't nice to us. If, on the other hand, you treat the other person as likable, the results are likely to be more positive.

In business the power of the self-fulfilling prophecy was proved as early as 1890. A new tabulating machine had just been installed at the U.S. Census Bureau in Washington, D.C. In order to use the machine, the bureau's staff had to learn a new set of skills that the machine's inventor believed to be quite difficult. He told the clerks that after some practice they could expect to punch about 550 cards per day; to process any more would jeopardize their psychological well-being. Sure enough, after two weeks the clerks were processing the anticipated number of cards and reported feelings of stress if they attempted to move any faster.

Later an additional group of clerks was hired to operate the same machines. These workers knew nothing of the devices, and no one had told them about the upper limit of production. After only three days the new employees were each punching over 2,000 cards per day with no ill effects. Again, the self-fulfilling prophecy seemed to be in operation. The original workers believed themselves capable of punching only 550 cards and so behaved accordingly, whereas the new clerks had no limiting expectations as part of their self-concepts and so behaved more productively.[7]

The self-fulfilling prophecy operates in families as well. If parents tell a child long enough that he can't do anything right, his self-concept will soon incorporate this idea, and he will fail at many or most of the tasks he attempts. On the other hand, if a child is told he is a capable or lovable or kind person, there is a much greater chance of his behaving accordingly.

The self-fulfilling prophecy is an important force in interpersonal communication, but we don't want to suggest that it explains all behavior. There are certainly times when the expectation of an event's outcome won't bring it about. Your hope of drawing an ace in a card game won't in any way affect the chance of that card turning up in an already shuffled deck, and your belief that good weather is coming won't stop the rain from falling. In the same way, believing you'll do well in a job interview when you're clearly not qualified for the position is unrealistic. Similarly, there will probably be people you don't like and occasions you won't enjoy, no matter what your attitude. To connect the self-fulfilling prophecy with the "power of positive thinking" is an oversimplification.

In other cases your expectations will be borne out because you're a good predictor and not because of the self-fulfilling prophecy. For example, children are not equally well equipped to do well in school, and in such cases it would be wrong to say that the child's performance was shaped by a parent or teacher even though the behavior did match that which was expected. In the same way, some workers excel and others fail, some patients recover and others don't, all according to our predictions but not because of them.

Keeping these qualifications in mind, you will find it important to recognize the tremendous influence that self-fulfilling prophecies play in our lives. To a great extent we are what we believe we are. In this sense we and those around us constantly create our self-concepts and thus ourselves.

. . . . the difference between a lady and a flower girl is not how she behaves, but how she's treated. I shall always be a flower girl to Professor Higgins, because he always treats me as a flower girl, and always will; but I know I can be a lady to you, because you always treat me as a lady, and always will.

G. B. Shaw,
Pygmalion

Changing Your Self-Concept

After reading this far, you know more clearly just what the self-concept is, how it is formed, and how it affects communication. But we still haven't focused directly on perhaps the most important question of all: How can you change the parts of your self-concept with which you aren't happy? There's certainly no quick method for becoming the person you'd like to be: Personal growth and self-improvement are a lifetime process. But we can offer several suggestions that will help you move closer to your goals.

Have Realistic Expectations   It's extremely important to realize that some of your dissatisfaction might come from expecting too much of yourself. If you demand that you handle every act of communication perfectly, you're bound to be disappointed. Nobody is able to handle every conflict productively, to be totally relaxed and skillful in conversations, always to ask perceptive questions, or to be 100 percent helpful when others have problems. Expecting yourself to reach such unrealistic goals is to doom yourself to unhappiness at the start.

Sometimes it's easy to be hard on yourself because everyone around you seems to be handling themselves so much better than you. It's important to realize that much of what seems like confidence and skill in others is a front to hide uncertainty. They may be suffering from the same self-imposed demands of perfection that you place on yourself.

Even in cases where others definitely seem more competent than you, it's important to judge yourself in terms of your own growth and not against the behavior of others. Rather than feel miserable because you're not as talented as an expert, realize that you probably are a better, wiser, or more skillful person than you used to be and that this is a legitimate source of satisfaction. Perfection is fine as an ideal, but you're being unfair to yourself if you expect actually to reach it.

Self-Appreciation Exercise

As a means of demonstrating the self-appreciation that can come from recognizing that you're growing, try the following:

1. Form a circle in your group. Your group size may be the group as a whole or several small groups.

2. Each group member in turn should complete the following statement:

   "I'm a long way from being perfect at _____, but I'm slowly getting better by _____."

   Here are some examples:

   "I'm a long way from being perfect at <u>my job,</u> but I'm slowly getting better by <u>taking on just one task at a time and persisting until I finish.</u>"

   "I'm a long way from being perfect at <u>approaching strangers,</u> but I'm slowly getting better by <u>going to more parties and once in a while actually starting to talk to people I don't know.</u>"

Have a Realistic Perception of Yourself   One source of a poor self-concept is an inaccurate self-perception. As you've already read, such unrealistic pictures sometimes come from being overly harsh on yourself, believing that you're worse than the facts indicate. By showing the self-concept list you developed on page 31 to others who know you, it will be possible to see whether you have been selling yourself short. Of course, it would be foolish to deny that you could be a better person than you are, but it's also important to recognize your strengths. A periodic session of bragging such as you tried earlier in this chapter is often a good way to put your strengths and short-comings into perspective.

An unrealistically poor self-concept can also arise from the inaccurate feedback of others. Perhaps you are in an environment where you receive an excessive number of downer messages, many of which are undeserved, and a minimum of upper messages. We've known many housewives, for example, who have returned to college after many years spent in homemaking, where they received virtually no recognition for their intellectual strengths. It's amazing that these women have the courage to come to college at all, so low are their self-concepts; but come they do, and most are thrilled to find that they are much brighter and more competent intellectually than they suspected. In the same way, workers with overly critical supervisors, children with cruel "friends," and students with unsupportive teachers all are prone to low self-concepts owing to excessively negative feedback.

If you fall into this category, it's important to put the unrealistic evaluations you receive into perspective and then to seek out more supportive people who will acknowledge your assets as well as point out your shortcomings. Doing so is often a quick and sure boost.

Have the Will to Change   Often we say we want to change, but we aren't willing to do the necessary work. In such cases it's clear that the responsibility for growing rests squarely on your shoulders, as the example following the exercise shows.

Reevaluating Your "Can'ts"

1. Choose a partner and for five minutes or so take turns making and listing statements that begin with "I can't. . . ." Try to focus your statements on your relationships with family, friends, co-workers, students, and even strangers: whomever you have a hard time communicating with.

   Sample statments:

   "I can't be myself with strangers I'd like to get to know at parties."

   "I can't tell a friend how much I care about her."

   "I can't bring myself to ask my supervisor for the raise I think I deserve."

   "I can't ask questions in class."

2. Notice your feelings as you make each statement: self-pity, regret, concern, frustration, and so on, and reveal these to your partner.

3. Now repeat aloud each statement you've just made; except this time change each "can't" to a "won't." After each sentence, tell your partner whatever thoughts you have about what you've just said.

4. After you've finished, decide whether "can't" or "won't" is more appropriate for each item, and explain your choice to your partner.

5. Are there any instances of the self-fulfilling prophecy in your list—times when your decision that you "couldn't" do something was the only force keeping you from doing it?

The point of this exercise should be clear. Often we maintain an unrealistic self-concept by claiming that we "can't" be the person we'd like to be when in fact we're simply not willing to do what's required. You *can* change in many ways, if only you are willing to make the effort.

You might, for instance, decide that you'd like to become a better conversationalist. Seeking the advice of your instructor or some other communication adviser, you receive two pieces of advice. First, you're instructed to spend the next three weeks observing people who handle themselves well in conversations and to record exactly what they do that makes them so skillful. Second, your adviser suggests that you read several books on the subject of conversational skills. You begin these tasks with the best intentions, but after a few days the task of recording conversations becomes a burden—it would be so much easier just to listen to others talk. And your diligent reading program becomes bogged down as the press of other work fills up your time. In other words, you find you just "can't" fit the self-improvement plan into your busy schedule.

Let's be realistic. Becoming a better communicator is probably one of many goals in your life. It's possible that other needs are more pressing, which is completely reasonable. However, you should realize that changing your self-concept often requires a good deal of commitment, and without that effort your good intentions alone probably won't get you much closer to this goal. In communication, as in most other aspects of life, "there's no such thing as a free lunch."

Have the Skill to Change   Often trying isn't enough. In some instances you would change if you knew of a way to do so. To see if this is the case for you,

go back to your list of *can'ts* and *won'ts,* and see if any items there are more appropriately "don't know how." If so, then the way to change is to learn how. You can do so in two ways.

First, you can seek advice—from books such as this one, the references listed at the end of each chapter, and other printed sources. You can also get advice from instructors, counselors, and other experts, as well as friends. Of course, not all the advice you receive will be useful, but if you read widely and talk to enough people, you have a good chance of learning the things you want to know.

A second method of learning how to change is to observe models—people who handle themselves in the ways you would like to master. It's often been said that people learn more from models than in any other way, and by taking advantage of this principle you will find that the world is full of teachers who can show you how to communicate more successfully. Become a careful observer. Watch what people you admire do and say, not so that you can copy them, but so that you can adapt their behavior to fit your own personal style.

At this point, you might be overwhelmed at the difficulty of changing the way you think about yourself and the way you act. Remember, we never said that this process would be an easy one (although it sometimes is). But even when change is difficult, you know that it's possible if you are serious. You don't need to be perfect, but you can improve your self-concept if you choose.

The Skin Horse had lived longer in the nursery than any of the others. He was so old that his brown coat was bald in patches and showed the seams underneath, and most of the hairs in his tail had been pulled out to string bead necklaces. He was wise, for he had seen a long succession of mechanical toys arrive to boast and swagger, and by-and-by break their mainsprings and pass away, and he knew that they were only toys, and would never turn into anything else. For nursery magic is very strange and wonderful, and only those playthings that are old and wise and experienced like the Skin Horse understand all about it.

"What is REAL?" asked the Rabbit one day, when they were lying side by side near the nursery fender, before Nana came to tidy the room. "Does it mean having things that buzz inside you and a stick-out handle?"

"Real isn't how you are made," said the Skin Horse, "it's a thing that happens to you. When a child loves you for a long, long time, not just to play with, but REALLY loves you, then you become Real."

"Does it hurt?" asked the Rabbit.

"Sometimes," said the Skin Horse, for he was always truthful. "When you are Real you don't mind being hurt."

"Does it happen all at once, like being wound up," he asked, "or bit by bit?"

"It doesn't happen all at once," said the Skin Horse. "You become. It takes a long time. That's why it doesn't often happen to people who break easily, or have sharp edges, or who have to be carefully kept. Generally, by the time you are Real, most of your hair has been loved off, and your eyes drop out and you get loose in the joints and very shabby. But these things don't matter at all, because once you are real you can't be ugly, except to people who don't understand."

Margery Williams,
The Velveteen Rabbit

More Readings on the Self-Concept

Briggs, Dorothy C. *Your Child's Self-Esteem.* Garden City, N.Y.: Doubleday, 1975.
   This is a down-to-earth guide for parents and other adults who work with children. It reminds us of the critical role we play in shaping the self-concept of children.

Campbell, Colin. "Our Many Versions of the Self: An Interview with M. Brewster Smith." *Psychology Today* 9 (February 1976): 74–79.
   Psychologist Smith discusses the many ways to view the self and the consequences of each.

Cushman, Donald P., and Dudley D. Cahn, Jr. *Communication in Interpersonal Relationships.* Albany: State University of New York Press, 1985.
   Several parts of this challenging book detail the theory and research that explain the role the self-concept plays in interpersonal communication. See especially Chapters 2 and 3.

Driscoll, Richard. "Their Own Worst Enemies." *Psychology Today* 16 (July 1982): 45–49.
   Clinical psychologist Driscoll provides a number of reasons why some people insist on disparaging themselves. The behavior he describes illustrates the extent to which people will go to maintain an unfavorable self-concept.

Gergen, Kenneth J. "Multiple Identity: The Healthy, Happy Human Being Wears Many Masks." *Psychology Today* 5 (May 1972): 31–35, 64–66.
   This article suggests that we wear a series of masks; instead of a single identity there is a whole series of "you's" that emerge in various situations.

Hayakawa, S.I. *Symbol, Status and Personality.* New York: Harcourt Brace Jovanovich, 1953.
   Written over thirty years ago, Hayakawa's description of the self-concept (in Chapter 4) is still one of the clearest and most interesting ones around.

Insel, Paul M., and Lenore Jacobson. *What Do You Expect? An Inquiry Into Self-Fulfilling Prophecies.* Menlo Park, Calif.: Cummings Publishing Co., 1975.
   This collection of essays and research articles describes some of the many ways the self-fulfilling prophecy operates. Especially valuable for educators.

Rosenthal, Robert, and Lenore Jacobson. *Pygmalion in the Classroom.* New York: Holt, Rinehart and Winston, 1968.
   This book contains a fascinating description of how self-fulfilling prophecies operate in education, social science research, medicine, and everyday life.

Rubin, Zick. "Does Personality Really Change after 20?" *Psychology Today* 15 (May 1981): 18–27.
   According to a large body of research, the answer to this question is both "yes" and "no." The information in this article will comfort people who say, "I am what I am" and encourage those who hope to change.

Snyder, Mark. "Self-Fulfilling Stereotypes." *Psychology Today* 16 (July 1982): 60–68.
   Snyder demonstrates how stereotyped expectations about others can actually create behavior that confirms prejudicial attitudes. This article illustrates the harmful consequences of some self-fulfilling prophecies.

Wells, Theodora. *Keeping Your Cool Under Fire: Communicating Non-Defensively.* New York: McGraw-Hill, 1980.
   This is a lengthy but readable treatment of defensiveness. In addition to

amplifying the material in this chapter, Wells discusses defensiveness in
organizations and relates the subject to some of the principles of emotions
you will read about in Chapter 4 of this book.

Wilmot, William W. *Dyadic Communication*, 3d ed. New York: Random House,
    1987.

Wilmot's second chapter, "Perception of Self," expands several concepts
introduced in the pages you have just read. The discussion of multiple selves
provides an especially valuable explanation of the nature of self-esteem.

Study the drawing on the opposite page. What does it look like to you? Do you see a half view of an old woman with a big nose? Or do you see a young woman looking away from you to the left? If you can't see them both, let us help you. The long vertical line that makes up the old lady's nose is the cheek and jaw of the girl; the old woman's mouth is the girl's neckband, and her left eye is the girl's ear. Can you see them both now?

Suppose you saw only one picture at first, the way most people do. What would you have thought about someone who saw the other one? If you weren't familiar with this type of experiment, if you didn't particularly like the person, or if you happened to be feeling impatient that day, you might be tempted to call anyone who disagreed with you wrong or even crazy. It's possible that you could end up in a nasty argument over who was right, each of you pushing your own view, never recognizing or admitting that both interpretations are correct.

Many communication problems follow this pattern: We ignore the fact that all of us are different and that these differences equip us to view the world from our very own vantage points. Usually we spend more energy defending our own position than understanding another's.

This chapter will help you deal with these problems by giving you some practice in seeing the world through other people's eyes as well as your own. We'll look at some of the reasons the world appears different to each of us. In our survey we'll explore several areas: how our psychological makeup, personal needs, interests, and biases shape our perceptions; the physiological factors that influence our view of the world; the social roles that affect our image of events; and finally the role culture plays in creating our ideas of what behavior is proper. In doing so, we'll cover many of the types of physiological and psychological noise that were described in the communication model in Chapter One.

The Perception Process

We need to begin our discussion of perception by examining the gap between "what is" and what we know. At one time or another you've probably seen photos of sights invisible to the unaided eye: perhaps an infrared photo of a familiar area or the vastly enlarged image of a minute object taken by an electron microscope. You've also noticed how certain animals are able to hear sounds and smell odors that are not apparent to humans. Experiences like these remind us that there is much more going on in the world than we are able to experience with our limited senses, that our idea of reality is in fact only a partial one.

Even within the realm of our senses we're only aware of a small part of what is going on around us. For instance, most people who live in large cities find that the noises of traffic, people, and construction soon fade out of their awareness. Others can take a walk through the forest without distinguishing one bird's call from another or noticing the differences between various types of vegetation. On a personal level, we've all had the experience of failing to notice something unusual about a friend—perhaps a new hairstyle or a sad expression—until it's called to our attention.

Sometimes our failure to recognize some events while noticing others comes from not paying attention to important information. But in other cases it's simply impossible to be aware of everything, no matter how attentive we might be: There is just too much going on.

William James said that "to the infant the world is just a big blooming, buzzing confusion." One reason for this is the fact that infants are not yet able to sort out the myriad impressions with which we're all bombarded. As we grow, we learn to manage all this data, and as we do so, we begin to make sense out of the world.

Since this ability to organize our perceptions in a useful way is such a critical factor in our ability to function, we need to begin our study of perception by taking a closer look at this process. We can do so by examining the three steps by which we attach meaning to our experiences.

Selection   Since we're exposed to more input than we can possibly manage, the first step in perception is to select what data we will attend to. There are several factors that cause us to notice some messages and ignore others.

Stimuli that are *intense* often attract our attention. Something that is louder, larger, or brighter stands out. This explains why—other things being equal— we're more likely to remember extremely tall or short people and why someone who laughs or talks loudly at a party attracts more attention (not always favorable) than do more quiet guests.

Repetitious stimuli, repetitious stimuli, repetitious stimuli, repetitious stimuli, repetitious stimuli, repetitious stimuli also attract attention.* Just as a quiet but steadily dripping faucet can come to dominate our awareness, people to whom we're frequently exposed become noticeable.

ATTENTION IS ALSO FREQUENTLY RELATED TO contrast OR change IN STIMULATION. Put differently, unchanging people or things become less noticeable. This principle gives an explanation (excuse?) for why we take wonderful people for granted when we interact with them frequently. It's only when they stop being so wonderful or go away that we appreciate them.

* We borrowed the graphic demonstrations in this and the following paragraph from Dennis Coon's *Introduction to Psychology,* 3d ed. (St. Paul, Minn.: West Publishing Co., 1983).

Motives also determine what information we select from our environment. If you're anxious about being late for a date, you'll notice whatever clocks may be around you; and if you're hungry, you'll become aware of any restaurants, markets, and billboards advertising food in your path. Motives also determine how we perceive people. For example, someone on the lookout for a romantic adventure will be especially aware of attractive potential partners, whereas the same person at a different time might be oblivious to anyone but police or medical personnel in an emergency.

Selection isn't an objective process: Paying attention to some things and ignoring others invariably distorts our observations. Some of these distortions are due to *omission.* Consider, for example, the times a friend has asked you to describe "what happened" at a party or some other event. We've already suggested that it would be impossible to describe everything that occurred: the clothes everyone wore, the number and type of drinks each person had, the sequence of musical numbers played, every word spoken by every guest, and so on.

As these examples show, many of the details we omit are trivial. In other cases, however, we leave out important information. This kind of omission results in oversimplification. A long, thoughtful explanation winds up being described simply as "he said, 'no.' " "What's she like?" you might ask and get the answer "She's from England and she's beautiful." Although this description may be true, it ignores the fact that the person being described may also be a single parent, a genius, a neurotic, a top-notch skier, along with a host of other significant characteristics. The tendency to oversimplify when selecting information to notice reminds us of the person who, when asked to describe the novel *War and Peace,* replied, "It's about Russia."

Organization   Along with selecting information from the environment, we must arrange it in some meaningful way. You can see how the principle of organization works by looking at Figure 3–1. You can view the picture either as one of a vase or as one of two twins, depending on whether you focus on the white or the black areas. In instances such as this we make sense of stimuli by noticing some data that stand out as a "figure" against a less striking "ground." The "vase-face" drawing is interesting because it allows us to choose between two sets of figure-ground relationships.

Figure 3–1

This principle of figure-ground organization operates in nonvisual ways, too. Recall, for instance, how certain speech can suddenly stand out from a babble of voices. Sometimes the words are noticeable because they include your name, whereas at other times they might be spoken by a familiar voice.

In examples like the ones we just mentioned, the process of organization is relatively simple. But there are other cases in which messages are ambiguous, having more than one possible way of being organized. You can see a visual example of such an ambiguous stimulus in Figure 3–2. How many ways can you view the boxes? One? Two? Three? Keep looking. If you're stumped, Figure 3–3 will help.

We can see the principle of alternative organizing patterns in human interaction. At a young age many children don't yet classify people according to their skin color. They are just as likely to identify a black person, for example, as being tall, wearing glasses, or being a certain age. As they become more socialized, they'll doubtless learn that one common organizing principle used in today's society is race, and when they do, their perceptions of others will

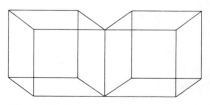

Figure 3–2

Figure 3—3

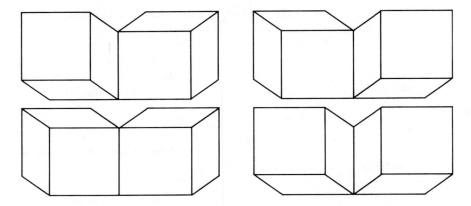

change. In the same way it's possible to classify people or behaviors according to many schemes, each of which will result in different consequences. Do you organize according to age, education, occupation, physical attractiveness, astrological sign, or some other scheme? Imagine how different your relationships would be if you didn't use these organizing methods.

Many interpersonal disputes arise from the different ways people organize a series of events.[1] This process of *punctuation* can be illustrated by visualizing a running quarrel between a husband and wife. The husband accuses the wife of being a nag, while she complains that he is withdrawing from her. Figure 3—4 describes this cycle.

Notice that the order in which each partner punctuates this cycle affects how the dispute looks. The husband begins by blaming the wife: "I withdraw because you nag." The wife organizes the situation differently, starting with the husband: "I nag because you withdraw." Once the cycle gets rolling, it is impossible to say which accusation is accurate. The answer depends on how the sequence is punctuated.

Recall a personal disagreement that escalated over time. Punctuate the dispute twice: first in a way that places blame on the other person, and then in a way that suggests your behavior caused the problem.

Figure 3—4

Interpretation   The third step in the perception process is interpretation. Consider the husband-wife quarrel we just discussed. Suppose the wife suggests that they go away for a weekend vacation. If the husband interprets his wife's idea as more nagging ("You never pay attention to me"), the fight will continue. If he views it as a romantic break from the past, his reaction is likely to be positive. It wasn't the event itself that shaped the outcome, but the way the husband interpreted it.

Interpretation plays a role in virtually every interpersonal act. Is the person who smiles at you across a crowded room interested in romance or simply being polite? Is a friend's kidding a sign of affection or irritation? Should you take an invitation to "drop by any time" literally or not?

Several factors cause us to interpret an event in one way or another:

—*Past experience.* What meaning have similar events held? If, for example, you've been gouged by landlords in the past, you might be skeptical about an apartment manager's assurances that careful housekeeping will assure the refund of your cleaning deposit.

—*Assumptions about human behavior.* "People generally do as little work as possible to get by." "In spite of their mistakes, people are doing the best they can." Beliefs like these will shape the way we interpret another's actions.

—*Expectations.* Anticipation shapes interpretations. If you imagine that your boss is unhappy with your work, you'll probably feel threatened by a request to "see me in my office first thing Monday morning." On the other hand, if you imagine that your work will be rewarded, your weekend will probably be pleasant.

—*Knowledge.* If you know that a friend has just been jilted by a lover or been fired from a job, you'll interpret his aloof behavior differently from your interpretation if you were unaware of what had happened. If you know that an instructor speaks sarcastically to all students, you won't be as likely to take her remarks personally.

—*Personal moods.* When you're feeling insecure, the world is a very different place from the world you experience when you're confident. The same goes for happiness and sadness or any other opposing emotions. The way we feel determines how we interpret events.

Of course, interpretations aren't always accurate; but whether they're correct or not, they shape our thoughts and behavior.

As factors like these suggest, the way we select, organize, and interpret data is often distorted. Consider statements you've heard (and made yourself) that were not complete or fair descriptions of people or events:

—She's a terrible person!
—You don't care about me at all!
—I did my best. It's not my fault!

As we saw in our discussion of selection, distortions like these can arise from *omission,* when we ignore important information. For example, the accusation "You never help out around here" might ignore the fact that the other person does help out sometimes, and the statement "Everybody in Pittsburgh was rude" could overlook the 75 percent of the people you encountered who were either polite or indifferent. In other cases, distortion can arise in the process of interpretation: *overemphasizing* certain facts and *downplaying* others. You might spice up your horror stories about Pittsburgh, for example, by exaggerating the

I've always admired those reporters who can descend on an area, talk to key people, ask key questions, take samplings of opinions, and then set down an orderly report very much like a road map. I envy this technique and at the same time do not trust it as a mirror of reality. I feel that there are too many realities. What I set down here is true until someone else passes that way and rearranges the world in his own style. In literary criticism the critic has no choice but to make over the victim of his attention into something the size and shape of himself. . . .

So much there is to see, but our morning eyes describe a different world than do our afternoon eyes, and surely our wearied evening eyes can only report a weary evening world.

John Steinbeck,
Travels with Charley

We usually see only the things we are looking for—so much that we sometimes see them where they are not.

Eric Hoffer

surliness of a cabdriver and minimizing the helpfulness of a shopkeeper. Likewise, in an effort to make yourself look good, you might exaggerate your role in an athletic victory or minimize your responsibility for a defeat. Finally, distortions sometimes actually lead us to *invent* facts that simply aren't true. "I tried my hardest" or "I meant to call you" you might say in a moment of self-justification when, in fact, you didn't do so at all.

Don't assume that distortions like these are always conscious or deliberate. Most of the time we offer them sincerely, deceiving ourselves as well as trying to convince others. Why do we make such distortions? We'll answer this question in a few pages when we discuss the powerful way the self-concept influences perception.

Perception Checking to Prevent Misunderstandings

Problems can arise when people treat interpretations as if they were matters of fact. Like most people, you probably resent others' jumping to conclusions about the reasons for your behavior:

"Why are you mad at me?" (Who said you were?)
"What's the matter with you?" (Who said anything was the matter?)
"Come on now. Tell the truth." (Who said you were lying?)

As you'll learn in Chapter Nine, even if your interpretation is correct, a dogmatic, mind-reading statement is likely to generate defensiveness.

The skill of **perception checking** provides a better way to handle your interpretations. A perception check has three parts:

1. A description of the behavior you have noticed.
2. Two possible interpretations of the behavior.
3. A request for feedback about how to interpret the behavior correctly.

Perception checks for the preceding three examples would look like this:

"When you stomped out of the room and slammed the door, I wasn't sure whether you were mad at me or just in a hurry. How *did* you feel?"

"You haven't laughed much in the last couple of days. It makes me wonder whether something's bothering you, or whether you're just feeling quiet. What's up?"

"You said you really liked the job I did, but there was something about your voice that made me think you may not like it. How do you really feel?"

Practice your perception checking ability by developing three-part verifications for the following situations:

1. You made what you thought was an excellent suggestion to an instructor. The professor looked uninterested but said she would check on the matter right away. Three weeks have passed and nothing has changed.

2. A neighbor and good friend has not responded to your "Good morning" for three days in a row. This person is usually friendly.

3. You haven't received the usual weekly phone call from the folks back home in over a month. The last time you spoke, you had an argument about where to spend the holidays.

4. An old friend with whom you have shared the problems of your love life for years has recently changed when around you: The formerly casual hugs and kisses have become longer and stronger; and the occasions where you "accidentally" brush up against one another, more frequent.

"*Relativity.*" Here we have three forces of gravity working perpendicularly to one another. Three earth-planes cut across each other at right-angles, and human beings are living on each of them. It is impossible for the inhabitants of different worlds to walk or sit or stand on the same floor, because they have differing conceptions of what is horizontal and what is vertical. Yet they may well share the use of the same staircase. On the top staircase illustrated here, two people are moving side by side and in the same direction, and yet one of them is going downstairs and the other upstairs. Contact between them is out of the question, because they live in different worlds and therefore can have no knowledge of each other's existence.

M. C. Escher

Influences on Perception

Now that we've explored the psychological processes by which we perceive, it's time to look at some of the influences that cause us to select, organize, and interpret information.

Physiological Influences   The first set of influences we need to examine involves our physical makeup. Within the wide range of human similarities, each of us perceives the world in a unique way because of physiological factors. In other words, although the same events exist "out there," each of us receives a different image because of our perceptual hardware. Consider the long list of factors that shape our views of the world:

The Senses   The differences in how each of us sees, hears, tastes, touches, and smells stimuli can affect interpersonal relationships. Consider the following everyday situations:

"Turn down that radio! It's going to make me go deaf."
"It's not too loud. If I turn it down, it will be impossible to hear it."

"It's freezing in here."
"Are you kidding? We'll suffocate if you turn up the heat!"

"Why don't you pass that truck? The highway is clear for half a mile."
"I can't see that far, and I'm not going to get us killed."

These disputes aren't just over matters of opinion. The sensory data we receive are different. Differences in vision and hearing are the easiest to recognize, but other gaps exist as well. There is evidence that identical foods taste different to various individuals.[2] Odors that please some people repel others.[3] Likewise, temperature variations that leave some of us uncomfortable are inconsequential to others. Remembering these differences won't eliminate them, but it will make it easier to remember that the other person's preferences aren't crazy, just different.

Age   One reason older people view the world differently than younger ones is because of a greater scope and number of experiences. There are also developmental differences that shape perceptions. Swiss psychologist Jean Piaget described a series of stages that children pass through on their way to adulthood.[4] According to Piaget, younger children are incapable of performing mental feats that are natural to the rest of us. Until they approach the age of seven, for example, they aren't able to take another person's point of view. This fact helps explain why children often seem egocentric, selfish, and uncooperative. A parent's exasperated plea, "Can't you see I'm too tired to play?" just won't make sense to a four-year-old full of energy, who imagines that everyone else must feel the same.

To a Laplander, a temperature of fifty-eight degrees may be "hot," to a South African it may be "cold." The statement "It is hot (or cold) is a statement about what is going on inside one's body. The statement "The temperature is now ninety degrees (or fifty-eight degrees)" is a statement about what is going on outside one's body....

This distinction is by no means trivial.... I can never prove to a Laplander that fifty-eight degrees is "cool," but I can prove to him that it is fifty-eight degrees. In other words, there is no paradox in two different people's concluding that the weather is both "hot" and "cold" at the same time. As long as they both know that each of them is talking about a different reality, their conversation can proceed in a fairly orderly way.

Neil Postman,
Crazy Talk, Stupid Talk

"This is nothing. When I was your age, the snow was so deep it came up to my chin!"

Health   Recall the last time you came down with a cold, flu, or some other ailment. Do you remember how different you felt? You probably had much less energy. It's likely that you felt less sociable, and that your thinking was slower than usual. These kinds of changes have a strong impact on how you relate to others. It's good to realize that someone else may be behaving differently because of illness. In the same way, it's important to let others know when you feel ill, so they can give you the understanding you need.

Fatigue   Just as being ill can affect your relationships, so can being overly tired. Again it's important to recognize the fact that you or someone else may behave differently when fatigued. Trying to deal with important issues at such a time can get you into trouble.

Hunger   People often get grumpy when they haven't eaten and sleepy after stuffing themselves. A number of physiological changes occur as we eat and become hungry again. Trying to conduct important business at the wrong time in this cycle can lead to problems.

Biological Cycles   Are you a "morning person" or a "night person"? Most of us can answer this question pretty easily, and there's a good physiological reason behind our answer. Each of us is in a daily cycle in which all sorts of changes constantly occur, including body temperature, sexual drive, alertness, tolerance to stress, and mood.[5] Most of these changes are due to hormonal cycles. For instance, adrenal hormones, which affect feelings of stress, are secreted at higher rates during some hours. In the same manner, the male and female sex hormones enter our systems at variable rates. We often aren't conscious of these changes, but they surely govern the way we relate toward each other. Once we're aware that our own daily cycles and those of others govern our feelings and behavior, it becomes possible to manage our lives so that we deal with important issues at the most effective times.

   For some women, the menstrual cycle plays an important role in shaping feelings and thus affects communication. Women aren't the only ones whose communication is affected by periodic changes in mood. Men, too, go through recognizable mood cycles, even though they aren't marked by obvious physical changes. Although they may not be aware of it, many men seem to go through biologically regulated periods of good spirits followed by equally predictable times of depression.[6] The average length of this cycle is about five weeks, although in some cases it's as short as sixteen days or as long as two months. However long it may be, this cycle of ups and downs is quite regular.

   Although neither men nor women can change these emotional cycles, simply learning to expect them can be a big help in improving communication. When you understand that a bad mood is predictable from physiological causes, you can plan for it. You'll know that every few weeks your patience will be shorter, and you'll be less likely to blame your bad moods on innocent bystanders. The people around you can also learn to expect your periodic lows. If they can attribute them to biology, maybe they won't get angry at you.

More than 40 years ago, the late Dr. Rex Hersey believed that male factory workers were incorrectly thought to be stable and unchanging in their daily capabilities. For a year, he observed both management and workers, concentrating on a group of men who seemed particularly well-adjusted and at ease in their jobs. Through a combination of four-times-a-day interviews with the workers, regular physical examinations, and a supplementary set of interviews with their families, he arrived at charts for each individual, showing that emotions varied predictably within the rhythm of 24 hours, and within the larger rhythm of a near-monthly cycle of four to six weeks. Low periods were characterized by apathy, indifference, or a tendency to magnify minor problems out of all proportion. High periods were often marked by a feeling of well-being, energy, a lower body weight, and a decreased need for sleep.

Each man tended to deny that he was more or less irritable, more or less amiable, at different points in his cycle, but standardized psychological tests established clearly that he responded very differently to the same life stresses at different times of his cycle. This denial by men of a cyclicity traditionally accepted by women may be an important factor: a two-edged sword for both men and women.

ESTELLE RAMEY, *MS.* MAGAZINE

New Body, New Perspective

You can get a clearer idea of how physiology influences perception by trying the following exercise.

1. Choose one of the following situations:
   An evening in a singles' bar
   A volleyball game
   A doctor's physical examination

2. How would the event you chose seem different if
   Your eyesight were much worse (or better).
   You had a hearing loss.
   You were eight inches taller (or shorter).
   You were coming down with a serious cold.
   You were a member of the opposite sex.
   You were ten years older (or younger).

Cultural Differences   So far you have seen how physical factors can make the world a different place for each of us. But there's another kind of perceptual gap that often blocks communication—the gap between people from different backgrounds. Every culture has its own world view, its own way of looking at the world. When we remember these differing cultural perspectives, they can be a good way of learning more about both ourselves and others. But at times it's easy to forget that people everywhere don't see things the way we do.

The most obvious cross-cultural problems arise out of poor translation from one language to another:

—Chevrolet was baffled when its Nova model did not sell well in Latin American countries. Officials from General Motors finally realized the problem: In Spanish, *no va* means "does not go."

—One airline lost customers when it promoted the "rendezvous lounges" on its planes flying Brazilian routes. In Portugese, *rendezvous* is a place to have sex.

—McDonald's Corporation was chagrined to learn that in French-Canadian slang "big macs" are large breasts.[7]

Nonverbal behaviors, too, differ from one part of the world to another. In many cultures, the American "OK" sign, made by touching the thumb and forefinger, is an obscene gesture representing the female genitalia. To a woman, it is a proposition for sex, and to a man it is an accusation of homosexuality.[8] It's easy to imagine the problems that could result in an unsuspecting American's innocent gesture.

The range of cultural differences is wide. In Middle Eastern countries, personal odors play an important role in interpersonal relationships. Arabs consistently breathe on people when they talk. As anthropologist Edward Hall explains,

> To smell one's friend is not only nice, but desirable, for to deny him your breath is to act ashamed. Americans, on the other hand, trained as they are not to breathe in people's faces, automatically communicate shame in trying to be polite. Who would expect that when our highest diplomats are putting on their best manners they are also communicating shame? Yet this is what occurs constantly, because diplomacy is not only "eyeball to eyeball" but breath to breath.[9]

"I don't understand it. Why didn't he marry both of them?"

It isn't necessary to travel overseas to encounter differing cultural perspectives. Within this country there are many subcultures, and the members of each one have backgrounds that cause them to see things in unique ways. Failure to recognize these differences can lead to unfortunate and unnecessary misunderstandings. For example, an uninformed Anglo teacher or police officer might interpret the downcast expression of a Latino female as a sign of avoidance, or even dishonesty, when in fact this is the proper behavior in her culture for a female being addressed by an older man. To make direct eye contact in such a case would be considered undue brashness or even a sexual come-on.

Eye contact also differs in black and white cultures. Whereas whites tend to look away from a conversational partner while speaking and at the other person when listening, blacks do just the opposite, looking at their companion more when talking and less when listening.[10] This difference can cause communication problems without either person's realizing the cause. For instance, whites are likely to use eye contact as a measure of how closely the other person is listening: The more others look, the more they seem to be paying attention. A white speaker, therefore, might interpret a black partner's lack of eye contact as a sign of inattention or rudeness when quite the opposite could be true. Since this sort of interpretation is usually unconscious, the speaker wouldn't even consider the possibility of testing his assumptions with the kind of perception check you learned earlier in this chapter.

BEWARE OF A CROCODILE BAG

There was a girl they all said later was American. She went stepping down the street ahead of me, young, with a good figure, well covered. She was well dressed too, and she had a way of working her haunches as she walked that rather singled her out. I had been specially conscious of her for the past hundred yards or so because there was a man following along close behind her who found her irresistible—it was clear to see in the way he was jockeying for position, sidling up on her right, whipping over to the left again, only to be foiled each time by some clumsy interfering pedestrian or a lamp-standard or whatever it might be. I knew what he planned to do, too.

This was in Athens and the three of us—first the girl, next the man I speak of, and then myself bringing up the rear—were walking across the top of Constitution Square along with a whole crowd of others. On we went, the girl wiggling, the man set on his little plan, head held rigid and a bit to one side, one arm behind his back—she must surely have been aware of him as over the road she wobbled and on to the further pavement, down the side of the Hotel Grande Bretagne. The man was most certainly Greek and I guessed that the girl could not be. He was coming right up alongside her now, very close . . . and then suddenly, without warning, the girl spun on her heel in a ninety-degree turn and the next moment she would be in at the Grande Bretagne side-entrance, safe in one of the little segments of those revolving doors. It all but caught the man off-balance: but the Greek mind is very

quick and he reacted instantly. He had to move before she could slip away for ever. So his arm shot out and he pinched her smartly on the behind.

What should a girl do when this happens in the public street? In Athens it is an occupational risk all girls run and I have had talks with several of them about it. They mostly give the same answer. Nothing. They are very sensible about it: They realize that if they dress provocatively and walk provocatively, someone is likely to be provoked into pinching them. An Athenian girl can recognize a pincher a block distant. He is quite easy to identify, it seems—the slightly furtive sideways advance, the hand behind the back symbolically out of sight, as it were, the manoeuvring—girls quickly learn to take evasive action, such as keeping away from shop-windows or points where they could get cornered, and the nervous ones certainly welcomed the full flaring skirts with the layers of stiff frilly petticoat underneath when that fashion came in. But those narrow, hobbling skirts. . . . I have questioned several Athenians. They say it is better to come up from behind if you can. I can see the sense in that. "A mezedaki," they are apt to call it: a little hors d'oeuvre. It is a game, really: a game for two persons, whether the second person wishes to play or not. And once the pincher has got his pinch in, or else the girl has outwitted him and escaped, he does not follow her up. He is content with his pinch, just as a picador is content with his pic, or the bande-rillero with banderillas. Most girls

say there is only one rule—if she loses she must do so with grace. No shrieks, no angry cries. She must just walk on as if nothing whatever had happened. The game is over. She has lost.

The game is not always very well understood by foreign ladies visiting Athens. The case of the American girl who had fled to the safety of the Grande Bretagne underlines my point. Her thinking was confused. She was not in the wrong, maybe, but she reacted wrongly. When the man landed his pinch and won, she lost her head as well as the game. She went black in the face and did something very shocking. Everyone present gasped. She was carrying a big crocodile travel-bag—a splendid thing with metal clasps and buckles, and so on. She swung this bag of hers in a great arc and caught the man over the head with it. He went to the ground instantly. She tossed her head furiously and as she turned to wobble through the revolving doors to refuge, the man was rising to his feet again and wagging his head in his bewilderment.

"I only pinched her . . ." he said plaintively, looking round at us.

We were quite a little crowd by now—the hotel doorman, taxi-drivers, other passersby, a policeman.

"Tch-tch! . . ." the people went, wagging their heads too and staring through the big plate-glass windows at the girl's retreating back. What sort of girl could she be? A taxi-driver helped the poor man up, brushing him down.

"Did she hurt you, then?" he asked with great solicitude.

Peter Mayne

82

Social Roles   So far you have seen how cultural and physiological variations can block communication. Along with these differences, another set of perceptual factors that can lead to communication breakdowns. From almost the time we're born, each of us is indirectly taught a whole set of roles that we'll be expected to play. In one sense this collection of prescribed parts is necessary because it enables a society to function smoothly and provides the security that comes from knowing what's expected of you. But in another way having roles defined in advance can lead to wide gaps in understanding. When roles become unquestioned and rigid, people tend to see the world from their own viewpoint, having no experiences that show them how other people view it. Naturally, in such a situation communication suffers.

Sex Roles   In every society one of the most important factors in determining roles is sex. How should a woman act? What kinds of behavior go with being a man? Until recently most of us never questioned the answers our society gave to these questions. Boys are made of "snips and snails and puppy-dog tails" and grow up to be the breadwinners of families; little girls are "sugar and spice and everything nice," and their mothers are irrational, intuitive, and temperamental. Not everyone fits into these patterns, but in the past the patterns became well established and were mainly unquestioned by most people.

*I have noticed
that men
somewhere around forty
tend to come in from the
field with a sigh
and removing their coat
in the hall
call into the kitchen
   you were right
   grace
   it ain't out there
   just like you've always
said
and she
with the children gone
at last
breathless
puts her hat on her head
   the hell it ain't
coming and going
they pass
in the doorway*

Ric Masten

But in recent years many men and women have found that following these roles caused them to live in different worlds that only partially meet, and they've found this kind of life unsatisfying. People are more and more willing to see themselves and others as **androgynous**—possessing a mixture of traits that have previously been considered exclusively masculine and feminine. Thus, it is becoming more common and acceptable for women to behave assertively, pursue careers, and choose not to take primary responsibility for raising children, whereas many men are beginning to feel comfortable expressing their emotions, becoming deeply involved in child care, and so on.

Occupational Roles The kind of work we do often governs our view of the world. Imagine five people taking a walk through the park. One, a botanist, is fascinated by the variety of trees and plants. The zoologist is looking for interesting animals. The third, a meteorologist, keeps an eye on the sky, noticing changes in the weather. The fourth companion, a psychologist, is totally unaware of nature, instead concentrating on the interaction between the people in the park. The fifth person, being a pickpocket, quickly takes advantage of the others' absorption to make some money. There are two lessons in this little story. The first, of course, is to watch your wallet carefully. The second is that our occupational roles govern our perceptions.

Even within the same occupational setting, the different roles that participants have can affect their experience. Consider a typical college classroom, for example: The experiences of the instructor and students often are quite dissimilar. Having dedicated a large part of their lives to their work, most professors see their subject matter—whether French literature, physics, or speech communication—as vitally important. Students who are taking the course to satisfy a general education requirement may view the subject quite differently: maybe as one of many obstacles that stand between them and a degree, maybe as a chance to meet new people. Another difference centers on the amount of knowledge possessed by the parties. To an instructor who has taught the course many times, the material probably seems extremely simple; but to students encountering it for the first time, it may seem strange and confusing. Toward the end of a semester or quarter the instructor might be pressing onward hurriedly to cover all the material in the course, whereas the students are fatigued from their studies and ready to move more slowly. We don't need to spell out the interpersonal strains and stresses that come from such differing perceptions.

Perhaps the most dramatic illustration of how occupational roles shape perception occurred in 1971.[11] Stanford psychologist Philip Zimbardo recruited a group of middle-class, well-educated young men, all white except for one Oriental. He randomly chose eleven to serve as "guards" in a mock prison set up in the basement of Stanford's psychology building. He issued the guards uniforms, handcuffs, whistles, and billy clubs. The remaining ten subjects became "prisoners" and were placed in rooms with metal bars, bucket toilets, and cots.

Zimbardo let the guards establish their own rules for the experiment. The rules were tough: No talking during meals, rest periods, and after lights out. Head counts at 2:30 A.M. Troublemakers received short rations.

Faced with these conditions, the prisoners began to resist. Some barricaded their doors with beds. Others went on hunger strikes. Several ripped off their identifying number tags. The guards reacted to the rebellion by clamping down hard on protesters. Some turned sadistic, physically and verbally abusing the prisoners. They threw prisoners into solitary confinement. Others forced prisoners to call each other names and clean out toilets with their bare hands.

Within a short time the experiment had become reality for both prisoners and guards. Several inmates had stomach cramps and lapsed into uncontrollable weeping. Others suffered from headaches, and one broke out in a head-to-toe rash after his request for early "parole" was denied by the guards.

The experiment was scheduled to go on for two weeks, but after six days Zimbardo realized that what had started as a simulation had become too intense. "I knew by then that they were thinking like prisoners and not like people," he said. "If we were able to demonstrate that pathological behavior could be produced in so short a time, think of what damage is being done in 'real' prisons. . . ."

This dramatic exercise in which twenty-one well-educated, middle-class citizens turned almost overnight into sadistic bullies and demoralized victims tells us that *how* we think is a function of our roles in society. It seems that *what* we are is determined largely by society's designation of *who* we are. Fortunately, many officials in the field of law enforcement are aware of the perceptual blindness that can come with one's job. These professionals have developed programs that help to overcome the problem, as the following reading illustrates.

The belief that one's own view of reality is the only reality is the most dangerous of all delusions.

Paul Watzlawick

Field Experiments: Preparation for the Changing Police Role

We are all aware that it is extremely difficult to immerse the average policeman into situations that will reveal the feelings of the down-and-outer, the social outcast, the have-nots, and show us their perspective of normal law-enforcement procedures. Obviously the officer, in his police role, would not fit into a ghetto of any kind. But suppose he were a man with a great deal of courage, willing for the sake of experimentation to become a bum, a skid row habitant.

Our Covina officers who were willing to become skid row habitants were carefully selected and conditioned for the role they were about to play. Each man was given three dollars with which to purchase a complete outfit of pawn shop clothing. The only new article of attire he was allowed was foot-wear—reject tennis shoes purchased for a few small coins. Among his other props were such items as a shopping bag filled with collected junk, and a wine bottle camouflaged with a brown paper sack.

Conditioned and ready, our men, assigned in pairs, moved into the Los Angeles skid row district. They soon discovered that when they tried to leave the area, walking a few blocks into the legitimate retail sections, they were told, "Go back where you belong!" Our men knew in reality they were not "bums," but they found that other citizens quickly categorized them and treated them accordingly. Some women, when approached on the sidewalk and asked for a match, stepped out into the street rather than offer a reply, much less a light for a smoke.

During the skid row experiment, our men ate in the rescue missions, and sat through the prayer services with other outcasts and derelicts. They roamed the streets and the alleys, and discovered many leveling experiences. Some were anticipated, others were not. Perhaps the most meaningful experience of the skid row exercise occurred to Tom Courtney, a young juvenile officer with five years' police service.

It was dusk, and Tom and his partner were sauntering back to a prearranged gathering place. Feeling a little sporty, the pair decided to "polish off" the bottle of wine. They paused in a convenient parking lot and Tom tipped the bottle up. As if from nowhere, two uniformed policemen materialized before the surprised pair. Tom and his partner were spread-eagled against a building and searched. Forgetting the admonishment not to reveal identities and purpose unless absolutely necessary, Tom panicked and identified himself.

Later, Tom found it difficult to explain why he was so quick in his revelation. "You wouldn't understand," he told me; then blurted out that he "thought he might get shot."

I found it difficult to receive this as a rational explanation, especially since Tom stated that the officers, while firm, were courteous at all times. With some additional prodding, Tom admitted that as he was being searched, he suddenly thought of every negative thing he had ever heard about a policeman. He even perceived a mental flash of a newspaper headline: "Police Officer Erroneously Shot While on Field Experiment."

"I know better now," Tom continued, "but when you feel that way about yourself, you believe—you believe."

I attempted to rationalize with Tom his reason for fear. I asked if he was certain that the officers were courteous. He replied in the affirmative, but added, "They didn't smile, or tell me what they were going to do next." Tom had discovered a new emotional reaction within his own personal make-up, and it left a telling impression.

Today, Tom Courtney is still telling our department personnel, "For God's sake, smile when you can. And above all, tell the man you're shaking down what you are going to do. Take the personal threat out of the encounter, if you can."

Equally important as Tom's experience, I believe, is the lesson we learned about personal judgments. Our men in the "Operation Empathy" experiment found they were adjudged by the so-called normal population as "being like" all the other inmates of skid row, simply because their appearance was representative.

Perhaps we would all do well to heed the lesson, for now, more than at any other time in our history, policemen must guard against the natural tendency to lump people into categories simply because they look alike.

The invisible barrier that stands between the law enforcer and the law breaker is being bridged through experimentation. Human beings are dealing with human beings, and successful field experiments, conducted by law enforcement, have shown that empathy, understanding another's emotions and feelings, can, in some potentially volatile situations, play an important role towards nonviolence in police-involved situations.

R. Fred Ferguson,
Chief of Police, Riverside Police Department, Riverside, California. Formerly Chief, Covina Police Department, Covina, California.

Role Reversal

Walk a mile in another person's shoes. Find a group that is foreign to you, and try to become a member of it for a while.

If you're down on the police, see if your local department has a ride-along program where you can spend several hours on patrol with one or two officers.

If you think the present state of education is a mess, become a teacher yourself. Maybe an instructor will give you the chance to plan one or more classes.

If you're adventuresome, follow the example of the men in the article on pages 87–88 and become a homeless person for a day. See how you're treated.

If you're a political conservative, try getting involved in a radical organization; if you're a radical, check out the conservatives.

Whatever group you join, try to become part of it as best you can. Don't just observe. Get into the philosophy of your new role and see how it feels. You may find that all those weird people aren't so strange after all.

23 JUDGES SHAKEN BY NIGHT IN NEVADA PRISON

RENO (UPI)—More than one of the 23 shaken judges from across the country who spent the night at the Nevada State Prison said Thursday it should be torn down along with others in the country.

"Appalling."

"My conscience is scarred."

"Am I glad to get out of there. I didn't get five minutes sleep."

These were typical comments from the judges as they climbed off the bus in the morning after returning to Reno from the state prison in Carson City.

The judges, all attending a graduate seminar at the University of Nevada in Reno, volunteered to spend the night in prison to learn more about the prisoners' point of view.

"After that experience I'm going to work for total reform of our prisons," vowed Tom Lee of Miami.

"I was in a cage like an animal," said Newton Vickers of Topeka, who complained the prisoners "screamed and rattled cans against the wall all night and I couldn't sleep."

"Ten years in there is like 100 or maybe 200," he said. "They should take two bull-dozers out there and tear it down."

> *"You're wrong" means "I don't understand you"—*
> *I'm not seeing what you're seeing. But there is*
> *nothing wrong with you, you are simply not me*
> *and that's not wrong.*
>
> Hugh Prather

Self-Concept   A final factor that influences how we think of ourselves and others is the self-concept. Extensive research shows that a person with high self-esteem is more likely to think well of others whereas someone with low self-esteem is likely to have a poor opinion of others.[12] Your own experience may bear this out: Persons with low self-esteem are often cynical and quick to ascribe the worst possible motives to others, whereas those who feel good about themselves are disposed to think favorably about the people they encounter. As one writer put it, "What we find 'out there' is what we put there with our unconscious projections. When we think we are looking out a window, it may be, more often than we realize, that we are really gazing into a looking glass."[13]

Besides distorting the facts about others, our self-concepts also lead us to have distorted views of ourselves. We already hinted at this fact when we explained in Chapter Two that the self-concept is not objective. "It wasn't my fault," you might be tempted to say, knowing deep inside that you were responsible. "I look horrible," you might think as you look into the mirror despite the fact that everyone around you sincerely insists you look terrific.

The egocentric tendency to rate ourselves more favorably than others see us has been demonstrated experimentally.[14] In one study, a random sample of men were asked to rank themselves on their ability to get along with others.[15] Defying mathematical laws, all subjects—every last one—put themselves in the top half of the population. Sixty percent rated themselves in the top 10 percent of the population, and an amazing 25 percent believed they were in the top 1 percent. In the same study, 70 percent of the men ranked their leadership in the top quarter of the population, whereas only 2 percent thought they were below average. Sixty percent said they were in the top quarter in athletic abilities, whereas only 6 percent viewed themselves as below average.

Distortions like these usually revolve around the desire to maintain a self-concept that has been threatened. The desire to maintain a favorable presenting image is often strong. If you want to view yourself as a good student or musician, for example, an instructor who gives you a poor grade or a critic who doesn't appreciate your music *must* be wrong, and you'll find evidence to show it. If you want to think of yourself as a good worker or parent, you'll find explanations for the problems in your job or family that shift the responsibility away from you. Of course, the same principle works for people with excessively negative self-images: They'll go out of the way to explain any information that's favorable to them in terms that show they really are incompetent or undesirable. The list of defense mechanisms in Chapter Nine shows how inventive people can be when a threatened presenting image is at stake.

92

It was six men of Indostan
    To learning much inclined,
Who went to see the elephant
    Though all of them were blind
That each by observation
    Might satisfy his mind.

The first approached the elephant
    And, happening to fall
Against the broad and sturdy side,
    At once began to bawl:
"Why, bless me! But the elephant
    Is very much like a wall!"

The second, feeling of the tusk,
    Cried: "Ho! What have we here
So very round and smooth and
        sharp?
    To me, 'tis very clear,
This wonder of an elephant
    Is very like a spear!"

The third approached the animal,
    And, happening to take
The squirming trunk within his
        hands
    Thus boldly up he spake:
"I see," quoth he, "the elephant
    Is very like a snake!"

The fourth reached out his eager
    hand
    And felt about the knee:
"What most this wondrous beast is
    like
    Is very plain," quoth he:
'Tis clear enough the elephant
    Is very like a tree!"

The fifth who chanced to touch the
    ear
    Said: "E'en the blindest man
Can tell what this resembles
    most—
    Deny the fact who can:
This marvel of an elephant
    Is very like a fan!"

The sixth no sooner had begun
    About the beast to grope
Than, seizing on the swinging tail
    That fell within his scope,
"I see," quoth he, "the elephant
    Is very like a rope!"

And so these men of Indostan
    Disputed loud and long,
Each in his own opinion
    Exceeding stiff and strong;
Though each was partly in the
    right,
    And all were in the wrong.

John G. Saxe

The Accuracy—and Inaccuracy—of Perception

By now you can see how self-concept can distort perceptions of both our own motives and those of others. Research has uncovered several other perceptual errors we need to guard against.[16]

We Are Influenced by What Is Most Obvious   The error of being influenced by what is most obvious is understandable. As you read at the beginning of this chapter, we select stimuli from our environment that are noticeable: intense, repetitious, unusual, or otherwise attention-grabbing. The problem is that the most obvious factor is not necessarily the only cause—or the most significant one for an event. For example,

—When two children (or adults, for that matter) fight, it may be a mistake to blame the one who lashes out first. Perhaps the other one was at least equally responsible, teasing or refusing to cooperate.

—You might complain about an acquaintance whose malicious gossiping or arguing has become a bother, forgetting that by putting up with such behavior in the past you have been at least partially responsible.

—You might blame an unhappy working situation on the boss, overlooking other factors beyond her control such as a change in the economy, the policy of higher management, or demands of customers or other workers.

We Cling to First Impressions, Even If Wrong   Labeling people according to our first impressions is an inevitable part of the perception process. These labels are a way of making interpretations. "She seems cheerful." "He seems sincere." "They sound awfully conceited."

If they're accurate, impressions like these can be useful ways of deciding how to respond best to people in the future. Problems arise, however, when the labels we attach are inaccurate; once we form an opinion of someone, we tend to hang onto it and make any conflicting information fit our image.

Suppose, for instance, you mention the name of your new neighbor to a friend. "Oh, I know him," your friend replies. "He seems nice at first, but it's all an act." Perhaps this appraisal is off-base. The neighbor may have changed since your friend knew him, or perhaps your friend's judgment is simply unfair. Whether the judgment is accurate or not, once you accept your friend's evaluation, it will probably influence the way you respond to the neighbor. You'll look for examples of the insincerity you've heard about . . . and you'll probably find them. Even if the neighbor were a saint, you would be likely to interpret his behavior in ways that fit your expectations. "Sure he *seems* nice," you might think, "but it's probably just a front." Of course, this sort of suspicion can create a self-fulfilling prophecy, transforming a genuinely nice person into someone who truly becomes an undesirable neighbor.

Given the almost unavoidable tendency to form first impressions, the best advice we can give is to keep an open mind and be willing to change your opinion as events prove it mistaken.

We Tend to Assume Others Are Similar to Us   In Chapter Two you read one example of this principle: that people with low self-esteem imagine others view them unfavorably, whereas people who like themselves imagine that

others like them, too. The frequently mistaken assumption that others' views are similar to our own applies in a wide range of situations:

   —You've heard a slightly raunchy joke that is pretty funny. You might assume that it won't offend a somewhat straight friend. It does.

   —You've been bothered by an instructor's tendency to get off the subject during lectures. If you were a professor, you'd want to know if anything you were doing was creating problems for your students, so you decide that your instructor will probably be grateful for some constructive criticism. Unfortunately, you're wrong.

   —You lost your temper with a friend a week ago and said some things you regret. In fact, if someone said those things to you, you'd consider the relationship was finished. Imagining that your friend feels the same way, you avoid making contact. In fact, your friend feels that he was partly responsible and has avoided you because he thinks you're the one who wants to end things.

   Examples like these show that others don't always think or feel the way we do and that assuming similarities exist can lead to problems. How can you find out the other person's real position? Sometimes by asking directly, sometimes by

The test of a first-rate intel-
ligence is the ability to hold two
opposed ideas in mind at the
same time and still retain the
ability to function.

F. Scott Fitzgerald

checking with others, and sometimes by making an educated guess after you've thought the matter out. All these alternatives are better than simply assuming everyone would react as you do.

We Tend to Favor Negative Impressions of Others Over Positive Ones

What do you think about Harvey? He's handsome, hardworking, intelligent, and honest. He's also very conceited.

Did the last quality make a difference in your evaluation? If it did, you're not alone. Research shows that when people are aware of both the positive and negative characteristics of another, they tend to be more influenced by the undesirable traits. In one study, for example, researchers found that job interviewers were likely to reject candidates who revealed negative information even when the total amount of information was highly positive.

Sometimes this attitude makes sense. If the negative quality clearly outweighs any positive ones, you'd be foolish to ignore it. A surgeon with shaky hands and a teacher who hates children, for example, would be unsuitable for their jobs whatever their other virtues. But much of the time it's a bad idea to pay excessive attention to negative qualities and overlook good ones. This is the mistake some people make when screening potential friends or dates: They find some who are too outgoing or too reserved, others who aren't intelligent enough, and still others who have the wrong sense of humor. Of course, it's important to find people you truly enjoy, but expecting perfection can lead to much unnecessary loneliness.

Poet Ric Masten may have said it best: While you're waiting for a prince (or princess) to come along and change your life, you might as well realize that frogs can be fun, too!

We Blame Innocent Victims for Their Misfortunes

The blame we assign for misfortune depends on who the victim is. When others suffer, we often blame the problem on their personal qualities. On the other hand, when we're the victims, we find explanations outside ourselves. Consider a few examples:

—When *they* botch a job, we might think they weren't listening well or trying hard enough; when *we* make the mistake, the problem was unclear directions or not enough time.

—When *he* lashes out angrily, we say he's being moody or too sensitive; when *we* blow off steam, it's because of the pressure we've been under.

—When *she* gets caught speeding, we say she should have been more careful; when *we* get the ticket, we deny we were driving too fast or say, "Everybody does it."

There are at least two explanations for this kind of behavior. Since most of us have an idealized presenting image, we defend ourselves by finding explanations for our own problems that make us look good. Basically what we're doing here is saying, "It's not *my* fault." And since looking good is so often a personal goal, putting others down can be a cheap way to boost our own self-esteem, stating in effect, "I'm better than he is."

Don't misunderstand: We don't always commit the kind of perceptual errors described in this section. Sometimes, for instance, people *are* responsible for their misfortunes, and our problems are not our fault. Likewise, the most obvious interpretation of a situation may be the correct one. Nonetheless, a large amount of research has proved again and again that our perceptions of others are often distorted in the ways listed here. The moral, then, is clear: Don't assume that your first judgment of a person is accurate.

Think about someone you've had a disagreement with lately or someone you dislike. See if any of your perceptions about that person might be mistaken in one of the ways you've just read about.

1. Were the person's actions motivated by some cause that isn't obvious?
2. Were your first impressions of the person mistaken?
3. Have you assumed that the person is thinking or acting the way you would?
4. Have you been placing too much emphasis on negative characteristics and downplaying positive ones?
5. Have you been unfairly blaming the person for his or her problems?

Empathy: The Road to Understanding

After reading the preceding list of perceptual errors, you can see that we do indeed select, organize, and interpret the behaviors of others in ways that are often inaccurate. What we clearly need to do, then, is improve our ability to understand others from their point of view as well as from our own. This ability to put ourselves into another person's shoes—view an experience from the other's perspective—is called *empathy*.

Empathy Defined   Empathy is the ability to project oneself into another person's point of view so as momentarily to think the same thoughts and feel the same emotions as the other person. The word *empathy* is derived from two Greek words (ἐν + πάθοσ) that mean "feeling in(side)."[17] These words suggest that empathy involves more than just intellectually understanding another person: It requires you to *experience* the other's perception.*

Empathy is quite different from sympathy. The roots for sympathy (σύν + πάθοσ) mean "feeling with." As this definition implies, when you feel sympathetic, you stand beside the other person, feeling compassion. But despite your concern, sympathy doesn't involve the degree of understanding that empathy does. When you sympathize, it is still the other's confusion, joy, or pain. When you empathize, the experience becomes your own, at least for the moment.

How important is empathy in interpersonal relationships? One simple experiment suggests the answer.[18] In this study, college students were asked to list their impression of people either shown in a videotaped discussion or described in a short story. Half the students were instructed to empathize with the person as much as possible, and the other half were not given any instructions about empathizing. The results were impressive: The students who did not practice empathy were prone to explain the person's behavior in terms of personality characteristics. For example, they might have explained a cruel statement by

*Technically speaking, *empathy* is the ability to experience *emotions* similar to another person, whereas *decentering* or *role taking* is the ability to experience the other's thoughts as well. In practice, however, *empathy* is used as the global, all-purpose term.

saying the speaker was mean, or they might have attributed a divorce to the partners' lack of understanding. The empathetic students, on the other hand, were more aware of possible elements in the situation that might have contributed to the reaction. For instance, they might have explained a person's unkind behavior in terms of job pressures or personal difficulties. In other words, practicing empathy seems to make people more tolerant.

You might argue here, "Why should I be more tolerant? Maybe behavior I disapprove of *is* due to the other person's personality defects and not just a result of outside factors. Maybe people are selfish, lazy, or stupid much of the time." Perhaps so, but research clearly shows that we are much more charitable when finding explanations for our own behavior.[19] When explaining our actions, we are quick to suggest situational causes: "I was tired." "She started it." "The instructions weren't clear." In other words, we often excuse ourselves by saying, "It wasn't my fault!" As we've already said, we're less forgiving when we judge others. Perhaps becoming more empathetic can help even the score a bit, enabling us to treat others at least as kindly as we treat ourselves.

Requirements for Empathy   Empathy may be valuable, but it isn't always easy. In fact, research shows that it's hardest to empathize with people who are different from us radically: in age, sex, socioeconomic status, intelligence, and so forth.[20] In order to make the kind of perceptual leaps we are talking about, you need to develop several skills and attitudes.

Open-Mindedness   Perhaps the most important ingredient of empathy is the ability and disposition to be open-minded—to set aside for the moment his or her own beliefs, attitudes, and values and consider those of the other person. This is especially difficult when the other person's position is radically different from your own. The temptation is to think (and sometimes say), "That's crazy!" "How can you believe that?" or "I'd do it this way. . . ." As you'll read in Chapter Seven, attitudes like these often aren't helpful even if your position is correct.

Being open-minded is often difficult because people confuse *understanding* another's position with *accepting* it. These are quite different matters. To understand why a friend might disagree with you, for example, doesn't mean you have to give up your position and accept hers.

Imagination   Being open-minded often isn't enough to allow empathy. You also need enough imagination to be able to picture another person's background and thoughts. A happily married or single person needs imagination to empathize with the problems of a friend considering divorce. A young person needs it to empathize with a parent facing retirement. A teacher needs it to understand fully the problems facing students, just as those students can't be empathetic without having enough imagination to understand how their instructor feels.

Commitment   Since empathizing is often difficult, a third necessary quality is the sincere desire to understand the other person. Listening to unfamiliar, often confusing information takes time and isn't always fun. If you aim to be empathetic, it's realistic to be willing to face the challenge.

Two Views

1. Choose a disagreement you presently have with another person or group. The disagreement might be a personal one—such as an argument about how to settle a financial problem or who is to blame for a present state of affairs—or it might be a dispute over a contemporary public issue, such as the right of women to obtain abortions on demand or the value of capital punishment.

2. In 300 words or so, describe your side of the issue. State why you believe as you do, just as if you were presenting your position to an impartial jury.

3. Now take 300 words or so to describe in the first-person singular how the other person sees the same issue. For instance, if you are a religious person, write this section as if you were an atheist: For a short while get in touch with how the other person feels and thinks.

4. Now show the description you wrote in step 3 to your "opponent," the person whose beliefs are different from yours. Have that person read your account and correct any statements that don't reflect his or her position accurately. Remember, you're doing this so that you can more clearly understand how the issue looks to the other person.

5. Make any necessary corrections in the account you wrote in step 3, and again show it to your partner. When your partner agrees that you understand his or her position, have your partner sign your paper to indicate this.

6. Now record your conclusions to this experiment. Has this perceptual shift made any difference in how you view the issue or how you feel about your partner?

Developing the Ability to Empathize   Being open-minded, imaginative, and committed is often easier said than done. What we often need is a tool that will help us practice these attitudes. The following reading offers just such a tool. Paul Reps's **pillow method** is paradoxical. Although on the one hand it seems too simple really to work, a few attempts will show that seeing other sides of an issue can be a difficult job. The results are worth the effort as you will see when you try it for yourself.

pillow education in rural japan

How do you solve your problems?

In growing up, as much as we do grow up mentally, each of us has personal difficulties and social problems in relation with those about us.

In rural Japan a group of children are meeting their difficulties in a splendid way and even teaching their parents how to do so.

They are using a method of thinking for themselves that works. If someone has done a child an injustice, if his feelings have been hurt, if he is in pain, if his or her father is quarreling—anything becomes the subject of the study. They have no name for it, but since it is done with a pillow it might be called pillow education.

A pillow has four sides and a middle. A problem has four approaches and a middle.

For example: A child is slow in his school work. It is his turn to show the group how he is thinking through this situation. He sits before the pillow, placing his hand at 1.

"Suppose I can't think quickly," he says. "If I place here at 1, 'I can't think quickly,' then this may change at some time."

"Here at 2," he continues, placing his hand in the 2 position, "is the place where I can think quickly and easily."

In doing this, the child has objectified a handicap. He takes a look at it instead of letting it corrode inside. He also has imagined the possibility of his difficulty resolving.

He continues: "If 1 is where I can't think quickly and 2 is the place where I can, then I will say that here, 3, is a situation where I can

think both slowly and quickly, where 1 and 2 are together."

This third step (the 3 place on the pillow) merges the opposites 1 and 2, just as 2 reverses the problem originally placed at 1. This is education in action done by the individual for himself or herself. There are as many girls as boys in the group.

It is a fact that most adults can only think to 2: white 1, black 2; right 1, wrong 2. "If I am right as I am, 1, you are wrong, 2." Entire lives are lived with this kind of thinking. Such dichotomy, either-or, right-wrong, often results in private and public unresolved differences.

When we consider the millions of dead in recent wars from a few leaders not being able to think beyond 2, we see how urgently such education is needed.

"You say you are right, father, and our neighbor is wrong," the child tells his father who is in a property dispute. "But may there not also be a place where you are wrong and he is right. And both of you may be wrong and both right. And at still another place, 4, all this may be forgotten."

"What are you talking about?" asks the father.

The child gets out a pillow. In a few weeks the father, considerably interested, has visited the school.

Such sharp thinking came from a very young child. He had a method of thinking. If he finds no difficulty to solve for himself during the week, he begins looking for one. When called on in class, he doesn't like to be without a subject he has worked on.

The child reasons not in numbers but in a relational sequence of four steps: wrong, 1; right, 2; both wrong and right, 3; and neither wrong nor right, 4. He does this as if walking a 4-step figure with his hand and with his mind.

In conclusion each child summarizes his presentation by cupping his hands in the middle of the pillow ( ), affirming an unnamed center from which 1, 2, 3, 4 emerge. It is as if he holds the complete problem in his own hands at the center of the pillow.

He then places the hand at 4, 3, 2, 1 and concludes by saying, "All these are gloriously affirmed," or "Each of these steps is good."

It is a tremendous relief to the child to be able to reverse his thinking and not be continually held in one viewpoint. In such kind of problem-solving, "nothing is the matter," their mentor says. A rebellious child joining the others invariably becomes gentle in a few weeks.

The number of students has grown from 3 to more than 30. The meetings are a happy time. Students are entirely unhesitant about making personal problems public.

All kinds of subjects come before the pillow: Hunger and not hungry, beauty and ugliness, environment and mood, a bucket of water and a sea of water, blood of Orientals and blood of Occidentals, after my death the world will be and will not be— anything that troubles or concerns the child.

Even the pillow itself is treated as a subject: "When 1, I first heard of this study, I grasped it easily. But 2, since I understand it, it never finishes in me."

Another child offers: "Here 1, I will say that American culture surpasses Japanese culture. But here 2, I will say Japanese culture surpasses American culture. And here 3, I will say that both American culture surpassing Japanese and Japanese culture surpassing American are correct. And here 4,

actually neither does any such surpassing.

"Moreover since all these spring from center ( ), in such a view 4, 3, 2, 1, each is fully affirmed by me."

The students' building is inadequate. They are poor. They share clothes and food with those still poorer. But they have declined publicity for the group, thinking it might only bring more problems.

"Someone else must tell others about our method, we don't know how," they say. They are too busy using it in their own lives.

Have you something troubling you? Have you a pillow? If so, you may join these children in their wide way of thinking. It is not easy to translate the feeling of one person into the language of another and to convey in words the sensible delight of gentle hands on a pillow showing parents how to think.

Paul Reps,
Square Sun, Square Moon

Apart from abstract propositions of comparison (such as two and two make four), propositions which tell us nothing by themselves about concrete reality, we find no proposition ever regarded by any one as evidently certain that has not either been called a falsehood, or at least had its truth sincerely questioned by some one else.

William James,
The Will to Believe

Pillow Talk

Try using the pillow method in your life. It isn't easy, but once you begin to understand it, the payoff in increased understanding is great.

1. Pick a person or viewpoint with whom or which you strongly disagree. If you've chosen a person, it's best to have him or her there with you; but if that's not possible, you can do it alone.

2. What disagreement should you choose? No doubt there are many in your life:

   > parent-child
   > teacher-student
   > employer-employee
   > brother-sister
   > friend-friend
   > nation-nation
   > Republican-Democrat

3. For each problem you choose, really place yourself in each position on the pillow as you encounter it:

   a. Your position is correct, and your opponent's is wrong.
   b. Your opponent's position is correct, and yours is wrong.
   c. Both your positions are correct, and both are wrong.
   d. It isn't important which side is right or wrong. Finally, affirm the fact that all four positions are true.

4. The more important the problem is to you, the harder it will be to accept positions 2, 3, and 4 as valid. But the exercise will work only if you can suspend your present position and imagine how it would feel to hold the other ones.

5. How can you tell if you've been successful with the pillow method? The answer is simple: If after going over the four steps you can understand—not necessarily accept but just understand—the other person's position, you've done it. After you've reached this understanding, do you notice any change in how you feel about the other person?

PILLOW EDUCATION IN ACTION

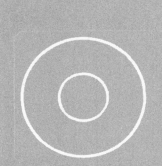

INTRODUCTION

The problem I decided to work on involves me and my boyfriend. We have trouble deciding how serious our relationship is. I want things more casual to give both of us some freedom. Bill wants things on a one-to-one basis, not allowing either of us to go out with anyone else.

POSITION 1: I'M RIGHT AND BILL IS WRONG

I am right in wanting the relationship more casual. Because of some bad past experiences I like my relationships to grow gradually, so that I don't get hurt as easily. Also, I like to be genuine when expressing feelings or commitments, and I don't want to say things to Bill before I really feel them. Bill should realize this and not push me.

POSITION 2: BILL IS RIGHT AND I'M WRONG

He's right for wanting the relationship his way because this is the only way he has ever had a relationship. He likes the security of having a steady girlfriend. Since it's hard to change old habits and Bill's reasons for wanting a steady relationship make sense for him, I'm wrong for not being more sympathetic.

POSITION 3: BOTH OF US ARE RIGHT AND BOTH ARE WRONG

I'm right to want a more casual relationship because of my past experiences and present needs, but I'm wrong to ignore Bill's needs. He's right to want the security of a one-to-one relationship because he feels best with this type of arrangement, but he's wrong to push me before I'm ready.

POSITION 4: IT DOESN'T MATTER

When both of us are together and enjoying each other, no thought is given to future commitments or the type of relationship we are involved in. At that moment no thought of this problem enters our minds, and for the moment it does not exist.

CONCLUSION: ALL POSITIONS ARE TRUE TOGETHER

I can see now that Bill and I are limiting ourselves by not going beyond steps 1 and 2. If we can see the rights and wrongs in each other's position, then maybe we can find an answer that both of us will feel good about.

INTRODUCTION

Last week I came to work expecting to work in my regular unit, but I was "floated" to another floor. When I reported there, I had a disagreement with the charge nurse over my assignment. I tried to explain to her that I felt she was giving me too heavy a workload, but she didn't seem to understand what I was trying to tell her. I was angry and upset, so I decided to give the pillow method a try to see if I could clarify the problem before I talked to her again.

POSITION 1: I AM RIGHT, AND SHE IS WRONG

The assignment she gave me was too heavy. Patient assignments should not be made by room numbers without regard to the type of patient and the amount of care needed. She was wrong to give me the patients needing the most care in order to give her staff a break. I am justified to feel used when treated in this manner.

POSITION 2: SHE IS RIGHT, AND I AM WRONG

I shouldn't expect any special treatment just because I'm from another floor. It is easier to assign patients by room number. It keeps the nurses in one area and saves working steps.

POSITION 3: WE ARE BOTH RIGHT AND BOTH WRONG

I am right in saying that she did give me the hardest assignment, but I can see now that she didn't do this with the intention of being unfair: Somebody had to do the work. She was right (or at least reasonable) in being cool to my complaints: They probably made me look as if I wanted special consideration. I am right in saying that assigning patients by room number is not an effective way to manage the workload.

POSITION 4: IT REALLY ISN'T IMPORTANT WHO WAS RIGHT OR WRONG

I was only working on that floor one night and probably won't work there for another year. The whole incident is over and not worth worrying about. There are always going to be times when things won't work out the way I'd like them. I must admit that the majority of my assignments are fair.

CONCLUSION

I found this assignment very interesting. When I started, I was still so angry that I felt totally dumped on! By the time I had gone through the four steps I could understand why the charge nurse behaved as she did. I didn't feel so angry at her and decided to talk to her again to see if we could clear the air. We did get a chance to do this, and I was able to explain clearly how I felt in a way that didn't threaten her. What's more important, I was able to truly listen to her without becoming defensive. The outcome of our conversation was that we parted feeling good about each other. I know I couldn't have done this before looking at the issue from all sides, using the pillow method.

INTRODUCTION

My husband, Rick, is a dreamer of dreams. His most recent idea was to give up our house and possessions and move onto a boat in the harbor. Since I am a fairly conventional person, the idea seemed crazy to me at first. But we talked about it many times, and eventually the idea became an adventure to me, and I was comfortable considering the real possibility of making the move. I shared our idea with my mother, expecting to get a favorable reaction. Instead, I got a very negative, emotional one. She saw the idea as being just one more crazy dream that Rick was forcing upon me. I, naturally, claimed she was wrong and defended Rick.

POSITION 1: I'M RIGHT AND SHE'S WRONG

After many years of close companionship I'm certain that I know Rick much better than my mother does. I have accepted the dreamer in him and realize that most of his ideas will never come to pass. When he arrives at the conclusion that one of his dreams is important enough to pursue, we discuss it. He doesn't shove the plan down my throat. We have a great deal of respect for each other, and our decision-making is always a joint effort. Therefore, I think my mother is wrong to say that any initiation of change in our marriage is always one-sided, in favor of Rick.

POSITION 2: SHE'S RIGHT, AND I'M WRONG

My mother looks at our relationship, first, from the standpoint of how it affects me, her daughter. She loves me and is genuinely concerned about how equal my part is in our relationship. She has known me all my life and sees me as lacking assertiveness in making my ideas known. Many times in the past she has seen me sacrifice my principles to keep in good standing with a person I care for. For this reason, she also sees me as being very fragile and easily hurt. No mother can stand by and watch her daughter walk into a possibly painful situation without trying, in some way, to shelter her from the blow. This is her way of reaching out to save me from what she thinks could be a big mistake and the hurt that would go with it.

She also admits that the idea of giving up our house and all our possessions to live on a boat rocks the very foundation upon which she has built her life. Coming from a background where security is a marriage, a house, comfortable furnishings, and kids in the future, she sees no sense in what we plan to do with our lives. She sees us throwing away a lot of positive, concrete things that we have worked hard to get, just to chase a rainbow. Therefore, she thinks that I am wrong for wanting to live out a fantasy that has potential for disappointment when I have all these comfortable, real things surrounding me and providing me with security.

POSITION 3: WE'RE BOTH RIGHT, BUT BOTH WRONG

I am right in defending Rick's position, as well as my own, in our relation-ship because I know that we share equally in ideas and decision-making. I am wrong in thinking that just because she is my mother and she tends always to take what she sees to be my side in issues, she lacks any real sound basis for her side of the argument in this case.

She is right in being concerned about my feelings in this situation. She is wrong in overlooking the fact that I have changed through the years. My attitudes have become more open and receptive to change, and I have the courage now to challenge many aspects of life that I would never even have approached when I was younger.

POSITION 4: IT DOESN'T MATTER

I know that my mother loves Rick and cares about his welfare, just as she cares about mine. If we pursue this dream, she won't love us any less. Even though she may disagree with us, her love is not based on whether or not we always see things her way. In the same way, I love her regardless of whether she accepts everything that I think or do. Looking at the overall picture, I can see that how we both feel about this issue really doesn't mat-ter because it doesn't affect our love for each other, now or in the future.

CONCLUSION

Now that I can see the truth in all four positions, the issue takes on a new kind of importance. It has been the tool to help me overcome my own selec-tive perception of the boat situation, as well as others. I have also attained a greater insight into the way my mother feels about things, but more importantly, why she feels as she does. In light of this discovery, the issue does matter a great deal to me and is important.

More Readings on Perception

Argyle, Michael. *Social Interaction.* Chicago: Aldine-Atherton, 1969.
  *Argyle offers a comprehensive treatment of the influences that shape our
  perceptions of others.*

Bartley, S. Howard. *Perception in Everyday Life.* New York: Harper & Row, 1972.
  *An interesting introduction to the field of psychobiology, covering a wide-
  ranging discussion of the physiological influences on perception. Anecdotes
  and informal discussion by the author make a potentially intimidating subject
  interesting and understandable.*

Dodd, Carley H. *Dynamics of Intercultural Communication.* Dubuque, Iowa:
  W. C. Brown, 1982.
  *Dodd provides a good overview of what happens when people from two
  cultures try to communicate. Especially relevant for readers interested in
  interpersonal communication is Chapter 6, which deals with matters such as
  self-disclosure, submission and dominance, formality, and interpersonal
  attraction across cultures.*

Goldstein, E. Bruce. *Sensation and Perception,* 2d ed. Belmont, Calif.:
  Wadsworth, 1984.
  *A detailed look at the subject of human perception. Chapters 7 and 14 are
  especially relevant to the material you have just read.*

Hammer, Richard. "Role Playing: A Judge Is a Con, A Con Is a Judge." *New York
  Times Magazine,* September 14, 1969.
  *The account of a role-reversal workshop that gave some judges and police a
  new perspective on what it means to be a prisoner.*

Hastrof, Albert H., and Hadley Cantril. "They Saw a Game: A Case Study."
  Journal of Abnormal and Social Psychology 49 (January 1954).
  *This study clearly illustrates how selective perception operates by showing
  how football fans view their home team as saints and the opposition as
  monsters.*

Laing, R. D., H. Phillipson, and A. R. Lee. *Interpersonal Perception: A Theory
  and a Method of Research.* New York: Harper & Row, 1966.
  *A thorough examination of the social and psychological factors that influence
  interpersonal perception.*

Loftus, Elizabeth. *Eyewitness Testimony.* Cambridge, Mass.: Harvard University
  Press, 1979.
  *Loftus describes the way in which events are retained in the memory and how
  factors can influence the way they are recalled.*

Ramey, Estelle. "Men's Cycles." *Ms.,* Spring 1972.
  *A description of men's emotional, physical, and sexual cycles as well as the
  daily rhythms that both men and women undergo.*

Rubin, Zick. "The Rise and Fall of First Impressions." In *Interpersonal Communication in Action,* 3d ed. Bobby R. Patton and Kim Giffin, eds. New York:
  Harper & Row, 1980.
  *Rubin presents a readable description of the factors that distort the accuracy
  of first impressions.*

Schneider, David J., Albert H. Hastrof, and Phoebe C. Ellsworth. *Person Perception,* 2d ed. Reading, Mass.: Addison-Wesley, 1979.
  Probably the best introduction to the subject available. The book covers

matters such as snap judgments, perceptual accuracy, bias, and self-perception.

Snyder, Mark. "Self-Fulfilling Stereotypes." *Psychology Today* 16 (July 1982): 60–68.

Snyder illustrates the power of perception by citing research that describes how expecting others to behave in stereotypical ways actually increases the likelihood that they will act according to the predictions.

Tyler, Leona. *The Psychology of Human Differences*. New York: Appleton-Century-Crofts, 1965.

A survey of the psychological differences between people. Covers intelligence, personality, sex, age, race, class.

Wilentz, Joan S. *The Senses of Man*. New York: Thomas Y. Crowell, 1968.

This book provides a good bridge between overly simple and technical work in perception.

Wilmot, William W. *Dyadic Communication*, 2d ed. Reading, Mass.: Addison-Wesley, 1979.

Chapter 3 covers much of the information discussed in the preceding pages, but the different emphasis and references make it worth reading.

It's hard to talk about communication without realizing the importance of emotions. Think about it: Feeling confident can make the difference between success and failure in everything from giving a speech to asking for a date, whereas insecurity can ruin your chances. Being angry or defensive can spoil your time with others, whereas feeling and acting calm will help prevent or solve problems. The way you share or withhold your feelings of affection can affect the future of your relationships. On and on the list of feelings goes: appreciation, loneliness, joy, insecurity, curiosity, irritation. The point is clear: Communication shapes our feelings, and feelings influence our communication.

Because this subject of emotions is so important, we'll spend this chapter taking a closer look. Just what are feelings, and how can we recognize them? How are feelings caused, and how can we control them, increasing the positive ones and decreasing the negative? When and how can we best share our feelings with others?

What Are Emotions?

Suppose an extraterrestrial visitor asked you to explain emotions. How would you answer? You might start by saying that emotions are things that we feel. But this doesn't say much, for in turn you would probably describe feelings as synonymous with emotions. Social scientists who have studied the role of affect generally agree that there are several components to the phenomena we label as feelings.

Physiological Changes   When a person has strong emotions, many bodily changes occur. For example, the physical components of fear include an increased heartbeat, a rise in blood pressure, an increase in adrenaline secretions, an elevated blood sugar level, a slowing of digestion, and a dilation of pupils. Some of these changes are recognizable to the person having them. These sensations are termed **proprioceptive stimuli,** meaning that they are activated by the movement of internal tissues. Proprioceptive messages can offer a significant clue to your emotions once you become aware of them. For instance, we know a woman who began focusing on her internal messages and learned that every time she returned to the city from a vacation, she felt an empty feeling in the pit of her stomach. From what she'd already learned about herself, she knew that this sensation always accompanied things she dreaded; and once aware of this knowledge, she realized she was much happier in the country. Now she is trying to find a way to make the move she knows is right for her.

Another friend of ours had always appeared easygoing and agreeable in even the most frustrating circumstances. But after focusing on internal messages, he discovered his mild behavior contrasted strongly with the tense muscles and headaches that he got during trying times. This new awareness led him to realize that he did indeed feel frustration and anger—and that he somehow needed to deal with these feelings if he were going to feel truly comfortable.

... Every thought, gesture, muscle tension, feeling, stomach gurgle, nose scratch, fart, hummed tune, slip of the tongue, illness—everything is significant and meaningful and related to the now. It is possible to know and understand oneself on all these levels, and the more one knows the more he is free to determine his own life.

If I know what my body tells me, I know my deepest feelings and I can choose what to do.... Given a complete knowledge of myself, I can determine my life; lacking that mastery, I am controlled in ways that are often undesirable, unproductive, worrisome, and confusing.

William Schutz,
Here Comes Everybody

How Does It Feel?

Here's a way to learn more about yourself from your body. You can do this exercise with a group or individually outside the classroom. If you do it alone, read all the steps ahead of time so that you can work through the whole experience without interrupting yourself. However, the exercise will have more impact if you do it for the first time in a group because in this way your facilitator can read the instructions for you. Also, in a group your feelings can be shared and compared.

The ellipses (. . .) in the instructions indicate points where you should pause for a moment and examine what you're feeling.

1. Wherever you are, find yourself a comfortable position, either lying or sitting. You'll need to find a quiet place with no distractions. You'll see that the exercise works better if you dim the lights.

2. Close your eyes. The visual sense is so dominant that it's easy to neglect your other senses.

3. Now that your eyes are closed and you're comfortable, take a trip through your body and visit its various parts. As you focus on each part, don't try to change what you find . . . just notice how you are, how you feel.

4. Now let's begin. Start with your feet. How do they feel? Are they comfortable, or do they hurt? Are your toes cold? Do your shoes fit well, or are they too tight?

   Now move your attention to your legs. . . . Is there any tension in them, or are they relaxed? . . . Can you feel each muscle? . . . Are your legs crossed? Is there pressure where one presses against the other? . . . Are they comfortable?

   Now pay attention to your hips and pelvis . . . the area where your legs and backbone join. Do you feel comfortable here, or are you not as relaxed as you'd like to be? If you're seated, direct your attention to your buttocks. . . . Can you feel your body's weight pressing against the surface you're sitting on?

   Now move on to the trunk of your body. How does your abdomen feel? . . . What are the sensations you can detect there? . . . Is anything moving? . . . Focus on your breathing. . . . Do you breathe off the top of your lungs, or are you taking deep, relaxed breaths? . . . Does the air move in and out through your nose or your mouth? Is your chest tight, or is it comfortable?

   Checking your breathing has probably led you to your throat and neck. Is your throat comfortable, or do you feel a lump there you need to keep swallowing? . . . How about your neck? . . . Can you feel it holding your head in its present position? . . . Perhaps moving your head slowly from side to side will help you feel these muscles doing their work. . . . Is there tension in your neck or shoulders?

   Now let's move to your face. . . . What expression are you wearing? . . . Are the muscles of your face tense or relaxed? Which ones? Your mouth . . . brow . . . jaw . . . temples? Take a few moments and see. . . .

   Finally, go inside your head and see what's happening there. . . . Is it quiet and dark, or are things happening there? . . . What are they? Does it feel good inside your head, or is there some pressure or aching? . . .

   You've made a trip from bottom to top. Try feeling your whole body now. . . .

See what new awareness of it you've gained. . . . Are there any special parts of your body that attract your attention now? . . . What are they telling you?

Now there's another very important part of your body to focus on. It's the part of you where you *feel* when you're happy or sad or afraid. Take a moment and find that spot. . . . See how you are now in there. . . . See what happens when you ask yourself, "How am I now? How do I feel?" . . . See what happens in that place when you think of a personal problem that's been bothering you lately. . . . Be sure it's something that's important to your life now. . . . Now see if you can get the feel of this problem there in the place where you feel things. . . . Let yourself feel all of it. . . . If the feeling changes as you focus on it, that's OK. Just stay with the feeling wherever it goes and see how it is. . . . If what you feel now makes a difference to you, see what that difference is. . . . Now, take a few minutes to use in whatever way you like, and then slowly open your eyes.

5. Now think about the following questions. If you're with a group, you may want to discuss them there.

a. Did you find out things about your body that you hadn't noticed before? Did you discover some tensions that you'd been carrying around? How long do you think you've been this way? Did recognizing them make any difference to you?

b. Could you find the part of yourself where you usually feel things? Where was it? Or are there different spots for different feelings? Did focusing on your problem make some kind of difference to you?

"What the hell was that? Something just swept over me— like contentment or something."

Drawing by Weber. © 1981 The New Yorker Magazine, Inc.

Nonverbal Reactions   Not all physical changes that accompany emotions are internal. Feelings are often apparent by observable changes. Some of these changes involve a person's appearance: blushing, sweating, and so on. Other changes involve behavior: a distinctive facial expression, posture, gestures, different vocal tone and rate, and so on.

Although it's reasonably easy to tell when someone is feeling a strong emotion, it's more difficult to be certain exactly what that emotion might be. A slumped posture and sigh may be a sign of sadness, or it may signal fatigue. Likewise, trembling hands might indicate excitement, or they may be an outward sign of fear. As you'll learn in Chapter Six, nonverbal behavior is usually ambiguous; and it's dangerous to assume that it can be "read" with much accuracy.

Although we usually think of nonverbal behavior as the reaction to an emotional state, there may be times when the reverse is true—when nonverbal behavior actually *causes* emotions. Research by Paul Ekman uncovered instances when experimental subjects were able to create various emotional states by altering their facial expressions.[1] When volunteers were coached to move their facial muscles in ways that appeared afraid, angry, disgusted, amused, sad, surprised, and contemptuous, the subjects' bodies responded as if they were having these feelings. Interestingly, the link between smiling and happiness was not as strong because, Ekman speculates, smiles can represent so many different emotions: happiness, anger, sadness, and so on.

Cognitive Interpretations   Although there may be cases in which there is a direct connection between physical behavior and emotional states, in most situations the mind plays an important role in determining how we feel. On page 111 you read that some physiological components of fear are a racing heart, perspiration, tense muscles, and elevated blood pressure. Interestingly enough, these symptoms are similar to the physical changes that accompany excitement, joy, and other emotions. In other words, if we were to measure the physical condition of someone having a strong emotion, we would have a hard time knowing whether that person was trembling with fear or quivering with excitement. The recognition that the bodily components of most emotions are similar led some psychologists to conclude that the experience of fright, joy, or anger comes primarily from the *label* we give to the same physical symptoms at a given time.[2] This cognitive explanation of emotion has been labeled **attribution theory.** Psychologist Philip Zimbardo offers a good example of attribution in action:

> I notice I'm perspiring while lecturing. From that I infer I am feeling nervous. If it occurs often, I might even label myself a "nervous person." Once I have the label, the next question I must answer is "Why am I nervous?" Then I start to search for an appropriate explanation. I might notice some students leaving the room, or being inattentive. I am nervous because I'm not giving a good lecture. That makes me nervous. How do I know it's not good? Because I'm boring my audience. I am nervous because I am a boring lecturer and I want to be a good lecturer. I feel inadequate. Maybe I should open a delicatessen instead. Just then a student says, "It's hot in here, I'm perspiring and it makes it tough to concentrate on your lecture." Instantly, I'm no longer "nervous" or "boring."[3]

In his book *Shyness,* Zimbardo discusses the consequences of making inaccurate or exaggerated attributions. In a survey of more than 5,000 subjects, over 80 percent described themselves as having been shy at some time in their lives, whereas more than 40 percent considered themselves presently shy. Most significantly, those who labeled themselves "not shy" behaved in virtually the *same way* as their shy counterparts. They would blush, perspire, and feel their hearts pounding in certain social situations. The biggest difference between the two groups seemed to be the label with which they described themselves.[4] This is a significant difference. Someone who notices the symptoms we've described and thinks, "I'm such a shy person!" will most likely feel more uncomfortable and communicate less effectively than another person with the same symptoms who thinks, "Well, I'm a bit shaky (or excited) here, but that's to be expected."

We'll take a closer look at ways to reduce unpleasant emotions through cognitive processes later in this chapter.

Types of Emotions

So far our discussion has implied that although emotions may differ in tone, they are similar in most other ways. In truth, emotions vary in many respects.

Primary and Mixed Emotions   Emotions are rather like colors: Some are simple, whereas others are blends. Robert Plutchik's "emotion wheel" illustrates the difference.[5] Plutchik has identified eight **primary emotions,** which are placed inside the perimeter of the wheel. He suggests that these primary feelings can combine to form other, **mixed emotions,** some of which are listed outside the circle.

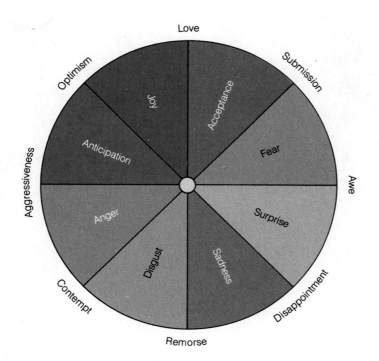

The emotion wheel: primary and mixed emotions

Whether or not you agree with the specific emotions Plutchik identifies as primary and secondary, the wheel suggests that many feelings need to be described in more than a single term. To understand why, consider the following examples. For each one, ask yourself two questions: How would you feel? What feelings might you express?

An out-of-town friend has promised to arrive at your house at six o'clock. When he hasn't arrived by nine, you are convinced that a terrible accident has occurred. Just as you pick up the phone to call the police and local hospitals, your friend breezes in the door with an offhand remark about getting a late start.

You and your companion have a fight just before leaving for a party. Deep inside you know you were mostly to blame, even though you aren't willing to admit it. When you arrive at the party, your companion leaves you to flirt with several other attractive guests.

In situations like these you would probably feel mixed emotions. Consider the case of the overdue friend. Your first reaction to his arrival would probably be relief: "Thank goodness, he's safe!" But you would also be likely to feel anger: "Why didn't he phone to tell me he'd be late?" The second example would probably leave you with an even greater number of mixed emotions: guilt at contributing to the fight, hurt and perhaps embarrassment at your friend's flirtations, and anger at this sort of vengefulness.

Intensity of emotions

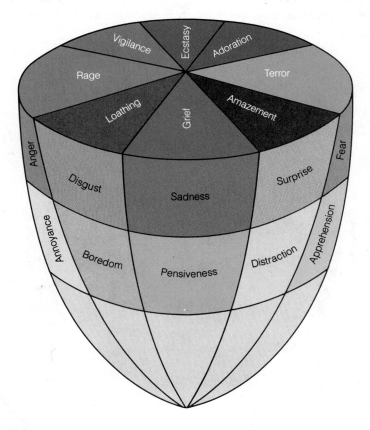

Despite the commonness of mixed emotions, we often communicate only one feeling . . . usually the most negative one. In both the preceding examples you might show only your anger, leaving the other person with little idea of the full range of your feelings. Consider the different reaction you would get by showing *all* your emotions in these cases, and others.

Intense and Mild Emotions   Another way emotions are like colors is in their intensity. The figure on page 116 illustrates this point clearly.[6] Each vertical slice represents the range of a primary emotion from its mildest to its most intense state. This model shows the importance not only of choosing the right emotional family when expressing yourself but also of describing the strength of the feeling. Some people fail to communicate clearly because they understate their emotions, failing to let others know how strongly they feel. To say you're "annoyed" when a friend breaks an important promise, for example, would probably be an understatement. In other cases, people chronically overstate the strength of their feelings. To them, everything is "wonderful" or "terrible." The problem with this sort of exaggeration is that when a truly intense emotion comes along, they have no words left to describe it adequately. If chocolate chip cookies from the local bakery are "fantastic," how does it feel to fall in love?

Recognizing Your Emotions

Keep a three-day record of your feelings. You can do this by spending a few minutes each evening recalling what emotions you felt during the day, what other people were involved, and the circumstances in which the emotion occurred.

At the end of the three-day period you can understand the role emotions play in your communication by answering the following questions:

1. How did you recognize the emotions you felt: through proprioceptive stimuli, nonverbal behaviors, or cognitive processes?

2. Did you have any difficulty deciding which emotion you were feeling?

3. What emotions do you have most often? Are they primary or mixed? Mild or intense?

4. In what circumstances do you or don't you express your feelings? What factors influence your decision to show or not show your feelings? The type of emotion? The person or persons involved? The situation (time, place)? The subject that the emotion involves (money, sex, and so on)?

5. What are the consequences of the type of communicating you just described in step 4? Are you satisfied with these consequences? If not, what can you do to become more satisfied?

Reasons for Not Expressing Emotions

Most people rarely express their emotions, at least verbally. You can verify this fact by counting the number of genuine emotional expressions you hear over a two- or three-day period. You'll probably discover that these sorts of expressions

An emotion without social rules of containment and expression is like an egg without a shell: a gooey mess.

Carol Tarvis

are extremely rare. People are generally comfortable making statements of fact and often delight in expressing their opinion, but they rarely disclose how they feel.

Why is it that people fail to express their feelings? Let's take a look at several reasons.

Social Rules   In our society the unwritten rules of communication discourage the direct expression of most emotions.[7] From a young age we learn that it is undesirable to voice negative feelings. Consider familiar statements like

"Don't get angry."
"There's nothing to worry about."
"There's no reason to feel bad."
"Control yourself—don't get excited."
"For heaven's sake, don't cry!"

Notice how each of these messages denies the right to feel a certain emotion. Anger isn't legitimate, and neither is fear. Feeling bad is silly. And don't make a scene by crying. Often parental admonitions like these are nothing more than coded requests for some peace and quiet. But when they are repeated often enough, the underlying instruction comes through loud and clear—only a narrow range of emotions is acceptable.

Surprisingly, social rules even discourage too much expression of positive feelings.[8] A hug and kiss for Mother is all right, though a young man should shake hands with Dad. Affection toward friends becomes less and less frequent as we grow older, so that even a simple statement such as "I like you" is seldom heard between adults.

Social Roles   Expression of emotions is also limited by the requirements of many social roles. Salespeople are taught always to smile at customers, no matter how obnoxious. Teachers are portrayed as paragons of rationality, supposedly representing their field of expertise and instructing their students with total impartiality. Students are rewarded for asking "acceptable" questions and otherwise being submissive creatures.

CATHY   **by Cathy Guisewite**

Furthermore, stereotyped sexual roles discourage people from freely expressing certain emotions. Men don't cry and are rational creatures. They must be strong, emotionally and physically. Aggressiveness is a virtue ("the Marine Corps builds men"). Women, on the other hand, are supposedly flighty, prone to tears and other emotional outbursts. They are often irrational and intuitive. A certain amount of female determination and assertiveness is appealing, but when faced with a man's resistance, women ought to defer lest they be accused of being a "bitch" or worse.

Inability to Recognize Emotions   The result of all these restrictions is that many of us lose the ability to feel deeply. Just as a muscle withers away when it is unused, our capacity to recognize and act on certain emotions decreases without practice. It's hard to cry after spending most of one's life fulfilling the role society expects of a man even when the tears are inside. After years of denying your anger, the ability to recognize that feeling takes real effort. For someone who has never acknowledged love for one's friends, accepting that emotion can be difficult indeed.

Fear of Self-Disclosure   In a society that discourages the expression of feelings, emotional self-disclosure can seem risky.[9] For a parent, boss, or teacher whose life has been built on the image of confidence and certainty, it may be frightening to say, "I'm sorry. I was wrong." A person who has made a life's work out of not relying on others has a hard time saying, "I'm lonesome. I want your friendship."

Moreover, someone who musters up the courage to share feelings such as these still risks unpleasant consequences. Others might misunderstand: An expression of affection might be construed as a romantic invitation, and a confession of uncertainty might appear to be a sign of weakness. Another risk is that emotional honesty might make others feel uncomfortable. Finally, there's always a chance that emotional honesty could be used against you, either out of cruelty or thoughtlessness.

Guidelines for Expressing Emotions

Emotions are a fact of life. Nonetheless, communicating them effectively isn't a simple matter. It's obvious that showing every feeling of boredom, fear, anger, or frustration would get you in trouble. Even the indiscriminate sharing of positive feelings—love, affection, and so on—isn't always wise. On the other hand, withholding emotions can be personally frustrating and can keep relationships from growing and prospering.

The following suggestions can help you decide when and how to express your emotions. Combined with the guidelines for self-disclosure in Chapter Nine, they can improve the effectiveness of your emotional expression.

Recognize Your Feelings   Answering the question "How do you feel?" isn't always easy. As you've already read, there are a number of ways in which feelings become recognizable. Physiological changes can be a clear sign of your emotional state. Monitoring nonverbal behaviors is another excellent way to keep in touch with your feelings. You can also recognize your emotions by monitoring your thoughts, as well as the verbal messages you send to others. It's not far from the verbal statement "I hate this!" to the realization that you're angry (or bored, nervous, or embarrassed).

Choose the Best Language   Most people suffer from impoverished emotional vocabularies. Ask them how they're feeling and the response will almost always include the same terms: *good* or *bad, terrible* or *great,* and so on. Take a moment now and see how many feelings you can write down. After you've done your best, look at the list on page 123 and see which ones you've missed.

Relying on a small vocabulary of feelings is as limiting as using only a few terms to describe colors. To say that the ocean in all its moods, the sky as it varies from day to day, and the color of your true love's eyes are all "blue" only tells a fraction of the story. Likewise, it's overly broad to use a term like *good* or *great* to describe how you feel in situations as different as earning a high grade, finishing a marathon, and hearing the words "I love you" from a special person.

There are several ways to express a feeling verbally:

—Through *single words:* "I'm angry" (or "excited," "depressed," "curious," and so on).

—By describing *what's happening to you:* "I feel like giving up," "My stomach is tied in knots," "I'm on top of the world."

—By describing *what you'd like to do:* "I feel like running away," "I'd like to give you a hug," "I feel like giving up."

Many communicators think they are expressing feelings when, in fact, their statements are emotionally counterfeit. For example, it sounds emotionally revealing to say, "I feel like going to a show" or "I feel we've been seeing too

much of each other." But in fact, neither of these statements has any emotional content. In the first sentence the word *feel* really stands for an intention: "I *want* to go to a show." In the second sentence the "feeling" is really a thought: "I *think* we've been seeing too much of each other." You can recognize the absence of emotion in each case by adding a genuine word of feeling to it. For instance, "I'm *bored* and I want to go to a show" or "I think we've been seeing too much of each other and I feel *confined*."

Share Mixed Feelings   Many times the feeling you express isn't the only one you're experiencing. For example, you might often express your anger but overlook the confusion, disappointment, frustration, sadness, or embarrassment that preceded it.

Recognize the Difference Between Feeling and Acting   Just because you feel a certain way doesn't mean you must always act on it. This distinction is important because it can liberate you from the fear that acknowledging and showing a feeling will commit you to some disastrous course of action. If, for instance, you say to a friend, "I feel so angry that I could punch you in the nose," it becomes possible to explore exactly why you feel so furious and then to resolve the problem that led to your anger. Pretending that nothing is the matter, on the other hand, will do nothing to diminish your resentful feelings, which can then go on to contaminate the relationship.

Accept Responsibility for Your Feelings   It's important to make sure that your language reflects the fact that you're responsible for your feelings. Instead of "You're making me angry," say, "I'm getting angry." Instead of "You hurt my feelings," say, "I feel hurt when you do that." Remember the fallacy of causation: People don't make us like or dislike them, and pretending that they do denies the responsibility each of us has for our own emotions.

Choose the Time and Place to Express Your Feelings   Often the first flush of a strong feeling is not the best time to speak out. If you're awakened by the racket caused by a noisy neighbor, storming over to complain might result in your saying things you'll regret later. In such a case, it's probably wiser to wait until you have thought out carefully how you might express your feelings in a way that would be most likely to be heard.

   Even after you've waited for the first flush of feeling to subside, it's still important to choose the time that's best suited to the message. Being rushed or tired or disturbed by some other matter are probably all good reasons for postponing the expression of your feeling. Often dealing with your emotions can take a great amount of time and effort, and fatigue or distraction will make it difficult to follow through on the matter you've started. In the same manner you ought to be sure that the recipient of your message is ready to hear you out before you begin.

Express Your Feelings Clearly   Either out of confusion or discomfort we sometimes express our emotions in an unclear way. One key to making your emotions clear is to realize that you most often can summarize them in a few words—*hurt, glad, confused, excited, resentful,* and so on. In the same way,

*I remember
when my body knew
when it was time
to cry
and it was all
right then
to explode
the world
and melt
everything
warm
and start new
washed clean*

Bernard Gunther

with a little thought you can probably describe very briefly any reasons you have for feeling a certain way.

In addition to avoiding excessive length, a second way to prevent confusion is to avoid overqualifying or downplaying your emotions—"I'm a *little* unhappy" or "I'm *pretty* excited" or "I'm *sort* of confused." Of course, not all emotions are strong ones. We do feel degrees of sadness and joy, for example, but some communicators have a tendency to discount almost every feeling. Do you?

A third danger to avoid is expressing feelings in a coded manner. This happens most often when the sender is uncomfortable about revealing the feeling in question. Some codes are verbal ones, as when the sender hints more or less subtly at the message. For example, an indirect way to say, "I'm lonesome" might be "I guess there isn't much happening this weekend, so if you're not busy, why don't you drop by?" Such a message is so indirect that the chances that your real feeling will be recognized are slim. For this reason, people who send coded messages stand less of a chance of having their emotions understood—and their needs met.

Finally, you can express yourself clearly by making sure that both you and your partner understand that your feeling is centered on a specific set of circumstances rather than being indicative of the whole relationship. Instead of saying, "I resent you," say, "I resent you when you don't keep your promises." Rather than "I'm bored with you," say "I'm bored when you talk about your money."

SOME FEELINGS

afraid	concerned	exhausted	hurried	nervous	sexy
aggravated	confident	fearful	hurt	numb	shaky
amazed	confused	fed up	hysterical	optimistic	shocked
ambivalent	content	fidgety	impatient	paranoid	shy
angry	crazy	flattered	impressed	passionate	sorry
annoyed	defeated	foolish	inhibited	peaceful	strong
anxious	defensive	forlorn	insecure	pessimistic	subdued
apathetic	delighted	free	interested	playful	surprised
ashamed	depressed	friendly	intimidated	pleased	suspicious
bashful	detached	frustrated	irritable	possessive	tender
bewildered	devastated	furious	jealous	pressured	tense
bitchy	disappointed	glad	joyful	protective	terrified
bitter	disgusted	glum	lazy	puzzled	tired
bored	disturbed	grateful	lonely	refreshed	trapped
brave	ecstatic	happy	loving	regretful	ugly
calm	edgy	harassed	lukewarm	relieved	uneasy
cantankerous	elated	helpless	mad	resentful	vulnerable
carefree	embarrassed	high	mean	restless	warm
cheerful	empty	hopeful	miserable	ridiculous	weak
cocky	enthusiastic	horrible	mixed up	romantic	wonderful
cold	envious	hostile	mortified	sad	worried
comfortable	excited	humiliated	neglected	sentimental	

Feelings and Phrases

You can try this exercise alone or with a group.

1. Choose a situation from Column A and a receiver from Column B.

2. Create a statement that would most effectively express your feeling for this combination.

3. Now create statements of feeling for the same situation with other receivers from Column B. How are the statements different?

4. Repeat the process with various combinations, using other situations from Column A.

Column A: Situations

a. You have been stood up for a date or appointment.

b. The other person pokes fun at your schoolwork.

c. The other person compliments you on your appearance, then says, "I hope I haven't embarrassed you."

d. The other person gives you a hug and says, "It's good to see you."

Column B: Receivers

a. An instructor

b. A family member (you decide which one)

c. A classmate you don't know well

d. Your best friend

There are, I know, cats that purr
loudly. Mine can be heard only
when your cheek rests against
the soft fur on her back—so
afraid is she to share her
pleasure with you.

The tree I fed, nurtured, watered so
faithfully that it grew taller than
the house, never bowed in the
breeze to me as I passed under
it—only sprinkled pale yellow
flowers in my hair that later
greeted me when I glanced in a
mirror.

People, too, keep within them their
purrs, their faintly scented
flowers, not returning a sign that
your stroking of their egos has
been noted and appreciated—and
a little bit more to the left, please.

Lenni Shender Goldstein

Managing Difficult Emotions

Although feeling and expressing many emotions adds to the quality of interpersonal relationships, not all feelings are beneficial. For instance, rage, depression, terror, and jealousy do little to help you feel better or improve your relationships. The following pages will give you tools to minimize these unproductive emotions.

Facilitative and Debilitative Emotions

We need to make a distinction between **facilitative emotions,** which contribute to effective functioning, and **debilitative emotions,** which keep us from feeling and relating effectively.

One big difference between the two types is their *intensity.* For instance, a certain amount of anger or irritation can be constructive because it often provides the stimulus that leads you to improve the unsatisfying conditions. Rage, on the other hand, will usually make matters worse. The same holds true for fear. A little bit of nervousness before an important athletic contest or job interview might give you the boost that will improve your performance. (Mellow athletes or employees usually don't do well.) But total terror is something else.

A second characteristic that distinguishes debilitative feelings from facilitative ones is their extended *duration.* Feeling depressed for a while after the breakup of a relationship or the loss of a job is natural. But spending the rest of your life grieving over your loss would accomplish nothing. In the same way, staying angry at someone for a wrong inflicted long ago can be just as punishing to you as to the wrongdoer. Our goal, then, is to find a method for getting rid of debilitative feelings while remaining sensitive to your more facilitative emotions, which can improve your relationships. Fortunately, there is such a method. Developed by cognitive psychologists such as Aaron Beck[10] and Albert Ellis,[11] it is based on the idea that the way to change feelings is to change unproductive thinking.

Thoughts Cause Feelings

For most people, emotions seem to have a life of their own. You wish you could feel calm when approaching strangers, yet your voice quivers. You try to appear confident when asking for a raise, yet your eye twitches nervously.

At times like these it's common to say that strangers or your boss *make* you feel nervous just as you would say that a bee sting causes you to feel pain. The apparent similarities between physical and emotional discomfort become clear if you look at them in the following way:

$$\textit{Event} \longrightarrow \textit{Feeling}$$

bee sting ⟶	physical pain
meeting strangers ⟶	nervous feelings

When looking at your emotions in this way, you seem to have little control over how you feel. However, this apparent similarity between physical pain and emotional discomfort (or pleasure) isn't as great as it seems to be. Cognitive psychologists argue that it is not *events* such as meeting strangers or being jilted by a lover that cause people to feel bad, but rather the *beliefs they hold* about these events.

Albert Ellis, who developed the cognitive approach called *rational-emotive therapy,* tells a story that makes this point clear. Imagine yourself walking by a friend's house and seeing your friend stick his head out of a window and call

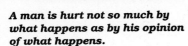

A man is hurt not so much by what happens as by his opinion of what happens.

Montaigne

you a string of vile names. (You supply the friend and the names.) Under these circumstances it's likely that you would feel hurt and upset. Now imagine that instead of walking by the house you were passing a mental institution when the same friend, who was obviously a patient there, shouted the same offensive names at you. In this case, your feelings would probably be quite different— most likely, sadness and pity. You can see that in this story the activating event of being called names was the same in both cases, yet the emotional consequences were very different. The reason for your different feelings has to do with your thinking in each case. In the first instance, you would most likely think that your friend was very angry with you; further, you might imagine that you must have done something terrible to deserve such a response. In the second case, you would probably assume that your friend had some psychological difficulty, and most likely you would feel sympathetic.

From this example you can start to see that it's the *interpretations* people make of an event that determine their feelings.* Thus, the model for emotions looks like this:

Event	*Thought*	*Feeling*
being called names	"I've done something wrong."	hurt, upset
being called names	"My friend must be sick."	concern, sympathy

Talking to Yourself

You can become better at understanding how your thoughts shape your feelings by completing the following steps.

1. Take a few minutes to listen to the silent voice you use when thinking. Close your eyes now and listen to it. . . . Did you hear the voice? Perhaps it was saying, "What voice? I don't have any voice. . . ." Try again, and pay attention to what the voice is saying.

2. Now think about the following situations, and imagine how you would react in each. How would you interpret them with your little voice? What feelings would follow from each interpretation?
   a. While sitting on a bus, in class, or on the street, you notice an attractive person sneaking glances at you.
   b. During a lecture your professor asks the class, "What do you think about this?" and looks toward you.
   c. You are telling friends about your vacation, and one yawns.
   d. You run into a friend on the street and ask how things are going. "Fine," he replies and rushes off.

3. Now recall three recent times when you felt a strong emotion. For each one, recall the activating event and then the interpretation that led to your emotional reaction.

*There are two other ways emotions are caused that do not involve self-talk. The first involves a conditioned response, in which a stimulus that was originally paired with an emotion-arousing event triggers the same emotion in future instances. You might, for instance, feel a wave of sadness when you catch a whiff of the perfume a former lover wore at the time of your breakup. The other cause of emotions that does not involve self-talk occurs when a person has learned that a certain feeling (or more correctly, behaviors that reflect that feeling) results in a desirable response from others. For example, some people cry or mope because doing so gets them a sympathetic response.

Irrational Thinking and Debilitative Emotions   Focusing on the self-talk that we use to think is the key to understanding debilitative feelings. Albert Ellis suggests that many debilitative feelings come from accepting a number of irrational thoughts—we'll call them *fallacies* here—which lead to illogical conclusions and in turn to debilitating feelings.

"There is nothing good or bad but thinking makes it so."

Shakespeare,
Hamlet

1. **The fallacy of perfection**   People who accept the **fallacy of perfection** believe that a worthwhile communicator should be able to handle every situation with complete confidence and skill.

    Once you accept the belief that it's desirable and possible to be a perfect communicator, the next step is to assume that people won't appreciate you if you are imperfect. Admitting your mistakes, saying, "I don't know," or sharing feelings of uncertainty seem like social defects when viewed in this manner. Given the desire to be valued and appreciated, it's tempting to try to *appear* perfect, but the costs of such deception are high. If others ever find you out, they'll see you as a phony. Even when your act isn't uncovered, such a performance uses up a great deal of psychological energy and thus makes the rewards of approval less enjoyable.

    Subscribing to the myth of perfection not only can keep others from liking you but also can act as a force to diminish your own self-esteem. How can you like yourself when you don't measure up to the way you ought to be? How liberated you become when you can comfortably accept the idea that you are not perfect, that

    Like everyone else, you sometimes have a hard time expressing yourself.

    Like everyone else, you make mistakes from time to time, and there is no reason to hide this.

    You are honestly doing the best you can to realize your potential, to become the best person you can be.

2. **The fallacy of approval**   The mistaken belief known as the **fallacy of approval** is based on the idea that it is not just desirable but *vital* to get the approval of virtually every person. People who accept this belief go to incredible lengths to seek acceptance from others even when they have to sacrifice their own principles and happiness to do so. Accepting this irrational myth can lead to some ludicrous situations:

    Feeling nervous because people you really don't like seem to disapprove of you

Feeling apologetic when others are at fault

Feeling embarrassed after behaving unnaturally to gain another's approval

In addition to the obvious discomfort that arises from denying your own principles and needs, the myth of approval is irrational because it implies that others will respect and like you more if you go out of your way to please them. Often this simply isn't true. How is it possible to respect people who have compromised important values just to gain acceptance? How is it possible to think highly of people who repeatedly deny their own needs as a means of buying approval? Though others may find it tempting to use these individuals to suit their ends or amusing to be around them, they hardly deserve genuine affection and respect.

   In addition, striving for universal acceptance is irrational because it's simply not possible. Sooner or later a conflict of expectations is bound to occur; one person will approve if you behave only in a certain way, but another will only accept the opposite course of action. What are you to do then?

> *I never was what you would call a fancy skater—and while I seldom actually fell, it might have been more impressive if I had. A good resounding fall is no disgrace. It is the fantastic writhing to avoid a fall which destroys any illusion of being a gentleman. How like life that is, after all!*
>
> Robert Benchley

Don't misunderstand: Abandoning the fallacy of approval doesn't mean living a life of selfishness. It's still important to consider the needs of others and to meet them whenever possible. It's also pleasant—we might even say necessary—to strive for the respect of those people you value. The point here is that when you must abandon your own needs and principles in order to seek these goals, the price is too high.

3. **The fallacy of shoulds**   One huge source of unhappiness is the **fallacy of shoulds,** the inability to distinguish between what *is* and what *should be.* You can see the difference by imagining a person who is full of complaints about the world:

"There should be no rain on weekends."

"People ought to live forever."

"Money should grow on trees."

"We should all be able to fly."

Beliefs like these are obviously foolish. However pleasant wishing may be, insisting that the unchangeable should be changed won't affect reality one bit. And yet many people torture themselves by engaging in this sort of irrational thinking when they confuse *is* with *ought*. They say and think things like this:

"My friend should be more understanding."

"She shouldn't be so inconsiderate."

"They ought to be more friendly."

"You should work harder."

The message in each of these cases is that you would *prefer* people to behave differently. Wishing that things were better is perfectly legitimate, and trying to change them is, of course, a good idea; but it's unreasonable to *insist* that the world operate just as you want it to or to feel cheated when things aren't ideal.

Becoming obsessed with shoulds has three troublesome consequences. First, it leads to unnecessary unhappiness, for people who are constantly dreaming about the ideal are seldom satisfied with what they have. A second drawback is that merely complaining without acting can keep you from doing anything to change unsatisfying conditions. A third problem with shoulds is

that this sort of complaining can build a defensive climate in others, who will resent being nagged. It's much more effective to tell people about what you'd like than to preach: Say, "I wish you'd be more punctual" instead of "You should be on time." We'll discuss ways of avoiding defensive climates in Chapter Nine.

4. **The fallacy of overgeneralization**   The **fallacy of overgeneralization** comprises two types. The first occurs when we base a belief on a *limited* amount of *evidence.* For instance, how many times have you found yourself saying something like

> "I'm so stupid! I can't even understand how to do my income tax."

> "Some friend I am! I forgot my best friend's birthday."

In cases like these, we focus on a limited type of shortcoming as if it represented everything about us. We forget that along with our difficulties we also have solved tough problems and that though we're sometimes forgetful, at other times we're caring and thoughtful.

A second related category of overgeneralization occurs when we *exaggerate* shortcomings:

"You *never* listen to me."

"You're *always* late."

"I can't think of *anything*."

On closer examination, absolute statements like these are almost always false and usually lead to discouragement or anger. You'll feel far better when you replace overgeneralizations with more accurate messages to yourself and others:

"You often don't listen to me."

"You've been late three times this week."

"I haven't had any ideas I like today."

Many overgeneralizations are based on abuse of the verb *to be*. For example, unqualified thoughts such as "He *is* an idiot [all the time?]" and "I *am* a failure [in everything?]" will make you see yourself and others in an unrealistically negative way, thus contributing to debilitative feelings.

5. **The fallacy of causation**   The **fallacy of causation** is based on the irrational belief that emotions are caused by others rather than by one's own self-talk.

  This fallacy causes troubles in two ways. The first plagues people who become overly cautious about communicating because they don't want to "cause" any pain or inconvenience for others. This attitude occurs in cases such as

  Visiting friends or family out of a sense of obligation rather than a genuine desire to see them

  Keeping quiet when another person's behavior is bothering you

  Pretending to be attentive to a speaker when you are already late for an appointment or feeling ill

  Praising and reassuring others who ask for your opinion even when your honest response would be negative

  There's certainly no excuse for going out of your way to say things that will result in pain for others, and there will be times when you choose to

A man said to the universe:
"Sir, I exist!"
"However," replied the universe,
"The fact has not created in me
A sense of obligation."

Stephen Crane

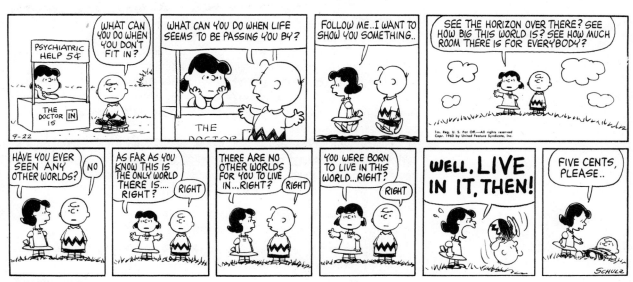

"The mind is its own place, and in itself can make a Heav'n of Hell, a Hell of Heav'n."

John Milton,
Paradise Lost

inconvenience yourself to make life easier for those you care about. It's essential to realize, however, that it's an overstatement to say that you are the one who causes others' feelings. It's more accurate to say that they *respond* to your behavior with feelings of their own. For example, consider how strange it sounds to suggest that you make others fall in love with you. Such a statement simply doesn't make sense. It would be closer to the truth to say that you act in one way or another, and some people might fall in love with you as a result of these actions whereas others wouldn't. In the same way, it's incorrect to say that you *make* others angry, upset—or happy, for that matter. It's better to say that others' responses are as much or more a function of their own psychological makeup as or than they are determined by our own behavior (respectively).

Restricting your communication because of the fallacy of causation can result in three types of damaging consequences. First, as a result of your caution you often will fail to have your own needs met. There's little likelihood that others will change their behavior unless they know that it's affecting you in a negative way. A second consequence is that you're likely to begin resenting the person whose behavior you find bothersome. Obviously, this reaction is illogical because you have never made your feelings known, but logic doesn't change the fact that burying your problem usually leads to a buildup of hostility.

Even when withholding feelings is based on the best intentions, it often damages relationships in a third way; for once others find out about your deceptive nature, they will find it difficult ever to know when you are really upset with them. Even your most fervent assurances that everything is fine sound suspicious because there's always the chance that you may be covering up resentments you're unwilling to express. Thus, in many respects taking responsibility for others' feelings is not only irrational but also counterproductive.

The fallacy of causation also operates when we believe that others cause *our* emotions. Sometimes it certainly seems as if they do, either raising or lowering our spirits by their actions. But think about it for a moment: The same actions that will cause you happiness or pain one day have little effect at other times. The insult or compliment that affected your mood strongly yesterday leaves you unaffected today. Why? Because in the latter case you attached less importance to either. You certainly wouldn't feel some emotions without others' behavior; but it's your thinking, not their actions, that determines how you feel.

6. **The fallacy of helplessness**   The irrational idea of the **fallacy of helplessness** suggests that satisfaction in life is determined by forces beyond your control. People who continuously see themselves as victims make such statements as

> "There's no way a woman can get ahead in this society. It's a man's world, and the best thing I can do is to accept it."

> "I was born with a shy personality. I'd like to be more outgoing, but there's nothing I can do about that."

> "I can't tell my boss that she is putting too many demands on me. If I did, I might lose my job."

The mistake in statements like these becomes apparent once you realize that there are many things you can do if you really want to. As you read in Chapter Two, most "can't" statements can be more correctly rephrased either as *"won't"* ("I can't tell him what I think" becomes "I won't be honest with him") or as *"don't know how"* ("I can't carry on an interesting conversation" becomes "I don't know what to say"). Once you've rephrased these inaccurate "can'ts," it becomes clear that they're either a matter of choice or an area that calls for your action—both quite different from saying that you're helpless.

When viewed in this light, it's apparent that many "can'ts" are really rationalizations to justify not wanting to change. Once you've persuaded yourself that there's no hope for you, it's easy to give up trying. On the other hand, acknowledging that there is a way to change—even though it may be difficult—puts the responsibility for your predicament on your shoulders. You *can* become a better communicator—this book is one step in your movement toward that goal. Don't give up or sell yourself short!

7. **The fallacy of catastrophic expectations**   Fearful communicators who subscribe to the irrational **fallacy of catastrophic expectations** operate on the assumption that if something bad can possibly happen, it will. Typical catastrophic fantasies include

> "If I invite them to the party, they probably won't want to come."

> "If I speak up in order to try and resolve a conflict, things will probably get worse."

> "If I apply for the job I want, I probably won't be hired."

> "If I tell them how I really feel, they'll probably laugh at me."

Although it's naive to think that all your interactions with others will meet with success, it's just as damaging to assume that you'll fail. One way to escape from the fallacy of catastrophic expectations is to think about the consequences that would follow even if you don't communicate successfully. Keeping in mind the folly of trying to be perfect and of living only for the approval of others, realize that failing in a given instance usually isn't as bad as it might seem. What if people do laugh at you? Suppose you don't get the job? What if others do get angry at your remarks? Are these matters really *that* serious?

Before moving on, we need to add a few thoughts about thinking and feeling. First, you should realize that thinking rationally won't completely eliminate debilitative feelings. Some debilitative feelings, after all, are very rational: grief over the death of someone you love, euphoria over getting a new job, and apprehension about the future of an important relationship after a serious fight, for example. Thinking rationally can eliminate many debilitative feelings from your life, but not all of them.

How Irrational Are You?

1. Return to the situations described in the exercise Talking to Yourself on page 126. Examine each one to see whether your self-talk contains any irrational thoughts.

2. Keep a two- or three-day record of your debilitative feelings. Are any of them based on irrational thinking? Examine your conclusions, and see if you repeatedly use any of the fallacies described in the preceding section.

3. Take a class poll to see which irrational fallacies are most "popular." Also, discuss what subjects seem to stimulate most of this irrational thinking (for example, schoolwork, dating, jobs, family, and so on).

Minimizing Debilitative Emotions   How can you overcome such irrational thinking? Albert Ellis and his associates have developed a simple, yet effective approach. When practiced conscientiously, it can help you cut down on the self-defeating thinking that leads to many debilitative emotions.

1. Monitor your emotional reactions   The first step is to recognize when you're having debilitative emotions. (Of course, it's also nice to be aware of pleasant feelings when they occur!) As we suggested earlier, one way to notice feelings is through proprioceptive stimuli: butterflies in the stomach, racing heart, hot flashes, and so on. Although such reactions might be symptoms of food poisoning, more often they reflect a strong emotion. You can also recognize certain ways of behaving that suggest your feelings: Stomping instead of walking normally, being unusually quiet, or speaking in a sarcastic tone of voice are some examples.

It may seem strange to suggest that it's necessary to look for emotions—they ought to be immediately apparent. The fact is, however, that we often suffer from debilitating feelings for some time without noticing them. For example, at the end of a trying day you've probably caught yourself frowning and realized that you've been wearing that mask for some time without realizing it.

2. **Note the activating event**   Once you're aware of how you're feeling, the next step is to figure out what activating event triggered your response. Sometimes it is obvious. For instance, a common source of anger is being accused unfairly (or fairly) of foolish behavior; being rejected by somebody important to you is clearly a source of hurt, too. In other cases, however, the activating event isn't so apparent. A friend of ours reported feeling much more irritable than usual though he couldn't figure out what led to these emotions. After some analysis he realized that his grumpiness increased shortly after his roommate began carrying on with a new woman. He felt like an intruder in his own apartment when he walked in to find the two lovers expressing their feelings.

Sometimes there isn't a single activating event but rather a series of small incidents that finally build toward a critical mass and trigger a debilitative feeling. This sort of thing happens when you're trying to work or sleep and are continually interrupted by a string of interruptions or when you suffer a series of small disappointments.

The best way to begin tracking down activating events is to notice the circumstances in which you have debilitative feelings. Perhaps they occur when you're around *specific* people. In other cases, you might be bothered by certain *types of individuals* owing to their age, role, background, or some other factor. Or perhaps certain *settings* stimulate unpleasant emotions: parties, work, school. Sometimes the *topic* of conversation is the factor that sets you off, whether it be politics, religion, sex, or some other subject.

3. **Record your self-talk**   This is the point at which you analyze the thoughts that are the link between the activating event and your feeling. If you're serious about getting rid of debilitative emotions, it's important actually to write down your self-talk when first learning to use this method. Putting your thoughts on paper will help you see whether or not they actually make any sense.

Monitoring your self-talk might be difficult at first. This is a new skill, and any new activity seems awkward. If you persevere, however, you'll find you will be able to identify the thoughts that lead to your debilitative feelings. Once you get in the habit of recognizing this internal monolog, you'll be able to identify your thoughts quickly and easily.

4. **Dispute your irrational beliefs**   Disputing your irrational beliefs is the key to success in the rational-emotive approach. Use the list of irrational fallacies on pages 127–134 to discover which of your internal statements are based on mistaken thinking.

You can do this most effectively by following three steps. First, decide whether each belief you've recorded is rational or irrational. Next, explain why the belief does or doesn't make sense. Finally, if the belief is irrational, you should write down an alternative way of thinking that is more sensible and that can leave you feeling better when faced with the same activating event in the future.

I believe that courage is all too often mistakenly seen as the absence of fear. If you descend by rope from a cliff and are not fearful to some degree, you are either crazy or unaware. Courage is seeing your fear in a realistic perspective, defining it, considering the alternatives and choosing to function in spite of risk.

Leonard Zunin,
Contact: The First Four Minutes

ACTIVATING EVENT

My friend Betsy dropped by last night when I was studying for an important exam. This is typical of her: She seems to be phoning or coming over to my place constantly and usually at times when I'm busy or have other guests.

BELIEFS AND SELF-TALK

1. After all the hints I've dropped, she should get the idea and leave me alone.
2. She's driving me crazy.
3. I'm a coward for not speaking up and telling her to quit bothering me.
4. If I do tell her, she'll be crushed.
5. There's no solution to this mess. I'm damned if I tell her to leave me alone and damned if I don't.

FEELINGS

I felt mad at Betsy and myself. I also felt cruel and heartless for wanting to turn away such a lonely person. I was frustrated at not being able to study.

DISPUTING IRRATIONAL BELIEFS

1. This is irrational. If Betsy were perfect, she would be more sensitive and get my hints. But she's an insensitive person, and she's behaving just as I'd expect her to do. I'd like her to be more considerate, though. That's rational!
2. This is a bit melodramatic. I definitely don't like her interruptions, but there's a big difference between being irritated and going crazy. Besides, even if I were losing my mind, it wouldn't be accurate to say that she was driving me crazy, but rather that I'm letting her get to me. (It's fun to feel sorry for myself sometimes, though.)
3. This is an exaggeration. I am afraid to tell her, but that doesn't make me a coward. It makes me a less than totally self-assured person. This confirms my suspicion that I'm not perfect.
4. There's a chance that she'll be disappointed if she knows that I've found her irritating. But I have to be careful not to catastrophize here. She would probably survive my comments and even appreciate my honesty once she got over the shock. Besides, I'm not sure that I want to take the responsibility of keeping her happy if it leaves me feeling irritated. She's a big girl, and if she has a problem, she can learn to deal with it.
5. I'm playing helpless here. There must be a way I can tell her honestly while still being supportive.

ACTIVATING EVENT

I was at my boyfriend Mike's house the other night when he received a phone call from his ex-wife (they've been separated about a year). After some superficial conversation she asked him if he was happy. His response was, "Yes, I'm happy <u>for now</u>" (emphasis mine). Toward the end of the conversation she asked him to tell her that he loved her. His response was, "I'd rather not. I don't want to talk now. I'll talk to you tomorrow when you call about shipping the furniture."

BELIEFS AND SELF-TALK

1. I wish she wouldn't call him! Why can't she leave him alone?
2. I wish she didn't exist!
3. What does he mean, "I'm happy <u>for now</u>?" Does he have doubts about us?
4. Why can't he tell her firmly that it's over between them? And why does he want to talk to her tomorrow about it? Maybe he has something to say that he wants to keep from me.
5. If he went back to her, I would die.

CONSEQUENCES

I felt angry toward Mike's wife and toward Mike. I felt hurt and jealous. I was also very fearful about losing Mike.

DISPUTING IRRATIONAL BELIEFS

1. My question, "Why can't she leave him alone?" is really another way of saying I wish she would quit phoning. This is a rational thing for me to want.
2. It's irrational to wish that she didn't exist. She does exist, and I can't change that. I have to learn to deal with it and quit trying to wish her away.
3. I'm not sure whether this is rational or not. Maybe Mike's "for now" meant nothing. On the other hand, that did seem like an odd thing to say. The only way I can find out whether he has doubts about our future is to ask him. It's stupid for me to worry before I see whether there's any reason for doing it.
4. What I'm really saying here is that he should tell her that it's over. Though I wish he'd do that, there's no reason why he should. He'll handle this the way he thinks is best. He doesn't want to hurt her, and he's trying to let her off lightly. He sees her in a different light than I do, of course, and so he'll speak to her in a different way. My fear that Mike is keeping things from me is irrational catastrophizing. Why do I always—oops! often—assume the worst?
5. I would definitely be hurt and sad if he went back to her, but I wouldn't die. I sure do get dramatic at times!

After reading about this method for dealing with unpleasant emotions, some readers have objections.

"This rational-emotive approach sounds like nothing more than trying to talk yourself out of feeling bad." This accusation is totally correct. After all, since we talk ourselves *into* feeling bad, what's wrong with talking ourselves *out* of bad feelings, especially when they are based on irrational thoughts? Rationalizing may be an excuse and a self-deception, but there's nothing wrong with being rational.

"The kind of disputing we just read sounds phony and unnatural. I don't talk to myself in sentences and paragraphs." There's no need to dispute your irrational beliefs in any special literary style. You can be just as colloquial as you want. The important thing is to clearly understand what thoughts led you into your debilitative feeling so you can clearly dispute them. When the technique is new to you, it's a good idea to write or talk out your thoughts in order to make them clear. After you've had some practice, you'll be able to do these steps in a quicker, less formal way.

"This approach is too cold and impersonal. It seems to aim at turning people into cold-blooded, calculating, emotionless machines." This is simply not true. A rational thinker can still dream, hope, and love: There's nothing necessarily irrational about feelings like these. Basically rational people even indulge in a bit of irrational thinking once in a while. But they usually know what they're doing. Like healthy eaters who occasionally treat themselves to a snack of junk food, rational thinkers indulge themselves emotionally once in a while, knowing that they'll return to their healthy lifestyle soon with no real damage done.

"This technique promises too much. There's no chance I could rid myself of all unpleasant feelings, however nice that might be." We can answer this by assuring you that rational-emotive thinking probably won't totally solve your emotional problems. What it can do is to reduce their number, intensity, and duration. This method is not the answer to all your problems, but it can make a significant difference—which is not a bad accomplishment.

Rational Thinking

1. Return to the diary of irrational thoughts you recorded on page 134. Dispute the self-talk in each case, and write a more rational interpretation of the event.

2. Now try out your ability to think rationally on the spot. You can do this by acting out the scenes listed in step 4. You'll need three players for each one: a subject, the subject's "little voice"—his or her thoughts—and a second party.

3. Play out each scene by having the subject and second party interact while the "little voice" stands just behind the subject and says what the subject is probably thinking. For example, in a scene where the subject is asking an instructor to reconsider a low grade, the voice might say, "I hope I haven't made things worse by bringing this up. Maybe he'll lower the grade after rereading the test. I'm such an idiot! Why didn't I keep quiet?"

4. Whenever the voice expresses an irrational thought, the observers who are watching the skit should call out, "Foul." At this point the action should stop while the group discusses the irrational thought and suggests a more rational line of self-talk. The players should then replay the scene with the voice speaking in a more rational way.

Here are some scenes. Of course, you can invent others as well.

a. A couple is just beginning their first date.

b. A potential employee has just begun a job interview.

c. A teacher or boss is criticizing the subject for showing up late.

d. A student and instructor run across each other in the market.

More Readings on Emotions

Beck, Aaron T. *Cognitive Therapy and the Emotional Disorders.* New York: International Universities Press, 1976.

Beck is one of the leading figures in the exploration of how thinking shapes emotions. Though this book is written for professionals, it gives a clear picture of one way to handle debilitative feelings.

Bowers, John W., Sandra M. Metts, and W. Thomas Duncanson. "Emotion and Interpersonal Communication." In *Handbook of Interpersonal Communication.* Beverly Hills, Calif.: Sage, 1985.

This is a scholarly review of theories of interpersonal emotion. Bowers and his associates also examine how emotions are interpreted through messages and the role of emotions in creating, maintaining, and dissolving interpersonal relationships.

Ellis, Albert. *A New Guide to Rational Living.* North Hollywood, Calif.: Wilshire Books, 1977.

Ellis is probably the best-known advocate of changing feelings by thinking rationally, and this is his most widely read book.

Izard, Carroll E. *Human Emotions.* New York: Plenum Press, 1977.

Although Izard spends a major part of the book defending his own theories about emotions, there is also a good explanation of the subject for interested readers.

Jakubowski, Patricia, and Arthur Lange. *The Assertive Option.* Champaign, Ill.: Research Press, 1978.

Jakubowski and Lange offer both a good review of the principles in this chapter and some specific suggestions on how to express feelings assertively.

Kranzler, Gerald. *You Can Change How You Feel.* Eugene, Ore.: RETC Press, 1974.

Many readers find the tone of this book somewhat irritating, but it does provide a brief and clear summary of the information in this chapter.

Lazarus, Arnold, and Allen Fay. *I Can If I Want To.* New York: Morrow, 1975.

The authors expand on the list of irrational fallacies described in this chapter, providing real-life examples of each and then suggesting corrective behavior. A useful book.

Tarvis, Carol. *Anger: The Misunderstood Emotion.* New York: Simon & Schuster, 1982.

Tarvis cites many studies to show that the "let it all hang out" approach to anger does little good for either sender or receiver. This doesn't mean that unassertiveness is desirable either. The most effective way to deal with anger in interpersonal disputes, Tarvis argues, is to express feelings clearly and politely.

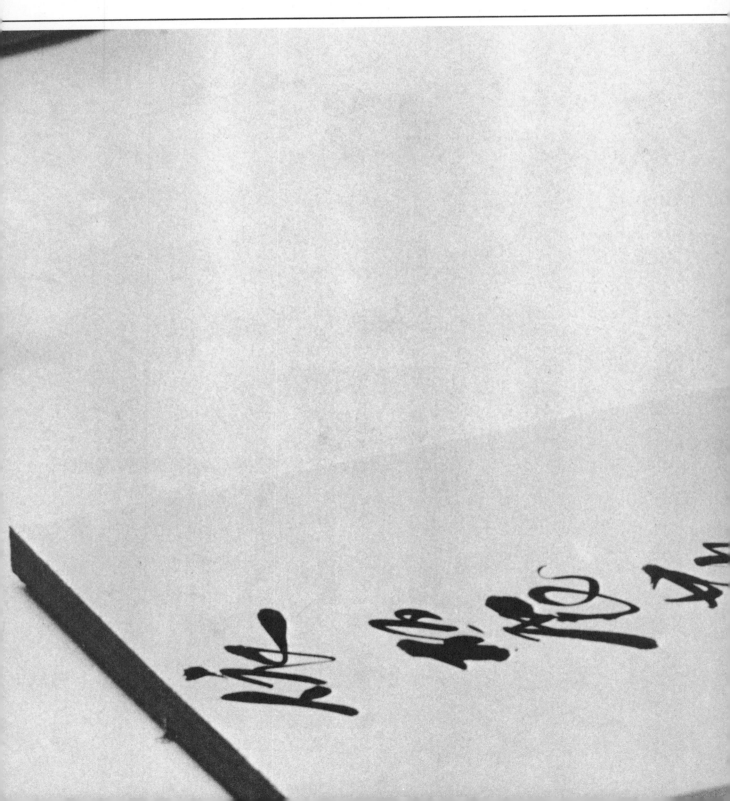

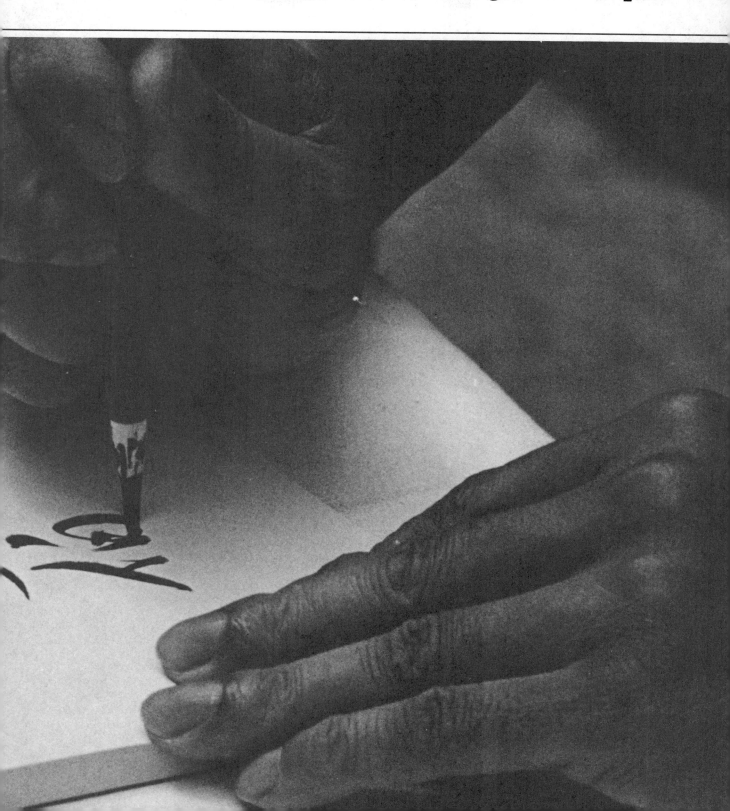

AND THE WHOLE EARTH WAS OF ONE LANGUAGE AND ONE SPEECH. AND IT CAME TO PASS, AS THEY JOURNEYED FROM THE EAST, THAT THEY FOUND A PLAIN IN THE LAND OF SHINAR; AND THEY DWELT THERE.

2 AND THEY SAID TO ONE ANOTHER, GO TO, LET US MAKE BRICK, AND BURN THEM THOROUGHLY. AND THEY HAD BRICK FOR STONE, AND SLIME HAD THEY FOR MORTAR.

3 AND THEY SAID, GO TO, LET US BUILD US A CITY AND A TOWER, WHOSE TOP MAY REACH UNTO HEAVEN; AND LET US MAKE US A NAME, LEST WE BE SCATTERED ABROAD UPON THE FACE OF THE WHOLE EARTH.

4 AND THE LORD CAME DOWN TO SEE THE CITY AND THE TOWER, WHICH THE CHILDREN OF MEN BUILDED.

5 AND THE LORD SAID, BEHOLD, THE PEOPLE IS ONE, AND THEY HAVE ALL ONE LANGUAGE; AND THIS THEY BEGIN TO DO: AND NOW NOTHING WILL BE RESTRAINED FROM THEM, WHICH THEY HAVE IMAGINED TO DO.

6 GO TO, LET US GO DOWN, AND THERE CONFOUND THEIR LANGUAGE, THAT THEY MAY NOT UNDERSTAND ONE ANOTHER'S SPEECH.

7 SO THE LORD SCATTERED THEM ABROAD FROM THENCE UPON THE FACE OF ALL THE EARTH; AND THEY LEFT OFF TO BUILD THE CITY.

8 THEREFORE IS THE NAME OF IT CALLED BABEL; BECAUSE THE LORD DID THERE CONFOUND THE LANGUAGE OF ALL THE EARTH; AND FROM THENCE DID THE LORD SCATTER THEM ABROAD UPON THE FACE OF ALL THE EARTH.

Genesis 11:1–9

> **"I don't know what you mean by 'glory,' " Alice said.**
>
> **Humpty Dumpty smiled contemptuously. "Of course you don't—till I tell you. I meant 'there's a nice knock-down argument for you!' "**
>
> **"But 'glory' doesn't mean 'a nice knock-down argument,' " Alice objected.**
>
> **"When I use a word," Humpty Dumpty said, in a rather scornful tone, "it means just what I choose it to mean—neither more nor less."**
>
> **"The question is," said Alice, "whether you can make words mean so many different things."**
>
> **"The question is," said Humpty Dumpty, "which is to be master—that's all."**
>
> Lewis Carroll,
> *Through the Looking Glass*

Sometimes it seems as if *none* of us speaks the same language. How often have you felt that nobody understood what you were saying? You knew what you meant, but people just didn't seem to understand you. And how often have the tables been turned—you couldn't understand someone else's ideas?

In this chapter we'll examine these problems by taking a quick look at the relationship between words and things. We'll try to show you some of the ways language can trip you up and some things you can do to make it work better. We'll also talk about how language not only describes how we see the world but also shapes our view of it.

Words and Meanings

Let's begin our study by looking at some characteristics of language. Because we use words almost constantly, we often assume that they are ideally suited to convey meaning. Actually, there are several points to keep in mind if your verbal messages are going to be accurate and successful.

Language Is Symbolic   As we said in Chapter One, words are symbols that represent things—ideas, events, objects, and so on.* Words are not the things themselves. For instance, it's obvious that the word *coat* is not the same as the piece of clothing it describes. You would be a fool to expect the letters *c-o-a-t* to keep you warm in a snowstorm. This point seems so obvious as to be hardly worth mentioning, yet people often forget the nature of language and confuse symbols with their referents.For example, some students will cram facts into their heads just long enough to regurgitate them into a blue book to earn a high grade, forgetting that letters like *A* or *B* are only symbols and that a few lines of ink on paper don't necessarily represent true learning. In the same way, simply saying the words "I care about you" isn't necessarily a reflection of the truth although many disappointed lovers have learned this lesson the hard way.

Language Is Rule-Governed   The elements of any language have no meaning by themselves. And in many combinations, they are also meaningless. For example, the letters *flme oo usi oysk* are pure gibberish. But when rearranged into a more recognizable pattern, they become understandable: "Kiss me, you fool!" This example illustrates the second characteristic of language, which is the existence of a body of *rules* that dictates the way in which symbols can be used.

Languages contain two types of rules. Syntactic rules govern the ways in which symbols can be arranged. For example, in English, syntactic rules require every word to contain at least one vowel and prohibit sentences such as "Have you the cookies brought?" which would be perfectly acceptable if translated into

---

* Some of these "things" or referents, do not exist in the physical world. For instance, some referents are mythical (such as unicorns), some are no longer tangible (such as the deceased Mr. Smith), and others are abstract ideas (such as "love").

a language such as German. Although most of us aren't able to describe the syntactic rules that govern our language, it's easy to recognize their existence by noting how odd a statement that violates them appears.

Semantic rules also govern our use of the language. But where syntax deals with structure, semantics governs meaning. Semantic rules reflect the ways in which speakers of a language respond to a particular symbol. Semantic rules are what make it possible for us to agree that "bikes" are for riding and "books" are for reading, and they help us know whom we will and won't encounter when we use rooms marked "men" or "women." Without semantic rules, communication would be impossible, for each of us would use symbols in unique ways, unintelligible to one another.

Meanings Are in People, Not Words Show a dozen people the same symbol, and ask them what it means, and you're likely to get twelve different answers. Does an American flag bring up associations of soldiers giving their lives for their country? Fourth of July parades? Institutionalized bigotry? Mom's apple pie? How about a cross: What does it represent? The gentleness and wisdom of Jesus Christ? Fire-lit rallies of Ku Klux Klansmen? Your childhood Sunday school? The necklace your sister always wears?

Like these symbols, words can be interpreted in many different ways. And, of course, this is the basis for many misunderstandings. It's possible to have an

COON!!

HONKIE!!

Words don't mean—people mean!

argument about feminism without ever realizing that you and the other person are using the word to represent entirely different things. The same goes for *communism, Republicans, health food,* and thousands on thousands of other symbols. Words don't mean; people do—and often in widely different ways.

It might seem as if one remedy to misunderstandings like these would be to have more respect for the dictionary meanings of words. You might think that if people would just consult a dictionary whenever they send or receive a potentially confusing message, there would be little problem.

This approach has two shortcomings. First, dictionaries show that many words have multiple definitions, and it isn't always clear which one applies in a given situation. The 500 words most commonly used in everyday communication have over 14,000 dictionary definitions, which should give you an idea of the limitations of this approach.

A second problem is that people often use words in ways you'd never be able to look up. Sometimes the misuse of words is due to a lack of knowledge, as when you might ask your auto parts dealer for a new generator when you really need an alternator. As you'll read later in this chapter, there are other cases in which people deliberately use words in unconventional ways to mislead or confuse.

The third shortcoming of dictionaries is that they define most words in terms of *other* words, and this process often won't tell you any more about a term than you already know. In fact, it's possible to talk endlessly about a subject and sound very knowledgeable without ever having the slightest idea of what your words refer to. The following quiz is an example. Read the paragraph, and see if you can answer the questions:[1]

"SHOOTING" REPORT CREATES A STIR

A report of a "shooting" created a major stir and a minor mystery yesterday afternoon when police cars and emergency vehicles converged on the 1000 block of Santa Barbara Street.

After questioning numerous witnesses, officers reconstructed this chain of events, according to Sgt. Nick Katzenstein.

About 2 P.M. an elderly man was walking along the sidewalk when he came upon three young women sitting on a wall next to a market. One of the women—boyish looking with short hair—was showing the others something that looked like a puncture mark on her upper arm. The man asked, "Are you all right?," but got no answer.

So he continued on until he met a woman friend and told her that a boy near the market was getting a shot. The woman misunderstood. She telephoned police and reported that a boy was being shot. That brought several officers in police cars, firemen in a rescue truck and paramedics in an ambulance with siren blaring to the scene.

Officers couldn't find either a victim or the woman who had reported the shooting. They questioned the three young women sitting on the wall. An auto had backfired in the parking lot, one of the three recalled. Perhaps that was the "shot." Several other people were questioned, but none could shed light on the shooting.

Finally officers found the woman who had made the report. She directed them to the "boy" on the wall, who then recalled having showed her friends a newly received innoculation on her arm as the elderly man was walking past.

SANTA BARBARA NEWS-PRESS

Because public opinion is sometimes marsiflate, empetricious insoculences are frequently zophilimized. Nevertheless, it cannot be overemphasized that carpoflansibles are highly traculate.

1. In the authors' opinion, carpoflansibles are
   a. Empetricious
   b. Traculate
   c. Zophilimized
2. Public opinion is sometimes
   a. Insoculent
   b. Variable
   c. Marsiflate
3. According to the text insoculences are zophilimized
   a. Often
   b. Never
   c. Sometimes

You can see that the correct answers are 1(b), 2(c), and 3(a). But even if you scored perfectly on the quiz, do you know the meaning of the paragraph? Of course not, for the words are gibberish. But if you look closely, you'll find that many people use their own language in the same way, talking in terms that they can define only by other terms.

After reading this far, you should be aware that language isn't the simple thing it at first seems to be. You've already seen that a failure to use language with the care and caution it deserves can lead to problems. Sometimes these problems are relatively minor, but in other cases they can be disastrous, as the following account shows.

"Well, at any rate it's a great comfort," she said as she stepped under the trees, "after being so hot, to get into the—into the—into what?" she went on, rather surprised at not being able to think of the word. "I mean to get under the—under the—under this, you know!" putting her hand on the trunk of the tree. "What does it call itself, I wonder? I do believe it's got no name—why to be sure it hasn't!"

Lewis Carroll,
Through the Looking Glass

The Great *Mokusatsu* Mistake

Was This the Deadliest Error of Our Time?

For many months after the Japanese collapse in 1945, people wondered whether it was the atomic bomb or Russia's entry into the war that had brought to an end the fighting in the Pacific. But it gradually became clear that the importance of these two events in persuading Japan to surrender had been overrated; that Japan had been a defeated nation long before August 1945.

"The Japanese had, in fact, already sued for peace before the Atomic Age was announced to the world with the destruction of Hiroshima, and before the Russian entry into the war," Fleet Admiral Chester W. Nimitz told Congress; and other American military leaders confirmed this report.

Why, then, did not Japan accept the Potsdam Declaration, which called upon Japan to surrender, when it was issued in late July of 1945, instead of waiting until the second week in August, after Hiroshima and Nagasaki had been blasted into radioactive rubble and the Russians had begun their drive into Manchuria? That question has never been satisfactorily answered.

The true story of Japan's rejection of the Potsdam Declaration *may* be the story of an incredible mistake—a mistake which so altered the course of history in the Far East that we shall never be able to estimate its full effect on our nation—a mistake which, ironically, was made by a Japanese and involved just one Japanese word.

I say that it "may be" because part of the actual truth lies buried in human motivations which will probably always puzzle historians. But another part of it is clearly demonstrable. Let me tell the story; then you can judge for yourself what really happened.

By the spring of 1945 there was no question in the minds of Japan's leaders that their nation had been badly beaten.

The plight of the nation was so desperate that the actual figures were kept secret even from some of the cabinet ministers. Japan's industrial complex had crumbled under the aerial assault. Steel production was down 79 percent, aircraft production down 64 percent. By September a lack of aluminum would halt the building of planes entirely.

Allied air attacks were destroying railroads, highways, and bridges faster than they could be replaced. Hundreds of thousands of bodies were buried in the smoking ruins of cities and towns. Millions were homeless. In Tokyo alone, almost half of the homes had been leveled. People were fleeing the cities. A combination of American surface, air, and undersea attack had cut off shipments from the occupied regions on which Japan depended for her life. Food was running out.

American planes destroyed the last of Japan's fleet in a battle off Kyushu on the very day in April when Suzuki took office. The aged Premier was an admiral without a navy.

"We must stop the war at the earliest opportunity," he said when he learned the true condition of his nation's war potential. The *jushin,* the senior statesmen, had advised the Emperor in February of 1945 that surrender was necessary *no matter what the cost.*

The Potsdam Declaration was issued on July 26, 1945. It was signed by the United States, Great Britain, and (to the surprise of the Japanese) China. The reaction among Japanese leaders was one of exultation. The terms were far more lenient than had been expected. The Japanese were quick to note that instead of demanding unconditional surrender from the *government,* the last item of the proclamation called upon the government to proclaim the unconditional surrender of the *armed forces.*

The document also promised that Japan would not be destroyed as a nation, that the Japanese would be free to choose their own form of government, that sovereignty over the home islands would be returned to them after occupation, that they would be allowed access to raw materials for industry, and that Japanese forces would be allowed to return home.

Most important of all, the phrasing of the proclamation hinted strongly that the Emperor would be left on the throne, the one point which had been of most concern to the cabinet in all its discussions of surrender. The Japanese were expected to read between the lines, which they very quickly did.

Upon receiving the text of the proclamation, the Emperor told Foreign Minister Togo without hesitation that he deemed it acceptable. The full cabinet then met to discuss the Allied ultimatum.

Despite the fact that the cabinet members were considering acceptance of the Potsdam terms, they could not at first decide whether the news of the Allied proclamation should be released to the Japanese public. Foreign Minister Togo, anxious to prepare the people for the surrender, argued for four hours for its prompt release to the press. At six in the evening he won his point over strong army objections and late that night the declaration was released to the newspapers.

But there was another factor which the cabinet also was forced to consider. As yet the Japanese had received news of the statement of Allied policy at Potsdam only through their radio listening posts. It was not addressed to their government and the ultimatum had not yet reached them through official channels. Could the cabinet act on the basis of such unofficial information?

"After mature deliberation the hastily convened cabinet decided to keep silence for a while about the Potsdam proclamation pending further developments," says Kase.

The delay in announcing acceptance of the Allied terms was not expected to be long, but Prime Minister Suzuki was to meet the very next day with the press. The Japanese newsmen undoubtedly would question him about the proclamation. What should he say?

Hiroshi Shimomura, president of the powerful Board of Information—counterpart of Germany's propaganda ministry—and a member of the cabinet, recalls in his account of this fateful session that it was decided that the prime minister, if asked, should treat the subject lightly.

"This was to be done in order not to upset the surrender negotiations then under way through Russia," says Shimomura.

Premier Suzuki was to say merely that the cabinet had reached no decision on the Allied demands and that the discussion was continuing. Although the policy was to be one of silence, the very fact that the cabinet did not reject the ultimatum at once would make it clear to the Japanese people what was in the wind.

When Premier Suzuki confronted the press on July 28, he said that the cabinet was holding to a policy of *mokusatsu*. The word *mokusatsu* not only has no exact counterpart in English but it is ambiguous even in Japanese. Suzuki, as we know, meant that the cabinet had decided to make no comment on the Potsdam proclamation, with the implication that something significant was impending. But the Japanese were tricked by their own language. For in addition to meaning "to withhold comment," *mokusatsu* may also be translated as "to ignore."

The word has two characters in Japanese. *Moku* means "silence" and *satsu* means "kill," thus implying in an absolutely literal sense "to kill with silence." This can mean—to a Japanese—either to ignore or to refrain from comment.

Unfortunately the translators at the Domei News Agency could not know what Suzuki had in mind. As they hastily translated the prime minister's statement into English, they chose the wrong meaning. From the towers of Radio Tokyo the news crackled to the Allied world that the Suzuki cabinet had decided to "ignore" the Potsdam ultimatum.

The cabinet was furious at Suzuki's choice of words and the subsequent error by Domei. The reaction of Kase, who had fought long and hard for peace, was one of dismay.

"This was a piece of foolhardiness," he says. "When I heard of this I strongly remonstrated with the cabinet chief secretary, but it was too late.... Tokyo radio flashed it—to America! The punishment came swiftly. An atomic bomb was dropped on Hiroshima on August 6 by the Allies, who were led by Suzuki's outrageous statement into the belief that our government had refused to accept the Potsdam proclamation."

But for this tragic mistake, Kase laments, Japan might have been spared the atomic attack and the Russian declaration of war.

William J. Coughlin

Where Words Go Astray

One word, one mistaken interpretation by a news reporter, and the cost may have been tens of thousands of lives. Add to this the literally hundreds of small misunderstandings that almost certainly come between you and other people every week, and you can probably begin to see the need for looking closely at how our language works.

What are some of our most common problems in understanding each other? We'll start our survey of semantics by listing the most important ones, and after doing so, try to show you how you can keep them from occurring in your life.

Attitude Survey

Begin by filling out the following questionnaire. It's a series of statements someone might make while discussing politics; you've probably heard comments like these many times. Signify your response by putting a number next to each statement according to the following scale:

5 strongly agree

4 agree

3 undecided

2 disagree

1 strongly disagree

1. ____In many cases revolutions are justifiable ways of getting rid of repressive governments.
2. ____All groups can live in harmony in this country without changing the system very much.
3. ____It's not really undemocratic to recognize that the world is divided into superior and inferior people.
4. ____If you start trying to change things very much, you usually make them worse.
5. ____You can usually depend more on a person who owns property than one who doesn't.
6. ____Freedom is worth fighting for—sometimes even to death.
7. ____I prefer the practical person anytime to the intellectual.
8. ____Private ownership of property is necessary if we're to have a strong nation.
9. ____No matter what ordinary people may think, political power doesn't come from them but from some higher source.
10. ____It's better to stick with what you have than to try new things you don't really know.
11. ____Increasing government control in our lives is taking away our freedom.
12. ____A person has the right to protect himself or herself from physical threats, no matter what the law says.

13. ____It's never wise to introduce changes rapidly, in government or in the economic system.

14. ____Our society is so complicated that if you try to reform parts of it, you're likely to upset the whole system.

15. ____A person doesn't really get much wisdom until he or she is well along in years.

16. ____If something grows up over a long time, there's bound to be much wisdom in it.

17. ____I'd want to be sure that something would really work before I'd be willing to take chances on it.

18. ____You can't change human nature.

19. ____The heart is as good a guide as the head.

After writing down your response to the questions, compare them with the answers of other people who have taken the survey. Where do you agree? Disagree? Talk over your responses, and see if anyone's mind is changed. Do you ever get the feeling in such conversations that all you're doing is talking in circles? Why do you think this is so?

What happened when you discussed the survey? It's likely that you found yourself in one of those unsatisfying arguments where you not only disagreed with other respondents about the answers you gave but also couldn't even be sure you were talking about the same questions.

If this did happen, you can probably see why. The statements you responded to were so vague that they meant different things to every person who read them. Take question 1, for example. What kind of revolution were you thinking about—violent or nonviolent? Are all revolutions alike? If so, to defend one means you have to defend them all. If you don't believe all revolutions are justified, did you explain in your discussion which ones you do support? And what about "repressive governments"? Do you think everybody you argued with shared the same idea of what constitutes one? Probably not, but did you take much time trying to find a common definition for this term? In discussions like the ones you probably had here, it almost seems sometimes that the people involved are speaking different languages that only look alike.

Now you might say that this vague kind of language in the survey was obvious, that in your everyday communications you'd never be this careless in your use of language. But would this really be true? How often do you recall arguing with someone about one or more of these topics, and how many times have such discussions turned into frustrating arguments?

In the next pages we'll take a look at some common semantic problems. As you read about them, think about how they influenced your response to the preceding survey and how they occur in your everyday encounters.

Equivocal Words   One kind of semantic misunderstanding is caused by equivocal words, that is, words that have more than one dictionary definition. Equivocal misunderstandings happen almost every day, usually when we least expect them. We were ordering dinner in a Mexican restaurant and noticed that

> *A motorist was driving on the Merritt Parkway outside New York City when his engine stalled. He quickly determined that his battery was dead and managed to stop another driver, a woman. She consented to push his car to get it started.*
>
> *"My car has an automatic transmission," he explained to her, "so you'll have to get up to 30 to 35 miles per hour to get me started."*
>
> *The woman smiled sweetly and walked back to her car. The motorist climbed into his own car and waited for her to line up her car behind his. He waited—and waited. Finally, he turned around to see what was wrong.*
>
> *There was the woman—coming at his car at 30 to 35 miles per hour!*
>
> William V. Haney

the menu described each item as being served with rice or beans. We asked the waitress for "a tostada with beans," but when the order came, we were surprised to find that instead of a beef tostada with beans on the side as we expected, the waitress had brought a tostada *filled* with beans. At first we were angry at her for botching a simple order, but then we realized that it was as much our fault for not making the order clear as it was hers for not checking.

Often equivocal misunderstandings are more serious. A nurse gave one of her patients a real scare when she told him that he "wouldn't be needing" his robe, books, and shaving materials anymore. After that statement the patient became quiet and moody for no apparent reason. When the nurse finally asked why, she found out that her statement had led the poor man to think he was going to die immediately; she really meant that he'd be going home soon.

As we mentioned earlier, most of the words we use can be interpreted in a number of ways. A good rule to remember if you want to keep misunderstandings to a minimum is "If a word can be interpreted in more than one way, it probably will be."

Relative Words   Relative words are ones that gain their meaning by comparison. For example, is the school you attend a large or small one? This depends on what you compare it to: Alongside a campus like UCLA, with its more than 30,000 students, it probably looks pretty small; but compared with a smaller institution, it might seem quite large. In the same way relative words like *fast* and *slow, smart* and *stupid, short* and *long* depend for their meaning upon what they're compared to. ("Large" size olives are among the smallest you can buy; the bigger ones are "giant," "colossal," and "supercolossal.")

The Semantics of "I Love You"

. . . "I love you" [is] a statement that can be expressed in so many varied ways. It may be a stage song, repeated daily without any meaning, or a barely audible murmur, full of surrender. Sometimes it means: I desire you or I want you sexually. It may mean: I hope you love me or I hope that I will be able to love you. Often it means: It may be that a love relationship can develop between us or even I hate you. Often it is a wish for emotional exchange: I want your admiration in exchange for mine or I give my love in exchange for some passion or I want to feel cozy and at home with you or I admire some of your qualities: A declaration of love is mostly a request: I desire you or I want you to gratify me, or I want your protection or I want to be intimate with you or I want to exploit your loveliness.

Sometimes it is the need for security and tenderness, for parental treatment. It may mean: My self-love goes out to you. But it may also express submissiveness: Please take me as I am, or I feel guilty about you, I want, through you, to correct the mistakes I have made in human relations. It may be self-sacrifice and a masochistic wish for dependency. However, it may also be a full affirmation of the other, taking the responsibility for mutual exchange of feelings. It may be a weak feeling of friendliness, it may be the scarcely even whispered expression of ecstasy. "I love you,"—wish, desire, submission, conquest; it is never the word itself that tells the real meaning here.

J. A. M. Meerloo, *Conversation and Communication*

Using relative terms without explaining them can lead to communication problems. Have you ever responded to someone's question about the weather by telling her it was warm, only to find out that she thought it was cold? Or have you followed a friend's advice and gone to a "cheap" restaurant, only to find that it was twice as expensive as you expected? Have you been disappointed to learn that classes you've heard were "easy" turned out to be hard, that journeys you were told would be "short" were long, that "unusual" ideas were really quite ordinary? The problem in each case came from failing to anchor the relative term used to a more precisely measurable one.

Emotive Language   To understand how emotive language works we need to distinguish between *denotative* and *connotative* meanings. **Denotation** describes an event in purely objective terms, whereas **connotations** contain an emotional element. Consider, for example, the term *pregnant*. The denotative meaning of this word involves a condition in which a female is carrying her offspring during a gestation period. When it is used in this purely biological sense, most people could hear the term without a strong emotional reaction. But imagine the additional turmoil this word would create when an unmarried teenage couple find it stamped on the young woman's lab report. Certainly the meaning to these people would go far beyond the dictionary definition.

Some words have little or no connotative meaning: *the, it, as,* and so on. Others are likely to evoke both denotative and connotative reactions: *cancer, income tax,* and *final examination,* for example. There are also terms that are almost exclusively connotative, such as the *damn!* (or other oath) you would probably utter if you hammered your thumb instead of a nail.

Connotative meanings are a necessary and important part of human communication. Since people are creatures with emotions, it is inevitable that they will use some words that will evoke strong reactions. Without connotative meanings we'd be unable to describe ourselves fully or to have others understand us.

Problems occur, however, when people claim to use words in a purely denotative way when they are really expressing their attitudes. **Emotive language,**

How to Tell a Businessman from a Businesswoman

A businessman	A businesswoman
He is aggressive	She is pushy
He is careful about details	She's picky
He loses his temper because he's so involved in his job	She's bitchy
He's depressed (or hung over), so everyone tiptoes past his office	She's moody, so it must be her time of the month
He follows through	She doesn't know when to quit
He's firm	She's stubborn
He makes wise judgments	She reveals her prejudices
He is a man of the world	She's been around
He isn't afraid to say what he thinks	She's opinionated
He exercises authority	She's tyrannical
He's discreet	She's secretive
He's a stern taskmaster	She's difficult to work for

then, contains words that sound as if they're describing something when they are really announcing the speaker's attitude toward something. Do you like that old picture frame? If so, you'd probably call it "an antique," but if you think its ugly, you'd likely describe it as "a piece of junk." Now whether the picture frame belongs on the mantel or in the garbage can is a matter of opinion, not fact, but it's easy to forget this when you use emotive words. You might have a long and bitter argument with a friend about whether a third person was "assertive" or "obnoxious" when a more accurate and peaceable way to handle the issue would be to acknowledge that one of you approves of that person's behavior and the other doesn't. Emotive words may sound like statements of fact, but they're always opinions.

Here's a list of other emotive words:

If You Approve, Say	If You Disapprove, Say
thrifty	cheap
traditional	old-fashioned
extrovert	loudmouth
cautious	coward
progressive	radical
information	propaganda
determined	stubborn
slender	skinny

Conjugating "Irregular Verbs"

Here's a way to see how emotive words work. According to S. I. Hayakawa, the idea of "conjugating irregular verbs" this way originated with Bertrand Russell.

1. The technique is simple: Just take an action or personality trait, and show how it can be viewed either favorably or unfavorably, according to the label we give it. For example,
> I'm casual.
> You're a little careless.
> He's a slob.

Or try this one:
> I read love stories.
> You read erotic literature.
> She reads pornography.

Or
> I'm thrifty.
> You're money conscious.
> He's a tightwad.

2. Now try a few conjugations yourself, using the following statements:
   a. I'm tactful.
   b. I'm conservative.
   c. I'm quiet.
   d. I'm relaxed.
   e. My child is high-spirited.
   f. I have a lot of self-pride.

3. Now recall at least two situations in which you used an emotive word as if it were a description of fact and not an opinion. A good way to remember these situations is to think of a recent argument you had and imagine how the other people involved might have described it. How would their words differ from yours?

Confusing Facts and Inferences   Some statements refer to things or acts we can observe ("She is driving a Volkswagen"), and some refer to things we can't observe directly ("She is seething with rage"). Although the two types of statements are grammatically identical, they are quite different semantically. **Factual statements** are based on direct observation and are usually easy to verify. **Inferential statements** are interpretations of sense data.

There's nothing wrong with making inferences as long as you identify them as such: "She stomped out and slammed the door. It looked to me as if she were seething with rage." The danger comes when we confuse inferences with facts and make them sound like the absolute truth.

One way to avoid fact-inference confusion is to use the perception checking skill described in Chapter Three to test the accuracy of your inferences. Recall that a perception check has three parts: a description of the behavior being discussed, your interpretation of that behavior, and a request for verification. For instance, instead of saying, "Why are you laughing at me?" you could say, "When you laugh like that [description of behavior], I get the idea you think something I did was stupid [interpretation]. *Are* you laughing at me [question]?"

Abstraction in Language

In the beginning of this chapter we said that words represent things rather than being things themselves. This fact leads to the critically important idea that language can describe events on many levels, some of which are more abstract than others.

To understand the concept of abstraction, consider the object you're reading now. What would you call it? Probably a book. But you could narrow your description by calling it a "communication book" or, even more specifically, *Looking Out/Looking In*. You could be even more precise than this if you wanted to: You could say that you're reading Chapter Five of *Looking Out/Looking In* or even page 161 of Chapter Five of *Looking Out/Looking In*. In each case, your description would be more precise, focusing more specifically on the object we asked you about while excluding other things that were members of the same categories but didn't apply in this case.

Instead of going down the abstraction ladder to more basic terms, you could go the other way. Rather than talking about this thing you're reading as a book, you could describe it as educational literature, nonfiction writing, or printed material, each description being less and less specific.

Semanticist S. I. Hayakawa created an **abstraction ladder** to describe this process.[2] This ladder consists of a number of descriptions of the same person, object, or event. The lowest description on the ladder describes the phenomenon at its most basic level: atoms and molecules interacting, nerve synapses operating, magnetic waves moving through space, and so on.

Further up the ladder are visually observable aspects of the event: specifically what words are said, what movements are made, what colors or sizes are

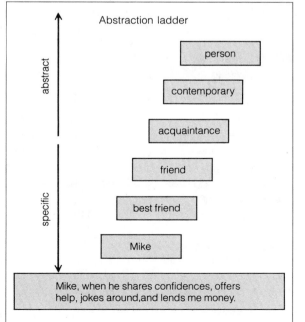

Figure 5–1
Abstraction ladder

Last night while Roy and I were preparing dinner, four-year-old Michael yelled from the family room, "Hey mom, how do you make love, again?" The expression on Roy's face clearly said, "What have you been teaching this kid?" I calmly answered Michael's question with "L-O-V-E." He had been drawing a picture for a friend and wanted to sign it "Love, Michael," but had forgotten how to "make" love. I wonder how Roy would have answered Michael's question if I hadn't been around!

present, and so on. Moving still higher up the ladder, we come to increasingly general descriptions. The sample abstraction ladder illustrated in Figure 5–1 is an example of the many levels on which a phenomenon can be described.

Higher-level abstractions are generalizations that serve as a useful kind of linguistic shorthand. It may be easier to use the word *yuppie* to describe some of your friends than to spell out the details: that Tony drives a BMW, skis most winter weekends, and is a wine connoisseur; that Bret is a fast-track attorney who is rehabilitating an urban loft; and that Marilyn is an M.B.A. from Columbia who plans to raise a family, pursue her career, and sharpen her tennis game.

Although abstractions like *yuppie, jerk, Christian,* or *conservative* make it easier to emphasize the similarities between people, objects, or events, they also lead us to ignore differences between them. This failure can lead to several problems, which we'll now examine.

Problems with Abstractions   Most problems with abstractions arise from using terms that are too high on the abstraction ladder. This lack of specificity causes trouble in four ways.

Stereotyping   Imagine someone who has had a bad experience while traveling abroad and as a result blames an entire country. "Those damn Hottentots are a bunch of thieves. If you're not careful, they'll steal you blind. I know, because one of 'em stole my camera last year." You can see here how lumping people into highly abstract categories ignores the fact that for every thieving Hottentot there are probably 100 honest ones. It's this kind of thinking that leads to mistaken assumptions that keep people apart: "None of those kids are any damn good!" "You can't trust anybody in business!" "The police are a bunch of goons." Each of these statements ignores the very important fact that sometimes our descriptions are too general, that they say more than we really mean.

When you think about examples like these, you begin to see how thinking in abstract terms can lead to ignoring individual differences, which can be as important as similarities. In this sense semantics isn't "just" a matter of words. People in the habit of using highly abstract language begin to *think* in generalities, ignoring uniqueness. And as we discussed in Chapter Two, expecting people to be a certain way can become a self-fulfilling prophecy. If I think all police officers are brutal, I'm more likely to react in a defensive, hostile way toward them, which in turn increases the chance that they'll react to me as a threat. If I think that no teachers care about their classes, then my defensive indifference is likely to make a potentially helpful instructor into someone who truly doesn't care.

Failing to recognize abstractions for what they are can lead to a great deal of unnecessary grief. We know a couple who were convinced that their child was abnormal because she hadn't learned to talk by the age of two. When we tried to tell them that some kids begin talking later than others and that there was nothing to worry about, the parents wouldn't accept our help. "But something must be wrong with Sally," they said, pointing to a book on child development. "It says right here that children should be talking by one year, and Sally only makes funny noises." What the parents had failed to do was read the first chapters of the book, in which the authors stressed that the term *child* is an abstraction—

> **A group of synonyms does not define an object. A careful description may help bring it into focus for the listener, but is not conclusive. Final identification is achieved only by pointing to the apple, touching it with the hand, seeing it with the eyes, tasting it with the mouth, and so recognizing it as nonverbal. Here is the base from which all our proud words rise—every last one of them—and to it they must constantly return and be refreshed. Failing this, they wander into regions where there are no apples, no objects, no acts, and so they become symbols for airy chunks of nothing at all. . . .**

Stuart Chase,
The Tyranny of Words

that there's no such thing as the "typical" child because each one is an individual.

Confusing Others   Have you ever been disappointed with the way a haircut turned out? In spite of your instructions—"not too short," for example—you got up from the chair with a style unlike anything you wanted. Although the problem might have come from choosing a stylist who should have become a butcher, it's more likely that your instructions weren't clear enough. Terms like "not too short" or "more casual" are just too abstract to paint a clear picture of what you had in mind.

   Of course, overly abstract explanations can cause problems of a more serious nature. Imagine the lack of understanding that could arise from vague complaints such as

A   We never do anything that's fun anymore.

B   What do you mean?

A   We used to do lots of unusual things, but now it's the same old stuff, over and over.

B   But last week we went on that camping trip, and tomorrow we're going to that party where we'll meet all sorts of new people. Those are new things.

A   That's not what I mean. I'm talking about *really* unusual stuff.

B   (becoming confused and a little impatient) Like what? Taking hard drugs or going over Niagara Falls in a barrel?

A   Don't be stupid. All I'm saying is that we're in a rut. We should be living more exciting lives.

B   Well, I don't know what you want.

**Words, strain,
crack, and sometime break,
under the burden.**

T. S. Eliot

Overly abstract language also leads to confusing directions:

Teacher   I hope you'll do a thorough job on this paper.

Student   When you say thorough, how long should it be?

T   Long enough to cover the topic thoroughly.

S   How many sources should I look at when I'm researching it?

T   You should use several—enough to show me that you've really explored the subject.

S   And what style should I use to write it?

T   One that's scholarly but not too formal.

S   Arrgh!!!

Along with unclear complaints and vague instructions, even compliments can suffer from being expressed in overly abstract terms. Psychologists have established that behaviors that are reinforced will recur with increased frequency—which means that your statements of appreciation will encourage others to keep acting in ways you like. But if they don't know just what it is that you appreciate, the chances of repetitive behavior are lessened. There's a big difference between "I appreciate your being so nice" and "I appreciate the way you spent that time talking to me when I was upset."

Bypassing   Bypassing occurs when people unintentionally use the same word to mean different things or use different words to represent the same thing. Have you ever gotten angry at a friend who calls to say, "I'll be a little late for our date" and then keeps you waiting an hour? This mixup about the relative term *little* typifies bypassing. So does the argument we once heard between two students, one black and one white, who were talking about a particular model of car. The black student insisted the car was "bad" whereas the white claimed it was "great." After a few minutes they finally realized that they both liked the auto, but that the terms they chose to express themselves suggested a disagreement. Problems of bypassing such as these are much more likely to occur when we use abstract language since there's less possibility of checking terms against observable events.

cathy   by Cathy Guisewite

Confusing Yourself   Overly abstract language can leave even you unclear about your own thoughts. At one time or another we've all felt dissatisfied with ourselves and others. Often these dissatisfactions show up as thoughts such as "I've got to get better organized" or "She's been acting strangely lately." Sometimes abstract statements such as these are shorthand for specific behaviors that we can easily identify, but in other cases we'd have a hard time clearly explaining what we'd have to do to get organized or what the strange behavior is. And without clear ideas of these concepts it's hard to begin changing matters. Instead, the tendency is to go around in mental circles, feeling vaguely dissatisfied without knowing exactly what is wrong or how to improve matters.

In many situations it's important to be specific, but I can't think of any examples offhand.

Ashleigh Brilliant

Down to Specifics: Avoiding Abstract Thinking and Language

If abstract language is often a problem, what can you do to reduce its inappropriate use in your life? Probably the best answer is to pay attention to your everyday conversations and thoughts. Every so often—especially when your emotions are strong—ask yourself whether you can transfer your language down the abstraction ladder to less vague terms.

You can do this by learning to make **behavioral descriptions** of your problems, goals, appreciations, complaints, and requests. We use the word *behavioral* because descriptions of this sort move down the abstraction ladder to describe the specific, observable objects and actions about which we're thinking.

It's hard to overestimate the value of specific, behavioral language because speaking in this way vastly increases the chance not only of thinking clearly about what's on your mind but also of others understanding you. A behavioral description should include three elements:

Who Is Involved   At first the answer to this question might seem simple. If you're thinking about a personal problem or goal, you might reply, "I am"; if you're expressing appreciation, complaining, or making a request of another person, he or she would be the one who is involved. Although the question of involvement may be easy, it often calls for more detail. Ask yourself whether the problem or goal you're thinking about involves an entire category of people (women, salespeople, strangers), a subclass of the group (attractive women, rude salespeople, strangers you'd like to meet), or a specific person (Jane Doe, the salesclerk at a particular store, a new person in your neighborhood). If you're talking to another person, consider whether your appreciation, complaint, or request is directed solely at him or her or whether it also involves others.

In What Circumstances Does the Behavior Occur?   You can identify the circumstances by answering several questions. In what places does the behavior occur? Does it occur at any particular times? When you are discussing particular subjects? Is there anything special about you when it occurs: Are you tired, embarrassed, busy? Is there any common trait shared by the other person or people involved? Are they friendly or hostile, straightforward or manipulative, nervous or confident? In other words, if the behavior you're describing doesn't occur all the time (and few behaviors do), you need to pin down what circumstances set this situation apart from other ones.

"In that case," said the Dodo solemnly, rising to its feet, "I move that the meeting adjourn, for the immediate adoption of more energetic remedies—"

"Speak English!" said the Eaglet. "I don't know the meaning of half those long words, and, what's more, I don't believe you do either!" And the Eaglet bent down its head to hide a smile: some of the other birds tittered audibly.

"What I was going to say," said the Dodo in an offended tone, "was that the best thing to get us dry would be a Caucus-race."

"What is a Caucus-race?" said Alice.

"Why," said the Dodo, "the best way to explain it is to do it."

Lewis Carroll,
Alice's Adventures in Wonderland

What Behaviors Are Involved?   Although terms such as *more cooperative* and *helpful* might sound as if they're concrete descriptions of behavior, they are usually too vague to explain clearly what's on your mind. Behaviors must be *observable,* ideally both to you and to others. For instance, moving down the abstraction ladder from the relatively vague term *helpful,* you might arrive at "does the dishes every other day," "volunteers to help me with my studies," or "fixes dinner once or twice a week without being asked." It's easy to see that terms like these are easier for both you and others to understand than are more vague abstractions.

There is one exception to the rule that behaviors should be observable, and that involves the internal processes of thoughts and emotions. For instance, in describing what happens to you when a friend has kept you waiting for a long time, you might say, "My stomach felt as if it were in knots—I was really worried. I kept thinking that you had forgotten and that I wasn't important enough to you for you to remember our date." What you're doing when offering such a description is to make unobservable events clear.

You can better understand the value of behavioral descriptions by looking at the examples we've provided in Table 5–1. Notice how much more clearly they explain the speaker's thought than do the more vague terms.

One valuable type of behavioral description is the **operational definition.** Instead of defining a word with more words, an operational definition points, as it were, to the behaviors, actions, or properties that a word signifies. The definition of *interpersonal communication* in Chapter One is an operational one, since it helps us identify what kinds of interactions do and don't qualify as we'll use the term in this book.

We use operational definitions all the time: "The student union is that building with all the bikes in front." "What I'd like more than anything is thirty acres of land on the Columbia River." "My idea of a good time is eating a triple-decker, three-flavor, chocolate-dipped ice cream cone." All these statements are relatively clear; rather than using vague, more abstract language, they tell in observable terms just what the speaker is talking about. Hayakawa points out that the best examples of operational definitions in our everyday lives are found in cookbooks. They describe a dish by telling you what ingredients are combined in what amounts by what operations. ("To make a pizza, begin with the crust. Mix ¼ cup water with 2 cups flour. . . .")

But as we've already seen, some definitions aren't operational. They never point down the ladder of abstraction to more clearly understandable operations; instead, they only explain words with more words. A nonoperational, highly abstract cookbook might define a pizza as "a delectable, flavorful treat that is both hearty and subtle."

This example illustrates both the advantages and limitations of operational definitions. On the one hand, they paint a very clear picture of what you're talking about, leaving very little to the listener's imagination. On the other hand, they leave out some qualities that lend an emotional element to communication. Although the recipe for pizza might tell you *how* to make one, it's not likely to make you *want* to eat it. Figurative language is appropriate at times. You're much more likely to win your true love's affection by reciting poetry than by talking about how your blood pressure changes whenever you're together. The trick, then, isn't to use just abstract or only specific language, but rather to use each when it will best suit your needs.

Table 5—1   Abstract vs. Behavioral Descriptions

	Abstract Description	Behavioral Description			Remarks
		Who Is Involved	In What Circumstances	Specific Behaviors	
Problem	I'm no good at meeting strangers.	People I'd like to date.	When I meet them at parties or at school.	Think to myself, "They'd never want to date me." Also, I don't originate conversations.	Behavioral description more clearly identifies thoughts and behaviors to change.
Goal	I'd like to be more assertive.	Telephone and door-to-door solicitors.	When I don't want the product or can't afford it.	Instead of apologizing or explaining, say, "I'm not interested" and keep repeating this until they go away.	Behavioral description clearly outlines how to act; abstract description doesn't.
Appreciation	"You've been a great boss."	(No clarification necessary.)	When I've needed to change my schedule because of school exams or assignments.	"You've rearranged my hours cheerfully."	Give both abstract and behavioral descriptions for best results.
Complaint	"I don't like some of the instructors around here."	Professors A and B.	In class when students ask questions the professors think are stupid.	Either answer in a sarcastic voice (you might demonstrate) or accuse us of not studying hard enough.	If talking to A or B, use only behavioral description. With others, use both abstract and behavioral descriptions.
Request	"Quit bothering me!"	You and your friends X and Y.	When I'm studying for exams.	Instead of asking me over and over to party with you, I wish you'd accept my comment that I need to study and leave me to do it.	Behavioral description will reduce defensiveness and make it clear that you don't *always* want to be left alone.

The problems crop up when we start talking about other types of deviant behavior. We say of a person who drinks too much that he "is" an alcoholic, and we say of people who think bizarre thoughts that they "are" schizophrenic. This person is a drug addict and that person is a homosexual. Others are sadomasochists, pedophiliacs, juvenile delinquents. The English language is constructed in such a way that we speak of people being (certain things) when all we know is that they do certain things. . . .

That kind of identity is a myth. Admittedly, if a person believes the myth, the chances rise that he will assume the appropriate, narrowly defined role. Believing that one is an addict, an alcoholic, a schizophrenic, or a homosexual can result in relinquishing the search for change and becoming imprisoned in the role.

Edward Sagarian

Language, Attitudes, and Behavior

The power of language goes beyond simply creating or preventing misunderstandings. Language also shapes the way we view the world and provides insights about how we view our relationships with others.

Language Shapes Our Attitudes   Anthropologists know that the culture in which we live influences our perception of reality. Some social scientists believe that this cultural perspective is at least partially shaped by the very language the members of that culture speak. This idea has been most widely circulated in the writings of Benjamin Lee Whorf and Edward Sapir, and identified as the **Whorf-Sapir hypothesis**.[3]

After spending several years studying various North American Indian cultures, Whorf found that their entire way of thinking was shaped by the language they spoke. For example, Nootka, a language spoken on Vancouver Island, contains no distinction between nouns and verbs. Therefore the Indians who speak it view the entire world as being constantly in process. Where we see a thing as fixed or constant (noun), they view it as constantly changing. Thus, instead of calling something a "fire," the Nootka speaker might call it a "burning"; where we see a house, he would see a "house-ing." In this sense our language operates much like a snapshot camera, whereas Nootka works more like a moving-picture camera.

What does this have to do with communication? How does our language influence the way we relate with each other? Because of the static, unchanging nature of English grammar, we often regard people and things as never changing. Someone who spoke a more process-oriented language would view people quite differently, better recognizing their changeable nature.

The Whorf-Sapir hypothesis has never been conclusively proved or disproved. In spite of its intellectual appeal, some critics point out that it is possible to conceive of flux even in static languages like English. They suggest that Whorf and Sapir overstated the importance of their idea. Supporters of the hypothesis respond that although it is *possible* to conceptualize an idea in different languages, some make it much easier to recognize a term than do others.

For example, suppose that you, an English speaker, have just returned from a visit to New York and someone asks you what kind of place it is. "Oh, it's a terrible place," you say. Now look at this response. By saying that New York *is* terrible (or great or any other adjective), your language implies two things: First, that your judgment is a total one—that it covers everything about the city—and second, that New York is an unchanging place. The word *is* implies eternal sameness, when in fact the "things" we give names to are really changing, dynamic processes. New York today isn't the same place it was last year or will be tomorrow, and your experiences there aren't the same ones that other people might have had. You'd have been more correct if you'd answered by saying, "My experiences while visiting New York in January 1981 were that the streets were crowded; the people I encountered behaved rudely; and the prices for food, lodging, and entertainment were too high." Now, of course, this way of talking isn't always practical, but it's certainly more accurate than judging New York in absolute terms.

The real culprit we're talking about is the word *is*. It leads us to think of people or things as if they were absolute and unchanging. Saying that "John *is* handsome, boring, or immature" isn't as correct as saying, "The John I encountered yesterday seemed to be. . . ." There's a big difference between saying, "Beth is a phony" and "Beth seemed phony the other night." The second statement describes the way someone behaved at one time, and the first categorizes her as if she had always been phony. It's this kind of verbal generalizing that causes teachers to think of students as "slow learners" or "troublemakers" because of past test scores or reports.

Alfred Korzybski, who originated the discipline of general semantics, suggested a linguistic device to remind us of the way all things change. He proposed that we qualify important words by attaching subscripts to them. For example, instead of saying "I didn't like Joe," you might say "I didn't like Joe $_{last Tuesday}$." This would make it harder to think in abstract, overly general terms.

The following article is one example of how subscripting helps avoid the idea that people act or should be expected to act consistently. As you read it, imagine how you could apply this way of thinking to one or two people you know. How would doing so affect your relationships with them?

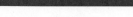

Is Is What Was Was?

An is is just a was that was and
  that is very small . . .
And is is was so soon it almost
  wasn't is at all.
For is is only is until it is a
  was—you see . . .
And as an is advances—to
  remain an is can't be . . .
'cause if is is to stay an is
  it isn't is because
another is is where it was and
  is is then a was.

Tom Hicks,
Etc. Magazine

A Greek named Heraclitus claimed that you never see the same river twice because the water that was there one minute is not there the next. In this respect, it seems to me, husbands are like rivers. For example, my husband Tom.

Tom_1 is of course the lover; Tom_2, the man of business. Both these Toms are substantially the same today as when we were married in 1948.

Tom_3, the father, is different. He wasn't born until 1950. I watched his birth with some pity, a little resentment, and a strong upsurge of motherly feeling toward him. He was almost as bewildered as was Tom, Jr. But, whereas the baby took strong hold in his new world, Tom_3 stood at the edge of fatherhood for a while, until I felt like taking him by the ear with an old-fashioned motherly grip and leading him to his son. Today, though, Tom_3 bears little resemblance to $Tom_{3\ (1950)}$. Actually, I feel a little shut out now when Tom_3 and Tom, Jr., are especially close, as when they're planning a fishing trip.

Tom_4, the fisherman, is a loathsome person—an adolescent, self-centered, unpredictable, thoughtless, utterly selfish braggart. Yesterday, he bought Junior a fishing rod.

"Pampering him," I said. "He needs other things so much more— his teeth straightened, summer camp."

"He needs a fishing rod," Tom_4 said.

"You're teaching him to become a thoughtless husband," I charged.

"Oh, I don't know," Tom_4 said. "Maybe he'll marry a girl who likes to fish."

That stopped me for a minute. I'd never thought of there being such girls. Perhaps Tom_4 was disappointed in me. I was just wondering what I could wear on a fishing trip when Tom_4 shattered my good intentions by saying, "A fishing trip for Junior is a good deal more important than a permanent for Nancy."

This came as a surprise. Tom_{3b} as father of Nancy was not the Tom_{3a} father of Junior. Usually Nancy could get away with anything. At five, she had known better than to cut up the evening paper before her father had seen it, but Tom_{3b} had just laughed. He was certainly no relation to the husband-at-breakfast Tom who would scream if his wife got the pages of the morning paper out of place. He'd always been a little too indulgent with Nancy and too severe with Junior, but now he was begrudging Nancy a permanent.

"Do you want to have an unattractive daughter?" I asked, but Tom_{3b} wasn't there. Tom_5, the amateur plumber and ardent do-it-yourselfer, had taken over. He was at the sink fussing with the garbage disposer, promising to fix it Saturday.

"Why don't you buy Nancy a fishing rod?" I suggested.

And who looked back at me? Tom_6 the bewildered husband. "Are you joking?" he asked.

"Certainly not," I said indignantly. "You should train her to make a good wife."

Tom_6 laughed. Then Tom_7 took over. Tom_7 is the appreciative husband. He's a very determined fellow. He laughs loud and long.

"Very funny," he said. "I always appreciate your sense of humor. I always tell my—"

"Don't overdo it," I snarled. "I'm not being funny. Maybe she should have a fishing rod."

"She has her permanent," Tom_8 said with a laugh. "When she gets a little older she can fish with that." Tom_8 is a clown, the life of the party. Some day I may murder him.

I poured the coffee and resisted the temptation to drip a little on Tom_8's balding head. "Polygamy's wonderful," I murmured with a sigh, as I set the coffee pot down.

Tom_7 looked at me with concern. "Have you seen your doctor lately?" he asked.

"No, there are enough men in my life," I answered. But Tom_2 was looking at his watch. I realized that my remark had been wasted. Not one of my husbands was listening.

Mary Graham Lund

Even within the confines of English, the words we use to describe people's roles or functions in society can also shape the way they feel about themselves. Much of people's self-esteem is derived from the importance they feel their work has, a perception that often comes from the titles for their roles. For example, a theater owner had trouble keeping ushers for more than a week or two. The ushers tired quickly of their work, which consisted mostly of taking tickets, selling popcorn, and showing people to their seats. Then with only one change, the manager ended the personnel problems. The manager simply "promoted" all the ushers to the "new" position of "assistant manager." And believe it or not, the new title was sufficient to make the employees happy. The new name encouraged them to think more highly of themselves and to take new pride in their work.

The significance of words in shaping our self-concept goes beyond job titles. Racist and sexist language greatly affects the self-concepts of those facing discrimination. An article in the *New York Times Magazine* by Casey Miller and Kate Swift points out some of the aspects of our language that suggest women are of lower status than men. Miller and Swift write that, except for words referring to females by definition, such as *mother* and *actress,* English defines many nonsexual concepts as male. The underlying assumption is that people in general are men. Also, words associated with males have positive connotations, such as *manly, virile, courageous, direct, strong,* and *independent,* whereas words related to females are fewer and have less positive connotations, such as *feminine wiles* and *womanish tears* [4]

Most dictionaries, in fact, define *effeminate* as the opposite of *masculine* although the opposite of *feminine* is closer to *unfeminine.* Any language expressing stereotyped sexual attitudes or assuming the superiority of one sex over another is sexist, so adding feminine endings to nonsexual words, such as *poetess* for female poet, is as sexist as *separate but equal* is racist.

Whereas sexist language usually defines the world as made up of superior men and inferior women, racist language usually defines it as composed of superior whites and other, inferior racial groups. Words and images associated with *white* are usually positive, whether it's the hero-cowboy in white or connotations of white as *pure, clean, honorable, innocent, bright,* and *shiny.* The words and images associated with black are often negative, a concept that reaches from the clothes of the villain-cowboy to connotations such as *decay, dirt, smudge, dismal, wicked, unwashed,* and *sinister.*

To the extent that our language is both sexist and racist, our view of the world is affected. For example, men are given more opportunity than women to see themselves as "good," and in the same way whites are given more opportunity than blacks. Language shapes the self-concepts of those it labels in such a way that members of the linguistically slighted group see themselves as inferior.

Many linguistic changes beginning in the late 1960s were aimed primarily at teaching speakers and writers a new vocabulary to change the destructive connotations that accompany many of our words. For example, "black is beautiful" is an effort to reduce perceived differences in status among blacks and whites.

Changes in writing style were also designed to counter the sexual prejudices inherent in language, particularly eliminating the constant use of *he* and introducing various methods either to eliminate reference to a particular sex or to

"It's called bananas flambeau, not a bunch of burned bananas."

refer to both sexes. Words that use *man* generically to refer to humanity at large often pose problems, but only to the unimaginative. Consider the following substitutions: *Mankind* may be replaced by *humanity, human beings, human race,* and *people; man-made* may be replaced by *artificial, manufactured,* and *synthetic; manpower* may be replaced by *human power, workers,* and *work force;* and *manhood* may be replaced by *adulthood.*

> *Congressmen* are *members of congress.*
> *Firemen* are *fire fighters.*
> *Chairmen* are *presiding officers, leaders,* and *chairs.*
> *Foremen* are *supervisors.*
> *Policemen* and *policewomen* are both *police officers.*
> *Stewardesses* and *stewards* are both *flight attendants.*

Throughout this book we have used a number of techniques for avoiding sexist language: switching to the sexually neutral plural (*they*), occasionally using the passive voice to eliminate sexed pronouns, employing the *he or she* structure, carefully balancing individual masculine and feminine pronouns in illustrative material, and even totally rewriting some parts to delete conceptual sexual bias. But many people believe that a more radical solution is appropriate. They suggest that since language shapes perceptions, we need to change our grammar in order to change our thinking. Read the article on page 175, and see whether you agree.

De-Sexing the English Language

On the television screen, a teacher of first-graders who has just won a national award is describing her way of teaching. "You take each child where you find him," she says. "You watch to see what he's interested in, and then you build on his interests."

A five-year-old looking at the program asks her mother, "Do only boys go to that school?"

"No," her mother begins, "she's talking about girls too, but—"

But what? The teacher being interviewed on television is speaking correct English. What can the mother tell her daughter about why a child, in any generalization, is always *he* rather than *she*? How does a five-year-old comprehend the generic personal pronoun?

The effect on personality development of this one part of speech was recognized by thoughtful people long before the present assault on the English language by the forces of Women's Liberation. Fifteen years ago, Lynn T. White, then president of Mills College, wrote:

> The grammar of English dictates that when a referent is either of indeterminate sex or both sexes, it shall be considered masculine. The penetration of this habit of language into the minds of little girls as they grow up to be women is more profound than most people, including most women, have recognized: for it implies that personality is really a male attribute, and that women are a human sub-species. . . . It would be a miracle if a girl-baby, learning to use the symbols of our tongue, could escape some wound to her self-respect: whereas a boy-baby's ego is bolstered by the pattern of our language.

Now that our language has begun to respond to the justice of Women's Liberation, a lot of people apparently are trying to kick the habit of using *he* when they mean anyone, male or female. In fact, there is mounting evidence that a major renovation of the language is in progress with respect to this pronoun. It is especially noticeable in the speeches of politicians up for election: "And as for every citizen who pays taxes, I say that he or she deserves an accounting!" A variation of the tandem form is also cropping up in print, like the copy on a coupon that offers the bearer a 20 percent saving on "the cost of his/her meal." A writer in the New York newspaper *The Village Voice* adopts the same form to comment "that every artist of major stature is actually a school in him/herself."

Adding the feminine pronoun to the masculine whenever the generic form is called for may be politically smart and morally right, but the result is often awkward.

Some of the devices used to get around the problem are even less acceptable, at least to grammarians. It is one thing for a student to announce in assembly that "Anybody can join the Glee Club as long as they can carry a tune," but when this patchwork solution begins to appear in print, the language is in trouble. In blatant defiance of every teacher of freshman English, a full-page advertisement in *The New York Times* for its college and school subscription service begins with this headline: "If someone you know is attending one of these colleges, here's something they should know that can save them money." Although the grammatical inconsistency of the *Times's* claim offends the ear—especially since "they" in the headline can refer only to "colleges"—the alternatives would present insurmountable problems for the writer. For example, the sentence might read, "If someone you know . . . etc., here's something he or she should know that can save him/her money." Or, in order to keep the plural subject in the second clause, the writer might have begun, "If several people you know are attending one or more of these colleges. . . ." But by that time will the reader still care?

In the long run, the problem of the generic personal pronoun is a problem of the status of women. But it is more immediately a matter of common sense and clear communication. Absurd examples of the burdens now placed upon masculine pronouns pop up everywhere. "The next time you meet a handicapped person, don't make up your mind about him in advance," admonishes a radio public service announcement. A medical school bulletin, apparently caught by surprise, reports that a certain scholarship given annually "to a student of unquestioned ability and character who has completed his first year" was awarded to one Barbara Kinder.

Since there is no way in English to solve problems like these with felicity and grace, it is becoming obvious that what we need is a new singular personal pronoun that is truly generic: a common-gender pronoun. Several have been proposed, but so far none appears to have the transparently logical relationship to existing pronouns that is necessary if a new word is to gain wide acceptance. Perhaps a clue to the solution is to be found in people's persistent use of *they* as a singular pronoun.

In the plural forms, both genders are included in one word: *they* can

	Singular		*Plural*
	Distinct Gender	Common Gender	Common Gender
Nominative *he* and *she*		*tey*	*they*
Possessive *his* and *her* (or *hers*)		*ter* (or *ters*)	*their* (or *theirs*)
Objective *him* and *her*		*tem*	*them*

refer to males or females or a mixed group. So why not derive the needed singular common-gender pronouns from the plural? *They, their,* and *them* suggest *tey, ter,* and *tem.* With its inflected forms pronounced to rhyme with the existing plural forms, the new word would join the family of third person pronouns as shown in the box. . . .

Someone will probably object to the idea of a common-gender pronoun in the mistaken belief that it is a neuter form and therefore underrates sexual differences. The opposite is true. Once *tey* or a similar word is adopted, *he* can become exclusively masculine, just as *she* is now exclusively feminine. The new pronoun will thus accentuate the significant and valuable

differences between females and males—those of reproductive function and form—while affirming the essential unity and equality of the two sexes within the species.

Language constantly evolves in response to need. It is groping today for ways to accommodate the new recognition of women as full-fledged members of the human race. If the new pronoun helps anyone toward that end, tey should be free to adopt it.

If anyone objects, it is certainly ter right—but in that case let tem come up with a better solution.

Casey Miller and Kate Swift

This power of labeling extends even to our personal names. Research shows that these names are more than just simple means of identification, that in fact they shape the way others think of us, the way we view ourselves and our behavior.[5]

Different names have different connotations. Psychologists Barbara Buchanan and James Bruning asked college students to rate over a thousand names according to their likability, how active or passive they seemed, and their masculinity or femininity. In spite of the large number of subjects, the responses were quite similar. Michael, John, and Wendy were likable and active and were rated as possessing the masculine or feminine traits of their sex. Percival, Isadore, and Alfreda were less likable, and their sexuality was more suspect. Other research also suggests that names have strong connotative meanings. More common names are generally viewed as being more active, stronger, and better than unusual ones.

The preconceptions we hold about people because of their names influence our behavior toward them. In a well-known study Herbert Harari and John McDavid asked a number of teachers to read several essays supposedly written by fifth-grade students. The researchers found that certain names—generally the most popular ones, such as Lisa, Michael, and Karen—received higher grades, regardless of which essay they were attached to, whereas other, less popular names—Elmer, Bertha, Hubert—were consistently graded as inferior. There was one exception to the link between popular names and high grades: Unpopular Adelle received the highest evaluation of all. Harari and McDavid speculated that the teachers saw her as more "scholarly."

It's not surprising to find that the attitudes others hold toward a person because of his or her name have an effect on that person's self-concept. Forty years ago, B. M. Savage and F. L. Wells found that students at Harvard who had unusual names were more likely to be neurotic and to flunk out of school. The negative effect of unusual names seems to be more damaging to men than to women, perhaps because of our social convention that makes such labels acceptable for females. At any rate, research such as this makes it clear that the question "What shall we name the baby?" is an important one for more than aesthetic reasons.

Language Reflects Our Attitudes

Besides shaping the way we view ourselves and others, language reflects our attitudes. Feelings of control, attraction, commitment, responsibility . . . all these and more are reflected in the way we use language.

Power   Communication researchers have identified a number of language patterns that add to or detract from a speaker's ability to influence others, as well as reflecting how a speaker feels about his or her degree of control over a situation.[6] Table 5–2 summarizes some of these findings by listing several types of "powerless" language.

You can see the difference between powerful and powerless language by comparing the following statements:

> "Excuse me, sir. I hate to say this, but I . . . uh . . . I guess I won't be able to turn in the assignment on time. I had a personal emergency and . . . well . . . it was just impossible to finish it by today. I'll have it in your mailbox on Monday, okay?"

> "I won't be able to turn in the assignment on time. I had a personal emergency and it was impossible to finish it by today. I'll have it in your mailbox on Monday."

Alice: "Must a name mean something?"
Humpty-Dumpty: "Of course it must . . .

My name means the shape I am . . .
With a name like yours, you might be any shape, almost."

Lewis Carroll,
Through the Looking Glass

Table 5—2   Examples of Powerless Language

Hedges	"I'm *kinda* disappointed..." "I *think* we should..." "I *guess* I'd like to..."
Hesitations	"*Uh,* can I have a minute of your time?" "*Well,* we could try this idea..." "I wish you would—*er*—try to be on time."
Intensifiers	"*So* that's how I feel..." "I'm not *very* hungry."
Polite forms	"Excuse me *sir*..."
Tag questions	"It's about time we got started, *isn't it?*" "*Don't you think* we should give it another try?"
Disclaimers	"*I probably shouldn't say this, but...*" "*I'm not really sure but...*"

Whether or not the professor finds the excuse acceptable, it's clear that the second speaker feels confident, whereas the first one is apologetic and uncertain. The first statement is a classic example of what social scientists have come to call "one-down" communication.[7]

Some relationships are characterized by what social scientists term *complementary* communication, in which one partner uses consistently powerful

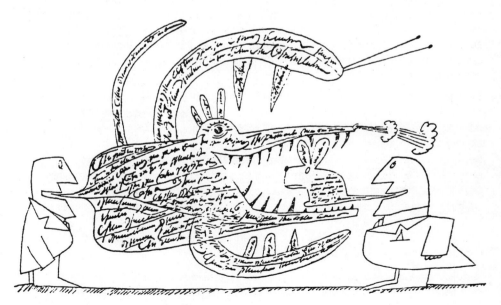

language while the other responds with powerless speech. A demanding boss and compliant employees or the stereotypically tyrannical husband and submissive wife are examples of complementary relationships. In other relationships, called *symmetrical,* the power is distributed more evenly between the partners: Both may use equally powerful or powerless speech. The locus of power isn't constant: As relationships pass through different stages, the distribution of power shifts, and so do the speech patterns of the partners.[8] You can test this principle for yourself. Recall situations in which you were feeling especially vulnerable, uncertain, confused, or powerless. Did your language include the characteristics listed in Table 5–2? Did these characteristics disappear when you felt more safe, confident, or powerful? What factors led to these changes? The subject being discussed? Your feelings about yourself at the moment? The way the other person was treating you?

Simply counting the number of powerful or powerless statements won't always reveal who has the most control in a relationship. Social rules often mask the real distribution of power. A boss who wants to be pleasant might say to a secretary, "Would you mind retyping this letter?" In truth, both boss and secretary know this is an order and not a request, but the questioning form makes the medicine less bitter.[9] Therefore, a knowledge of the context and the personalities of the speakers is necessary before it's safe to make any assumptions about who controls whom.

Attraction and Interest   Social customs discourage us from expressing like or dislike in many situations. Only a clod would respond to the question "What do you think of the cake I baked for you?" by saying "It's terrible." Bashful or cautious suitors might not admit their attraction to a potential partner. Even when people are reluctant to speak candidly, the language they use can suggest their degree of interest and attraction toward a person, object, or idea. Morton Wiener and Albert Mehrabian outline a number of linguistic clues that reveal these attitudes.[10]

Demonstrative Pronoun Choice   Although several pronouns can correctly refer to a person, some are more positive than others. Consider the difference between saying, "These people want our help" and the equally accurate, "Those people want our help." Most people would probably conclude that the first speaker is more sympathetic than the second. In the same way, speakers sound more positive when they say, "Here's Tom" than if they say, "There's Tom." The difference in such cases is one of grammatical *distance*. People generally suggest attraction by indicating closeness and dislike by linguistically removing themselves from the object of their conversation.

Sequential Placement   Another way to signify attitude is to place positive items earlier in a sequence. For example, notice the difference between discussing "Jack and Jill" and referring to "Jill and Jack." Likewise, consider how people respond to questions about courses they are taking or friends they intend to invite to an upcoming party. In many cases the first person or subject mentioned is more important or better liked than subsequent ones. (Of course, sequential placement isn't always significant. You may put "toilet bowl cleaner" at the top of your shopping list simply because it's closer to the door than champagne.)

The most powerful stimulus for changing minds is not a chemical. Or a baseball bat. It is a word.

George A. Miller,
Past President,
American Psychological Association

Wiener and Mehrabian point out an interesting example of the sequencing principle that often occurs in psychotherapy, where the patient mentions a certain subject first, not because it is most important but because it's the easiest one to discuss. Even here the same principle applies: Positive subjects often precede negative ones.

Negation   People usually express liking in a direct, positive manner whereas they use more indirect, negative language with less favorable subjects. Imagine, for instance, that you ask a friend's opinion about a book, movie, or restaurant. Consider the difference between the responses, "It was good" and "It wasn't bad." In the same way, the positive "I'd like to get together with you" may be a stronger indication of liking than the more negative "Why don't we get together?"

Duration   The length of time people spend discussing a person or subject can also be a strong indicator of attraction either to the subject or to the person with whom they're talking. If you ask a new acquaintance about work and receive the brief response "I'm a brain surgeon" with nothing more, you would probably suspect either that the subject was a sensitive one or that this person wasn't interested in you. Of course, there may be other reasons for short answers, such as preoccupation, but one good yardstick for measuring liking is the time others spend communicating with us.

Intimacy   Beyond simple interest and liking, language can also reflect the degree of intimacy between two partners. The most obvious indications are terms of affection or endearment. In romantic relationships, labels such as *honey* or *babe* suggest a new degree of intimacy. Even nonromantic friends often begin to use special labels for one another as their relationship becomes stronger: "Okay, buddy"; "See you later, amigo." Friends, lovers, and family members also create "personal idioms" that are unique to their relationship. The pet names children often use for their grandparents are a clear example. J. Berrisford Worthington may be the terror of the board room, but to his loving grandchildren

Drawing by Lorenz. © 1985 The New Yorker Magazine, Inc.

he's "Baba." At a party you might introduce an old friend as "Barbara," but to your circle of friends she's "Babs."

Responsibility   Besides indicating liking or interest, language can also reflect a speaker's unconscious willingness to take responsibility for statements, as the following categories show.

The "It" Statement   Notice the difference between the sentences of each set:

> "It bothers me when you're late."
> "I'm worried when you're late."
>
> "It's nice to see you."
> "I'm glad to see you."
>
> "It's a boring class."
> "I'm bored in the class."

"It" statements externalize the subject of the conversation. The subject is neither the person talking nor the one listening but some "it" that is never really identified. Whenever people hear the word *it* used this way, they should ask themselves what *it* refers to. They inevitably find that the speaker uses *it* to avoid clearly identifying to whom the thought or feeling belongs.

The "We" Statement   The word *we* can sometimes bring people together by pointing out their common beliefs. But in other cases the word becomes a device for diffusing the speaker's responsibility, a device that refers to a nebulous collection of people that doesn't really exist. Like *it* and *you, we* often really means *I.* "We all believe . . ." means "I believe . . ." and "We ought to . . ." means "I want to. . . ." (You might notice that this text uses a lot of *we's.* Do you find your beliefs included enough to think the word is justified?)

The "You" Statement   The word *you* also allows the speaker to disown comments that might be difficult to express:

> "You get frightened" instead of
> "I get frightened . . ."
>
> "You wonder . . ." instead of
> "I wonder . . ."
>
> "You start to think . . ." instead of
> "I'm starting to think . . ."

Questions   In the manner of "you" statements, questions often pass responsibility to the other person. They can also be used as a form of flattery ("Where did you get that lovely tie?") or as a replacement of "I" statements (the most common). Some therapists argue that there are very few *real* questions; most questions hide some statement that the person does not want to make, possibly out of fear.

"What are we having for dinner?" may hide the statement "I want to eat out" or "I want to get a pizza."

"How many textbooks are assigned in that class?" may hide the statement "I'm afraid to get into a class with too much reading."

"My hand is doing this movement . . ."

"Is it doing the movement?"

"I am moving my hand like this . . . and now the thought comes to me that . . ."

"The thought 'comes' to you?"

"I have the thought."

"You have it?"

"I think. Yes. I think that I use 'it' very much, and I am glad that by noticing it I can bring it all back to me."

"Bring it back?"

"Bring myself back. I feel thankful for this."

"This?"

"Your idea about the 'it.' "

"My idea?"

"I feel thankful towards you."

Claudio Naranjo

"Are you doing anything tonight?" can be a less risky way of saying, "I want to go out with you tonight."

"Do you love me?" safely replaces the statement "I love you," which may be too embarrassing, too intimate, or too threatening for the person to state directly.

The "But" Statement   Statements that take the form *X* but *Y* can be quite confusing. A closer look at this construction explains why. *But* has the effect of canceling the thought that precedes it:

> "You're a really swell person, but I think we ought to stop seeing each other."
> "You've done good work for us, but we're going to have to let you go."
> "This paper has some good ideas, but I'm giving it a grade of D because it's late."

These *buts* often mask the speaker's real meaning behind more pleasant-sounding ideas. A more accurate and less confusing way of expressing complex ideas is to replace *but* with *and.* In this way you can express a mixture of attitudes without eliminating any of them.

More Readings on Language

Benderly, Beryl Lieff. "Thinking/The Multilingual Mind." *Psychology Today* 15 (March 1981): 9–12.
> *Recent neurolinguistic research indicates that bilingual speakers process information in ways different from those who understand only one language. Preliminary findings seem to support the Whorf-Sapir hypothesis: Electroencephalograms of Hopi-speaking children indicate more right-brain activity whereas English speakers rely more heavily on left-hemisphere processing. Although research in this area is still scanty, the implications for semanticists are exciting.*

Carroll, John B., ed. *Language, Thought, and Reality: Selected Writings of Benjamin Lee Whorf.* Cambridge, Mass.: M.I.T. Press, 1966.
> *Writings of the most widely recognized authority about how language shapes our world view.*

Chase, Stuart. *The Tyranny of Words.* New York: Harvest Books, 1938.
> *A very readable account of the many ways in which semantic problems cause fuzzy thinking and get us into trouble.*

Condon, John C. *Semantics and Communication,* 3d ed. New York: Macmillan, 1984.
> *The clearest introduction to the field of semantics we've found.*

Harré, R., ed. *Life Sentences: Aspects of the Social Role of Language.* New York: Wiley, 1976.
> *Another collection of readings, mostly written by sociologists and social psychologists. The material here is challenging but interesting for the serious reader. Topics include rituals for incorporating strangers into a group, how physicians and psychiatrists identify deviance by speech, and thoughts on how Julius Caesar and Jesus Christ dealt with crowds.*

Hayakawa, S.I. *Language in Thought and Action.* New York: Harcourt Brace Jovanovich, 1964.

A clear, detailed treatment of many topics introduced in this chapter.
————. *The Use and Misuse of Language.* New York: Fawcett Books, 1962.
A collection of essays from ETC.: A Review of General Semantics, *which illustrate how topics introduced in this chapter apply to everyday situations.*
Kramarae, Cheris. *Women and Men Speaking.* Rowley, Mass.: Newbury House, 1981.
A detailed look at the similarities and differences between male and female speech. The conclusions are based more on the personal experiences of individual women than on observations of large-scale research studies. Although parts of the book are difficult to follow, Women and Men Speaking *does highlight the influence of gender in person-to-person communicaton.*
Kramarae, Cheris, Muriel Schulz, and William M. O'Barr, eds. *Language and Power.* Beverly Hills, Calif.: Sage, 1984.
This collection of articles examines the nature of linguistic power in a variety of contexts—medicine, courtrooms, family settings—and in various ethnic groups.
Mager, Robert. *Goal Analysis.* Belmont, Calif.: Fearon, 1972.
An entertaining, valuable guide for defining vague, abstract aims (called "Fuzzies") into specific behavioral targets. The book was written primarily for teachers to use in improving their instruction, but you should have no problem applying the ideas here to your own communication goals.
Marcus, Mary G. "The Power of a Name." *Psychology Today* 10 (October, 1976): 75–77, 108.
This interesting article illustrates how the principle of language-shaping perception applies to the names parents give their children. Do you want your son or daughter to be regarded as intelligent, clumsy, well adjusted, or neurotic? The name you choose may make a difference.
Miller, Casey, and Kate Swift. *Words and Women.* Garden City, N.Y.: Anchor Press, 1976.
Miller and Swift provide the evidence that points out how our everyday language communicates much about male and female role biases.
Pearson, Judy C. *Gender and Communication.* Dubuque, Iowa: W. C. Brown, 1985.
Chapter 6, "Language Usage of Women and Men," compares stereotyped perceptions of male-female language differences with the actual differences as revealed by social scientists. Pearson also offers explanations about why these differences exist, and she suggests some corrective actions.
Rothwell, J. Dan. *Telling It Like It Isn't: Language Misuse and Malpractice/What We Can Do About It.* Englewood Cliffs, N.J.: Prentice-Hall, 1982.
An interesting, readable catalog of the semantic abuses that interfere with satisfying personal relationships. Rothwell cites diverse sources such as The Anatomy of Swearing, *Sartre's* Being and Nothingness, *and advertisements for Perrier mineral water to illustrate the many ways language affects perception.*
Sagarian, Edward. "The High Cost of Wearing a Label." *Psychology Today* 10 (March, 1976): 25–27.
This article shows some of the dangers of the word is, *as described in this chapter. As Sagarian suggests, believing oneself to be a deviant can lead to an unnecessary self-fulfilling prophecy.*

Nonverbal Communication Means:

smiling, frowning
laughing, crying, sighing
standing close to others
being stand-offish
the way you look:
your hair, your clothing
your face, your body

your handshake (sweaty palms?)
your postures
your gestures
your mannerisms

your voice:
soft-loud
fast-slow
smooth-jerky

the environment you create:
your home, your room
your office, your desk
your kitchen
your car

One night—it was on the twentieth of March, 1888—I was returning from a journey to a patient (for I had now returned to civil practice), when my way led me through Baker Street. As I passed the well-remembered door, which must always be associated in my mind with my wooing, and with the dark incidents of the *Study in Scarlet,* I was seized with a keen desire to see Holmes again, and to know how he was employing his extraordinary powers. His rooms were brilliantly lit, and, even as I looked up, I saw his tall, spare figure pass twice in a dark silhouette against the blind. He was pacing the room swiftly, eagerly, with his head sunk upon his chest and his hands clasped behind him. To me, who knew his every mood and habit, his attitude and manner told their own story. He was at work again. He had risen out of his drug-created dreams and was hot upon the scent of some new problem. I rang the bell and was shown up to the chamber which had formerly been in part my own.

His manner was not effusive. It seldom was; but he was glad, I think, to see me. With hardly a word spoken, but with kindly eye, he waved me to an armchair, threw across his case of cigars, and indicated a spirit case and a gasogene in the corner. Then he stood before the fire and looked me over in his singular introspective fashion.

"Wedlock suits you," he remarked. "I think, Watson, that you have put on seven and a half pounds since I saw you."

"Seven!" I answered.

"Indeed, I should have thought a little more. Just a trifle more, I fancy, Watson. And in practice again, I observe. You did not tell me that you intended to go into harness."

"Then, how do you know?"

"I see it, I deduce it. How do I know that you have been getting yourself very wet lately, and that you have a most clumsy and careless servant girl?"

"My dear Holmes," said I, "this is too much. You would certainly have been burned, had you lived a few centuries ago. It is true that I had a country walk on Thursday and came home in a dreadful mess, but as I have changed my clothes I can't imagine how you deduce it. As to Mary Jane, she is incorrigible, and my wife has given her notice; but there, again, I fail to see how you work it out."

He chuckled to himself and rubbed his long, nervous hands together.

"It is simplicity itself," said he; "my eyes tell me that on the inside of your left shoe, just where the firelight strikes it, the leather is scored by six almost parallel cuts. Obviously they have been caused by someone who has very carelessly scraped round the edges of the sole in order to remove crusted mud from it. Hence, you see, my double deduction that you had been out in vile weather, and that you had a particularly malignant boot-slitting specimen of the London slavey. As to your practice, if a gentleman walks into my rooms smelling of iodoform, with a black mark of nitrate of silver upon his right forefinger, and a bulge on the right side of his top hat to show where he has secreted his stethoscope, I must be dull, indeed, if I do not pronounce him to be an active member of the medical profession."

I could not help laughing at the ease with which he explained his process of deduction. "When I hear you give your reasons," I remarked, "the thing always appears to me to be so ridiculously simple that I could easily do it myself, though at each successive instance of your reasoning I am baffled until you explain your process. And yet I believe that my eyes are as good as yours."

"Quite so," he answered, lighting a cigarette, and throwing himself down into an armchair. "You see, but you do not observe."

Sir Arthur Conan Doyle,
A Scandal in Bohemia

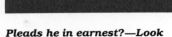

*Pleads he in earnest?—Look
   upon his face,
His eyes do drop no tears; his
   prayers are jest;
His words come from his
   mouth; ours, from our breast;
He prays but faintly, and would
   be denied;
We pray with heart and soul.*

William Shakespeare,
Richard II

Sometimes it's difficult to know how other people really feel. Often they don't know for sure themselves, and other times they have some reason for not wanting to tell you. In either case there are times when you can't find out what is going on inside another's mind simply by asking.

What should you do in these cases? They happen every day and often in the most important situations. Sherlock Holmes said the way to understand people was to watch them—not only to see, but to observe.

Observing yourself and others is what this chapter is about. In the following pages you'll become acquainted with the field of nonverbal communication—the way we express ourselves, not by what we say but by what we *do*. Psychologist Albert Mehrabian claims that 93 percent of the emotional impact of a message comes from nonverbal sources whereas only 7 percent is verbal.[1] Anthropologist Ray Birdwhistell describes a 65–35 percent split between actions and words, again in favor of nonverbal messages.[2] Whether or not we choose to argue with these precise figures, the point still remains: Nonverbal communication contributes a great deal to conveying meanings. It stands to reason, then, that one skill we need to develop is the ability to understand and respond to nonverbal messages.

Nonverbal Communication Defined

We need to begin our study of nonverbal communication by defining that term. At first this might seem like a simple task: If *non* means "not" and *verbal* means "words," *nonverbal communication* means "communicating without words." In fact, this literal definition isn't completely accurate. For instance, most communication scholars don't define American Sign Language (used by many people with hearing impairments) as nonverbal even though the messages are unspoken. On the other hand, you'll soon read that certain aspects of the voice aren't really verbal. (Can you think of any?)

This isn't the place to explore the rather complex debate about exactly what is and what isn't nonverbal. Interesting as that subject may be, we can move along in this introduction by defining **nonverbal communication** as "those messages expressed by other than linguistic means." This rules out not only sign languages but written words as well, but it includes messages transmitted by vocal means that don't involve language—the sighs, laughs, and other assorted noises we alluded to a moment ago. In addition, our definition allows us to explore the nonlinguistic dimensions of the spoken word—volume, rate, pitch, and so on.

Our brief definition only hints at the richness of nonverbal messages. You can begin to understand their prevalence by trying a simple experiment.

Verbal and Nonverbal Communication

Here's an experiment you can try either at home or in class. It will help you begin learning how nonverbal communication works.

1. Pick a partner, and find a place where you have some space to yourselves.
2. Now sit back-to-back with your partner, making sure that no parts of your bodies are touching. You should be seated so that you can talk easily without seeing each other.

3. Once you're seated, take two minutes to carry on a conversation about whatever subject you like. The only requirement is that you not look at or touch each other. Communicate by using words only.

4. Next, turn around so that you're facing your partner, seated at a comfortable distance. Now that you can both see and hear each other, carry on your conversation for another two minutes.

5. Continue to face each other, but for the next two minutes don't speak. Instead, join hands with your partner and communicate whatever messages you want to through sight and touch. Try to be aware of how you feel as you go through this step. There isn't any right or wrong way to behave here—there's nothing wrong with feeling embarrassed, silly, or any other way. The only requirement is <u>to remain silent</u>.

After you've finished the experiment, take some time to talk it over with your partner. Start by sharing how you felt in each part of the experience. Were you comfortable, nervous, playful, affectionate? Did your feelings change from one step to another? Could your partner tell these feelings without your expressing them? If so, how? Did your partner communicate his or her feelings too?

Characteristics of Nonverbal Communication

If this experiment seemed strange to you, we hope you still went through with it because it points out several things about nonverbal communication.

Nonverbal Communication Exists   Even when you were in the nontalking stage, you probably could pick up some of your partner's feelings by touching hands and noting posture and expressions—maybe more than you could during your conversation. We hope that this exercise showed you that there are other languages besides words that carry messages about your relationships.

The point isn't so much *how* you or your partner behaved during the exercises—whether you were tense or relaxed, friendly or distant. We wanted to show you that even without any formal experience you can recognize and to some degree interpret messages that other people send nonverbally. In this chapter we want to sharpen the skills you already have, to give you a better grasp of the vocabulary of nonverbal language and to show you how this knowledge can help you understand yourself and others better.

You Can't Not Communicate   The fact that communication without words took place between you and your partner brings us to this second important feature of nonverbal communication. To understand what we mean here, think about the exercise you just finished. Suppose we'd asked you not to communicate any messages at all while with your partner. What would you have done? Closed your eyes? Withdrawn into a ball? Left the room? You can probably see that even these behaviors communicate messages—that you're avoiding contact.

Take a minute now to try <u>not</u> communicating. Join with a partner, and spend some time trying not to reveal any messages to one another. What happens?

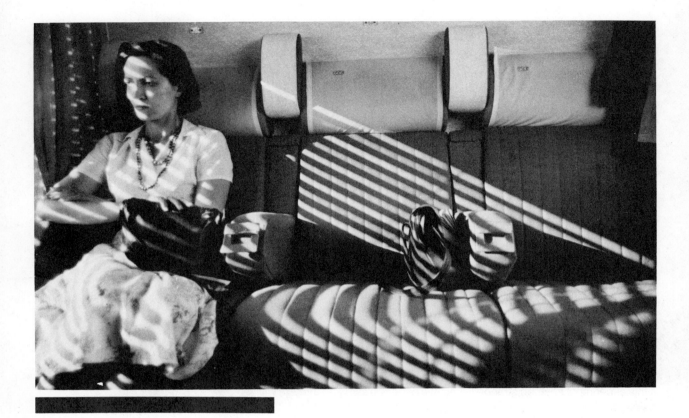

This impossibility of not communicating is extremely important to understand because it means that each of us is a kind of transmitter that cannot be shut off. No matter what we do, we give off information about ourselves.

Stop for a moment, and examine yourself as you read this. If someone were observing you now, what nonverbal clues would they get about how you're feeling? Are you sitting forward or reclining back? Is your posture tense or relaxed? Are your eyes wide open, or do they keep closing? What does your facial expression communicate? Can you make your face expressionless? Don't people with expressionless faces communicate something to you?

Of course, we don't always intend to send nonverbal messages. Consider, for instance, behaviors like blushing, frowning, sweating, or stammering. We rarely try to act in these ways, and often we're not aware of doing so. Nonetheless, others recognize signs like these and make interpretations about us based on their observations.

The fact that you and everyone around you is constantly sending nonverbal clues *is* important because it means that you have a constant source of information available about yourself and others. If you can tune into these signals, you'll be more aware of how those around you are feeling and thinking, and you'll be better able to respond to their behavior.

Nonverbal Communication Is Culture-bound   The significance of many nonverbal behaviors varies from one culture to another. The "A-okay" gesture made by joining thumb and forefinger to form a circle is a cheery affirmation to most Americans, but it has less positive meanings in other parts of the world.[3] In France and Belgium it means "You're worth zero." In Greece and Turkey it is a vulgar sexual invitation, usually meant as an insult. Given this sort of cross-cultural ambiguity, it's easy to imagine how an innocent tourist might wind up in serious trouble.

Less obvious cross-cultural differences can damage relationships without the parties ever recognizing exactly what has gone wrong. Edward Hall points out that whereas Americans are comfortable conducting business at a distance of roughly four feet, people from the Middle East stand much closer.[4] It is easy to visualize the awkward advance and retreat pattern that might occur when two diplomats or businesspeople from these cultures meet. The Middle Easterner would probably keep moving forward to close the gap that feels so wide, whereas the American would continually back away. Both would feel uncomfortable, probably without knowing why.

Like distance, patterns of eye contact vary around the world.[5] A direct gaze is considered appropriate for speakers in Latin America, the Arab world, and southern Europe. On the other hand, Asians, Indians, Pakistanis, and northern Europeans gaze at a listener peripherally or not at all. In either case, deviations from the norm are likely to make a listener uncomfortable.

Even within a culture, various groups can have different nonverbal rules. For example, research in the 1970s revealed that many blacks avoid looking others directly in the eyes.[6] The findings also showed that whites in the study interpreted this lack of eye contact as a signal of disinterest and withdrawal. Another difference involved taking turns in conversations: White listeners (following their

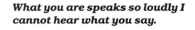

What you are speaks so loudly I cannot hear what you say.

Ralph Waldo Emerson

own cultural rules) began to speak when black speakers paused with a sustained gaze, whereas the blacks had not actually finished their statements. As long as cultural differences exist, this sort of awkwardness can be decreased when communicators are aware of the different nonverbal rules they bring to a conversation.

Nonverbal Communication Transmits Feelings and Attitudes

As you study this subject, you'll find that even though feelings are communicated quite well nonverbally, thoughts don't lend themselves to nonverbal channels.

Recall the exercise at the beginning of the chapter. Do you remember the different kinds of messages that you sent and received in the talking and non-talking parts of it? Most people find that in the first parts (where they communicate verbally) they talk about what they *think:* "Does the exercise seem like a good or bad one?" "What have you been doing lately?" "Did you do your reading?" and so on. Quite different kinds of messages usually come across in the last step, however. Without being able to use words, peoples' bodies generally express how they *feel*—nervous, embarrassed, playful, friendly, and the like.

You can test this finding in another way. Here's a list that contains both thoughts and feelings. Try to express each item nonverbally, and see which ones come most easily:

You're tired.
You're in favor of capital punishment.
You're attracted to another person in the group.
You think marijuana should be legalized.
You're angry at someone in the group.

From this experiment you can see that nonverbal channels do indeed express feelings and attitudes. Sometimes these sorts of messages focus on the *subject* under discussion ("I think this is a great class!"), and sometimes they reflect the sender's feelings about the *relationship* with the receiver ("I'm bored talking to you").

Nonverbal Communication Serves Many Functions

Just because this chapter deals with nonverbal communication, don't get the idea that our words and our actions are unrelated. Quite the opposite is true: Verbal and nonverbal communication are interconnected elements in every act of communication. Nonverbal behaviors can operate in several relationships with verbal messages.[7]

1. **Repeating** If someone asked you for directions to the nearest drugstore, you could say, "North of here about two blocks" and then repeat your instructions nonverbally by pointing north. Pointing is an example of what social scientists call **emblems**—deliberate nonverbal behaviors that have a very precise meaning, known to virtually everyone within a cultural group. For example, we all know that a head nod means "yes," a head shake means "no," a wave means "hello" or "goodbye," and a hand to the ear means "I can't hear you."

©1963 United Media, Inc.

2. **Substituting** Emblems also can replace a verbal message. When a friend asks, "What's up?" you might shrug your shoulders instead of answering in words. Not all substituting consists of emblems, however. Sometimes substituting responses are more ambiguous and less intentional. A sigh, smile, or frown may substitute for a verbal answer to your question "How's it going?" As this example suggests, nonverbal substituting is especially important when people are reluctant to express their feelings in words.

3. **Complementing** If you saw a student talking to a teacher, and his head was bowed slightly, his voice was low and hesitating, and he shuffled slowly from foot to foot, you might conclude that he felt inferior to the teacher, possibly embarrassed about something he did. The nonverbal behaviors you observed provided the context for the verbal behaviors—they conveyed the relationship between the teacher and student. Complementing nonverbal behaviors signal the attitudes the interactants have for one another.

   Much complementing behavior consists of **illustrators**—nonverbal behaviors that accompany and support spoken words. Scratching your head when searching for an idea and snapping your fingers when it occurs are examples of illustrators that complement verbal messages. Research shows that North Americans use illustrators more often when they are emotionally aroused—trying to explain ideas that are difficult to put into words when they are furious, horrified, very agitated, distressed, or excited.[8]

4. **Accenting** Just as we use italics to highlight an idea in print, we use nonverbal devices to emphasize oral messages. Pointing an accusing finger adds emphasis to criticism (as well as probably creating defensiveness in the receiver). Stressing certain words with the voice ("It was *your* idea!") is another way to add nonverbal accents.

5. **Regulating** Nonverbal behaviors can control the flow of verbal communication. For example, parties in a conversation often unconsciously send and receive turn-taking cues.[9] When you are ready to yield the floor the unstated rule is this: Create a rising vocal intonation pattern, then use a falling intonation pattern or draw out the final syllable of the clause at the end of your statement. Finally, stop speaking. If you want to maintain your turn when another speaker seems ready to cut you off, you can suppress the attempt by taking an audible breath, using a sustained intonation pattern (since rising and falling patterns suggest the end of a statement), and avoid any pauses in your speech. There are other nonverbal clues for gaining the floor and for signaling that you do not want to speak.

6. **Contradicting** People often simultaneously express different and even contradictory messages in their verbal and nonverbal behaviors. A common example of this sort of "double message" is the experience we've all had of hearing someone with a red face and bulging veins yelling, "Angry? No, *I'm not angry!*"

Usually, however, the contradiction between words and nonverbal clues isn't this obvious. At times we all try to seem different from what we are. There are many reasons for this contradictory behavior: to cover nervousness when giving a speech or in a job interview, to keep someone from worrying about us, or to appear more attractive than we believe we really are.

Even though some of the ways in which people contradict themselves are subtle, **double messages** have a strong impact. Research suggests that when a receiver perceives an inconsistency between verbal and nonverbal messages, the unspoken one carries more weight.[10]

As we discuss the different kinds of nonverbal communication throughout this chapter, we'll point out a number of ways in which people contradict themselves by either conscious or unconscious behaviors. Thus, by the end of this chapter you should have a better idea of how others feel, even when they can't or won't tell you with their words. Although double messages are an important type of nonverbal communication, don't get the idea that their absence means a sender is being totally candid. Table 6–1 summarizes research on when nonverbal cues to deception are most and least likely.

Table 6–1 Leakage of Nonverbal Cues to Deception

Deception Cues Are Most Likely When the Deceiver	*Deception Cues Are Least Likely When the Deceiver*
Wants to hide emotions being felt at the moment.	Wants to hide information unrelated to his or her emotions.
Feels strongly about the information being hidden.	Has no strong feelings about the information being hidden.
Feels apprehensive about the deception.	Feels confident about the deception.
Feels guilty about being deceptive.	Experiences little guilt about the deception.
Gets little enjoyment from being deceptive.	Enjoys the deception.
Needs to construct the message carefully while delivering it.	Knows the deceptive message well and has rehearsed it.

Based on material from "Mistakes When Deceiving" by Paul Ekman, in *The Clever Hans Phenomenon: Communication with Horses, Whales, Apes, and People,* ed. Thomas A. Sebeok and Robert Rosenthal (New York: New York Academy of Sciences, 1981), pp. 269–78.

she dresses in flags
comes on
like a mack truck
she paints
her eyelids green
and her mouth
is a loud speaker
rasping out
profanity

at cocktail parties
she is everywhere
like a sheep dog
working a flock
nipping at your sleeve
spilling your drink
bestowing
wet sloppy kisses

but i
have received
secret messages
carefully written
from the shy
quiet woman
who hides
in this
bizarre
gaudy castle

Ric Masten

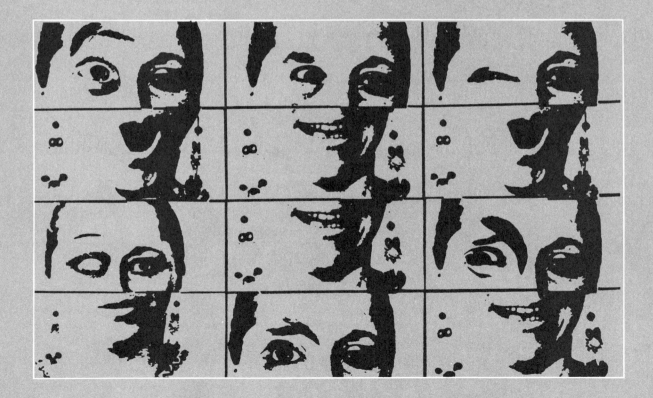

*I suppose it was something
you said
That caused me to tighten and
pull away.
And when you asked,
"What is it?"
I, of course, said,
"Nothing."*

*Whenever I say, "Nothing,"
You may be very certain there
is something.
The something is a cold, hard
lump of
Nothing.*

Lois Wyse

Nonverbal Communication Is Ambiguous   Before you get the idea that merely reading this chapter will turn you into some sort of mind reader, we want to caution you and in so doing introduce a fifth feature of nonverbal communication: A great deal of ambiguity surrounds nonverbal behavior. To understand what we mean, how would you interpret silence from your spouse, date, or companion after an evening in which you both laughed and joked a lot? Can you think of at least two possible meanings for this behavior? Or suppose that a much admired person with whom you've worked suddenly begins paying more attention to you than ever before. What could the possible meanings of this behavior be?

The point is that although nonverbal behavior can be very revealing, it can have so many possible meanings that it's foolish to think your interpretation will always be correct.

Some people are more skillful than others at accurately decoding nonverbal behavior.[11] Those who are better senders of nonverbal messages are also better receivers. Decoding ability also increases with age and training, though there are still differences in ability because of personality and occupation. For instance, extroverts are relatively accurate judges of nonverbal behavior, whereas dogmatists are not. Interestingly, women seem to be better than men at decoding nonverbal messages. Over 95 percent of the studies examined in one analysis showed that women are more accurate at interpreting nonverbal signals.[12] Despite these differences, even the best nonverbal decoders do not approach 100 percent accuracy.

When you do try to make sense out of ambiguous nonverbal behavior, you need to consider several factors: The *context* in which they occur (for example, smiling at a joke suggests a different feeling from smiling at another's misfortune); the *history of your relationship* with the sender (friendly, hostile, and so on); the *other's mood* at the time; and *your feelings* (when you're feeling insecure, almost anything can seem like a threat).

Reading "Body Language"

In your journey through the supermarket checkout stand or while waiting for a plane, you've probably noticed books that promise to teach you how to read "body language." These books claim that you can become a kind of mind reader, learning the deepest secrets of everyone around you. But it's not quite as simple as it sounds. Here's an exercise that will both increase your skill in observing nonverbal behavior and show you the dangers of being too sure that you're a perfect reader of body language. You can try the exercise either in or out of class, and the period of time over which you do it is flexible, from a single class period to several days. In any case, begin by choosing a partner, and then follow these directions:

1. For the first period of time (however long you decide to make it), observe the way your partner behaves. Notice how she moves, her mannerisms, postures, the way she speaks, how she dresses, and so on. To remember your observations, jot them down. If you're doing this exercise out of class over an extended period of time, there's no need to let your observations interfere with whatever you'd normally be doing: Your only job here is to compile a list of

your partner's behaviors. In this step you should be careful not to interpret your partner's actions; just record what you see.

2. At the end of the time period share what you've seen with your partner, who should do the same with you.

3. For the next period of time your job is not only to observe your partner's behavior but also to interpret it. This time in your conference you should tell your partner what you thought her actions said about her. For example, if she dressed carelessly, did you think this meant that she overslept, that she's losing interest in her appearance, or that she was trying to be more comfortable? If you noticed her yawning frequently, did you think this meant she was bored, tired from a late night, or sleepy after a big meal? Don't feel bad if your guesses weren't all correct. Remember, nonverbal clues tend to be ambiguous. You may be surprised how checking out the nonverbal clues you observe can help build a relationship with another person.

This exercise should have shown you the difference between merely observing somebody's behavior and actually interpreting it. Noticing someone's shaky hands or smile is one thing, but deciding what such behaviors mean is quite another. If you're like most people, you probably found that a lot of your guesses were incorrect. Now, if that was true here, it may also be true in your daily life. Being a sharp nonverbal observer can give you some good hunches about how people are feeling, but the only way you can find out if these hunches are correct is to *check them out* verbally, using the skill of perception checking you learned in Chapter Three.

Types of Nonverbal Communication

Keeping the five characteristics of nonverbal communication in mind, let's take a look at some of the ways we communicate in addition to words.

The first area of nonverbal communication we'll discuss is the broad field of **kinesics,** or body motion. In this section we'll explore the role that posture, gestures, body orientation, facial expressions, and eye behaviors play in our relationships with each other.

Body Orientation   We'll start with body orientation—the degree to which we face toward or away from someone with our body, feet, and head. To understand how this kind of physical positioning communicates nonverbal messages, you might try an experiment.

You'll need two friends to help you. Imagine that two of you are in the middle of a personal conversation when a third person approaches and wants to join you. You're not especially glad to see this person, but you don't want to sound rude by asking him to leave. Your task is to signal to the intruder that you'd rather be alone, using only the position of your bodies. You can talk to the third person if you wish, but you can't verbally tell him that you want privacy.

When you've tried this experiment or if you've ever been in a real situation similar to it, you know that by turning your body slightly away from an intruder

Fie, fie upon her!
There's language in her eyes,
her cheek, her lip.
Nay, her foot speaks; her wan-
ton spirits look out at every
joint and motive in her body.

William Shakespeare,
Troilus and Cressida

you can make your feelings very clear. An intruder finds himself in the difficult position of trying to talk over your shoulder, and it isn't long before he gets the message and goes away. The nonverbal message here is "Look, we're interested in each other right now and don't want to include you in our conversation." The general rule this situation describes is that facing someone directly signals your interest, and facing away signals a desire to avoid involvement. This explains how we can pack ourselves into intimate distance with total strangers in places like a crowded elevator without offending others. Because there's a very indirect orientation here (everyone is usually standing shoulder to shoulder, facing in the same direction), we understand that despite the close quarters everyone wants to avoid personal contact.

By observing the way people position themselves you can learn a good deal about how they feel. Next time you're in a crowded place where people can choose whom to face directly, try observing who seems to be included in the action and who is being subtly shut out. And in the same way, pay attention to your own body orientation. You may be surprised to discover that you're avoiding a certain person without being conscious of it or that at times you're "turning your back" on people altogether. If this is the case, it may be helpful to figure out why. Are you avoiding an unpleasant situation that needs clearing up, communicating your annoyance or dislike for the other, or sending some other message?

Posture   Another way we communicate nonverbally is through our posture.

To see if this is true, stop reading for a moment, and notice how you're sitting. What does your position say nonverbally about how you feel? Are there any other people near you now? What messages do you get from their present posture? By paying attention to the postures of those around you, as well as your own, you'll find another channel of nonverbal communication that can furnish information about how people feel about themselves and each other.

An indication of how much posture communicates is shown by our language. It's full of expressions that link emotional states with body postures:

I won't take this lying down!
He can stand on his own two feet.
She has to carry a heavy burden.
Take a load off your back.
He's all wrapped up in himself.
Don't be so nervous

Such phrases show that an awareness of posture exists for us even if it's often unconscious. The main reason we miss most posture messages is that they aren't very obvious. It's seldom that a person who feels weighted down by a problem hunches over so much that he stands out in a crowd, and when we're bored, we usually don't lean back and slump enough to embarrass the other person. In the reading of posture, then, the key is to look for small changes that might be shadows of the way people feel.

For example, a teacher who has a reputation for interesting classes told us how he uses his understanding of postures to do a better job. "Because of my

The Look of a Victim

Little Red Riding Hood set herself up to be mugged. Her first mistake was skipping through the forest to grandma's house. Her second mistake was stopping to pick flowers. At this point, as you might remember in the story, the mean, heavy wolf comes along and begins to check her out. He observes, quite perceptively, that she is happy, outgoing, and basically unaware of any dangers in her surrounding environment. The big bad wolf catches these nonverbal cues and splits to grandma's house. He knows that Red is an easy mark. From this point we all know what happens.

Body movements and gestures reveal a lot of information about a person. Like Little Red Riding Hood, pedestrians may signal to criminals that they are easy targets for mugging by the way they walk. When was the last time you assessed your "muggability rating"? In a recent study two psychologists set out to identify those body movements that characterized easy victims. They assembled "muggability ratings" of sixty New York pedestrians from the people who may have been the most qualified to judge—prison inmates who had been convicted of assault.

The researchers unobtrusively videotaped pedestrians on weekdays between 10:00 A.M. and 12 P.M. Each pedestrian was taped for six to eight seconds, the approximate time it takes for a mugger to size up an approaching person. The judges (prison inmates) rated the "assault potential" of the sixty pedestrians on a ten-point scale. A rating of one indicated someone was "a very easy rip-off," of two, "an easy dude to corner." Toward the other end of the scale, nine meant a person "would be heavy; would give you a hard time," and ten indicated that the mugger "would avoid it, too big a situation, too heavy." The results revealed several body movements that characterized easy victims: "Their strides were either very long or very short; they moved awkwardly, raising their left legs with their left arms (instead of alternating them); on each step they tended to lift their whole foot up and then place it down (less muggable sorts took steps in which their feet rocked from heel to toe). Overall, the people rated most muggable walked as if they were in conflict with themselves; they seemed to make each move in the most difficult way possible."

Loretta Malandro and Larry Barker

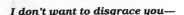

I don't want to disgrace you—

I've shined up my bones and smoothed my skin in quiet folds around me, arranged my limbs tastefully in elegant lines that none may see elbow or knee, I've instructed my jaw not to grin nor jape, my lips to stay firmly in place:

I shall not blink nor stare nor will a hair upon my head move, and I can hold my feet still, that not a toe will tumble:

I don't want to disgrace you—

but my hands have their own history and instinctively at your entrance

rise to your face

Gerald Huckaby

large classes I have to lecture a lot," he said. "And that's an easy way to turn students off. I work hard to make my talks entertaining, but you know that nobody's perfect, and I do have my off days. I can tell when I'm not doing a good job of communicating by picking out three or four students before I start my talk and watching how they sit throughout the class period. As long as they're leaning forward in their seats, I know I'm doing OK, but if I look up and see them starting to slump back, I know I'd better change my approach."

Psychologist Albert Mehrabian has found that other postural keys to feelings are tension and relaxation. He says that we take relaxed postures in non-threatening situations and tighten up when threatened.[13] Based on this observation he says we can tell a good deal about how others feel simply by watching how tense or loose they seem to be. For example, he suggests that watching tenseness is a way of detecting status differences: The lower-status person is generally the more rigid, tense-appearing one, whereas the one with higher status is more relaxed. This is the kind of situation that often happens when an employee sits ramrod straight while the boss leans back in her chair. The same principle applies to social situations, where it's often possible to tell who's uncomfortable by looking at pictures. Often you'll see someone laughing and talking as if he were perfectly at home, but his posture almost shouts nervousness. Some people never relax, and their posture shows it.

Sometimes posture communicates vulnerability in situations far more serious than mere social or business ones. One study revealed that rapists sometimes use postural clues to select victims they believe are easy to intimidate.[14] Easy targets are more likely to walk slowly and tentatively, stare at the ground, and move their arms and legs in short, jerky motions.

Try spending an hour or so observing the posture of those around you. See if you can get some idea of how they're feeling by the way they carry themselves. Also, pay attention to your own posture. In what situations do you tense up? Is this a sign of anger, aggressiveness, excitement, fear? Do you ever find yourself signaling boredom, interest, attraction, or other emotions by your posture? Do the feelings you find yourself expressing posturally ever surprise you?

Gestures   We have already discussed how emblems and illustrators convey messages. Sometimes gestures like these are intentional—a cheery wave or thumbs up, for example. In other cases, however, our gestures are unconscious. Occasionally an unconscious gesture will consist of an unambiguous emblem, such as a shrug that clearly means "I don't know." Another revealing set of gestures is what psychiatrist Albert Scheflen calls "preening behaviors"— stroking or combing one's hair, glancing in a mirror, and rearranging one's clothing. Scheflen suggests that these behaviors signal some sort of interest in the other party: perhaps an unconscious sexual come-on or perhaps a sign of less intimate interest.[15] More often, however, gestures are ambiguous. In addition to illustrators, another group of ambiguous gestures consists of what we usually call *fidgeting*—movements in which one part of the body grooms, massages, rubs, holds, fidgets, pinches, picks, or otherwise manipulates another part. Social scientists call these behaviors **manipulators**.[16] Social rules may discourage us from performing most manipulators in public, but people still do so without noticing.

Research reveals what common sense suggests—that increased use of manipulators is often a sign of discomfort.[17] But not *all* fidgeting signals uneasiness. People also are likely to use manipulators when relaxed. When they let their guard down (either alone or with friends), they will be more likely to fiddle with an earlobe, twirl a strand of hair, or clean their fingernails. Whether or not the fidgeter is hiding something, observers are likely to interpret manipulators as a signal of dishonesty. Since not all fidgeters are liars, it's important not to jump to conclusions about the meaning of manipulations.

Actually, *too few* gestures may be as significant an indicator of double messages as *too many*.[18] Lack of gesturing may signal a lack of interest, sadness, boredom, or low enthusiasm. Illustrators also decrease whenever someone is cautious about speaking. For these reasons, a careful observer will look for either an increase or a decrease in the usual level of gestures.

Face and Eyes   The face and eyes are probably the most noticed parts of the body, but this doesn't mean that their nonverbal messages are the easiest to read. The face is a tremendously complicated channel of expression for several reasons.

First, it's hard even to describe the number and kind of expressions we commonly produce with our face and eyes. For example, researchers have found that there are at least eight distinguishable positions of the eyebrows and forehead, eight more of the eyes and lids, and ten for the lower face.[19] When you multiply this complexity by the number of emotions we feel, you can see why it would be almost impossible to compile a dictionary of facial expressions and their corresponding emotions.

Another reason for the difficulty in understanding facial expressions is the speed with which they can change. For example, slow-motion films show

> *"Come on, Zorba," I cried, "teach me to dance!"*
> *Zorba leaped to his feet, his face sparkling . . .*
> *"Watch my feet, boss," he enjoined me. "Watch!"*
> *He put out his foot, touched the ground lightly with his toes, then pointed the other foot; the steps were mingled violently, joyously, the ground reverberated like a drum.*
> *He shook me by the shoulder.*
> *"Now then, my boy," he said. "Both together!"*
> *We threw ourselves into the dance. Zorba instructed me, corrected me gravely, patiently, and with great gentleness. I grew bold and felt my heart on the wing like a bird.*
> *"Bravo! You're a wonder!" cried Zorba, clapping his hands to mark the beat. "Bravo, youngster! To hell with paper and ink! To hell with goods and profits! To hell with mines and workmen and monasteries! And now that you, my boy, can dance as well and have learnt my language, what shan't we be able to tell each other!"*
> *He pounded on the pebbles with his bare feet and clapped his hands.*
> *"Boss," he said, "I've dozens of things to say to you. I've never loved anyone as much before. I've hundreds of things to say, but my tongue just can't manage them. So I'll dance them for you!"*
>
> Nikos Kazantzakis,
> *Zorba the Greek*

expressions fleeting across a subject's face in as short a time as it takes to blink an eye.[20] Also, it seems that different emotions show most clearly in different parts of the face: happiness and surprise in the eyes and lower face; anger in the lower face, brows, and forehead; fear and sadness in the eyes; and disgust in the lower face.

Ekman and Friesen have identified six basic emotions that facial expressions reflect—surprise, fear, anger, disgust, happiness, and sadness. Expressions reflecting these feelings seem to be recognizable in and between members of all cultures. Of course, affect blends—the combination of two or more expressions in different parts of the face—are possible. For instance, it's easy to imagine how someone would look who is fearful and surprised or disgusted and angry.

Research also indicates that people are quite accurate at judging facial expressions for these emotions. Accuracy increases when judges know the target or the context in which the expression occurs or when they have seen several samples of the target's expressions.

In spite of the complex way in which the face shows emotions, you can still pick up messages by watching it. One of the easiest ways is to look for expressions that seem to be overdone. Often when someone is trying to fool himself or another, he'll emphasize his mask to a point where it seems too exaggerated to be true. Another way to detect a person's feelings is by watching his expression at moments when he isn't likely to be thinking about his appearance. We've all had the experience of glancing into another car while stopped in a traffic jam or looking around at a sporting event and seeing expressions that the wearer would probably never show in more guarded moments. At other times it's possible to watch a **microexpression** as it flashes across a person's face. For just a moment we see a flash of emotion quite different from the one a speaker is trying to convey. Finally, you may be able to spot contradictory expressions on different parts of someone's face: Her eyes say one thing, but the expression of her mouth or eyebrows might be sending quite a different message.

The eyes themselves can send several kinds of messages. Meeting someone's glance with your eyes is usually a sign of involvement, whereas looking away often signals a desire to avoid contact. As we mentioned earlier, this is why solicitors on the street—panhandlers, salespeople, petitioners—try to catch our eye. Once they've managed to establish contact with a glance, it becomes harder for the approached person to draw away. A friend explained how to apply this principle to hitchhiking. "When I'm hitching a ride, I'm always careful to look each driver in the eye as he comes toward me. Most of them will try to look somewhere else as they pass, but if I can catch somebody's eye, he'll almost always stop." Most of us remember trying to avoid a question we didn't understand by glancing away from the teacher. At times like these we usually became very interested in our textbooks, fingernails, the clock—anything but the teacher's stare. Of course, the teacher always seemed to know the meaning of this nonverbal behavior and ended up calling on those of us who signaled our uncertainty.

Another kind of message the eyes communicate is a positive or negative attitude. When someone glances toward us with the proper facial expression, we get a clear message that the looker is interested in us—hence the expression "making eyes." At the same time, when our long glances toward someone else are avoided by him, we can be pretty sure that the other person isn't as interested in us as we are in him. (Of course, there are all sorts of courtship games in which the receiver of a glance pretends not to notice any message by glancing away yet signals interest with some other part of the body.)

The eyes communicate both dominance and submission. We've all played the game of trying to stare down somebody, and in real life there are also times when downcast eyes are a sign of giving in. In some religious orders, for example, subordinate members are expected to keep their eyes downcast when addressing a superior.

Even the pupils of our eyes communicate. E. H. Hess and J. M. Polt of the University of Chicago measured the amount of pupil dilation while showing men and women various types of pictures.[21] The results of the experiment were very interesting: A person's eyes grow larger in proportion to the degree of interest one has in an object. For example, men's pupils grew about 18 percent larger when looking at pictures of a naked woman, and the degree of dilation for women looking at a naked man's picture was 20 percent. Interestingly enough, the greatest increase in pupil size occurred when women looked at a picture of a mother and an infant. A good salesperson can increase profits by being aware of pupil dilation, as Edward Hall describes. He was once in a Middle Eastern bazaar, where an Arab merchant insisted that a customer looking at his jewelry buy a certain piece that the shopper hadn't been paying much attention to. But the vendor had been watching the pupils of the buyer's eyes and had known what the buyer really wanted.[22]

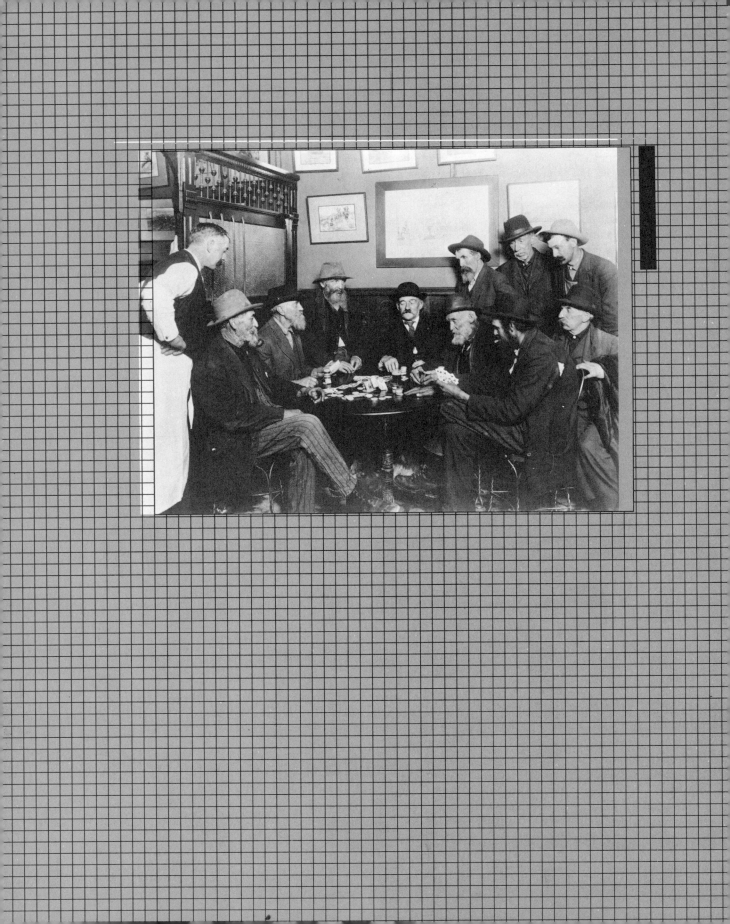

...the expert [poker player] is a psychologist.

He is continually studying the other players to see, first, if they have any telltale habits, and second, if there are any situations in which they act automatically.

In connection with general habits, I divide poker players into three classes

(a) the ingenuous player,

(b) the tricky, or coffee-housing player,

(c) the unreadable player.

The ingenuous player

When the ingenuous player looks worried, he probably is worried.

When he takes a long time to bet, he probably doesn't think much of his hand.

When he bets quickly, he fancies his hand.

When he bluffs, he looks a little guilty, and when he really has a good hand, you can see him mentally wishing to be called.

This ingenuousness, incidently, is seldom found in veteran players. A player of this type usually quits poker at an early stage on account of his "bad luck."

The tricky or coffee-housing player

At least ninety percent of all poker players fall into this category.

The tricky player has a great tendency to act just opposite of the way he really feels. Thus with a very good hand, he trembles a little as he bets, while with a poor hand, he fairly exudes confidence. O course, he may be triple-crossing, but year-in and year-out I have played in a great many games, and have found that at least two times out of three when another player makes a special effort to look confident, he has nothing, while when he tries to look nervous, he is loaded.

There is one mild little coffee-housing habit that practically never fails to act as a giveaway.

That is showing too much nonchalance. For instance, it is my turn to bet, and as I am about to put my chips in the pot, one of the other players casually lights a cigarette. Experience tells me that this casual player is at least going to call me, and is very likely to raise me if I bet.

Accordingly, if I do see that sign, unless my hand is really very good, I refuse to bet for him and simply check.

The unreadable player

This particular individual is, of course, the hardest opponent of all.

Invariably, he knows all the rules of correct play, but departs from all of them on occasion. Unlike the ingenuous player who acts the way he feels, or the coffee-house, who acts the way he doesn't feel, this player has no consistency.

Accordingly, the fact that he exudes confidence or looks nervous gives no clue to the nature of his hand.

The preceding discussion has been of a very general nature. Here are a few specific giveaway habits I have noticed.

(It should be borne in mind that poker has no ethics, except in a few obvious and specific instances and that short of actually cheating, which, by the way, includes attempting to peek at another player's hand, you have the right to any advantage you can gain.)

Glancing to the left

In the early stages of betting, a player with a normal calling hand usually comes into the pot with no fuss whatsoever. However, a player with a good hand is going to consider raising and before betting, is likely to cast a covert glance toward the players in back of him (on his left) to see if he can get any idea of what they are going to do.

If it looks to him as if two or three of them are going to call, he sandbags. If it looks as if they are all going to drop, he raises.

Accordingly, when I see this glance, even though the player merely calls, I am fairly sure that his hand is fully strong enough for a raise.

Looking at the hole card the second time

The very best stud players, of course, look at their hole card once, and then know it for the rest of the hand, but the average player, particularly with a low card in the hole, is likely to be careless and not remember it.

Accordingly, there are many instances where a second glance at the hole card gives a lot of information.

For instance:

The first bettor shows an ace. On the next card, he receives a six, and promptly looks at his hole card. At this point, there is a very strong presumption that his hole card is a six or very close to it.

Piling chips on your hole card

This is probably the most telltale giveaway habit of all.

Before the second card is dealt, a player looks at his hole card. If it is a low card, he pays no attention to it, but if it is a high card he is quite likely to put it down and pile some chips on top of it immediately, to prevent any possibility of it blowing over.

I know I must have seen chips piled on top of the hole card in that situation hundreds of times, and I do not recall more than two or three instances where the card was lower than a jack, and very few when it was not an ace or a king.

Looking at your draw

In Draw Poker, it is the exceptional player who will simply pick up the cards and look at them. The average player has various methods of mixing his draw with his hand, squeezing the cards, looking at them one at a time, etc.

While little can be learned about the nature of a player's hand from the manner in which he looks at his draw, there is one pretty general giveaway in connection with a one-card draw.

A player drawing to a flush or two pair is likely to put the card he draws in the middle of his hand. A player drawing to an open straight invariably puts the card either on top or bottom.

Oswald Jacoby,
Oswald Jacoby on Poker

He that has eyes to see and ears to hear may convince himself that no mortal can keep a secret. If his lips are silent, he chatters with his finger tips; betrayal oozes out of him at every pore.

Sigmund Freud

> **When a husband comes home from the office, takes off his hat, hangs up his coat, and says "Hi" to his wife, the way in which he says "Hi" reinforced by the manner in which he sheds his overcoat, summarizes his feelings about the way things went at the office. If his wife wants the details she may have to listen for a while, yet she grasps in an instant the significant message for her: namely, what kind of evening they are going to spend and how she is going to have to cope with it.**
>
> Edward Hall
> *The Silent Language*

Voice   The voice itself is another channel of nonverbal communication. We don't mean the words we say, which after all make up verbal communication, but rather *how* we say them. If you think about it for a moment, you'll realize that a certain way of speaking can give the same word or words many meanings. For example, look at the possible meanings from a single sentence just by changing the emphasis:

This is a fantastic communication book.
  (Not just any book, but *this* one in particular.)

This is a *fantastic* communication book.
  (This book is superior, exciting.)

This is a fantastic *communication* book.
  (The book is good as far as communication goes; it may not be so great as literature, drama, and the like.)

This is a fantastic communication *book.*
  (It's not a play or record; it's a book.)

It's possible to convey an idea without ever expressing it outright by emphasizing a certain word in a sentence. For example, a State Department official in the Nixon administration was able to express the government's position in an off-the-record way when answering questions. He had three different ways of saying, "I would not speculate." When he added no accent, he meant the department didn't really know; when he emphasized the *I,* he meant, "I wouldn't, but *you* may—and with some assurance"; when he emphasized *speculate,* he meant that the questioner's premise was probably wrong.[23]

There are many other ways a voice communicates—through its tone, speed, pitch, number and length of pauses, volume, **disfluencies**—nonlinguistic verbalizations, such as stammering, use of *uh, um, er,* and so on. All these factors together can be called **paralanguage,** and they can do a great deal to reinforce or contradict the message our words convey. Researchers have identified the

> *Shortly after I returned to my table I realized that now in the same room above a spirited argument was in progress. It had come with phenomenal speed, this dark and stormy mood. I couldn't hear the words, due to some accoustical quirk. As with the marathon venery just completed, I could hear the action in almost baroque detail but the speech stayed muffled and indistinct, so I got the impression of shuffling angry feet, chairs wrenched around impatiently, banged doors, and voices rising in rage uttering words I was only partly able to comprehend. The male's voice was dominant—a husky and furious baritone that all but drowned out the limpid Beethoven. By contrast the voice of the female seemed plaintive, defensive, growing shrill at moments as if in fright but generally submissive with an undertone of pleading. Suddenly a glass or china object—an ashtray, a tumbler, I knew not what—crashed and shattered against a wall, and I could hear the heavy male feet stamping toward the door, which flew open in the upstairs hallway. Then the door went shut with a tremendous clatter, and I heard the man's footsteps tramping off into one of the other second-floor rooms. Finally the room was left—after these last twenty minutes of delirious activity—in what might be termed provisional silence, amid the depths of which I could hear only the soft heartsick adagio scratching on the phonograph, and the woman's broken sobs on the bed above me.*

William Styron,
Sophie's Choice

communicative value of paralanguage through the use of content-free speech—ordinary speech that has been electronically manipulated so that the words are unintelligible but the paralanguage remains unaffected. (Hearing a foreign language that we do not understand has the same effect.) Subjects who hear content-free speech can consistently identify the emotion being expressed as well as its strength.[24]

In sarcasm we use both emphasis and tone of voice to change a statement's meaning to the opposite of its verbal message. Try this yourself with the following three statements. The first time, mean them literally, and then say them sarcastically.

"Darling, what a beautiful little gown!"
"I really had a wonderful time on my blind date."
"There's nothing I like better than calves' brains on toast."

Albert Mehrabian and others have conducted experiments that indicate that when the vocal factors (tone of voice, disfluencies, emphasis, and so on) contradict the verbal message (words), the vocal factors carry more meaning.[25] They had subjects evaluate the degree of liking communicated by a message in which vocal clues conflicted with the words; they found that the words had very little effect on the interpretation of the message.

Communication through paralanguage isn't always intentional. Often our voices give us away when we're trying to create an impression different from our actual feelings. For example, you've probably tried to sound calm and serene when you were really exploding with inner nervousness. Maybe your deception went along perfectly for a while—just the right smile, no telltale fidgeting of the hands, posture relaxed—and then, without your being able to do a thing about it, right in the middle of your relaxed comments, your voice squeaked! The charade was over.

Vocal changes that contradict spoken words are not easy to conceal. If the speaker is trying to conceal fear or anger, the voice will probably sound higher and louder, and the rate of talk may be faster than normal. Sadness produces the opposite vocal pattern: quieter, lower-pitched speech delivered at a slower rate.[26]

The derivation of the word "personality" proves that there was originally a profound understanding of the close connection between voice and personality. The word comes from the Latin persona, *which originally meant the mouthpiece of a mask used by actors (*persona: *the sound of the voice passes through). From the mask the term shifted to the actor; the "person" in drama. The word eventually came to mean any person and finally "personality," but over the centuries it lost its symbolic connection with the voice.*

Paul Moses, M.D.,
The Voice of Neurosis

Voice Messages

Here's an experiment that can give you an idea of some messages your voice communicates.

1. Choose a partner, and find a space for yourselves.

2. Now close your eyes. You'll be focusing on the voice as a means of communication; this will help screen out other kinds of nonverbal messages.

3. For five minutes carry on a conversation about whatever you want. As you talk, listen to your partner's voice. Try not to concentrate as much on the words as the way your partner sounds. Imagine what messages you'd receive if you were listening to a foreign language.

4. Now with your eyes still shut tell your partner what messages you received from the sound of her voice. Did it sound tired, relaxed, happy, tense? Share your perceptions.

5. Still keeping your eyes closed, take turns performing the following step. The first person begins a sentence with the words "I am my voice . . ."—completing the statement by describing whatever he hears his voice communicating. For example, "I am my voice and I'm very excited. I'm high-pitched and fast, and I can go on and on without stopping"; or "I am my voice, and I'm tired. I hardly ever say anything, and when I do, it's very quietly. It hardly takes anything to make me stop."

6. After both partners have completed the previous step, take turns sharing your perceptions of your partner's description of her voice. Do you agree with the interpretation, or did you pick up different messages?

I understand a fury in your words, but not the words.

William Shakespeare,
Othello

7. As you talk with others both in and outside of class, try to listen to the messages your voice sends. Can you tell when you're sincere and when you're being untruthful? Do you have a different voice for certain occasions with parents, employers, teachers, certain friends? Do you have a happy, bored, angry voice? What do these different voices say about the relationships in which you use them?

An interesting variation of this exercise is to spend five minutes or so holding a conversation with your partner in gibberish. Say whatever nonsense syllables come to your mind, and see what happens. If you can get over the fear of sounding foolish for a few minutes (is this so horrible?), you'll probably find that you can communicate a great deal with your voice, even without words.

Touch   Besides being the earliest means we have of making contact with others, touching is essential to our healthy development. During the nineteenth and early twentieth centuries a large percentage of children born every year died from a disease then called *marasmus,* which translated from Greek means "wasting away." In some orphanages the mortality rate was nearly 100 percent, but even children in the most "progressive" homes, hospitals, and other institutions died regularly from the ailment. When researchers finally tracked down the causes of this disease, they found that the infants suffered from lack of physical contact with parents or nurses, rather than lack of nutrition, medical care, or other factors. They hadn't been touched enough, and as a result they died. From this knowledge came the practice of "mothering" children in institutions—picking the baby up, carrying it around, and handling it several times each day. At one hospital that began this practice, the death rate for infants fell from between 30 to 35 percent to below 10 percent.[27]

As a child develops, the need for being touched continues. In his excellent

The unconscious parental feelings communicated through touch or lack of touch can lead to feelings of confusion and conflict in a child. Sometimes a "modern" parent will say all the right things but not want to touch his child very much. The child's confusion comes from the inconsistency of levels: If they really approve of me so much like they say they do, why won't they touch me?

William Schutz,
Here Comes Everybody

book *Touching: The Human Significance of the Skin,* Ashley Montagu describes research that suggests that allergies, eczema, and other health problems are in part caused by a lack of infant-mother contact. Although Montagu says that these problems develop early in life, he also cites cases where adults suffering from conditions as diverse as asthma and schizophrenia have been successfully treated by psychiatric therapy that uses extensive physical contact.[28]

Touch seems to increase a child's mental functioning as well as physical health. L. J. Yarrow has conducted surveys that show that babies who have been given plenty of physical stimulation by their mothers have significantly higher IQs than those receiving less.[29]

The society we live in places less importance on touch than on other, less immediate senses such as sight or hearing. Our language is full of visual and aural figures of speech such as "Seeing is believing," "I'll be hearing from you," "Here's looking at you," and "sounding something out." As Bernard Gunther points out, when leaving someone we say, "See you later," never "touch," "smell," or "taste" you later.[30]

Touch can communicate many messages. In addition to the nurturing/caring function we just discussed, it can signify many relationships:[31]

functional/professional (dental exam, haircut)
social/polite (handshake)
friendship/warmth (clap on back, Spanish *abrazo*)
love/intimacy (some caresses, hugs)
sexual arousal (some kisses, strokes)*

You might object to the examples following each of these categories, saying that some nonverbal behaviors occur in several types of relationships. A kiss, for example, can mean anything from a polite but superficial greeting to the most intense arousal. What makes a given touch more or less intense? Researchers have suggested a number of factors:

What part of the body does the touching
What part of the body is touched
How long the touch lasts
How much pressure is used
Whether there is movement after contact is made
Whether anyone else is present
The situation in which the touch occurs
The relationship between the persons involved[32]

From this list you can see that there is, indeed, a complex language of touch. Since nonverbal messages are inherently ambiguous, it's no surprise that this language can often be misunderstood. Is a hug playful or suggestive of stronger feelings? Is a touch on the shoulder a friendly gesture or an attempt at domination? Research suggests the interpretation can depend on a variety of factors, including the sex of the people involved, ethnic background, and marital status, among others.[33] This sort of ambiguity shows the importance of using the perception checking skills you learned in Chapter Three to be sure your interpretations are accurate.

In our now more than slightly cockeyed world, there seems to be little provision for someone to get touched without having to go to bed with whoever does the touching. And that's something to think about. We have mixed up simple, healing, warm touching with sexual advances. So much so, that it often seems as if there is no middle way between "Don't you dare touch me!" and "Okay, you touched me, so now we should make love!"

A nation which is able to distinguish the fine points between offensive and defensive pass interference, bogies, birdies, and par, a schuss and a slalom, a technical, a personal, and a player-control foul should certainly be able to make some far more obvious distinctions between various sorts of body contact.

Sidney Simon
Caring, Feeling, Touching

---

* Other types of touch can indicate varying degrees of aggression.

Our little girl was retreating into a walled-off world until we found the key to unlock her love.

"Debbie, please brush that hair out of your face. It's even getting into the food on your fork!"

It was suppertime; I had been late getting home from work, and I was edgy. My irritation was apparent in my voice. Slowly, mechanically, Debbie reached up and pushed her hair back. Then The Look began to come over her face.

I had seen it before. She had been perhaps four years old when it began. Her eyes became flat and expressionless, her face lost all animation. Even her coloring seemed to fade, and with her pale lashes and brows, she looked like an unpainted wooden doll. I knew that I could pass my hand in front of her face and she wouldn't even see it. Nor would she respond to anything that was said to her.

"There she goes again, feeling sorry for herself," commented Don, her big brother.

And so it appeared. The middle child in a family of seven children, it was understandable that she might feel sorry for herself. The older children bossed her around, nagged her, and seemed to pick on everything she said. The younger children demanded their own way, and often got it through the privilege of their ages. Pushed from above, threatened from below, Debbie didn't feel that she mattered to anyone.

The rest of the family continued with supper, ignoring Debbie. From past experience, we knew that it was useless to try to bring her back into the group. As the others were excused I led Debbie away from her half-eaten dinner to the living room, where I sat her down in front of the television set. Here she would gradually forget her grievances and join in again.

I couldn't help but have mixed feelings, though. Poor little thing! Six years old, and so unhappy! I wished desperately that I had more time to spend with her as an individual. I knew I had nagged her again. But why must she resort to that "Sorrowful Sal" act at every offense, either real or imagined? It was positively exasperating for her to tune us all out when it was quite clear that she could see and hear everything around her.

When Debbie had first begun to get The Look, we thought she was funny. "Isn't she cute when she's angry? See how she refuses to pay any attention to you! She's got a mind of her own!" But as time passed, it was no longer funny. It was angering to be intentionally ignored. We coaxed. We reasoned. We scolded. We even spanked her for her stubbornness, all to no avail.

But as long as it didn't happen often, we didn't pay much attention to such behavior. In a large family, it's easy to put a problem aside when a minor crisis has passed. Our older children were starting school; we had one in the "terrible twos" and an infant, as well as a chronic invalid who required extensive home nursing care. Our hands

were full. The more-urgent-appearing problems received our attention, and Debbie's increasing needs went unrecognized.

Debbie was in the first grade when one of the older children said to me one afternoon, "Mom, Debbie's teacher wants to talk to you." The normal pangs of worry hit me that night. What trouble had Debbie gotten herself into? I made an appointment for the next afternoon with her teacher.

"I'm worried about Debbie," Mrs. Voorhees told me. "She's so . . . alone. She craves attention and she desperately needs more of it from you." She was telling me as gently as she could that I was failing my daughter.

I turned the problem over and over in my mind. How could I give Debbie more attention without incurring the resentment of the other children? Knowing that siblings in a large family are intensely competitive, I decided it would be best to enlist their help. I called the older children together and repeated what Mrs. Voorhees had told me. "So I'm going to try to give Debbie what she needs. It means that she has a greater need for attention at this time, and I'm trying to help her. I'd do the same for any of you."

For a while this seemed to help. But as weeks went by, I found that even the knowledge of reasons for my actions could not compensate for the unequal distribution of my attention. Don began to take pokes and pinches at his little sister, or to kick her as she went by, for no apparent reason.

Denise would keep track of every favor that I might give Debbie, and accused me, "You've read to her four times in the past month, and only once to me."

It was true. I was now working full time and trying to divide the remaining time between the children. With the small amount of time that there was to be divided, the inequality was obvious. The resentment of the other children over the extra time given to Debbie alone only made them more quarrelsome and belittling toward her. It was defeating my original purpose.

Still, I wondered, what could I do? What should I do? Debbie was getting good grades in school, so it didn't seem that she was too badly in need of attention. I began to spend more time in group activities with the family and less time with Debbie as an individual.

The Look returned more frequently, and Debbie ran away that summer—several times. "Where will you live?" I asked her. "Under a bush," she would reply poignantly. My heart ached for her.

Her comments began to reveal her feelings. "I wish I'd never been born."; "I wish I was dead."; Or "Some day I'm going to kill myself."

One afternoon she climbed up on the family car, and walked around on it in her gritty shoes, scratching the paint. Her exasperated father spanked her vigorously. Afterward I sat down beside her at the foot of the stairway, where she sat sobbing. "Why ever did you do that, Debbie? You knew Daddy would get angry and spank you," I asked her.

"Because I don't like myself."

"Why don't you like yourself?"

"Because nobody likes me." Because nobody likes me. Oh, Debbie!

"I like you, Debbie. I love you. You're my little girl." Words. Just words. Again, The Look. She tuned me out. She didn't see or hear me.

What a desperate cry for help! A little girl, six years old, invoking the wrath of her parents because she didn't think she was a person worth liking!

It took me a long time to acknowledge that Debbie—that WE—needed help. "How could a six-year-old have any serious problems?" I would ask myself. "How could so young a child be too much for you to manage? Don't bring outsiders into it. We can handle our own problems if we work on them."

But we weren't handling them. By the time Debbie was seven years old, The Look became a routine part of our daily life.

After a long inner struggle I finally decided to go to the county mental-health center. "What if someone sees me there and thinks I'm a kook?" I wondered. But I swallowed my pride and went. It was the turning point in Debbie's life.

After I discussed the problem with the psychiatric social worker, he set up an appointment for the entire family. "I want to see how they interact," he told me. After several such appointments, he began to see Debbie alone. A few weeks later he was able to give some help.

"She's a very unhappy little girl," he told me. "You must give her the love and attention she needs. If you don't, her problems will probably come to a head when she is a teenager. Then there is a strong chance that she will either commit suicide, or turn for affection to the first fellow who will give her a little attention. And you know what that means. These girls often become unwed mothers in their teens."

"But how?" I asked. "I'm working full time; I must work. I've so little time to give any of the children and when I try to give Debbie a little extra attention, the other children become jealous and are cruel to her. And how do I cope with her when she tunes me out?"

"She's tuning you out to protect herself. Think about it," the social worker said, "When does she do it? When you scold her or criticize her? When the other children argue with her or deride her? These things hurt her so much that she can't cope with them. But if she can't see you or hear you, then you can't hurt her like that any more. So she withdraws. It's a defense mechanism she uses to keep from being hurt by other people."

He paused, then continued gently, "But you can reach her. There is one means you haven't tried yet. And that is—touch."

Touch? A strange thought. Communication without words. She could close her eyes and her ears, but she could still feel love.

"Touch her every chance you get. Ruffle her hair when you go by her. Pat her bottom. Touch her arm when you talk to her. Caress her. Put your hand on her shoulder, your arm around her. Pat her back. Hold her. Every chance you get. Every time you talk to her."

"Even when she refuses to see or hear you, she will feel you. And, incidently, this is something you can use to communicate with all your children. But pour it on Debbie."

Pour it on I did. And in a short time the results began to show noticeably. Debbie gradually became alive again. She smiled. She laughed. She had fun. She began to talk with me again. The Look became less and less fre-quent. And the other children never seemed to notice a thing, nor did they show any resentment of Debbie, possibly because I was touching them too.

Debbie is nine now, and she is like a different child. In addition to her new cheerful outlook on life, she has begun to discover some self-esteem. She stood in front of the mirror recently and told me, "I like my hair. It's pretty." What she was really telling me was that she has learned to like herself again. How far she has come! How far we all have come since I finally admitted that we needed professional help for a problem we hadn't been able to solve by ourselves.

The social worker's suggestion that I begin to communicate my love to my children by touching them was not guarantee to be a miracle cure for Debbie's problems—or anyone else's. It did work for us, but not without a serious reevaluation of ourselves as individuals and as a family unit. We have had to learn a lot about ourselves, and we had to try hard to understand one another better, to accept one another as distinctly different human beings, each with intense feelings and needs.

I know the road ahead of us will have many rough spots and that the struggle to work out family difficulties is not an easy one. Debbie's problems are not over yet by any means. Strong rivalry remains among the children and she is still right in the middle of it. She has many crucial years in front of her, and we'll have to continue to boost her ego. We'll have to pay attention to her; give her the opportunity to express her feelings and listen to her when she does.

But no matter what the future holds, I have learned at least one invaluable lesson: to let my children feel my love. Love can be shown in many ways—in facial expressions, in attitudes, in actions. Love can be heard. But—and perhaps this is most important of all—love can be felt, in one of the simplest means of communication there is: touch.

Phyllis Spangler

> *We can turn now to the safer and more tender intimacies of the dance-floor. At parties, discotheques, dance-halls and ballrooms, adults who are strangers to one another can come together and move around the room in an intimate frontal embrace. Individuals who are already friendly can also use the situation to escalate a nontouching relationship into a touching one. The special role that social dancing plays in our society is that it permits, in its special context, a sudden and dramatic increase in body intimacy in a way that would be impossible elsewhere. If the same full frontal embrace were performed between strangers, or partial strangers, outside the context of the dance-floor, the impact would be entirely different. Dancing, so to speak, devalues the significance of the embrace, lowering its threshold to a point where it can lightly be indulged in without fear of rebuff. Having permitted it to occur, it then gives a chance for it to work its powerful magic. If the magic fails to work, the formalities of the situation also permit retreat without ignominy.*

Desmond Morris, *Intimate Behaviour*

Clothing   Besides protecting us from the elements, clothing is a means of nonverbal communication. One writer has suggested that clothing conveys at least ten types of messages to others.[34]

1. Economic level
2. Educational level
3. Trustworthiness
4. Social position
5. Level of sophistication
6. Economic background
7. Social background
8. Educational background
9. Level of success
10. Moral character

Research shows that we do make assumptions about people based on their style of clothing. In one study, a male and female were stationed in a hallway so that anyone who wished to go by had to avoid them or pass between them. In one condition the conversationalists wore "formal daytime dress"; in the other, they wore "casual attire." Passers-by behaved differently toward the couple, depending on the style of clothing: They responded positively with the well-dressed couple and negatively when the same people were casually dressed.[35] Similar results in other situations show the influence of clothing. We are more likely to obey people dressed in a high-status manner. Pedestrians were more likely to return lost coins to well-dressed people than to those dressed in low-status clothing.[36] We are also more likely to follow the lead of high-status dressers, even when it comes to violating social rules. Eighty-three percent of the pedestrians in one study followed a well-dressed jaywalker who violated a "wait" crossing signal, whereas only 48 percent followed a confederate dressed in lower-status clothing.[37]

Despite the frequency with which we make them, our clothing-based assumptions aren't always accurate. The stranger wearing wrinkled, ill-fitting old clothes might be a worker on vacation, a normally stylish person on the way to clean a fireplace, or even an eccentric millionaire. As we get to know others better the importance of clothing shrinks.[38] This fact suggests that clothing is especially important in the early stages of a relationship, when making a positive first impression is necessary to encourage others to know us better. This advice is equally important in personal situations and in employment interviews. In both cases, our style of dress (and personal grooming) can make all the difference between the chance to progress further and outright rejection.

John T. Molloy believes in the old saw that clothes make the man. He believes it so much that two years ago he became America's first wardrobe engineer, a veritable B. F. Skinner of haberdashery who believes that a man's clothing can be chosen to evoke conditioned responses from anyone he meets. Operating out of a cluttered office in Manhattan, Molloy teaches dress habits that, he says, enable salesmen to sell more insurance, trial lawyers to win more cases and executives to exert more authority. Wardrobe engineering, Molloy says, "is just putting together the elements of psychology, fashion, sociology and art."

Molloy began to develop his theory in the late 1950s, when as an instructor at a prep school in Connecticut, he discovered that a teacher's dress could subtly affect student performance. In one case, two teachers taught the same class in separate half-day sessions: one consistently wore penny loafers while the other wore traditional lace-up shoes. The students, it turned out, worked longer and harder for the teacher in lace-ups, and Molloy concluded that the shoes were responsible. "I felt we were on to something big," he recalls, "but nobody noticed." Nobody, that is, but Molloy. Over the next decade, he refined his techniques and conducted other experiments that convinced him he was right. During his early research, for example, he discovered that the Boston Strangler invariably wore beige or gray

repairman-like outfits; the light colors tended to reassure housewives and helped him get into their homes. Last year Molloy planted an actor posing as a trainee in a New York City corporate office, and instructed him to ask 100 secretaries to retrieve some information from their files. First the actor dressed in "lower-middle-class" style: black shoes with large buckles, a greenish-blue suit, a white shirt and a chintzy blue polyester tie, thick glasses and a gold expansion watch band. In that garb, he was able to get only twelve secretaries out of 50 to go to the files for him. Later, in an "upper-middle-class" outfit—styled hair, expensive blue suit, beige shirt, silk polka-dot tie and brown cordovan shoes—he visited 50 more secretaries. This time, 42 of the 50 did as they were bade.

Based on such findings, Molloy has put together a number of courses designed to teach clients how to dress more effectively. For $300, he will teach an "upper-middle-class set of color and pattern values" that will help boost the wearer in the corporate world. For those with three years and $1,000 to invest, he will conduct a full-fledged, complex "credibility study" designed to find the "clothing trend" that will best project a desired image.

Molloy has already had plenty of takers. At his suggestion, the owner of an insurance agency in a Boston suburb replaced his flashily attired sales force with men in gray suits, simple ties and button-down collars—and sales boomed. A trial lawyer with a folksy courtroom man-

ner and a losing record was persuaded to abandon his pin-stripe suits and wire-rimmed spectacles (which were more suitable for a remote "authority figure") in favor of solid blue suits and glasses with thicker frames that gave him a friendlier image. He is now winning more cases.

One of Molloy's most satisfying experiences occurred a few years ago, when a conservatively dressed corporate recruiter at Columbia University insisted to him that clothes did not matter. It was a time when militant students were throwing recruiters off campus, and Molloy guaranteed that he could dress him so that a student would punch him in the nose. Dressed in dark blue clothing "just like a cop," the recruiter ventured back onto campus—and caught a fast one in the chops. Molloy collected his fee and won a convert.

Time Magazine

Proxemics—Distance as Nonverbal Communication   Proxemics is the study of the way people and animals use space. As you'll see by the end of this chapter, you can sometimes tell how people feel toward each other simply by noting the distance between them. To begin to understand how this is so, try this exercise:

Distance Makes a Difference

1. Choose a partner, and go to opposite sides of the room and face each other.
2. Very slowly begin walking toward each other while carrying on a conversation. You might simply talk about how you feel as you follow the activity. As you move coser, try to be aware of any change in your feelings. Continue moving slowly toward each other until you are only an inch or so apart. Remember how you feel at this point.
3. Now, while still facing each other, back up until you're at a comfortable distance for carrying on your conversation.
4. Share your feelings with each other and/or the whole group.

During this experiment your feelings probably changed at least three times. During the first phase, when you were across the room from your partner, you probably felt unnaturally far away. Then as you neared a point about three feet from him, you probably felt like stopping; this is the distance at which two people in our culture normally stand while conversing socially. If your partner wasn't someone you're emotionally close to, you probably began to feel quite uncomfortable as you moved through this normal range and came closer; it's possible that you had to force yourself not to move back. Some people find this phase so uncomfortable that they can't get closer than twenty inches or so to their partner.

What was happening here? Each of us carries around a sort of invisible bubble of personal space wherever we go. We think of the area inside this bubble as our private territory—almost as much a part of us as our own bodies. As you moved closer to your partner, the distance between your bubbles narrowed and at a certain point disappeared altogether: Your space had been invaded, and this is the point at which you probably felt uncomfortable. As you moved away again, your partner retreated out of your bubble, and you felt more relaxed.

Of course, if you were to try this experiment with someone very close to you—your mate, for example—you might not have felt any discomfort at all, even while touching. The reason is that our willingness to get close to others—physically as well as emotionally—varies according to the person we're with and the situation we're in. And it's precisely the distance that we voluntarily put between ourselves and others that gives a nonverbal clue about our feelings and the nature of the relationship.

Anthropologist Edward T. Hall has defined four distances that we use in our everyday lives.[39] He says that we choose a particular one depending on how we feel toward the other person at a given time, the context of the conversation, and what our interpersonal goals are.

1. Intimate distance The first of Hall's zones begins with skin contact and ranges out to about eighteen inches. We usually use **intimate distance** with people who are emotionally very close to us, and then mostly in private situations— making love, caressing, comforting, protecting. By allowing someone to move into our intimate distance we're letting them enter our territory. When we do this voluntarily, it's usually a sign of trust: We've willingly lowered our defenses. On the other hand, when someone invades this most personal area without our consent, we usually feel threatened. This explains the feeling you may have had during the last exercise when your partner intruded into your space without any real invitation from you. It also explains the discomfort we sometimes feel when forced into crowded places like buses or elevators with strangers. At times like these the standard behavior in our society is to draw away or tense our muscles and avoid eye contact. This is a nonverbal way of signaling, "I'm sorry for invading your territory, but the situation forced it."

In courtship a critical moment usually occurs when one member of a couple first moves into the other's intimate zone. If the partner being approached does not retreat, it usually signals that the relationship is moving into a new stage. On the other hand, if the reaction to the advance is withdrawal to a greater distance, the initiator should get the message that it isn't yet time to become more intimate. We remember from our dating the significance of where on the car seat our companions chose to sit. If they moved close to us, it meant one thing; if they stayed jammed against the passenger's door, we got quite a different message.

2. Personal distance The second spatial zone, **personal distance**, ranges from eighteen inches at its closest point to four feet at its farthest. Its closer phase

Some thirty inches from
my nose
The frontier of my Person
goes,
And all the untilled air
between
Is private <u>pagus</u> or
demesne.
Stranger, unless with
bedroom eyes
I beckon you to frater-
nize,
Beware of rudely cross-
ing it:
I have no gun, but I can
spit.

W. H. Auden

Once I heard a hospital nurse describing doctors. She said there were beside-the-bed doctors, who were interested in the patient, and foot-of-the-bed doctors, who were interested in the patient's condition. They unconsciously expressed their emotional involvement—or lack of it—by where they stood.

Edward T. Hall

is the distance at which most couples stand in public. But if someone of the opposite sex stands this near one partner at a party, the other partner is likely to feel uncomfortable. This "moving in" often is taken to mean that something more than casual conversation is taking place. The far range of personal distance runs from about two and a half to four feet. It's the zone just beyond the other person's reach. As Hall puts it, at this distance we can keep someone "at arm's length." This choice of words suggests the type of communication that goes on at this range: The contacts are still reasonably close, but they're much less personal than the ones that occur a foot or so closer.

Test this for yourself. Start a conversation with someone at a distance of about three feet, and slowly move a foot or so closer. Do you notice a difference? Does the distance affect your conversation?

3. **Social distance** Social distance ranges from four to about twelve feet. Within it are the kinds of communication that usually occur in business. Its closer phase, from four to seven feet, is the distance at which conversations usually occur between salespeople and customers and between people who work together. Most people feel uncomfortable when a salesclerk comes as close as three feet, whereas four or five feet nonverbally signals "I'm here to help you, but I don't mean to be too personal or pushy."

Take a minute now to role-play a customer-salesperson scene. Try it first at five feet and then at three. Which one seems most natural?

We use the far range of social distance—seven to twelve feet—for more formal and impersonal situations. This is the distance at which we sit from our boss (or other authority figure) as he stares across his desk at us. Sitting at this distance signals a far different and less relaxed type of conversation than if we were to pull a chair around to the boss's side of the desk and sit only three or so feet away.

4. **Public distance** Public distance is Hall's term for the farthest zone, running outward from twelve feet. The closer range of public distance is the one that most teachers use in the classroom. In the farther reaches of public space—twenty-five feet and beyond—two-way communication is almost impossible. In some cases, it's necessary for speakers to use public distance because of the size of their audience, but we can assume that anyone who voluntarily chooses to use it when he or she could be closer is not interested in having a dialog.

Physical invasion isn't the only way people penetrate our spatial bubble; we're just as uncomfortable when someone intrudes on our visual territory. If you've had the unpleasant experience of being stared at, you know that it can be just as threatening as having someone get too close. In most situations, however, people respect each others' visual privacy. You can test this the next time you're walking in public. As you approach another person, notice how this person will shift his or her glance away from you at a distance of a few paces, almost like a visual dimming of headlights. Generally, strangers maintain eye contact at a close distance only when they want something—information, assistance, signatures on a petition, recognition, a handout, and so on.

> *The interrogator should sit fairly close to the subject, and between the two there should be no table, desk, or other piece of furniture. Distance or the presence of an obstruction of any sort constitutes a serious psychological barrier and also affords the subject a certain degree of relief and confidence not otherwise attainable....*
>
> *As to the psychological validity of the above suggested seating arrangement, reference may be made to the commonplace but yet meaningful expressions such as "getting next" to a person, or the "buttonholing" of a customer by a salesman. These expressions signify that when a person is close to another one physically, he is closer to him psychologically. Anything such as a desk or a table between the interrogator and the subject defeats the purpose and should be avoided.*
>
> Inbau and Reid,
> *Criminal Interrogation and Confessions*

Territoriality   Whereas personal space is the invisible bubble we carry around as an extension of our physical being, territory remains stationary. Any geographical area such as a room, house, neighborhood, or country to which we assume some kind of "rights" is our territory. What's interesting about territoriality is that there is no real basis for the assumption of proprietary rights of "owning" some area, but the feeling of "owning" exists nonetheless. Your room in the house is *your* room whether you're there or not (unlike personal space, which is carried around with you), and it's your room because you say it is. Although you could probably make a case for your room's *really being* your room (and not the family's or that of the mortgage holder on the house), what about the desk you sit at in each class? You feel the same way about the desk, that it's yours even though it's certain that the desk is owned by the school and is in no way really yours.

The way people use space can communicate a good deal about power and status. Generally we grant people with higher status more personal territory and greater privacy. We knock before entering our boss's office, whereas she can usually walk into our work area without hesitating. In traditional schools professors have offices, dining rooms, and even toilets that are private, whereas the students, who are presumably less important, have no such sanctuaries. Among the military greater space and privacy usually come with rank: Privates sleep forty to a barracks, sergeants have their own private rooms, and generals have government-provided houses.

Physical Environment　To conclude our look at nonverbal communication, we want to emphasize the ways in which physical settings, architecture,
and interior design affect our communication. Begin by recalling for a moment
the different homes you've visited lately. Were some of these homes more
comfortable to be in than others? Certainly a lot of these kinds of feelings are
shaped by the people you were with, but there are some houses where it seems
impossible to relax, no matter how friendly the hosts are. We've spent what
seemed like endless evenings in what Mark Knapp calls "unliving rooms," where
the spotless ashtrays, furniture coverings, and plastic lamp covers seem to send
nonverbal messages telling us not to touch anything, not to put our feet up, and
not to be comfortable. People who live in houses like this probably wonder why
nobody ever seems to relax and enjoy themselves at their parties. One thing is

quite certain: They don't understand that this environment they have created can communicate discomfort to their guests.

A large amount of research shows how the design of an environment can shape the kind of communication that takes place in it. In one experiment at Brandeis University, A. Maslow and N. Mintz found that the attractiveness of a room influenced the happiness and energy of people working in it.[40] The experimenters set up three rooms: an "ugly" one, which resembled a janitor's closet in the basement of a campus building; an "average" room, which was a professor's office; and a "beautiful" room, which was furnished with carpeting, drapes, and comfortable furniture. The subjects in the experiment were asked to rate a series of pictures as a way of measuring their energy and feelings of well-being while at work. Results of the experiment showed that while in the ugly room, the subjects became tired and bored more quickly and took longer to complete their task. When they moved to the beautiful room, however, they rated the faces they were judging higher, showed a greater desire to work, and expressed feelings of importance, comfort, and enjoyment. The results teach a lesson that isn't surprising: Workers generally feel better and do a better job when they're in an attractive environment.

Many businesspeople show an understanding of how environment can influence communication. Robert Sommer, a leading environmental psychologist, described several such cases. In his book *Personal Space: The Behavioral Basis for Design,* he points out that dim lighting, subdued noise levels, and comfortable seats encourage people to spend more time in a restaurant or bar.[41] Knowing this, the management can control the amount of customer turnover. If the goal is to run a high-volume business that tries to move people in and out quickly, it's necessary to keep the lights shining brightly and not worry too much about soundproofing. On the other hand, if the goal is to keep customers in the bar or restaurant for a long time, the proper technique is to lower the lighting and use absorbent building materials that will reduce the noise.

Furniture design can control the amount of time a person spends in an environment, too. From this knowledge came the Larsen chair, which was designed for Copenhagen restaurant owners who thought their customers were occupying their seats too long without spending enough money. The chair is constructed to put an uncomfortable pressure on the sitter's back if occupied for more than a few minutes. (We suspect that many people who are careless in buying furniture for their homes get much the same result without trying. One environmental psychologist we know refuses to buy a chair or couch without sitting in it for at least half an hour to test its comfort.)

Sommer also describes how airports are designed to discourage people from spending too much time in waiting areas. The uncomfortable chairs, bolted shoulder to shoulder in rows facing outward, make conversation and relaxation next to impossible. Faced with this situation, travelers are forced to move to restaurants and bars in the terminal, where they're not only more comfortable but also likely to spend money.

Casino owners in places such as Las Vegas also know how to use the environment to control behavior. To keep gamblers from noticing how long they've been shooting craps, playing roulette and blackjack, and feeding slot machines, they build their casinos without windows or clocks. Unless they have their own watch, customers have no way of knowing how long they have been gambling or, for that matter, whether it's day or night.

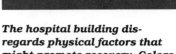

The hospital building disregards physical factors that might promote recovery. Colors are bland, but instead of being restful, are more often depressing; space is badly distributed, so that a patient may be stranded in a large room, or crowded in a small one; private and semi-private patients often feel isolated in their rooms.... Windows are badly placed, and the view most often shows an adjacent large hospital building or a parking lot....

One may immediately object that despite all this, the majority of patients adjust well to the hospital, recover, and go home. That is a little like saying that the world got on perfectly well without electricity, which is also true.

Michael Crichton, M.D.,
Five Patients

On the Grand Avenue corner is the Hearing Room, a sloping auditorium big enough for 706 people, and it was there, at one of the regular weekly meetings of the board, that we began our tour—and began to see the cause of the problem.

Citizens who want to address the board stand at two micro-phones in front of the first row of spectator seats. Beyond them, behind a solid oak fence running the width of the room and raised three steps, sit the supervisors' top aides: the clerk, the county counsel and the chief administrative officer. Beyond them, still another step up, sit the supervisors them-selves, arrayed behind a curving bench like justices of some high court, each one rock-ing in his own reclining chair.

Bob Abernathy and Art White,
West Magazine—Los Angeles Times

In a more therapeutic and less commercial way, physicians have also shaped environments to improve communications. One study showed that simply re-moving a doctor's desk made patients feel almost five times more at ease during office visits. Sommer found that redesigning a convalescent ward of a hospital greatly increased the interaction between patients. In the old design, seats were placed shoulder to shoulder around the edges of the ward. Grouping the chairs around small tables so that patients faced each other at a comfortable distance doubled the number of conversations.

The exterior design of a building often communicates a message about its occupants. Banks, for example, have traditionally used imposing elements such as large marble columns and open spaces to convey an image of strength and security to their customers. As tastes and attitudes change, however, architec-ture follows. (Some architects would argue that it also leads at times.) Banks built within the last ten or fifteen years reflect a newer approach, which stresses the institution's friendliness and openness, as conveyed by greater use of glass, landscaping, and lower barriers between customers and personnel.

The design of an entire building can shape communication among its users. Architects have learned that the way housing projects are designed will control to a great extent the contact neighbors will have with each other. People who live in apartments near stairways and mailboxes have many more contacts than do those living in less heavily traveled parts of the building, and tenants generally have more contacts with immediate neighbors than with people even a few doors away. Architects now use this information to design buildings that either encour-age communication or increase privacy, and house hunters can use the same knowledge to choose a home that gives them the neighborhood relationships they want.

So far we've talked about how designing an environment can shape com-munication, but there's another side to consider. Watching how people use an already existing environment can reveal what kind of relationships they want. For example, Sommer watched students in a college library and found that there's a definite pattern for people who want to study alone. While the library was uncrowded, students almost always chose corner seats at one of the empty rectangular tables. Finally, each table was occupied by one reader. New readers would then choose a seat on the opposite side and far end of an occupied table, thus keeping the maximum distance between themselves and the other readers. One of Sommer's associates tried violating these "rules" by sitting next to and across from other female readers when more distant seats were available. She found that the approached women reacted defensively, either by signaling their discomfort through shifts in posture, by gesturing, or by eventually moving away.

A person's position in a room can also communicate his status. Research shows that during conferences people who take leadership roles usually seat themselves at the ends of the table. This pattern carries over to many house-holds, where the father as head of the family sits at the end of the dinner table.

As this discussion of nonverbal communication draws to a close, several points deserve restating. First, in a normal two-person conversation the words or verbal components of the message carry far less of the social meaning of the situation than do the nonverbal components. This statistic may have been difficult for you to believe when we cited it at the beginning of the chapter, but by this time you know how many channels nonverbal communication includes: spatial distance, touch, body posture and tension, facial expression, hand and body movement, dress, physique, tone of voice, speed of speech, as well as disfluencies of speech and even the environment we create. Our hope is that the information in the chapter has placed some importance on nonverbal communication in your life.

Also remember that when we compare nonverbal behavior with verbal language, it's very limited. Nonverbal communication is concerned mostly with the expression of feelings, for example, preferences, and these usually *reinforce* or *contradict* the message we're expressing verbally.

Third, it is vital to realize that although nonverbal behaviors are more powerful in expressing feelings than are words, they're ambiguous and difficult to "read" accurately. They should always be verified.

A fourth point to remember is that many of the gestures, glances, postures, and other behaviors we've discussed here are culturally learned and don't necessarily apply to other cultures or even to subcultures within our society. At this point most nonverbal research has been done on middle- and upper-middle-class college students and shouldn't be automatically generalized to other groups.

Finally, we hope you now understand the importance of *congruency*—the matching of your verbal and nonverbal expressions. Contradicting messages from two channels are a pretty good indication of deliberate or unconscious deception, and matching signals reinforce your messages.

We haven't tried to teach you how to communicate nonverbally in this chapter—you've always known this. What we do hope you've gained here is a greater *awareness* of the messages you and others send, and we further hope that you can use this new awareness to understand and improve your relationships.

A good house is planned from the inside out. First, you decide what it has to do for its occupants. Then, you let the functions determine the form. The more numerous and various those functions, the more responsive and interesting the house should be. And it may not look at all like you expect.

Dan MacMasters,
Los Angeles Times

More Readings on Nonverbal Communication

Burgoon, Judee. "Nonverbal Signals." In *Handbook of Interpersonal Communi-cation.* Mark L. Knapp and Gerald R. Miller, eds. Beverly Hills, Calif.: Sage, 1985.
A thorough state-of-the-art appraisal by a leading scholar in the field. This survey focuses less on the types of nonverbal communication than on the characteristics they share: their functions, rules, relationship to verbal behavior, and structure of nonverbal code systems.

Ekman, Paul. *Telling Lies: Clues to Deceit in the Marketplace, Politics, and Marriage.* New York: Norton, 1985.
Ekman summarizes hundreds of research studies examining the role of nonverbal communication in deception. The focus is on detecting others' lies rather than becoming a more effective liar oneself.

Ekman, Paul, and Wallace V. Friesen. *Unmasking the Face.* Englewood Cliffs, N.J.: Prentice-Hall, 1975.
Two leading researchers in nonverbal communication discuss the research and speculation surrounding this highly visible means of expression.

Goleman, Daniel. "Can You Tell When Someone Is Lying to You?" *Psychology Today* 16 (August 1982): 14-23.
This article summarizes the research on nonverbal indicators of deception and describes how accurate people are at detecting others' lies.

Hall, Edward T. *The Hidden Dimension.* Garden City, N.Y.: Anchor Books, Doubleday, 1969.
Hall has probably done more work on proxemics than anyone else, and this book gives you a good survey of the field, including the research with animals that led to our knowledge about how humans use space. It also contains chapters on how different cultures handle space.

—————. *The Silent Language.* New York: Fawcett Books, 1959.
A good blend of theory and anecdotes, this book introduces several kinds of nonverbal communication and their cultural implications. As a quote on the cover says, "Diplomats could study this book with profit."

Hickson, Mark L., and Don W. Stacks. *NVC: Nonverbal Communication: Studies and Applications.* Dubuque, Iowa: W. C. Brown, 1985.
A recent survey of the subject. In addition to surveying the various nonverbal channels, Hickson and Stacks examine the role of nonverbal communication in same-sex and opposite-sex relationships, in the family, and on the job. A final chapter also discusses research methodology.

Mehrabian, Albert. *Silent Messages,* 2d ed. Belmont, Calif.: Wadsworth, 1981.
A prominent researcher's introduction to nonverbal communication. Mehra-bian briefly discusses nonverbal messages in a variety of contexts, including sales, political campaigns, and romance.

Montagu, Ashley. *Touching: The Human Significance of the Skin.* New York: Harper & Row, 1971.
Montague has written 335 fascinating pages about skin and the importance it has in our development. It's a book you'll probably want to read before you plan to have children.

Scheflen, Albert E. *How Behavior Means.* Garden City, N.Y.: Anchor Books, 1974.
This book explores kinesics, posture, interaction, setting, and culture, describing their importance in human communication.

Sebeok, Thomas A., and Robert Rosenthal, eds. *The Clever Hans Phenomenon: Communication with Horses, Whales, Apes, and People.* New York: New York Academy of Sciences (Vol. 364), 1981.

Clever Hans was a horse whose alertness to human nonverbal communication kept some of the best minds of Europe fooled for years. The articles in this book were delivered in a symposium named in Hans's honor and deal with such varied areas of nonverbal communication as conversational strategies, psychic readings, and deception.

Sommer, Robert. *Personal Space: The Behavioral Basis of Design.* Englewood Cliffs, N.J.: Prentice-Hall, 1969.

Sommer is a leading authority on environmental psychology, and this book is a good introduction to the field. It shows how manipulating space influences communication.

Wiemann, John M., and Randall P. Harrison, eds. *Nonverbal Interaction.* Beverly Hills, Calif.: Sage, 1983.

A collection of papers dealing with various dimensions of nonverbal communication and methodologies for understanding the phenomenon. Some articles are most appropriate for students who already have some background in the field, and others can be appreciated by serious readers exploring the subject for the first time.

Chapter Seven

Listening vs. Hearing

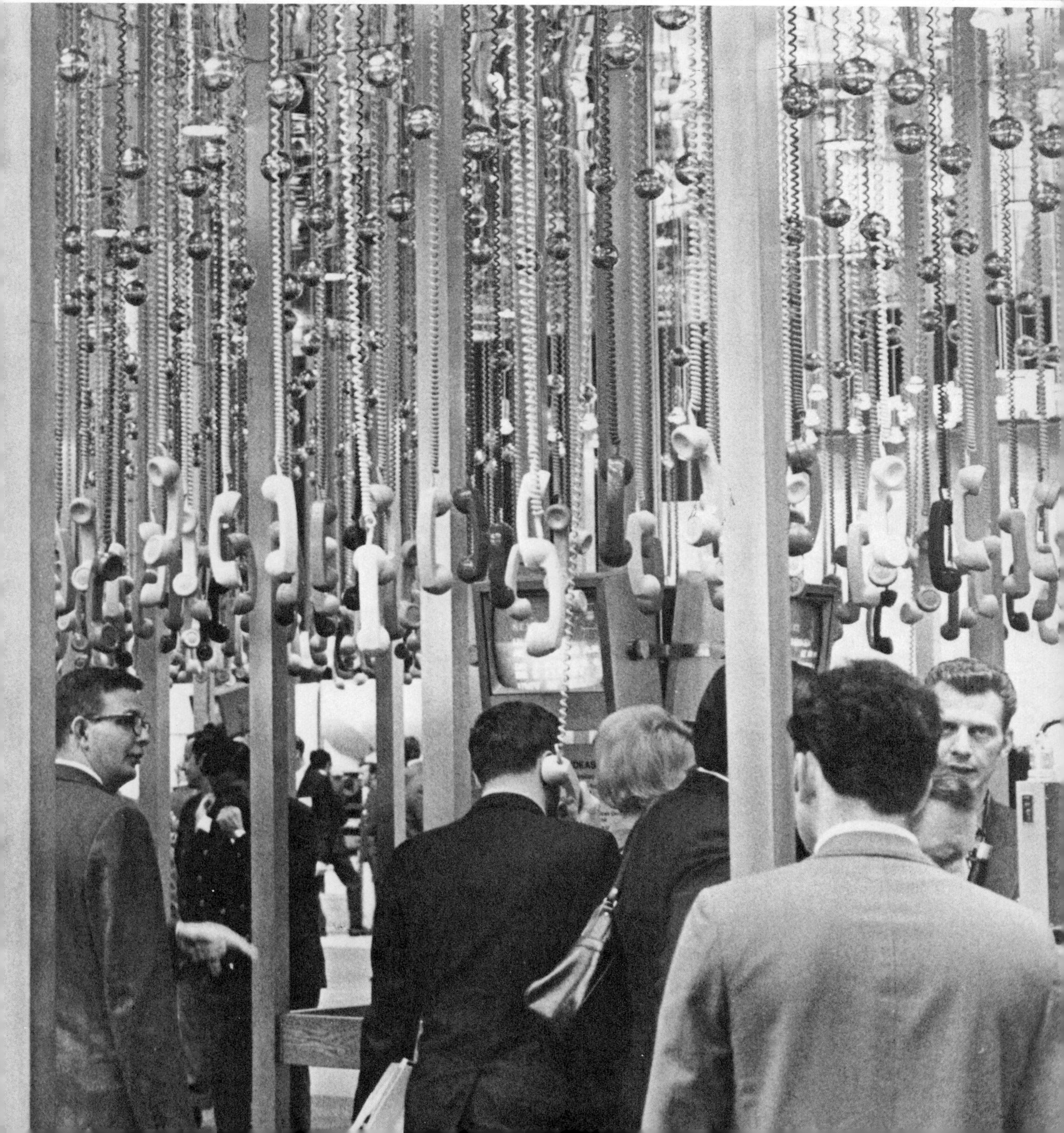

i have just
wandered back
into our conversation
and find
that you
are still
rattling on
about something
or other
i think i must
have been gone
at least
twenty minutes
and you
never missed me
now this might say
something
about my acting ability
or it might say
something about
your sensitivity
one thing
troubles me tho
when it
is my turn
to rattle on
for twenty minutes
which i
have been known to do
have you
been missing too

Ric Masten

There's more to listening than gazing politely at a speaker and nodding your head every so often. All of us know the frustration of not being heard, and unfortunately all of us are guilty of not listening to others at times. In fact, as you'll find out for yourself shortly, it's likely that more than half the things you say every day might as well have never been spoken because they're not understood clearly.

Poor receiving skills are especially unfortunate when you realize that we spend more time listening than in any other type of communication. A recent study (summarized in Figure 7–1) revealed that college students spent an average of 14 percent of their communicating time writing, 16 percent speaking, 17 percent reading, and a whopping 53 percent listening. Listening was broken down further into listening to mass communication media, such as radio and television, and listening to face-to-face messages. The former category accounted for 32 percent of the students' communication time, whereas the latter accounted for 21 percent—still more than any other type of face-to-face communication.[1]

This chapter will help you use this time most effectively by exploring the nature of listening. First, we'll talk about poor listening. You will see just how often you truly listen to others and how often you simply pretend—the results may surprise you. You'll learn why we don't listen much of the time, and you'll see some of the bad habits we've developed in this area. After looking at this rather gloomy picture, you'll learn some ways to improve your listening skills, making sure that you understand others and that they understand you. And finally we'll show you the technique of active listening, which not only lets you understand others better but also can actually show you how to help them solve their own problems.

Before we start talking about better ways of listening, here's an exercise that may remind you of some bad habits in this area.

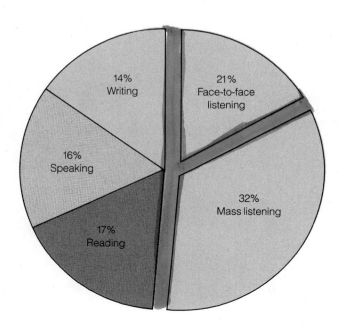

Figure 7–1
Types of communication activities

Not Listening

1. Divide the class into groups of four or five people.

2. Each person in turn should take two minutes to discuss with the group his ideas about a current issue (abortion, capital punishment, or some other idea that is personally important.) But as the talker shares his ideas, the other group members should think about the unfinished business in their lives—incomplete assignments, on-the-job work, things to discuss with the family. They should try to decide what they're going to do about these situations. The group members shouldn't be rude; they should respond politely every so often to the speaker, putting on a good appearance of paying close attention to him. But they should keep their mind on their personal concerns, not the speaker's remarks.

3. After everyone in your group completes step 2, spend some time discussing how you felt when you were talking and being listened to by the others. Also discuss how you felt as you thought about your problems instead of listening to the speaker.

4. For five minutes try to have a discussion in which each member of your group shares one personal communication problem she hopes to solve. Try to be as sincere and open with your feelings as you can. But as you all talk, try to keep the discussion focused on your problem. Every time someone reveals an idea or experience, try to turn it around to relate to your situation. Don't get sidetracked by anyone's comments. Your task is to tell the others about your communication problem.

5. After your discussion, take a few minutes to talk about how you felt during the conversation—when others ignored your message and when you ignored theirs.

Everybody's talkin' at me
I don't hear a word they're
*   sayin'*
Only the echoes of my mind.

Fred Neil,
Everybody's Talkin'

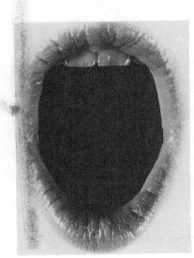

America has better means of communication than any nation on earth. We are constantly developing splendid new techniques for the dissemination of sound, pictures, and print. The only problem is that on the most basic level of communication—person-to-person, live, mouth-to-ear, low-frequency conversation—we're still in the dark ages; for everyone sends well enough, but very few of us are receiving.

Last week in the elevator of my mother's apartment house, a man asked her, "How are you?"

Since Mother had just spent three hours with a tax collector, she smiled graciously and said, "Lousy, thank you."

The man returned the smile and said, "That's nice."

Mother suspected that he either had misunderstood her or was simply a sadist. However, later the same day, she passed a woman who said, "How are you?"

"Suicidally distraught," said Mother.

"Fine," said the woman. "Hope the family's well, too."

This second exchange gave Mother the kind of revelation that only scientists have known when discovering great truths. Because that man and woman weren't people who would have wanted to see Mother out of the way (neither is in her will), she reached a profound conclusion: If you are well enough to be talking, people consider your condition superb, even if you colorfully describe an internal hemorrhage.

Mother's pioneering experimentation in the amenities has so inspired me that I have dedicated myself to continuing her work. Yesterday, I made real progress.

"How are you?" asked a man in front of my house.

"I'll be dead in a week," I said.

"Glad to hear it. Take care now."

There is no known way to shake the composure of the man who makes a perfunctory inquiry about your health; he loves his lines so well that the grimmest truth can't make him revise them. Never is human communication so defeated as when someone asks casually about your condition.

Some day, perhaps when I'm under a bus getting the last rites, I expect such a man to throw me a breezy, "How are you?"

"As well as can be expected," I'll say.

"Good. And the kids?"

"The older one goes to the chair tomorrow. The little one was lost on a Scout hike."

"Swell. The wife okay?"

"She just ran off with the milkman."

"Glad to hear it. You'll have to bring the whole family over one night soon."

Ralph Schoenstein,
Time Lurches On

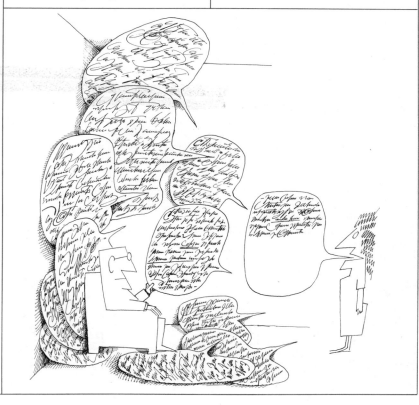

Types of Nonlistening

The preceding exercise demonstrated some of the most common types of poor listening. As you read on, you'll begin to recognize them as behaviors that you and those around you probably use quite often. Although you'll soon learn that a certain amount of inaccurate listening is understandable and sometimes even desirable, it's important to be aware of these types so that you can avoid them when understanding others is important to you.

Pseudolistening   Pseudolistening is an imitation of the real thing. Good pseudolisteners give the appearance of being attentive. They look you in the eye, nod and smile at the right times, and may even answer you occasionally. Behind that appearance of interest, however, something entirely different is going on, for pseudolisteners use a polite façade to mask thoughts that have nothing to do with what the speaker is saying. Often pseudolisteners ignore you because of something on their mind that's more important to them than your remarks. Other times they may simply be bored or think that they've heard what you have to say before and so tune out your remarks. Whatever the reasons, the significant fact is that pseudolistening is really counterfeit communication.

Stage-hogging   Stage-hogs are interested only in expressing their ideas and don't care about what anyone else has to say. These people will allow you to speak from time to time, but only so that they can catch their breath, use your remarks as a basis for their own babbling, or keep you from running away. Stage-hogs really aren't having a conversation when they dominate others with their talk; they're making a speech and at the same time probably making an enemy.

Selective Listening   Selective listeners respond only to the parts of your remarks that interest them, rejecting everything else. All of us are selective listeners from time to time, as, for instance, when we screen out radio commercials and music and keep an ear cocked for a weather report or an announcement of the time. In other cases, selective listening occurs in conversations with people who expect a thorough hearing but only pay attention to their partner when the subject turns to their favorite topic—perhaps money, sex, a hobby, or some particular person. Unless and until you bring up one of these pet subjects, you might as well talk to a tree.

© 1985 United Media, Inc.

AT A LECTURE—ONLY 12% LISTEN

Bright-eyed college students in lecture halls aren't necessarily listening to the professor, the American Psychological Association was told yesterday.

If you shot off a gun at sporadic intervals and asked the students to encode their thoughts and moods at that moment, you would discover that:

· About 20 percent of the students, men and women, are pursuing erotic thoughts.

· Another 20 percent are reminiscing about something.

· Only 20 percent are actually paying attention to the lecture; 12 percent are actively listening.

· The others are worrying, daydreaming, thinking about lunch or—surprise—religion (8 percent).

This confirmation of the lecturer's worst fears was reported by Paul Cameron, 28, an assistant professor at Wayne State University in Detroit. The annual convention, which ends Tuesday, includes about 2,000 such reports to 10,000 psychologists in a variety of meetings.

Cameron's results were based on a nine-week course in introductory psychology for 85 college sophomores. A gun was fired 21 times at random intervals, usually when Cameron was in the middle of a sentence.

SAN FRANCISCO SUNDAY EXAMINER AND CHRONICLE

Insulated Listening   Insulated listeners are almost the opposite of their selective cousins just mentioned. Instead of looking for something, these people avoid it. Whenever a topic arises that they'd rather not deal with, insulated listeners simply fail to hear or acknowledge it. You remind them about a problem, perhaps an unfinished job, poor grades, or the like, and they'll nod or answer you and then promptly forget what you've just said.

Defensive Listening   Defensive listeners take things you intended as innocent comments as personal attacks. The teenager who perceives her parents' questions about her friends and activities as distrustful snooping is a defensive listener, as is the insecure breadwinner who explodes any time his mate mentions money or the touchy parent who views any questioning by her children as a threat to her authority and parental wisdom. As your reading in Chapter Nine will suggest, it's fair to assume that many defensive listeners are suffering from shaky presenting images and avoid admitting it by projecting their own insecurities onto others.

Ambushing   Ambushers listen carefully to you, but only because they're collecting information they'll use to attack what you say. The cross-examining prosecution attorney is a good example of an ambusher. Needless to say, using this kind of strategy will justifiably initiate defensiveness in the other person.

Insensitive Listening   Insensitive listeners offer the final example of people who don't receive another person's messages clearly. As we've said before, people often don't express their thoughts or feelings openly but instead communicate them through a subtle and unconscious choice of words or nonverbal clues or both. Insensitive listeners aren't able to look beyond the words and behavior to understand their hidden meanings. Instead, they take a speaker's remarks at face value. The kind of companions Ralph Schoenstein describes on page 233 are insensitive listeners.

At the Party

Unrhymed, unrhythmical, the chatter goes:
Yet no one hears his own remarks as prose.

Beneath each topic tunelessly discussed
The ground-bass is reciprocal mistrust.

The names in fashion shuttling to and fro
Yield, when deciphered, messages of woe.

You cannot read me like an open book.

I'm more myself than you will ever look.

Will no one listen to my little song?

Perhaps I shan't be with you very long.

A howl for recognition, shrill with fear,
Shakes the jam-packed apartment,
     but each ear
Is listening to its hearing, so none hear.

W. H. Auden

Why We Don't Listen

After thinking about the styles of nonlistening described in the previous pages, most people begin to see that they listen carefully only a small percentage of the time. It's pretty discouraging to realize that much of the time you aren't hearing others and they aren't getting your messages, but this is a fact of life. Sad as it may be, it's impossible to listen *all* the time, for several reasons.

Message Overload   The amount of speech most of us encounter every day makes careful listening to everything we hear impossible. As you have already read, many of us spend almost half the time we're awake listening to verbal messages—from teachers, co-workers, friends, family, salespeople, and total strangers, not to mention radio and television. This means that we often spend five hours or more a day listening to people talk. It's impossible to keep our attention totally focused for this amount of time. Therefore, we have to let our attention wander at times.

Preoccupation   Another reason we don't always listen carefully is that we're often wrapped up in personal concerns that are of more immediate importance to us than the messages others are sending. It's hard to pay attention to someone else when you're anticipating an upcoming test or thinking about the wonderful time you had last night with good friends. Yet we still feel we have to "listen" politely to others, and so we continue with our charade.

Rapid Thought   Listening carefully is also difficult for a physiological reason. Although we're capable of understanding speech at rates up to 600 words per minute, the average person speaks between 100 and 140 words per minute.[2] Thus, we have a lot of "spare time" to spend with our minds while someone is talking. And the temptation is to use this time in ways that don't relate to the speaker's ideas, such as thinking about personal interests, daydreaming, planning a rebuttal, and so on. The trick is to use this spare time to understand the speaker's ideas better rather than letting your attention wander.

Effort   Listening effectively is hard work. The physical changes that occur during careful listening show the effort it takes: The heart rate quickens, respiration increases, and body temperature rises.[3] Notice that these changes are similar to the body's reaction to physical effort. This is no coincidence, for listening carefully to a speaker can be just as taxing as more obvious efforts.

External Noise   The physical world in which we live often presents distractions that make it hard to pay attention to others. The sound of traffic, music, others' speech, and the like, interfere with our ability to hear well. Also, fatigue or other forms of discomfort can distract us from paying attention to a speaker's remarks. Consider, for example, how the efficiency of your listening decreases when you are seated in a crowded, hot, stuffy room that is surrounded by traffic and other noises. In such circumstances even the best intentions aren't enough to ensure clear understanding.

> ### Duet
>
> **When we speak we do not listen, my son and I.**
> **I complain of slights, hurts inflicted on me.**
> **He sings a counterpoint, but not in harmony.**
> **Asking a question, he doesn't wait to hear.**
> **Trying to answer, I interrupt his refrain.**
> **This comic opera excels in disharmony only.**
>
> Lenni Shender Goldstein

Hearing Problems Sometimes a person's listening ability suffers from a physiological hearing problem. Once a hearing problem has been diagnosed, it's often possible to treat it. The real tragedy occurs when a hearing loss goes undetected. In such cases both the person with the defect and others can become frustrated and annoyed at the ineffective communication that results. If you suspect that you or someone you know suffers from a hearing loss, it's wise to have a physician or audiologist perform an examination.

Faulty Assumptions We often make incorrect assumptions that lead us to believe we're listening attentively when quite the opposite is true. When the subject is a familiar one, it's easy to think that you've "heard it all before" although in fact the speaker is offering new information. A related problem arises when you assume that a speaker's thoughts are too simple or obvious to deserve careful attention when the truth is that you ought to be listening carefully. At other times just the opposite occurs: You think that another's comments are too complex to be able to understand (as in some lectures), and so you give up trying to make sense of them. A final mistake people often make is to assume that a subject is unimportant and to stop paying attention when they ought to be listening carefully.

Lack of Apparent Advantages It often appears that we have more to gain by speaking than by listening. One big advantage of speaking is that it gives you a chance to control others' thoughts and actions. Whatever your goal—to be hired by a prospective boss, to convince others to vote for the candidate of your choice, or to describe the way you want your hair cut—the key to success seems to be the ability to speak well.

Another apparent advantage of speaking is the chance it provides to gain the admiration, respect, or liking of others. Tell jokes, and everyone will think you're a real wit. Offer advice, and they'll be grateful for your help. Tell them all you know, and they'll be impressed by your wisdom. But keep quiet . . . and you think you'll look like a worthless nobody.

Finally, talking gives you the chance to release energy in a way that listening can't. When you're frustrated, the chance to talk about your problems can often help you feel better. In the same way, you can often lessen your anger by letting it out verbally. It is also helpful to share your excitement with others by talking about it, for keeping it inside often makes you feel as if you might burst.

Although it's true that talking does have many advantages, it's important to realize that listening can pay dividends, too. As you'll soon read, being a good listener is one good way to help others with their problems; and what better way is there to have others appreciate you? As for controlling others, it may be true that it's hard to be persuasive while you're listening, but your willingness to hear others out will often encourage them to think about your ideas in return. Like defensiveness, listening is often reciprocal: You get what you give.

We have been given two ears and but a single mouth in order that we may hear more and talk less

Zeno of Citium

Lack of Training

Even if we want to listen well, we're often hampered by a lack of skill. A common but mistaken belief is that listening is like breathing—an activity that people do well naturally. "After all," the common belief goes, "I've been listening since I was a child. I don't need to study the subject in school."

The truth is that listening is a skill much like speaking: Virtually everybody does it, though few people do it well. As you read this chapter, you'll see that one reason so much poor listening exists is because most people fail to follow the important steps that lead to real understanding.

Styles of Listening

Before going any further, we want to make clear that it isn't always desirable to listen intently even when the circumstances permit. Given the number of messages to which we're exposed, it's impractical to expect yourself to listen well 100 percent of the time. This fact becomes even more important when you consider how many of the messages sent at us aren't especially worthwhile: boring stories, deceitful commercials, remarks we've heard many times before, and so on. Given this deluge of relatively worthless information, it's important for you to realize that behaviors such as insulated listening, pseudolistening, and selective listening are often reasonable. But there are times when you do want very much to understand others. At times like these you may try hard to get the other person's meaning and yet *still* seem to wind up with misunderstandings.

What can you do in such cases? It takes more than good intentions to listen well—there are skills that you can learn. To begin understanding these skills we need to look at two styles of listening.

Momma

By Mell Lazarus

© 1977 News America Syndicate.

One-Way Listening   One-way communication occurs when a listener tries to make sense out of a speaker's remarks without actively trying to provide feedback. Another term that describes this style of communication is **passive listening.** Probably the most familiar examples of passive listening occur when students hear a professor lecture or when viewers watch television. One-way communication also takes place in interpersonal settings, as when one person dominates a conversation while the others fall into the role of an audience or when some parents lecture their children without allowing them to respond.

The most important feature of one-way communication is that it contains little or no feedback. The receiver may deliberately or unintentionally send *nonverbal* messages that show how the speaker's ideas are being received—nods and smiles, stifled yawns, more or less eye contact—but there's no *verbal* response to indicate how—or even whether—the message has been received.

Since the speaker isn't interrupted in this type of lecture-conversation, one-way communication has the advantage of being relatively quick. We've all felt like telling someone, "I'm in a hurry. Just listen carefully and don't interrupt." What we're asking for here is one-way communication.

Sometimes one-way communication is an appropriate way of listening. As you'll soon read, sometimes the best way to help people with problems is to hear

them out. In many cases they're not looking for, nor do they need, a verbal response. At times like these, when there's no input by the receiver, *anybody* who will serve as a sounding board will do as a "listener." This explains why some people find relief talking to a pet or a photograph.

One-way communication also works well when the listener wants to ease back mentally and be entertained. It would be a mistake to interrupt a good joke or story or to stand up in the middle of a play and shout out a question to the performers.

But outside of these cases one-way listening isn't very effective for the simple reason that it almost guarantees that the listener will misunderstand at least some of the speaker's ideas. There are at least three types of misunderstandings. As you read about each of them, think about how often they occur in your life.

The first kind of misunderstanding happens when a speaker sends a clear, accurate message that the receiver simply gets wrong. Somehow a quarter cup of sugar is transformed into four cups or "I'll see you at twelve" is translated into "I'll see you at two."

In other cases, the receiver is listening carefully enough, but the speaker sends an incorrect message. These instances are the reverse of the ones just mentioned, and their results can be just as disastrous.

The third mixup that comes from one-way communication is probably the most common: The speaker sends a message that may not be incorrect but is overly vague, and the receiver interprets the words in a manner that doesn't match the speaker's ideas. In Chapter One we talked about the problems that arise from failing to check interpretations. In the statement "I'm a little confused," does *little* mean "slightly," or is it an understatement that could be translated into "very"? When a lover says, "You're my best friend," is this synonymous with the message "Besides your being such a romantic devil, I also feel comfortable with you," or does it mean, "I want to become less of a lover and more of a pal"? You could make your own personal list of confusing messages and in doing so prove the point: Understanding another's words isn't always a sure thing. Fortunately, there's another, usually better, way of listening.

Two-Way Listening   The element that distinguishes two-way from one-way communication is verbal feedback. You'll recall from the communication model in Chapter One that feedback occurs whenever a listener sends some sort of message to the sender indicating how the original idea was received. When the feedback is deliberate and verbal, we can say that two-way communication has occurred. There are at least two types of verbal feedback you can use as a listener.

1. **Questioning**   In a questioning response you ask for additional information to clarify your idea of the sender's message. If you ask directions to a friend's house, typical questions might be "Is your place an apartment?" or "How long does it take to get there from here?" In more serious situations, questions could include "What's bothering you?" or "Why are you so angry?" or "Why is that so important?" Notice that one key element of these questions is that they ask the speaker to elaborate on information already given.

Questioning is often a valuable tool for increasing understanding. Some-

"I have a pet at home"

"Oh, what kind of a pet?"

"It is a dog."

"What kind of a dog?"

"It is a St. Bernard."

"Grown up or a puppy?"

"It is full grown."

"What color is it?"

"It is brown and white."

"Why didn't you say you had a full-grown, brown and white St. Bernard as a pet in the first place?"

Listening is a rare happening among human beings. You cannot listen to the word another is speaking if you are preoccupied with your appearance, or with impressing the other, or are trying to decide what you are going to say when the other stops talking, or are debating about whether what is being said is true or relevant or agreeable. Such matters have their place, but only after listening to the word as the word is being uttered.

Listening is a private act of love in which a person gives himself to another's word, making himself accessible and vulnerable to that word.

William Stringfellow,
Friend's Journal

times, however, it won't help you receive a speaker's ideas any more clearly, and it can even lead to further communication breakdown. Consider again our example of asking directions to a friend's home. Suppose the instructions you've received are to "drive about a mile and then turn left at the traffic signal." Now imagine that there are a few common problems in this simple message. First, suppose that your friend's idea of a mile is different from yours: Your mental picture of the distance is actually closer to two miles whereas hers is closer to 300 yards. Next, consider the very likely occurrence that while your friend said, "traffic signal," she meant "stop sign"; after all, it's common for us to think one thing and say another. Keeping these problems in mind, suppose you tried to verify your understanding of the directions by asking, "After I turn at the light, how far should I go?" to which your friend replied that her house is the third from the corner. Clearly, if you parted after this exchange, you would encounter a lot of frustration before finding the elusive residence.

What was the problem here? It's easy to see that questioning didn't help, for your original idea of how far to drive and where to turn were mistaken. And contained in such mistakes is the biggest problem with questioning, for such inquiries don't tell you whether you have accurately received the information that has *already* been sent.

2. **Active listening**   Now consider another kind of feedback—one that would tell you whether you understand what had already been said before you asked additional questions. In this sort of feedback you restate in your own words the message you thought the speaker has just sent, without adding anything new. In the example of seeking directions we've been using, such rephrasing might sound like this: "So you're telling me to drive down to the traffic light by the high school and turn toward the mountains, is that it?" Immediately

So the first simple feeling I want to share with you is my enjoyment when I can really hear someone. I think perhaps this has been a long-standing characteristic of mine. I can remember this in my early grammar school days. A child would ask the teacher a question and the teacher would give a perfectly good answer to a completely different question. A feeling of pain and distress would always strike me. My reaction was, "But you didn't hear him!" I felt a sort of childish despair at the lack of communication which was (and is) so common.

Carl R. Rogers

sensing the problem, your friend could then reply, "Oh no, that's way too far. I meant that you should drive to the four-way stop by the park and turn there. Did I say stop light? I always do that when I mean stop sign!"

This simple step of restating what you thought the speaker has said before going on is commonly termed active listening, and it is a very important tool for effective listening. The thing to remember in active listening is to *paraphrase* the sender's words, not parrot them. In other words, restate what you think the speaker has said in your own terms as a way of cross-checking the information. If you simply repeat the speaker's comments *verbatim,* you'll sound as if you're foolish or hard of hearing, and just as important, you still might be misunderstanding what's been said.

At first, active listening might seem to have little to recommend it. It's an unfamiliar tool, which means that you'll have to go through a stage of awkwardness while learning it. And until you become skillful at responding in this new way, you run the risk of getting odd reactions from the people to whom you're responding. In spite of these very real problems, learning to listen actively is worth the effort, for it offers some very real advantages.

First, it boosts the odds that you'll accurately and fully understand what others are saying. We've already seen that one-way listening or even asking

questions may lead you to think you've understood a speaker when in fact you haven't. Active listening, on the other hand, serves as a way of double checking your interpretation for accuracy. Second, active listening guides you toward sincerely trying to understand another person instead of using nonlistening styles such as stage-hogging, selective listening, and so on. If you force yourself to reflect the other person's ideas in your own words, you'll have to spend your energy trying to understand that speaker instead of using your mental energy elsewhere: planning retorts, daydreaming, or defending yourself.

You can see for yourself what a difference active listening can make by trying the following exercise, either in class or with a companion on your own.

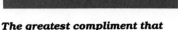

The greatest compliment that was ever paid me was when one asked me what I thought, and attended to my answer.

Henry David Thoreau

Active Listening

1. Find a partner; then move to a place where you can talk comfortably. Designate one person as *A* and the other *B*.

2. Find a subject on which you and your partner apparently disagree—a current events topic, a philosophical or moral issue, or perhaps simply a matter of personal taste.

3. *A* begins by making a statement on the subject. *B*'s job is then to paraphrase the idea back, beginning by saying something like "What I hear you saying is. . . ." It is very important that in this step *B* feeds back only what she heard *A* say without adding any judgment or interpretation. *B*'s job is simply to understand here, and doing so in no way should signify agreement or disagreement with *A*'s remarks.

4. *A* then responds by telling *B* whether or not her response was accurate. If there was some misunderstanding, *A* should make the correction, and *B* should feed back her new understanding of the statement. Continue this process until you're both sure that *B* understands *A*'s statement.

5. Now it's *B*'s turn to respond to *A*'s statement and for *A* to help the process of understanding by correcting *B*.

6. Continue this process until each partner is satisfied that she has explained herself fully and has been understood by the other person.

7. Now discuss the following questions:
   a. As a listener, how accurate was your first understanding of the speaker's statements?
   b. How did your understanding of the speaker's position change after you used active listening?
   c. Did you find that the gap between your position and that of your partner narrowed as a result of active listening?
   d. How did you feel at the end of your conversation? How does this feeling compare to your usual emotional state after discussing controversial issues?
   e. How might your life change if you used active listening at home? At work? With friends?

Listening to Help: Common Styles

So far, we've talked about how becoming a better listener can help you to understand other people more often and more clearly. If you use the skills presented so far, you should be rewarded by communicating far more accurately with others every day. But there's another way in which listening can improve your relationships. Strange as it may sound, often you can help other people solve their own problems simply by learning to listen—actively and with concern.

To understand how listening to others can be so helpful, you need to realize that many times you can't solve people's problems for them. You can, however, help them work things out for themselves. This is a difficult lesson to learn. When someone you care for is in trouble and feeling bad, your first tendency is to try and make things better—to answer questions, soothe hurts, fix whatever seems to be the problem. But even when you're sure you know what's right for a person, it's often necessary to let that person discover the solution independently.

This need to let people find their own answers doesn't mean that you have to stand by and do nothing when a friend is in trouble. Fortunately there's a way of responding that you can use to help others find solutions to their problems—even when you don't know these solutions yourself. But before we introduce this technique, take a few moments to explore your present style of responding to others' problems and see how well it works. You should complete this exercise right now, before continuing.

What Would You Say?

1. In a moment you'll read a list of situations in which someone tells you of a problem. In each case, write out the words you'd use in responding to this person.

2. Here are the statements:
   a. I don't know what to do about my parents. It seems as if they just don't understand me. Everything I like seems to go against their values, and they just won't accept my feelings as being right for me. It's not that they don't love me—they do. But they don't accept me.
   b. I've been pretty discouraged lately. I just can't get a good relationship going with any guys. . . . I mean a romantic relationship . . . you know. I have plenty of men whom I'm good friends with, but that's always as far as it goes. I'm tired of being just a pal. . . . I want to be more than that.
   c. (child to parents) I hate you guys! You always go out and leave me with some stupid sitter. Why don't you like me?
   d. I'm really bummed out. I don't know what I want to do with my life. I'm pretty tired of school, but there aren't any good jobs around, and I sure don't want to join the service. I could just drop out for a while, but that doesn't really sound very good either.
   e. Things really seem to be kind of lousy in my marriage lately. It's not that we fight too much or anything, but all the excitement seems to be gone. It's like we're in a rut, and it keeps getting worse. . . .
   f. I keep getting the idea that my boss is angry at me. It seems as if lately he hasn't been joking around very much, and he hasn't said anything at all about my work for about three weeks now. I wonder what I should do.

3. Once you've written your response to each of these messages, imagine the probable outcome of the conversation that would have followed. If you've tried this exercise in class, you might have two group members role-play each statement. Based on your idea of how the conversation might have gone, decide which responses were helpful and which were unproductive.

Most of the responses you made probably fell into one of several categories. None of these ways of responding is good or bad in itself, but it often happens that we use these ways when they aren't best suited to helping someone we care about solve a problem. There's a proper time and place for each kind of response. The problem usually occurs, however, when we use them in the wrong situations or depend on one of two styles of responses for all situations.

As you read the following description of these ways of responding, see which ones you used most frequently in the previous exercise, and think about the results that probably would have occurred from your response.

Advising   When approached with another's problem, the most common tendency is an **advising response:** to help by offering a solution. Although such a response is sometimes valuable, often it isn't as helpful as you might think.

Often your suggestion may not offer the best course to follow, in which case it can even be harmful. There's often a temptation to tell others how we would behave in their place, but it's important to realize that what's right for one person may not be right for another. A related consequence of advising is that it often allows others to avoid responsibility for their decisions. A partner who follows a suggestion of yours that doesn't work out can always pin the blame on you. Finally, often people simply don't want advice: They may not be ready to accept it, needing instead simply to talk out their thoughts and feelings.

Before offering advice, then, you need to be sure that three conditions are present. First, you should be confident that your advice is correct. It's essential to resist the temptation to act like an authority on matters about which you know little. It's equally important to remember that just because a course of action worked for you doesn't guarantee that it will be correct for everybody. Second, you need to be sure that the person seeking your advice is truly ready to accept it. In this way you can avoid the frustration of making good suggestions, only to find that the person with the problem had another solution in mind all the time. Finally, when offering advice, you should be certain that the receiver won't blame

B. C.   **by Johnny hart**

DR. PETER ← → HEAD SHRINKER

I'VE BEEN HAVING TROUBLE COMMUNICATING WITH PEOPLE...

HOW LONG HAS IT BEEN GOING ON?

...SO I THOUGHT MAYBE YOU COULD HELP ME.

5·24

> ## It is always a silly thing to give advice, but to give good advice is absolutely fatal.
>
> Oscar Wilde

you if the advice doesn't work. You may be offering the suggestions, but the choice and responsibility of following them is up to the other person.

Judging   A judging response evaluates the sender's thoughts or behaviors in some way. The judgment may be favorable—"That's a good idea" or "You're on the right track now"—or unfavorable—"An attitude like that won't get you anywhere." But in either case it implies that the person doing the judging is in some way qualified to pass judgment on the speaker's thoughts or actions.

Sometimes negative judgments are purely critical. How many times have you heard such responses as "Well, you asked for it!" or "I *told* you so!" or "You're just feeling sorry for yourself"? Although comments like these can sometimes serve as a verbal slap that brings problem-holders to their senses, they usually make matters worse.

In other cases negative judgments are less critical. These involve what we usually call *constructive criticism*, which is intended to help the problem-holder improve in the future. This is the sort of response given by friends about everything from the choice of clothing to jobs to friends. Another common setting for constructive criticism occurs in school, where instructors evaluate students' work to help them master concepts and skills. But whether it's justified or not, even constructive criticism runs the risk of arousing defensiveness since it may threaten the self-concept of the person at whom it is directed.

Judgments have the best chance of being received when two conditions exist. First, the person with the problem should have requested an evaluation from you. In addition, your judgments should be genuinely constructive and not designed to be disparaging. If you can remember to follow these two guidelines, your judgments will probably be less frequent and better received.

Analyzing   In an **analyzing statement,** the listener offers an interpretation to a speaker's message. Analyses like these are probably familiar to you:

"I think what's really bothering you is. . . ."
"She's doing it because. . . ."
"I don't think you really meant that."
"Maybe the problem started when she. . . ."

Interpretations are often effective ways to help people with problems to consider alternative meanings—ways they would have never thought of without your help. Sometimes a clear analysis will make a confusing problem suddenly clear, either suggesting a solution or at least providing an understanding of what is occurring.

In other cases, an analysis can create more problems than it solves. There are two problems with analyzing. First, your interpretation may not be correct, in which case the speaker may become even more confused by accepting it.

N-17

Second, even if your analysis is accurate, telling it to the problem-holder might not be useful. There's a chance that it will arouse defensiveness (since analysis implies superiority and evaluativeness), and even if it doesn't, the person may not be able to understand your view of the problem without working it out personally.

How can you know when it's helpful to offer an analysis? There are several guidelines to follow. First, it's important to offer your interpretation in a tentative way rather than as absolute fact. There's a big difference between saying, "Maybe the reason is . . ." and insisting, "This is the truth." Second, your analysis ought to have a reasonable chance of being correct. We've already said that a wild, unlikely interpretation can leave a person more confused than before. Third, you ought to be sure that the other person will be receptive to your analysis. Even if you're completely accurate, your thoughts won't help if the problem-holder isn't ready to consider what you say. Finally, you should be sure that your motive is truly to help the other person. It's sometimes tempting to offer an analysis to show how brilliant you are or even to make the other person feel bad for not having thought of the right answer in the first place. Needless to say, an analysis offered under these conditions isn't very helpful.

Questioning   A few pages ago we talked about questioning as one way for you to understand others better. A questioning response can also be a way to help others think about their problem and understand it more clearly. For example, questioning can help a problem-holder define vague ideas more precisely. You might respond to a friend with a line of questioning: "You said Greg has been acting 'differently' toward you lately. What has he been doing?" Another example of a question that helps clarify is as follows: "You told your roommates that you wanted them to be more helpful in keeping the place clean. What would you like them to do?"

Questions can also encourage a problem-holder to examine a situation in more detail by talking either about what happened or about personal feelings, for example, "How did you feel when they turned you down? What did you do then?" This type of questioning is particularly helpful when you are dealing with someone who is quiet or is unwilling under the circumstances to talk about the problem very much.

Although asking questions can definitely be helpful, two dangers can arise from using this style too much or at the wrong times. The first is that your questions may lead the problem-holder on a wild goose chase, away from a solution to the problem. For instance, asking, "When did the problem begin?" might provide some clue about how to solve it—but it could also lead to a long digression that would only confuse matters. As with advice, it's important to be sure you're on the right track before asking questions.

A second danger is that questioning can also be a way of disguising advice or criticism. We've all been questioned by parents, teachers, or other figures who seemed to be trying to trap or indirectly to guide us. In this way, questioning becomes a strategy and often implies that the person doing the asking already has some idea of what direction the discussion should take.

Supporting   A supporting response can take several forms. Sometimes it involves reassuring: "You've got nothing to worry about—I know you'll do a good

Most conversations seem to be carried out on two levels, the verbal level and the emotional level. The verbal level contains those things which are socially acceptable to say, but it is used as a means of satisfying emotional needs. Yesterday a friend related something that someone had done to her. I told her why I thought the person had acted the way he had and she became very upset and started arguing with me. Now, the reason is clear. I had been listening to her words and had paid no attention to her feelings. Her words had described how terribly this other person had treated her, but her emotions had been saying, "Please understand how I felt. Please accept my feeling the way I did." The last thing she wanted to hear from me was an explanation of the other person's behavior.

Hugh Prather

job." In other cases, support comes through comforting: "Don't worry. We all love you." We can also support people in need by distracting them with humor, kidding, and joking.

Sometimes a person needs encouragement, and in these cases a supporting response can be the best thing. But in many instances this kind of comment isn't helpful at all; in fact, it can even make things worse. Telling a person who is obviously upset that everything is all right or joking about what seems like a serious problem can communicate the idea that you don't think the problem is really worth all the fuss. People might see your comments as a putdown, leaving them feeling worse than before. As with the other styles we've discussed, supporting *can* be helpful . . . but only in certain circumstances.

You can get an idea of some problems that come from using the preceding helping styles by reading this dialog:

Tom   Boy, there must be something wrong with me. Last night I blew it on my first date with Linda. That's the way it always goes—I never seem to do anything right. I'm really a clod.

Bill   Oh, well, cheer up; you'll probably forget about it in a few days. (*supporting*)

Tom   No I won't. This dating thing really has me depressed. I feel like a social outcast or something.

Bill   Well, I think you're worrying about it too much. Just forget about it. It's probably your worrying that messes things up in the first place. (*judging, advising, analyzing*)

Tom   But I can't help worrying about it. How would you feel if you hadn't had a woman really like you in about three years?

Bill   Well, what do you think the problem is? Have you been polite to them? Do you get drunk or something? There must be some reason why you blow it. (*questioning*)

Tom   I don't know. I've tried all kinds of approaches, and none of them works.

Bill   Well, there's your problem. You're just not being yourself. You have to be natural, and then women will like you for what you are. There's really nothing to it—just be yourself, and everything will be cool. (*judging, analyzing, supporting*)

We've used this example to illustrate how good intentions aren't always helpful. Bill may have been right about what caused Tom's dating problem and how he could solve it, but because Tom didn't discover the answer himself, it most likely wasn't useful to him. As you know, people can often ignore the truth even when it's so obvious that you'd think they would trip over it.

This example shows that good intentions aren't always helpful. Even if your advice, judgments, and analysis are correct and your questions are sincere, and even if your support comes from the best motives, these responses often fail to help. One recent survey demonstrates how poorly such traditional responses work.[4] Mourners who had recently suffered from the death of a loved one reported that 80 percent of the statements made to them were unhelpful. Nearly half of the "helpful" statements were advice: "You've got to get out more." "Don't question God's will." Despite their frequency, these suggestions were only helpful 3 percent of the time. The next most frequent response was reassurance,

So Penseroso

Come, megrims, mollygrubs and collywobbles!
Come, gloom that limps, and misery that hobbles!
Come also, most exquisite melancholiage,
As dank and decadent as November foliage!
I crave to shudder in your moist embrace,
To feel your oystery fingers on my face.
This is my hour of sadness and of soulfulness,
And cursed be he who dissipates my dolefulness.
I do not desire to be cheered,
I desire to retire, I am thinking of growing a beard,
A sorrowful beard, with a mournful, a dolorous hue in it,
With ashes and glue in it.
I want to be drunk with despair,
I want to caress my care,
I do not wish to be blithe,
I wish to recoil and writhe,
I will revel in cosmic woe,
And I want my woe to show.
This is the morbid moment,
This is the ebony hour.
Aroint thee, sweetness and light!
I want to be dark and sour!
Away with the bird that twitters!
All that glitters is jitters!
Roses, roses are gray,
Violets cry Boo! and frighten me.
Sugar is stimulating,
And people conspire to brighten me.
Go hence, people, go hence!
Go sit on a picket fence!
Go gargle with mineral oil,
Go out and develop a boil!
Melancholy is what I brag and boast of,
Melancholy I mean to make the most of,
You beaming optimists shall not destroy it.
But while I am at it, I intend to enjoy it.
Go, people, stuff your mouths with soap,
And remember, please, that when I mope, I mope!

Ogden Nash

such as "She's out of pain now." Like advice, this kind of support was only helpful 3 percent of the time. Far more helpful were expressions that acknowledged the mourner's feelings. To understand how to communicate this kind of understanding, read on.

Active Listening: Another Helping Response

What can you say when none of the styles we've discussed so far seem to be right? Fortunately there is another way of responding that can often be helpful in showing your support while letting others solve their own problems. This style involves active listening, building on the techniques of paraphrasing introduced earlier in this chapter.[5]

Active listening lets others know that you're interested in what they have to say and that you care about them. And amazingly enough, simply feeding back others' ideas often helps them sort out and solve problems for themselves. If you're lucky, you probably know people who can help you understand things better simply by listening. These people are probably active listeners even though they don't know it.

You can begin to see how active listening works by imagining how the previous conversation might have gone if Bill had used this method.

Tom   Boy, there must be something wrong with me. Last night I blew it on my first date with Linda. That's the way it always goes—I never seem to do anything right. I'm really a clod.

Bill   You're pretty upset because things never seem to work out on your dates, huh?

Tom   Yeah. And I don't know what my problem is. I'm not stupid or anything. I always take them to nice places, and I don't get loaded and act like a fool or anything. But I always blow it.

Bill   So you always try to do everything just right—be a gentleman and all that, but it never works out.

Tom   Yeah. I really want to make it work, and so I wind up maybe being too much of a gentleman. I don't act natural. And then when that doesn't work, I get even more nervous the next time, which makes the woman nervous, and on it goes. It's a vicious circle.

Bill   So it's your nervousness that you think hangs you up? You're afraid of not being a good date, and so you try too hard, which the women don't like.

Tom   Yeah. I guess what I have to do is just be myself—not try to force things or act like I'm right out of some suave movie or something. Maybe I'll try that. . . .

Although active listening won't always be this successful, it's easy to see how this style of reflecting could often work. Active listening is a useful way of responding; combined with your other ways of reacting, it can turn you into a better helper.

Active Listening Defined   When you use active listening as a helping tool, your reflection should contain two elements. The first is a restatement of the speaker's *thoughts*. Though it might seem unnecessary to restate something the other person just uttered, your playing it back can often help the speaker to take a more objective look at what's been said, possibly to clarify the idea. Look at a simple example:

Other   I can't believe my boss! She keeps piling the work on, and I'll never get caught up. What does she think I am?

You   It doesn't seem fair, is that it?

Other   Well, she isn't exactly picking on me; everybody is loaded with work, including her. It's just that I didn't expect the job would be such a hassle when I took it, and I'm wondering if it's worth the money.

You   So you're thinking about quitting.

Other   Well, not right now. But maybe after the school year is over and I have more time, I'll look around. I can handle it for a few more months, but not another year!

In many cases you need to go beyond reflecting thoughts and also paraphrase the often unspoken *emotions* that accompany the verbal message. This kind of paraphrasing is especially true when someone has a problem. Since many people aren't aware of how they feel, your statement can help bring the troublesome emotion to the surface and clarify it. Look at this example:

Other   I can't believe what a thoughtless jerk my brother is. Whenever I call him to talk, he always tell me that I'm his "special little sister," but he hasn't called me or written in over a year. I'm always the one who's reaching out. He's such a phony!

The reality of the other person is not in what he reveals to you, but in what he cannot reveal to you.

Therefore, if you would understand him, listen not to what he says but rather to what he does not say.

Kahlil Gibran

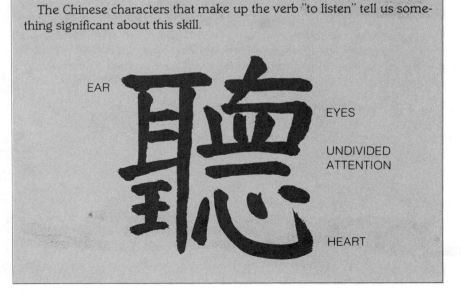

The Chinese characters that make up the verb "to listen" tell us something significant about this skill.

EAR

EYES

UNDIVIDED ATTENTION

HEART

In the Hospital one of my nursing patients said to me "I'm so much thinner—look at my arms and legs. I said "great," assuming that he was pleased. Later I found out that he was depressed about losing so much weight. Instead of offering support, my reply had left him feeling worse than before.

If I had paraphrased ("Sounds like you're glad to have lost weight"), he could have cleared up the misunderstanding, and maybe I could have helped him.

You   It sounds as if you're really mad at him for not making any effort to keep in touch.

Other   Oh, I suppose it isn't the letters themselves that matter. It just makes me think he doesn't care about me.

You   So you're not mad so much as hurt, huh?

Other   That's the truth. I'm not mad at all. I just wish I knew how much I really do matter to him.

Types of Active Listening   Counseling psychologist Gerard Egan describes several types of active listening (which he calls *accurate empathetic understanding*).[6] For the sake of simplicity, we can divide them into two categories.

1. **Simple reflection**   In **simple reflection,** you rephrase what the speaker has *explicitly* stated. There is no digging at hidden meanings or implied messages; rather, you simply put into your own words what you've heard. You may have to verbalize a feeling that the speaker only suggests, but beyond this your goal is to serve as a verbal sounding board.

Other   My friend keeps inviting me to go to church with her even though I've told her politely that it's not for me. I wish she'd lay off.

You   You're getting irritated at her for not respecting your decision.

Other   I can't decide whether to stay in school or skip a year to travel. The trip sounds great, but I know that if I quit, I might not go back.

You   So you're afraid that this wouldn't be just a vacation.

Although this type of simple reflecting might seem to be of little help, we'll soon explain several of its advantages.

2. **Interpretative reflection**   With **interpretative reflection,** you go beyond simply restating what the speaker has said by reflecting what appears to you to be an underlying message. There are two types of interpretative reflections. The first calls for you to summarize what the other person has been saying and to identify themes in these messages. Here are some sample interpretative reflections:

> "You've been talking for almost a half hour now about whether or not to move out of the apartment, and during that time the only reason you gave for staying was that moving would be a hassle. From what you've said, I get the idea that you'd really like to move. Does that make sense?"

> "I've been trying to boil down what you've been saying—tell me if this is it. You're sorry that you said those things last night, but you do think you had a reason for getting angry."

In a second variety of interpretative reflection, you try to paraphrase thoughts or feelings the speaker hasn't stated but that you suspect are the real message.

> "You keep telling me that everything is fine, but every time the subject of school comes up, all the enthusiasm goes out of your voice. I get the idea that something there is bothering you. Does that seem right?"

"When you talk about all the petty tasks your boss gives you and the questions he asks, I hear you saying that you're hurt and disappointed that he hasn't given you more responsibility."

You can see that responses like these contain an element of analysis. The feature that transforms them into active listening is their *tentative* quality. Notice that all the examples you just read are phrased tentatively rather than being dogmatic, mind-reading pronouncements. This conditional approach is more than a matter of choosing words carefully, for it indicates that you're simply giving an interpretation and allowing the speaker to decide whether or not it is accurate. This approach is very different from that of the analyzer who states with great certainty, "I know what you're *really* thinking. . . ."

As with analyzing, there's a danger in doing too much interpretative reflecting. Most often your simple paraphrasing of thoughts and emotions will be sufficient to let the speaker sort out the problem. Going overboard with your helpful perceptions might add to, rather than decrease, the speaker's confusion. Most important, before you give your interpretations, you should feel confident that they are accurate. This style of listening should not turn into a guessing game in which you try out every interpretation that occurs to you.

Advantages of Active Listening   When we talked about active listening as a way of understanding others, we discussed two of its advantages. We saw then that it increases the chances that you're receiving a message accurately, and it also makes you pay attention. In addition to these benefits, listening reflectively has advantages as a tool for helping others.

First, it takes the burden off you as a friend. Simply being there to understand what's on other peoples' minds often makes it possible for them to clarify their own problems. This means you don't have to know all the answers to help. Also, helping by active listening means you don't need to guess at reasons or solutions that might not be correct. Thus, both you and your friend are saved from going on a wild goose chase.

A second advantage is that active listening is a great way to get through layers of hidden meanings. Often people express their ideas, problems, or feelings in strangely coded ways. Active listening can sometimes help cut through to the real message.

The third advantage is that it's usually the best way to encourage others to share more of themselves with you. Knowing that you're interested will decrease the sense of threat, and they will let down some defenses. In this sense active listening is simply a good way to learn more about others and a good foundation on which to build a relationship.

Another benefit is the catharsis active listening provides for the person with a problem. Even when there's no apparent solution, simply having the chance to talk about what's wrong can be a tremendous relief. This sort of release often makes it easier to accept unchangeable situations rather than complaining about or resisting them.

Finally, at the very least active listening lets the other person know that you understand the problem. Although this might seem true of other helping styles, understanding isn't always present. For instance, you've probably had well-intentioned helpers reassure you or offer advice in a way that proved they didn't know what was upsetting you. Because it requires paraphrasing, active listening is the surest way to help you understand others' problems.

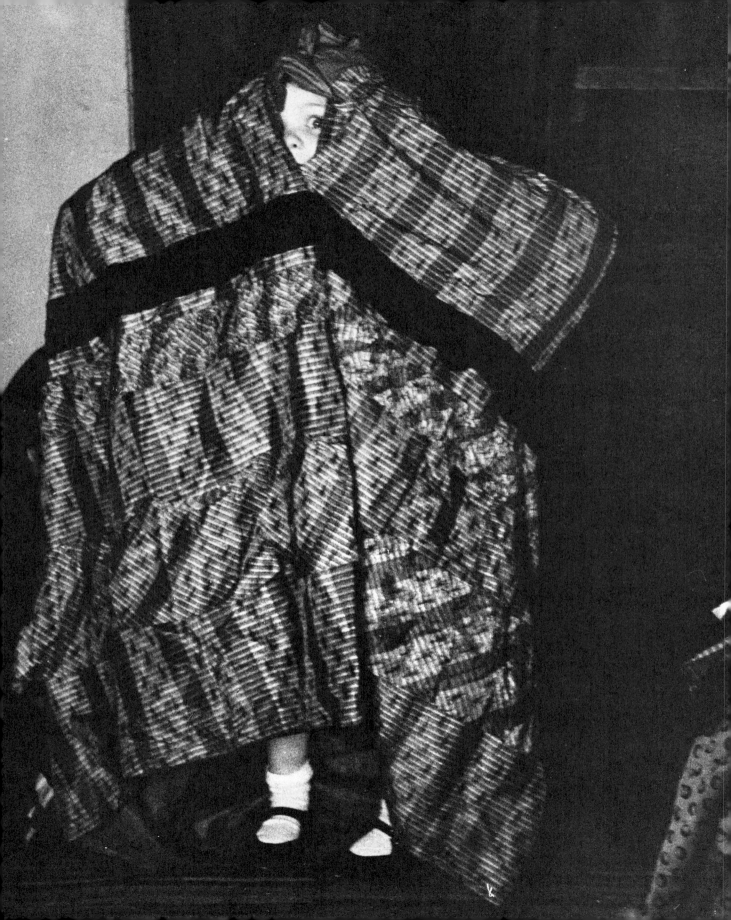

Danny

Mother   It's late. Turn out the light and go to sleep.

Danny   I'm not going to sleep.

Mother   You have to, it's late. You'll be tired tomorrow.

Danny   I'm not going to sleep.

Mother   (harshly)   Turn that light off immediately!

Danny   (flatly) I'm *never* going to sleep.

Mother   (I feel like strangling him. I'm so tired, I can't stand this tonight . . . I go into the kitchen, smoke a cigarette, decide that I'm going in there and try active listening even if it kills me! Entering Danny's room) C'mon, it's late but I'll sit on your bed for a while and rest my feet before I do the dishes [She takes the book from him, turns off the light, closes the door, and sits on the bed beside him, leaning back against the wall.]

Danny   Gimme that book! Don't turn off the light. Get out of here. I don't want you in here. I'm not going to sleep. I hate you!

Mother   You're feeling angry.

Danny   Yeah, I hate school and I'll never go back, never!

Mother   (He loves school.) You're fed up with school.

Danny   It's horrible. I'm not good in school. Don't know anything. I ought to be in second grade. [He's in third.] Math, I don't know it. [He is very good at it.] The teacher must think we're in a high school or something.

Mother   Math's pretty hard for you.

Danny   No! It's easy. Just don't feel like doing it.

Mother   Oh.

Danny   (sudden shift) I sure like baseball. Much rather play baseball than go to school.

Mother   You really like baseball.

Danny   Do you *have* to go to college? [Oldest brother will soon enter college, and there is much family talk about it.]

Mother   No.

Danny   How long do you have to go to school?

Mother   You have to finish high school.

Danny   Well, I'm not going to college. Don't have to, right?

Mother   Right.

Danny   Good, I'll play baseball.

Mother   Baseball's really fun.

Danny   Sure is. [Completely calmed down, talking comfortably, no anger.] Well, good night.

Mother   Good night.

Danny   Will you sit up with me some more?

Mother   Uh huh.

Danny   (pulls up covers which had been kicked off; carefully covers up Mother's knees and pats them) Comfortable?

Mother   Yes, thank you.

Danny   You're welcome [Period of quiet, then Danny starts snorting and sniffing with much exaggerated clearing of throat and nose.] Snort, snort, snort. [Danny does have slight allergy with stuffy nose, but the symptoms are never acute. Mother had never heard Danny snort like this before.]

Mother   Nose bugging you?

Danny   Yeah, sure is. Think I need the stuffy nose medicine?

Mother   Do you think it would help?

Danny   No. [Snort, snort.]

Mother   Nose really bugs you.

Danny   Yeah [snort]. [Sigh of anguish.] Oh, I wish you didn't have to breathe through your nose when you sleep.

Mother   (very surprised at this, tempted to ask where that idea came from) You think you have to breathe through your nose when you sleep?

Danny   I *know* I have to.

Mother   You feel sure about it.

Danny   I know it. Tommy told me, a long time ago. [Much admired friend, two years older.] He said you have to. You can't breathe through your mouth when you sleep.

Mother   You mean you aren't supposed to?

Danny   You just *can't* [snort]. Mommy, that's so, isn't it? I mean, you *gotta* breathe through your nose when you sleep, don't you? [Long explanation—many questions from Danny about admired friend. "He wouldn't lie to me."]

Mother   (explains that friend is probably trying to help but kids get false information sometimes. Much emphasis from Mother that everyone breathes through the mouth when sleeping.)

Danny   (very relieved) Well, good night.

Mother   Good night. [Danny breathing easily through mouth.]

Danny   (suddenly) [Snort.]

Mother   Still scary.

Danny   Uh huh. Mommy, what if I go to sleep breathing through my mouth—and my nose is stuffy—and what if in the middle of the night when I'm sound asleep—what if I closed my mouth?

Mother   (realizes that he has been afraid to go to sleep for years because he is afraid he would choke to death; thinks, "Oh, my poor baby") You're afraid you might choke maybe?

Danny   Uh huh. You *gotta* breathe. [He couldn't say, "I might die."]

Mother   (more explaining) It simply couldn't happen. Your mouth would open—just like your heart pumps blood or your eyes blink.

Danny   Are you *sure?*

Mother   Yes, I'm sure.

Danny   Well, good night.

Mother   Good night, dear. [Kiss. Danny is asleep in minutes.]

Thomas Gordon,
Parent Effectiveness Training

They Learn to Aid Customers by Becoming Good Listeners

Do you need someone to listen to your troubles?

Have your hair done.

Beauty salon chairs may be to today's women what conversation-centered backyard fences were to their grandmothers and psychiatrists' couches are to their wealthier contemporaries.

"We are not as family-oriented as our ancestors were," says counselor-trainer Andy Thompson. "They listened to and helped each other. Now that we have become a society of individuals isolated from one another by cars, telephones, jobs and the like, we have had to find other listeners."

Community training program director for Crisis House, Thompson has designed and is conducting human relations training sessions for workers to whom customers tend to unburden their woes most frequently—cosmetologists, bartenders and cab-drivers.

"People can definitely help others just by letting them talk," he said. "Relatives, friends or spouses who listen do a lot to keep the mental health of this country at a reasonable rate. Workers in situations that encourage communications can make the same meaningful contribution."

Thompson explained that his training is not meant to replace, or be confused with, professional treatment or counseling. His students fill a gap between family and professionals.

"There are not enough psychiatrists or psychologists to go around," he said. "And some professionals become so technical that

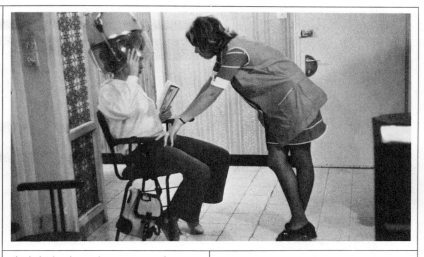

their help doesn't mean much to persons who just need a someone who will let them get problems and questions out in the open where they can look at them."

Thompson's first course of training, completed recently, was for cosmetologists.

The human relations training program attempts to make the most of these built-in assets by using a method Thompson calls "reflective listening."

"The purpose is to let the customer talk enough to clarify her own thinking," he said. "We are not interested in having cosmetologists tell women what to do, but to give them a chance to choose their own course of action.

"There is a tendency among listeners to try to rescue a person with problems and pull them out of negative situations. People don't really want that. They just want to discuss what is on their minds and reach their own conclusions."

Cosmetologists are taught to use phrases that aid customers in ana-

lyzing their thoughts. Some of the phrases are, "You seem to think..." "You sound like..." "You appear to be..." "As I get it, you..." and "It must seem to you that..."

There also are barriers to conversation that the cosmetologists are taught to avoid.

"A constant bombardment of questions can disrupt communications," Thompson said. "Commands will have the same effect. Many of them are impossible to follow anyway.

"How many can respond to orders to 'Stop feeling depressed,' 'Don't be so upset,' or 'Don't think about it.'

"The same applies to negative criticism, 'That's dumb,' for instance; and evaluations, such as 'Oh, you're just confused.'

"Comments that seem threatening—'You had better stop feeling sad,' as an example—will end a conversation as quickly as changing the subject or not paying attention."

San Diego Union

When to Use Active Listening   Active listening isn't appropriate in all situations. There are several factors to consider before you choose to use this style.

1. *Is the problem complex enough?* Sometimes people are simply looking for information and not trying to work out their feelings. At times like this, active listening would be out of place. If someone asks you for the time of day, you'd do better simply to give her the information than to respond by saying, "You want to know what time it is." If you're fixing dinner and someone wants to know when it will be ready, it would be exasperating to reply "You're interested in knowing when we'll be eating."

2. *Do you have the necessary time and concern?* The kind of paraphrasing we've been discussing here takes a good deal of time. Therefore, if you're in a hurry to do something besides listen, it's wise to avoid starting a conversation you won't be able to finish. Even more important than time is concern. It's not necessarily wrong to be too preoccupied to help or even to be unwilling to exert the considerable effort that active listening requires: You can't

© 1978 United Media, Inc.

help everyone with every problem. It's far better to state honestly that you're
unable or unwilling to help than to pretend to care when you really don't.

3. **Can you withhold judgment?** You've already seen that an active listener allows
   other people to find their own answers. You should only use this style if you
   can comfortably paraphrase without injecting your own judgments. It's
   sometimes tempting to rephrase others' comments in a way that leads them
   toward the solution you think is best without ever clearly stating your intentions. As you will read in Chapter Nine, this kind of strategy is likely to
   backfire by causing defensiveness if it's discovered. If you think the situation
   meets the criteria for advice described earlier in this chapter, you should offer
   your suggestions openly.

4. **Is your active listening in proportion to other responses?** Although active
   listening can be a very helpful way of responding to others' problems, it can
   become artificial and annoying when it's overused. This is especially true if
   you suddenly begin to use it as a major response. Even if such responses
   are potentially helpful, this sudden switch in your behavior will be so out of

The Superactive Listener

Just as there are those who seek cheap psychotherapy, there are others who are bent on dispensing it. Having a conversation with such an individual is like trying to punch a hole in a pond—you can try as hard as you like, but when you're done, there's just an unruffled surface reflecting your own face. "You're feeling under some pressure" is just not an appropriate response to a request for directions to the bathroom. These people are often immune to feedback. Tell them "I thought the point you made in the meeting was off-target," and they'll reply, "You thought my point was not quite on target." Get mad at them and they reflect your feelings: "You're saying you're angry because I didn't get the report I promised you in on time." You don't have to worry about excessive self-disclosure from such a person, but after dealing with him or her for a time, you may find yourself beating your head rhythmically against a wall.

Kristin Sheridan Libbee and Michael Libbee

character that others might find it distracting. A far better way to use active listening is gradually to introduce it into your repertoire of helpfulness, so that you can become comfortable with it without appearing too awkward. Another way to become more comfortable with this style is to start using it on real but relatively minor problems, so that you'll be more adept at knowing how and when to use it when a big crisis does occur.

More Readings on Listening

Axline, Virginia M. *Dibs: In Search of Self.* New York: Ballantine Books, 1967.
  This is a fascinating account of a child's transition from isolation to happy normality. Beautifully illustrates how active listening can be a therapeutic tool.
———. *Play Therapy.* New York: Ballantine Books, 1969.
  A description of the author's technique for working with troubled children. An important part of her work involves the skillful use of active listening.
Beier, Ernst G., and Evans G. Valens. *People-Reading: How We Control Others, How They Control Us.* New York: Stein and Day, 1975.
  Chapter 2, "How to Listen," Chapter 3, "How Not to Listen," and Chapter 4, "Listening to Feelings," expand on the information that we have been able to include in our one chapter. The many examples are extremely helpful in adding to your understanding of the art of listening.
Egan, Gerard. *Interpersonal Living.* Monterey, Calif.: Brooks/Cole, 1976.
  Egan gives a detailed description of the various types of active listening as a helping tool. Especially useful are Chapters 6, 7, and 9.
Floyd, James J. *Listening: A Practical Approach.* Glenview, Ill.: Scott, Foresman, 1985.
  A brief, skills-oriented introduction to the subject of listening. Coverage includes the importance of listening, ineffective listening habits, and guidelines for both listening to acquire information and listening to help others.

Glatthorn, Allan A., and Herbert R. Adams. *Listen Your Way to Management Success*. Glenview, Ill.: Scott, Foresman, 1983.
As its title suggests, this book is written for current and would-be managers. There is less emphasis on research than in other listening surveys but more attention to communication in on-the-job settings. Glatthorn and Adams also discuss how listening operates in conflicts and in dealing with power in organizations.

Gordon, Thomas. *Parent Effectiveness Training*. New York: Wyden, 1970.
Although Gordon's method is aimed at parents, the principles of communication he discusses are equally appropriate for other types of relationships. His treatment of active listening is clear and detailed.

_____. *P.E.T. in Action*. New York: Wyden, 1976.
In a question-and-answer format, Gordon covers most of the problems and misunderstandings that occur when people first try active listening.

Rogers, Carl R. *On Becoming a Person*. Boston: Houghton Mifflin, 1961.
The best-known practitioner of active listening describes the process.

Steil, Lyman K., Larry L. Barker, and Kittie W. Watson. *Effective Listening: Key to Your Success*. Reading, Mass.: Addison-Wesley, 1983.
Another book that emphasizes listening in business settings. Self-quizzes, quotations, and many examples make the book both informative and interesting.

Wolff, Florence I., Nadine C. Marsnik, William S. Tacey, and Ralph G. Nichols. *Perceptive Listening*. New York: Holt, Rinehart and Winston, 1983.
A prescriptive approach to improving listening skills. The book also clarifies ten common misconceptions about listening.

Wolvin, Andrew W., and Carolyn G. Coakley. *Listening*, 2d ed. Dubuque, Iowa: W. C. Brown, 1985.
Wolvin and Coakley describe the process of listening and examine the functions it serves: for entertainment, understanding, criticism, and so on.

Part Three Looking at Relationships

Chapter Eight

"We have a terrific relationship."
"I'm looking for a better relationship."
"Our relationship has changed a lot."

Relationship is one of those words that people use a great deal yet have a hard time defining. Take a moment to see if you can explain the term. It isn't as easy as it might seem.

The dictionary defines a relationship as "the mode in which two or more things stand to one another." This is true enough: You are tall in relation to some people and short in relation to others, and we are more or less wealthy only in comparison to others. But physical and economic relationships don't tell us much that is useful about interpersonal communication.

Interpersonal relationships involve the way people deal with one another *socially*. But what is it about their social interaction that defines a relationship? What makes some relationships "good" and others "bad"? We can answer this question by recalling the three kinds of social needs introduced in Chapter One: inclusion, control, and affection. When we judge the quality of personal relationships, we are usually describing how well those social needs are being met. Having come this far, we can define the term **interpersonal relationship** as an association in which the parties meet each other's social needs to a greater or lesser degree.

In this chapter we will take a close look at the nature of interpersonal relationships. We will examine the various ways a relationship can be defined. You will read a number of explanations for why we form positive relationships with some people and not with others. We will look at the stages through which relationships commonly progress. Finally, we will examine the subject of self-disclosure, looking at its effects on interpersonal relationships and offering guidelines about when it is and is not appropriate.

Dimensions of Interpersonal Relationships

What qualities define a relationship? Is it the amount of time we spend together? The things we say and do? The way we feel about each other? By examining several ways of categorizing relationships we can take a fresh look at what makes some communication truly interpersonal.

Context The most obvious way to classify relationships is by the contexts in which they occur. For example, the family provides a rich set of relationships for most of us. We also form relationships on the job, with fellow workers and in some cases with members of the public. School, neighborhood, religious faith, sports, and hobbies—all these contexts form bases for relationships.

Despite the visibility of the communication setting, context doesn't play much role in shaping *interpersonal* relationships. Recall from Chapter One that we defined interpersonal communication as possessing three unique qualities: a minimum of stereotyping, development of unique rules, and increased self-disclosure. Once we consider these factors, it's apparent that no context guarantees them. Sadly, even husbands and wives or parents and children can have impersonal, superficial relationships. The parties go through the motions,

> *For communication to have meaning it must have a life. It must transcend "you" and "me" and become "us." . . . In a small way we then grow out of our old selves and become something new.*
>
> Hugh Prather

rarely revealing themselves or working to create a unique arrangement that reflects their personalities. Clearly, then, context isn't useful as a basis for categorizing interpersonal relationships.

Time   The length of time a relationship lasts is one measure of its importance. We have all heard the line "our relationship goes back a long way," and we usually consider such statements as indicating how strong and valuable the relationship is. The same principle holds true for enemies. The length of time a dispute lasts is one measure of its importance. Not *all* long-standing relationships are important, however. Some can last for years and remain relatively superficial, like the neighbors who politely exchange clichés about the weather from time to time.

A better indicator of importance is the amount of time we *choose* to spend with others. You might work—or even party—with certain people out of obligation but avoid them whenever possible. Time voluntarily spent is a partial indicator of a relationship's importance, but *how* the parties communicate when together is even more important, as we will now see.

Intimacy   The dictionary defines *intimate* as "closely personal, characterized by close union, contact, association, acquaintance, or the like." This characterization makes it obvious why intimacy is such an important dimension of interpersonal relationships: By definition interpersonal relationships *are* intimate in one way or another. And for the most part, intimacy is achieved through communication.

The word *intimacy* can describe three very different kinds of relationships: intellectual, emotional, and physical. Few relationships are intimate in every

"Actually, I'm seeking a meaningless relationship."

Drawing by Richter. © 1970 The New Yorker Magazine, Inc.

respect—which explains why our relationships with people we describe as "close" differ so much. Consider your own interpersonal relationships with friends, family members, and others. In what ways is each one intimate? Total intimacy—emotional, intellectual, and physical—is rare. When it does occur the bond between partners is a strong one. This explains why good marriages become the most important relationship for many people. It also explains why marriages that don't achieve intimacy on some or all of these levels are less satisfying.

Most intimacy arises from communication of personal information. We will look at this sort of personal communication when we explore the subject of self-disclosure.

Affinity   Another dimension of relationships is affinity—the degree to which the partners like or appreciate one another. Not all interpersonal relationships are friendly. Colleagues who have worked together for years and who have struggled for most of that time may not like one another much, but they are still intensely involved with one another. Likewise, friends who disagree or lovers who argue constanty are partners in relationships. As long as these relationships possess all the characteristics that distinguish them as interpersonal—minimal stereotyping, unique rules, and self-disclosure—we can say they are interpersonal. In this sense, liking and disliking (both signs that we *care* about the other person) are much more closely related to one another than either is to indifference.

Control   A final way to look at relationships involves the question of control—the degree to which the parties in a relationship have the power to influence one another.

Types of Control   Communication researchers have commonly identified the balance of relational control in two ways. *Decision control* revolves around who has the power to determine what will happen in the relationship. What will we do Saturday night? Shall we use our savings to fix up the house or to take a vacation? How much time should we spend together and how much should we spend apart? As these examples suggest, some decisions are small, whereas

others are major. It's important to realize that even the smallest decisions reveal something about the balance of power in the relationship.

A very different way to see how partners influence one another is to examine *conversational control.* Some common indicators of conversational control include who talks the most, who interrupts whom, and who changes the topic most often. The person who exercises the greatest amount of conversational control doesn't always make decisions. A roommate who chatters constantly might not persuade you to accept his beliefs. Nonetheless, the ability to determine who talks about what does constitute one type of influence.

Distribution of Control   Control can be distributed in three ways within a relationship.[1] As you read each of these ways, decide which pattern describes each of your relationships.

A **complementary relationship** exists when the distribution of power is unequal. One partner says, "Let's go dancing tonight," and the other says, "Fine." The boss asks several employees to work late, and they all agree. You know your friend has been feeling low lately, and so you're willing to listen to her problems—even though you have other things to do.

In complementary situations like these, one party exercises control and the other is willing to go along. This structure explains why the controller is often labeled in communication jargon as "one up," whereas the party who is being controlled is termed "one down." As long as both parties are comfortable with their roles, a complementary relationship can be stable. On the other hand, relational problems are guaranteed if both parties struggle to occupy one-up positions.

Whereas power is unequal in complementary relationships, in **symmetrical relationships** the parties agree on the desirability of being equals in every situation. Neither person dominates the conversations, and every decision is made jointly. Although this approach sounds desirable in theory, it isn't easy to put into practice. Imagine the time and struggle required to balance the needs of two people who insisted on equal power in every decision. On trivial issues (what to eat for dinner, whether to buy green or yellow tennis balls) equal decision making often isn't worth the effort. On major issues (whether or not to move to a new city, how many children to have) it may not be possible. Despite these difficulties, the shared power of a symmetrical relationship is a goal in many relationships, especially for "modern" couples who object to the unequal, complementary power structure of traditional marriages.

Unlike the lopsidedness of complementary relationships and the total equality of symmetrical ones, **parallel relationships** handle power in a much more fluid way. Partners shift between one-up controlling positions and one-down roles, so that each person leads in some areas and follows in others. John may handle the decisions about car repairs and menu planning, as well as taking the spotlight at parties with their friends. Mary manages the finances and makes most of the decisions about child care, as well as controlling the conversation when she and John are alone. When a decision is very important to one partner, the other willingly gives in, knowing that the favor will be returned later. When issues are important to both partners, they try to share power equally. But when an impasse occurs, they will give in or compromise in a way that keeps the overall balance of power equal.

Understanding Your Relationships

As the preceding pages show, interpersonal relationships take many forms. You can understand the dimensions of your important relationships by answering the following questions about each of the important interpersonal relationships in your life.

1. How long has each one lasted?

2. How much time do you choose to spend with the other person?

3. What kinds of intimacy characterize each relationship: intellectual, emotional, physical? How deep is this intimacy in each relationship?

4. How much affinity exists in each relationship? In other words, how much do you *like* the other person?

5. How is control distributed in each relationship? Is the structure complementary, symmetrical, or parallel? How does this control occur: in terms of decision making or conversational influence?

After answering these questions for your important relationships, ask yourself how satisfied you are with each one. If you are not satisfied with your answers, consider what you can do to change each relationship.

Communicating About Relationships

By now you understand the dimensions that characterize an interpersonal relationship: context, time, intimacy, affinity, and control. But how are these dimensions communicated?

Content and Relational Messages   Virtually every verbal statement has a **content** dimension, containing the subject being discussed. The content of such statements as "It's your turn to do the dishes" or "I'm busy Saturday night" is obvious.

Content messages aren't the only thing being exchanged when two people communicate. In addition, almost every message—both verbal and nonverbal—also has a second, **relational** dimension, which makes statements about how the parties feel toward one another.[2] These relational messages deal with one or more social needs, most commonly inclusion, control, affection, or respect. Consider the two examples we just mentioned:

—Imagine two ways of saying, "It's your turn to do the dishes": one that is demanding and another that is matter-of-fact. Notice how the different nonverbal messages make statements about how the sender views control in this part of the relationship. The demanding tone says, in effect, "I have a right to tell you what to do around the house," whereas the matter-of-fact one suggests, "I'm just reminding you of something you might have overlooked."

—You can easily visualize two ways to deliver the statement "I'm busy Saturday night": one with little affection and the other with much liking.

Notice that in each of these examples the relational dimension of the message was never discussed. In fact, most of the time we aren't conscious of the many relational messages that bombard us every day. Sometimes we are unaware of relational messages because they match our belief about the amount of respect, inclusion, control, and affection that is appropriate. For example, you probably won't be offended if your boss tells you to do a certain job because you agree that supervisors have the right to direct employees. In other cases, however, conflicts arise over relational messages even though content is not disputed. If your boss delivers the order in a condescending, sarcastic, or abusive tone of voice, you probably will be offended. Your complaint wouldn't be with the order itself but with the way it was delivered. "I may work for this company," you might think, "but I'm not a slave or an idiot. I deserve to be treated like a human being."

How are relational messages communicated? As the boss-employee example suggests, they are usually expressed nonverbally. To test this fact for yourself, imagine how you could act while saying, "Can you help me for a minute?" in a way that communicates each of the following relationships:

superiority	friendliness	sexual desire
helplessness	aloofness	irritation

Although nonverbal behaviors are a good source of relational messages, remember that they are ambiguous. The sharp tone you take as a personal insult might be due to fatigue, and the interruption you take as an attempt to ignore your ideas might be a sign of pressure that has nothing to do with you. Before you jump to conclusions about relational clues, it's a good idea to practice the skill of perception checking that you learned in Chapter Three, for instance, "When you use that tone of voice to tell me it's my turn to do the dishes I get the idea you're mad at me. Is that right?" If your interpretation was indeed correct, you can talk about the problem. On the other hand, if you were overreacting, the perception check can prevent a needless fight.

Metacommunication   As this example of perception checking shows, not all relational messages are nonverbal. Social scientists use the term **metacommunication** to describe messages that refer to other messages.[3] In other words, metacommunication is communication about communication. Whenever we discuss a relationship with others, we are metacommunicating: "I wish we could stop arguing so much" or "I appreciate how honest you've been with me." Verbal metacommunication is an essential ingredient in successful relationships. Sooner or later there are times when it becomes necessary to talk about what is going on between you and the other person. The ability to focus on the kinds of issues described in this chapter can be the tool for keeping the relationship on track.

Metacommunication is an important method for solving conflicts in a constructive manner. It provides a way to shift discussion from the content level to relational questions, where the problem often lies. For example, consider the bickering couple described in the selection "TV or No TV" on page 277. Imagine how much better the chances of a positive outcome would have been if they had used metacommunication to examine the relational problems that were behind their quarrel: "Look, it's not the TV watching itself that bothers me. It's that I imagine you watch so much because you're mad at me or bored. Are you feeling bad about us?"

Metacommunication isn't just a tool for handling problems. It is also a way to reinforce the good aspects of a relationship: "I really appreciate it when you compliment me about my work in front of the boss." Comments like this serve two functions: First, they let others know that you value their behavior. Second, they boost the odds that the other person will continue the behavior in the future.

TV OR NO TV: CONTENT, RELATIONSHIP, AND COMMUNICATION

The following dialog shows how even the most ordinary conversations operate on both content and relational levels. Notice that three dimensions of the couple's relationship are at issue. At the outset the wife is seeking inclusion in her husband's spare time as well as hoping for more affection from him. As the conflict escalates, control becomes the central issue.

Imagine how much more constructive the exchange might have been if the husband and wife had realized that television watching was really only a symptom of several relational issues they needed to resolve.

Wife: "You watch too much TV."

While the content addresses a specific behavior, the relationship level is saying: I wish you didn't have so many things which take time and attention away from me. TV is only one minor example which happened to strike me at the moment.

Husband: "I do not."

The relationship message has been ignored completely and the husband prepares himself for the impending battle over TV watching.

Wife: "C'mon, honey . . . you do too."

The wife feels obligated to defend her initial statement. She cannot or will not verbalize the major problem with the relationship, but tries not to be too argumentative at this point. She is still hoping her husband will respond to her cues that reveal the relationship message—sitting on the arm of his chair with her arm around his shoulders.

Husband: "All right, then, I won't watch any TV for a whole week, damn it!"

He is still trying to win on the content level. His kick-me-while-I'm-down strategy is clever because if she agrees, she is really a bitch—knowing what a sacrifice it would be. (The "damn it" dramatized the sacrifice.) Besides, if she agrees, he will still "win" because she will feel guilty for having caused him to be one-down—which, of course, puts him one-up.

Wife: "Oh, just forget it. Do what you want."

The wife sees the trap her husband has prepared on the content level. She gives up on the possibility of positive communication on the relationship level and removes herself from his chair and starts to leave the scene.

Husband: "Forget it! How can I forget it? You come in here and make a big deal out of my TV habits. Then, to satisfy you, I agree to cut it out completely and you say, 'Forget it'! What's wrong with you, anyway?"

He realizes he has "won" on the content level and finally tunes in the relationship level—only to find negative cues. As if enjoying a relationship where he dominates, he tries to prolong his "winning" streak by urging continued argument—never realizing he is also prolonging his counterpart's losing streak.

Now the wife assesses her marital relationship. Her husband does not pay enough attention to her; he was insensitive to her metacommunication about their relationship; he enjoys dominating her; and now he has impugned her sanity for wishing to drop an issue she raised in the first place. The forecast for the immediate future is a long, miserable argument about TV watching. The long-range forecast is a frustrated and confused husband who can't understand why his wife is leaving him, especially since the only thing they fought about was so trivial—TV watching.

Mark Knapp

Interpersonal Attraction: Why We Form Relationships

What makes us want to build relationships with some people and not with others? What attracts us to one another? This is a question social scientists have studied extensively.[4] Though it would take an entire book to describe their findings, we can summarize a number of explanations. As you read them, consider which ones fit you.

We Like People Who Are Similar to Us—Usually   This should come as no surprise. One of the first steps in getting acquainted with a stranger is the search for common ground—interests, experiences, or other factors you share. When we find similarities, we usually feel some kind of attraction toward the person who is like us.

This doesn't mean that the key to popularity is to agree with everyone about everything. Research shows that attraction is greatest when we are similar to others in a high percentage of important areas. For example, a couple who support each other's career goals, like the same friends, and have similar beliefs about human rights can tolerate trivial disagreements about the merits of sushi or Miles Davis. With enough similarity in key areas, they can even survive disputes about more important subjects, such as how much time to spend with their families or whether separate vacations are acceptable. But if the number and content of disagreements become too great, the relationship may be threatened.

Similarity turns from attraction to repulsion when we encounter people who are like us in many ways but who behave in a strange or socially offensive manner. For instance, you have probably disliked people others have said were "just like you" but who talked too much, were complainers, or had some other unappealing characteristic. In fact, there is a tendency to have stronger dislike for similar but offensive people than for those who are offensive but different. One likely reason is that such people threaten our self-esteem, causing us to fear that we may be as unappealing as they are. In such circumstances, the reaction is often to put as much distance as possible between ourselves and this threat to our ideal self-image.

We Like People Who Are Different from Us—in Certain Ways
The fact that "opposites attract" seems to contradict the principle of similarity we just described. In truth, though, both are valid. Differences strengthen a relationship when they are *complementary*—when each partner's characteristics satisfy the other's needs. Couples, for instance, are often likely to be attracted to each other when one partner is dominant and the other passive. Relationships also work well when the partners agree that one will exercise control in certain areas ("You make the final decisions about money") and the other will take the lead in different ones ("I'll decide how we ought to decorate the place"). Strains occur when control issues are disputed.

Studies that have examined successful and unsuccessful couples over a twenty-year period show the interaction between similarities and differences. The research demonstrates that partners in successful marriages were similar enough to satisfy each other physically and mentally but were different enough to meet each other's needs and keep the relationship interesting. The successful couples found ways to keep a balance between their similarities and differences, adjusting to the changes that occurred over the years.

We Like People Who Like Us—Usually   This source of attraction is especially strong in the early stages of a relationship. At that time we are attracted to people who we believe are attracted to us. Conversely, we will probably not care for people who either attack or seem indifferent toward us. After we get to know others, their liking becomes less of a factor. By then we form our preferences more from the other reasons listed in this section.

"It would work with us, Francine. We share the same
narrow personal interests and concerns."

Drawing by Dana Freden. © 1979 The New Yorker Magazine, Inc.

It's no mystery why reciprocal liking builds attractiveness. People who approve of us bolster our feelings of self-esteem. This approval is rewarding in its own right, and it can also confirm a presenting self-concept that says, "I'm a likable person."

However, you can probably think of cases where you haven't liked people who seemed to like you. These experiences usually fall into two categories. Sometimes we think the other person's supposed liking is counterfeit—an insincere device to get something from us. The acquaintance who becomes friendly whenever he needs to borrow your car or the employee whose flattery of the boss seems to be a device to get a raise are examples. This sort of behavior really isn't "liking" at all. The second category occurs when the other person's approval doesn't fit with our own self-concept. As you read in Chapter Two, we cling to an existing self-concept even when it is unrealistically unfavorable. When someone says you're good-looking, intelligent, and kind, but you believe you are ugly, stupid, and mean, you may choose to disregard the flattering information and remain in your familiar state of unhappiness. Groucho Marx summarized this attitude when he said he would never join any club that would consider having him as a member.

We Are Attracted to People Who Can Help Us   Some relationships are based on a semieconomic model called **exchange theory.** It suggests that we often seek out people who can give us rewards—either physical or emotional—that are greater than or equal to the costs we encounter in dealing with them. When we operate on the basis of exchange, we decide (often unconsciously) whether dealing with another person is "a good deal" or "not worth the effort."

At its most blatant level, an exchange approach seems cold and calculating, but in some dimensions of a relationship it can be reasonable. A healthy business relationship is based on how well the parties help one another, and some friendships are based on an informal kind of barter: "I don't mind listening to the ups and downs of your love life because you rescue me when the house needs repairs." Even close relationships have an element of exchange. Husbands and wives tolerate each other's quirks because the comfort and enjoyment they get make the unhappy times worth accepting. Most deeply satisfying relationships, however, are built on more than just the benefits that make them a good deal.

We Like Competent People—Particularly When They're "Human"
We like to be around talented people, probably because we hope their skills and abilities will rub off on us. On the other hand, we are uncomfortable around those who are *too* competent—probably because we look bad by comparison.

Given these contrasting attitudes, it's no surprise that people are generally attracted to those who are talented but who have visible flaws that show they are human, just like us. There are some qualifications to this principle. People with especially high or low self-esteem find "perfect" people more attractive than those who are competent but flawed, and some studies suggest that women tend to be more impressed by uniformly superior people of both sexes, whereas men find desirable but "human" subjects especially attractive. On the whole, though, the principle stands: The best way to gain the liking of others is to be good at what you do but to admit your mistakes.

The fact that a certain degree of imperfection is attractive drives another nail into the coffin of the perfectionistic myth described in Chapter Four. We mistakenly believe that we need to appear flawless in order to gain the respect and affection of others when, in fact, acting perfect may drive away the people we want to draw closer.

We Are Attracted to People Who Disclose Themselves to Us—Appropriately
Telling others important information about yourself can help build liking. Sometimes the basis of this attraction comes from learning about how we are similar, either in experiences ("I broke off an engagement myself") or in attitudes ("I feel nervous with strangers, too"). Another reason why self-disclosure increases liking is because it is a sign of regard. When people share private information with you, it suggests they respect and trust you—a kind of liking that we've already seen increases attractiveness.

Not all disclosure leads to liking. People whose sharing is poorly timed often meet with bad results. It's probably unwise, for example, to talk about your sexual insecurities with a new acquaintance or to express your pet peeves to a friend at her birthday party. In addition to bad timing, opening up too much can also be a mistake. Research shows that people are judged as attractive when they match the amount and content of what they share with that of the other person in a relationship. See pages 299–300 for more guidelines about when and how to self-disclose.

We Feel Strongly About People We Encounter Often
As common sense suggests, we are likely to develop relationships with people we interact with frequently. In many cases, proximity leads to liking. We're more likely to develop friendships with close neighbors than with distant ones, for instance;

I do have some fears. Everybody does. But I want to keep them to myself because when you have an intimate friendship, one of the ways you know you have such a friendship is you trade secrets about yourself. And if I have nothing that's private to me at all, I wouldn't have anything to trade with other people.

Alan Alda

and several studies show that the chances are good that we'll choose a mate whom we cross paths with often. Facts like these are understandable when we consider that proximity allows us to get more information about the other people and benefit from a relationship with them.

Familiarity, on the other hand, can also breed contempt. Evidence to support this fact comes from police blotters as well as university laboratories. Thieves frequently prey on nearby victims even though the risk of being recognized is greater. Most aggravated assaults occur within the family or among close neighbors. Within the law, the same principle holds: You are likely to develop strong personal feelings of either like or dislike regarding others you encounter frequently.

Analyzing Interpersonal Attraction

1. List the names of five people with whom you have strong positive personal relationships. Use the list that follows to identify the basis of your attraction.
   a. Are their interests, attitudes, values, beliefs, or backgrounds similar to yours?
   b. Do they fill a complementary need for you?
   c. Are they attracted to you?
   d. Is your relationship a fair exchange of rewards?
   e. Are they competent but human?
   f. Have they shared personal information with you?
   g. Do you encounter them frequently?
2. Now consider five people with whom you would like to build a stronger relationship. Use the same list to decide whether you are the kind of person they would be attracted to.

Stages of Interpersonal Relationships

The process of interpersonal attraction is only the beginning of a relationship. As attraction motivates us to become more involved with another person, our relationship seems to pass through several stages.[5]

Although Table 8–1 on page 283 suggests that each of these stages is separate, in truth they usually blend together. There are occasions when relationships seem to reach a milestone and change almost immediately—from experimenting to intensifying or from bonding to differentiating, for example. In most cases, however, our relationships evolve more gradually. A relationship that has reached a stage of integrating probably still has some elements of experimenting, and one that consists of a great deal of avoiding may still have moments of bonding. Nonetheless, most relationships do seem to progress through the following stages.

Although the following description is most recognizable for mixed-gender couples, it also applies to other types of interpersonal relationships. It is likely that the following stages fit the people you work with, your close friends, and with

Table 8—1   An Overview of Relational Stages

Process	Stage	Representative Dialog
	Initiating	"Hi, how ya doin'?" "Fine. You?"
	Experimenting	"Oh, so you like to ski … so do I." "You do?! Great. Where do you go?"
Coming Together	Intensifying	"I … I think I love you." "I love you too."
	Integrating	"I feel so much a part of you." "Yeah, we are like one person. What happens to you happens to me."
	Bonding	"I want to be with you always." "Let's get married."
	Differentiating	"I just don't like big social gatherings." "Sometimes I don't understand you. This is one area where I'm certainly not like you at all."
	Circumscribing	"Did you have a good time on your trip?" "What time will dinner be ready?"
Coming Apart	Stagnating	"What's there to talk about?" "Right. I know what you're going to say and you know what I'm going to say."
	Avoiding	"I'm so busy, I just don't know when I'll be able to see you." "If I'm not around when you try, you'll understand."
	Terminating	"I'm leaving you … and don't bother trying to contact me." "Don't worry."

Reprinted with permission from Mark L. Knapp, *Interpersonal Communication and Human Relationships* (Boston: Allyn and Bacon, 1984).

some modification in the early stages, even members of your family. Not all relationships progress through every step, of course. Many never grow beyond the stage of experimenting, whereas others stabilize at a point of differentiation without ever deteriorating.

Initiating   The goals in the first stage are to show that you are interested in making contact and to show that you are the kind of person worth talking to. Communication during this stage is usually brief, and it generally follows conventional formulas: handshakes, remarks about innocuous subjects like the weather, and friendly expressions. These kinds of behavior may seem superficial and meaningless, but they are a way of signaling that we're interested in building

some kind of relationship with the other person. They allow us to say without saying, "I'm a friendly person, and I'd like to get to know you."

Experimenting   After making contact with a new person, we generally begin the search for common ground. This search usually begins with the basics: "Where are you from? What's your major?" From there we look for other similarities: "You're a runner too? How many miles do you do a week?"

The hallmark of experimenting is small talk. As Mark Knapp says, this small talk is like Listerine: "We hate it, but we take large quantities every day."[6] We tolerate the ordeal of small talk because it serves several functions. First, it is a useful way to find out what interests we share with the other person. It also provides a way to "audition" the other person—to help us decide whether a relationship is worth pursuing. In addition, small talk is a safe way to ease into a relationship. You haven't risked much as you decide whether to proceed further. Finally, small talk *does* provide some kind of link to others. It's often better than being alone.

Intensifying   At the next stage the kind of truly interpersonal relationship defined in Chapter One begins. The amount of personal disclosure increases as the partners move away from stereotyped ways of behaving. The degree of risk here is matched by the potential for gain.

Several changes occur during intensifying. Forms of address become more informal: "Come over here, honey," "Hey Gordo, pass me a beer." The parties begin to refer to themselves as "we": "We'll see you at the picnic." Increased familiarity leads to verbal shortcuts. Instead of saying "You look tired. Did you have a hard day at work?" it's only necessary to ask, "The boss again?" It is also during the intensifying stage that we begin to express directly feelings of commitment to one another: "I'm sure glad we met." "You're the best thing that's happened to me in a long time."

Integrating   As the relationship strengthens, the parties begin to take on an identity as a social unit. Invitations begin to be addressed to the couple. Social circles merge. The partners begin to take on each other's commitments: "Sure we'll spend Thanksgiving with your family." Common property may begin to be designated—our apartment, our car, our song. In this sense, the integration stage is a time when we give up some characteristics of our old selves and become different persons.

Bonding   During the bonding stage the parties make symbolic public gestures to show the world that their relationship exists. These gestures can take the form of a contract to be business partners or a license to be married. Bonding generates social support for the relationship. Custom and law both impose certain obligations on partners who have officially bonded.

Differentiating   Now that the two people have formed this commonality, they need to reestablish individual identities. How are we different? How am I unique? Former identifications as "we" now emphasize "I." Differentiation often first occurs when a relationship begins to feel the first, inevitable stress. Whereas a happy employee might refer to "our company," the description might change to "their company" when a raise or some other request isn't forthcoming. We see this kind of differentiation when parents argue over the misbehavior of a child: "Did you see what *your* son just did?"

Differentiation can be positive, too, for people need to be individuals as well as parts of a relationship. The key to successful differentiation is the need to maintain commitment to a relationship while creating the space for members to be individuals as well.

Circumscribing   So far we have been looking at the growth of relationships. Although some reach a plateau of development, going on successfully for as long as a lifetime, others pass through several stages of decline and dissolution. In the circumscribing stage communication between members decreases in quantity and quality. Restrictions and restraints characterize this stage, and dynamic communication becomes static. Rather than discuss a disagreement (which requires some degree of energy on both parts), members opt for withdrawal: either mental (silence or daydreaming and fantasizing) or physical (where people spend less time together). Circumscribing doesn't involve total avoidance, which comes later. Rather, it entails a certain shrinking of interest and commitment.

Stagnating   If circumscribing continues, the relationship begins to stagnate. Members behave toward each other in old, familiar ways without much feeling. No growth occurs. The relationship is a hollow shell of its former self. We see stagnation in many workers who have lost enthusiasm for their job yet continue

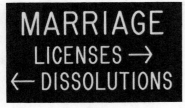

to go through the motions for years. The same sad event occurs for some couples who unenthusiastically have the same conversations, see the same people, and follow the same routines without any sense of joy or novelty.

Avoiding   When stagnation becomes too unpleasant, parties in a relationship begin to create distance between each other. Sometimes they do it under the guise of excuses ("I've been sick lately and can't see you") and sometimes directly ("Please don't call me; I don't want to see you now"). In either case by this point the handwriting is on the wall about the relationship's future.

Terminating   Characteristics of this final stage include summary dialogs of where the relationship has gone and the desire to dissociate. The relationship may end with a cordial dinner, a note left on the kitchen table, a phone call, or a legal document stating the dissolution. Depending on each person's feelings, this stage can be quite short, or it may be drawn out over time, with bitter jabs at each other. In either case, termination doesn't have to be totally negative. Understanding each other's investments in the relationship and needs for personal growth may dilute the hard feelings.

Self-Disclosure in Relationships

We have already seen that one way to judge the strength of a relationship is by the amount of personal information the parties share with one another. Furthermore, we have cited research showing that appropriate self-disclosure can increase a person's attractiveness. Given these facts, we need to take a closer look at the subject of self-disclosure. Just what is it? When is it desirable? How is it best done?

The best place to begin is with a definition. **Self-disclosure** is the process of deliberately revealing information about oneself that is significant and that would not normally be known by others. Let's take a closer look at some parts of this definition. Self-disclosure must be *deliberate.* If you accidentally mention to a friend that you're thinking about quitting a job or proposing marriage, that information doesn't qualify as self-disclosure. Besides being intentional, the information must also be *significant.* Volunteering trivial facts, opinions, or feelings— that you like fudge, for example—hardly count as disclosure. The third requirement is that the information being disclosed is *not known by others*. There's nothing noteworthy about telling others that you are depressed or elated if they already know that.

Degrees of Self-Disclosure   Although our definition of self-disclosure is helpful, it doesn't reveal the important fact that not all self-disclosure is equally revealing—that some disclosing messages tell more about us than others.

Social psychologists Irwin Altman and Dalmas Taylor describe two ways in which communication can be more or less disclosing.[7] Their **social penetration** model is pictured in Figure 8–1. The first dimension of self-disclosure in this model involves the *breadth* of information volunteered—the range of subjects being discussed. For example, the breadth of disclosure in your relationship with a fellow worker will expand as you begin revealing information about your life away from the job, as well as on-the-job details. The second dimension of

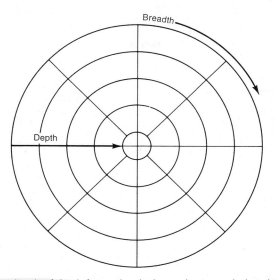

Figure 8—1
Social penetration model

disclosure is the *depth* of the information being volunteered, the shift from relatively nonrevealing messages to more personal ones.

Depending on the breadth and depth of information shared, a relationship can be defined as casual or intimate. In a casual relationship the breadth may be great, but not the depth. A more intimate relationship is likely to have high depth in at least one area. The most intimate relationships are those in which disclosure is great in both breadth and depth. Altman and Taylor see the development of a relationship as a progression from the periphery of their model to its center, a process that typically occurs over time. Each of your personal relationships probably has a different combination of breadth of subjects and depth of disclosure. Figure 8–2 pictures a student's self-disclosure in one relationship.

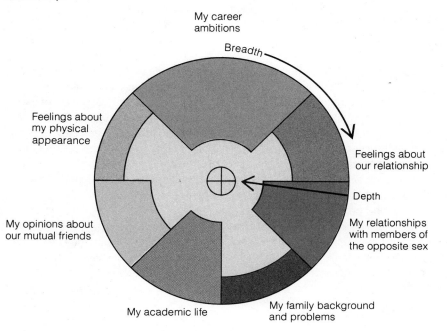

Figure 8—2
Sample model of social penetration

Figure 8—3
Levels of self-disclosure

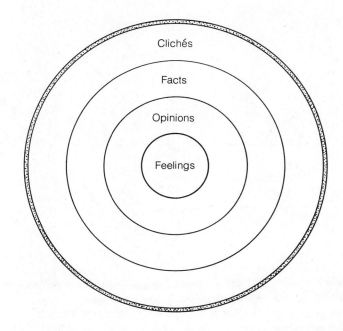

What makes some disclosing messages deeper than others? One way to understand the various levels of self-disclosure is to picture a series of four concentric circles.[8] Each circle represents a different type of communication. As a rule, the inner levels are more revealing than the outer ones. An examination of each level will explain their differences.

Clichés   The outermost layer consists of clichés: "How are you doing?" "Fine!" "We'll have to get together some time."

Remarks such as these usually aren't meant to be taken literally; in fact, the other person would be surprised if you responded to a casual "How are you?" with a lengthy speech on your health, state of mind, love life, or finances. Yet it's a mistake to consider clichés meaningless, for they serve several useful functions. For instance, they can give two speakers time to size each other up and decide whether it's desirable to carry their conversation any further. Our first impressions are generally based more on the nonverbal characteristics of the other person than on the words we hear spoken. Things like eye contact, vocal tone, facial expression, posture, and so on can often tell us more about another person than can the initial sentences in a conversation. Given the value of these nonverbal cues and the awkwardness of actually saying, "I want to take a few minutes to look you over before I commit myself to getting acquainted," the exchange of a few stock phrases can be just the thing to get you through this initial period comfortably.

Clichés can also serve as codes for other messages we don't usually express directly, such as "I want to acknowledge your presence" (for instance, when two acquaintances walk past each other). Additional unstated messages often contained in clichés are "I'm interested in talking if you feel like it" or "Let's keep the conversation light and impersonal; I don't feel like disclosing much about myself right now." Accompanied by a different set of nonverbal cues, a cliché can say, "I don't want to be impolite, but you'd better stay away from me for now." In all these cases clichés serve as a valuable kind of shorthand that makes it easy to keep the social wheels greased and indicates the potential for further, possibly more profound conversation.

Facts Moving inward from clichés on our self-disclosure model brings us to the level of volunteering *facts*. Not all factual statements qualify as self-disclosure: They must fit the criteria of being intentional, significant, and not otherwise known:

"This isn't my first try at college. I dropped out a year ago with terrible grades."

"I'm practically engaged." (On meeting a stranger while away from home.)
"That idea that everyone thought was so clever wasn't really mine. I read it in a book last year."

Facts like these can be meaningful in themselves, but they also have a greater significance in a relationship. Disclosing important information suggests a level of trust and commitment to the other person that signals a desire to move the relationship to a new level.

"If you want to talk, get a paper, and we'll talk about what's in the paper."

Drawing by Drucker. © 1985 The New Yorker Magazine, Inc.

Opinions   Still more revealing is the level of opinions:

"I used to think abortion was no big deal, but lately I've changed my mind."
"I really like Karen."
"I don't think you're telling me what's on your mind."

Opinions like these usually reveal more about a person than facts alone. If you know where the speaker stands on a subject, you can get a clearer picture of how your relationship might develop. Likewise, every time you offer a personal opinion, you are giving others valuable information about yourself.

Feelings   The fourth level of self-disclosure—and usually most revealing one—is the realm of feelings. At first glance, feelings might appear to be the same as opinions, but there is a big difference. As we saw, "I don't think you're telling me what's on your mind" is an opinion. Now notice how much more we learn about the speaker by looking at three different feelings that might accompany this statement:

"I don't think you're telling me what's on your mind, *and I'm suspicious.*"
"I don't think you're telling me what's on your mind, *and I'm angry.*"
"I don't think you're telling me what's on your mind, *and I'm hurt.*"

The difference between these four levels of communication suggests why relationships can be frustrating. One reason has to do with the depth of disclosure, which may not lead to the kind of relationship one or both parties are seeking. Sometimes the communicators might remain exclusively on the level of facts. This might be suitable for a business relationship but wouldn't be very likely in most other circumstances. Even worse, other communicators never get off the level of clichés. And just as a diet of rich foods can become unappealing if carried to excess, the overuse of feelings and opinions can also become disagreeable. In most cases the successful conversation is one in which the participants move from one level to another, depending on the circumstances.

B.C. by Johnny Hart

By permission of John Hart and News America Syndicate.

Another common problem occurs when two communicators want to relate to each other on different levels. If one is willing to deal only with facts and perhaps an occasional opinion and the other insists on revealing personal feelings, the results are likely to be uncomfortable for both. Consider the following meeting between Jack and Roger at a party.

J   Hi. My name's Jack. I don't think we've met before. (*cliché*)

R   I'm Roger. Nice to meet you. (*cliché*)

J   Do you know anybody here? I've just moved in next door and don't know a soul except for the host. What's his name . . . Lou? (*fact*)

R   Lou's right. Well, I'm here with my wife—that's her over there—and we know a few other people. (*fact; both speakers are comfortable so far*)

J   Well, I used to have a wife, but she split. She really did me in. (*fact and opinion*)

R   Oh? (*cliché; he doesn't know how to reply to this comment*)

J   Yeah. Everything was going along great—I thought. Then one day she told me she was in love with her gynecologist and that she wanted a divorce. I still haven't gotten over it. (*feeling and fact*)

R   Well, uh, that's too bad. (*cliché; Roger is now very uncomfortable*)

J   I don't think I'll ever trust another woman. I'm still in love with my wife, and it's killing me. She really broke my heart. (*feeling and fact*)

R   I'm sorry. Listen, I've got to go. (*cliché*)

Clearly, Jack moved to the level of disclosing feelings long before Roger was prepared to accept this kind of communication. Though this type of discussion might have helped a friendship if it had come at a later time, Jack only succeeded in driving Roger away by coming on too fast. Remember the hazards of moving too quickly to a level your partner is likely to find uncomfortable.

Examining Your Self-Disclosure

Here's a chance to explore the levels of self-disclosure you use with some important people in your life.

1. Choose a "significant other" as the subject of this exercise.

2. Spend a three-day period recording the number of statements you make in each category: clichés, facts, opinions, and feelings.

3. Try to be aware of the topics that you discuss on each level, along with the number of statements in each category.

4. Based on your findings, answer these questions:

   a. Which categories of self-disclosure do you engage in most frequently? Least often?

   b. What type of disclosure (cliché, fact, opinion, or feeling) do you use in each topic area?

   c. Explain the reason for omitting topical categories (for example, conflicts, the future) or levels of disclosure or both (for example, feelings).

   d. Explain the consequences of any omissions described in part c.

Figure 8—4

Figure 8—5

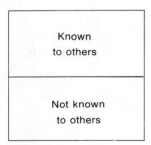

Figure 8—6

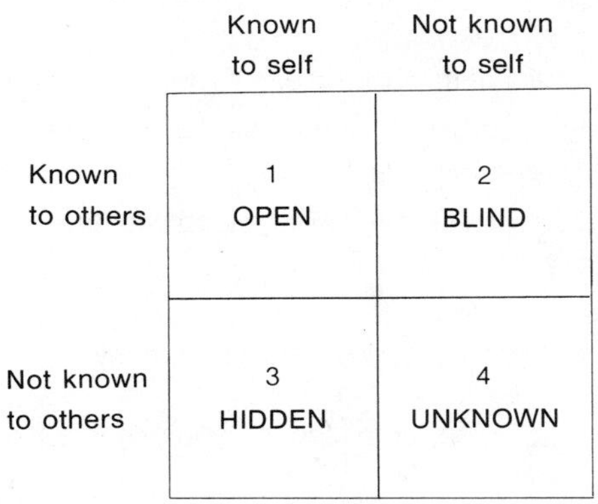

The Johari Window Model of Self-Disclosure   One way to look at the important part self-disclosure plays in interpersonal communication is by means of a device called the **Johari Window**.[9] (The window takes its name from the first names of its creators, Joseph Luft and Harry Ingham.) Imagine a frame inside which is everything there is to know about you: your likes and dislikes, your goals, your secrets, your needs—everything.

Of course, you aren't aware of everything about yourself. Like most people, you're probably discovering new things about yourself all the time. To represent this, we can divide the frame containing everything about you into two parts: the part you know about and the part you're not aware of, as in Figure 8–5.

We can also divide this frame containing everything about you in another way. In this division one part represents the things about you that others know, and the second part contains the things about you that you keep to yourself. Figure 8–6 represents this view.

When we impose these two divided frames one atop the other, we have a Johari Window. By looking at Figure 8–7 you can see the *everything about you* divided into four parts.

Part 1 represents the information of which both you and the other person are aware. This part is your *open area*. Part 2 represents the *blind area:* information of which you are unaware but the other person knows. You learn about information in the blind area primarily through feedback. Part 3 represents your *hidden area:* information that you know but aren't willing to reveal to others. Items in this hidden area become public primarily through self-disclosure, which is the focus of this chapter. Part 4 represents information that is *unknown* to both you and others. At first the unknown area seems impossible to verify. After all, if neither you nor others know what it contains, how can you be sure it exists? We can deduce its existence because we are constantly discovering new things about ourselves. It is not unusual to discover, for example, that you have an unrecognized talent, strength, or weakness. Items move from the unknown area either directly into the open area when you disclose your insight or through one of the other areas first.

The relative size of each area in our personal Johari Windows changes from time to time, according to our moods, the subject we are discussing, and our

	Known to self	Not known to self
Known to others	1 OPEN	2 BLIND
Not known to others	3 HIDDEN	4 UNKNOWN

Figure 8—7

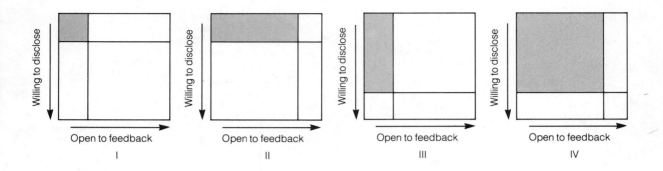

Figure 8–8
Four styles of disclosure

relationship with the other person. Despite these changes, most people's overall style of disclosure could be represented by a single Johari Window. Figure 8–8 pictures windows representing four extreme interaction styles.

Style I depicts a person who is neither receptive to feedback nor willing to self-disclose. This person takes few risks and may appear aloof and uncommunicative. The largest quadrant is the unknown area: Such people have a lot to learn about themselves, as do others. Style II depicts a person who is open to feedback from others but does not voluntarily self-disclose. This person may fear exposure, possibly because of not trusting others. People who fit this pattern may appear highly supportive at first. They want to hear *your* story and appear willing to deny themselves by remaining quiet. Then this first impression fades, and eventually you see them as distrustful and detached. A Johari Window describing such people has a large hidden area.

Style III in Figure 8–8 describes people who discourage feedback from others but disclose freely. Like the people pictured in diagram II, they may distrust others' opinions. They certainly seem self-centered. Their largest quadrant is the blind area: They do not encourage feedback, and so fail to learn much about how others view them.

Diagram IV depicts people who are both willing to disclose information about themselves and open to others' ideas. They are trusting enough to seek the opinions of others and disclose their own. In extreme, this communication style can be intimidating and overwhelming because it violates the usual expectations of how nonintimates ought to behave. In moderation, however, this open style provides the best chance for developing highly interpersonal relationships.

Interpersonal communication of any depth is virtually impossible if the individuals involved have little open area. Going a step further, you can see that a relationship is limited by the individual who is less open, that is, who possesses the smaller open area. Figure 8–9 illustrates this situation with Johari Windows. A's window is set up in reverse so that A's and B's open areas are adjacent. Notice that the amount of communication (represented by the arrows connecting the two open areas) is dictated by the size of the smaller open area of A. The arrows originating from B's open area and being turned aside by A's hidden and blind areas represent unsuccessful attempts to communicate.

You have probably found yourself in situations that resemble Figure 8–9. Perhaps you have felt the frustration of not being able to get to know someone who was too reserved. Perhaps you have blocked another person's attempts to build a relationship with you in the same way. Whether you picture yourself more

Figure 8—9

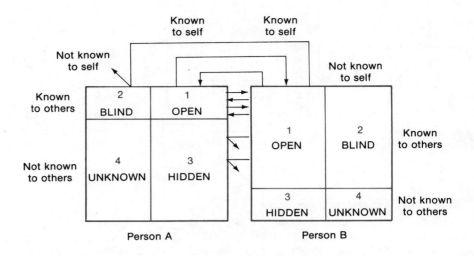

Person A   Person B

like Person A or Person B, the fact is that self-disclosure on both sides is necessary for the development of any interpersonal relationship. This chapter will describe just how much self-disclosure is optimal and of what type.

Building a Johari Window

You can use the Johari Window model to examine the level of self-disclosure in your own relationships.

1. Use the format described in the preceding section to draw two Johari Windows, representing the relationship between you and one other person. Remember to reverse one of the windows so that your open areas and those of the other person face each other.

2. Describe which parts of yourself you keep in the hidden area. Explain your reasons for doing so. Describe the costs or benefits or both of not disclosing these parts of yourself.

3. Look at the blind area of your model. Is this area large or small because of the amount of feedback (much or little) that you get from your partner or because of your willingness to receive the feedback that is offered?

4. Explain whether or not you are satisfied with the results illustrated by your answers. If you are not satisfied, explain what you can do to remedy the problem.

Characteristics of Self-Disclosure   The Johari Window suggests several characteristics of self-disclosure.

Self-Disclosure Usually Occurs in Dyads   Although it is possible for people to disclose a great deal about themselves in groups, such communication usually occurs in one-to-one settings. Since revealing significant information about yourself involves a certain amount of risk, limiting the disclosure to one person at a time minimizes the chance that your revelations will lead to unhappy consequences.

Self-Disclosure Is Usually Symmetrical   Note in Figure 8–9 that the amount of successful, two-way communication (represented by the arrows connecting the two open areas) is dictated by the size of the smaller open area of A. The arrows that are originating from B's open area and being turned aside by A's hidden and blind areas represent unsuccessful attempts to communicate. In situations such as this it's easy to imagine how B would soon limit the amount of disclosure to match that of A. On the other hand, if A was willing to match the degree of disclosure given by B, the relationship would move to a new level of intimacy. In either case we can expect that most often the degree of disclosure between partners will soon stabilize at a symmetrical level.

Self-Disclosure Occurs Incrementally   Although occasions do occur in which partners start their relationship by telling everything about themselves to each other, such instances are rare. In most cases the amount of disclosure increases over time. We begin relationships by revealing relatively little about ourselves; then if our first bits of self-disclosure are well received and bring on similar responses from the other person, we're willing to reveal more. This principle is important to remember. It would usually be a mistake to assume that the way to build a strong relationship would be to reveal the most private details about yourself when first making contact with another person. Unless the circumstances are unique, such baring of your soul would be likely to scare potential partners away rather than bring them closer.

Relatively Few Transactions Involve High Levels of Self-Disclosure   Just as it's unwise to seek great self-disclosure too soon, it's also unproductive to reveal yourself too much. Except for unique settings—such as in therapy—there's usually no need to disclose frequently or steadily.

Self-Disclosure Usually Occurs in the Context of Positive Relationships   This principle makes sense. We're generally more willing to reveal information about ourselves when we feel accepted by the other person. This doesn't mean that you should avoid making disclosing statements that contain negative messages (for example, "I feel uncomfortable about what happened last night"). Such explanations are likely to be successful if they're designed to be constructive, to help your relationship grow. On the other hand, disclosure that has the effect of attacking the other person ("You sure aren't very bright") is almost guaranteed to be destructive. For this reason, it's especially important to phrase negative messages in the supportive, assertive ways described in Chapters Nine and Ten.

Reasons for Self-Disclosure   Self-disclosure has the potential to improve and expand interpersonal relationships, but it serves other functions as well.[10] As you read each of the following reasons why people reveal themselves, see which apply to you.

Before I built a wall I'd ask to know
What I was walling in or walling out.
And to whom I was like to give offense.
Something there is that doesn't love a wall,
That wants it down.

Robert Frost

he stripped
the dark circles
of mystery off
revealed his eyes
and thus
he waited
exposed

and I
did sing the song
around
until I found
the chorus
that speaks
of windows

looking out
means looking in
my friend
and I'm all right
now
I'm fine
I have seen
the beauty
that is mine

you can
watch the sky
for signals
but look
to the eyes
for signs

Ric Masten

Catharsis   Sometimes you might disclose information in an effort to "get it off your chest." In a moment of candor you might, for instance, reveal your regrets about having behaved badly in the past.

Self-Clarification   Sometimes you can clarify your beliefs, opinions, thoughts, attitudes, and feelings by talking about them with another person. This sort of "talking the problem out" occurs with psychotherapists, but it also goes on with others, all the way from good friends to bartenders or hairdressers.

Self-Validation   If you disclose information ("I think I did the right thing...") with the hope of seeking the listener's agreement, you are seeking validation of your behavior—confirmation of a belief you hold about yourself. On a deeper level, this sort of self-validating disclosure seeks confirmation of important parts of your self-concept.

Reciprocity   A well-documented conclusion from research is that one act of self-disclosure begets another.[11] Thus, in some situations you may choose to disclose information about yourself to encourage another person to do so also.

Impression Formation   In some situations you may choose to reveal yourself to create a particular impression. Dating behavior, particularly on the first few dates, is often aimed at creating a favorable impression. To look good, we

"I'm a very sensual person. How about you, Mr. Gellerman?"

Drawing by Stan Hunt. © 1982 The New Yorker Magazine, Inc.

sometimes share selected bits of information about ourselves—for example, our accomplishments or goals.

Relationship Maintenance and Enhancement

Relationships need disclosure to stay healthy and develop. If you don't reveal how you're feeling about your partner, not to mention other parts of your life—the subjects of your interaction become limited and shallow.

Social Control

Revealing personal information may increase your control over the other person, and sometimes over the situation in which you and the other person find yourselves. For example, an employee who tells the boss that another firm has made overtures probably will have an increased chance of getting raises and improvements in working conditions.

Manipulation

Although most of the preceding reasons might strike you as being manipulative, they often aren't premeditated strategies. There are cases, however, when an act of self-disclosure is calculated in advance to achieve a desired result. Of course, if a disclosure's hidden motive ever becomes clear to the receiver, the results will most likely be quite unlike those intended.

The reasons for disclosing vary from one situation to another, depending on several factors. The strongest influence on why people disclose seems to be how well we know the other person.[12] When the target of disclosure is a friend, the most frequent reason people give for volunteering personal information is relationship maintenance and enhancement. In other words, we disclose to friends in order to strengthen the relationship. The second important reason is self-clarification—to sort out confusion to understand ourselves better.

With strangers, reciprocity becomes the most common reason for disclosing. We offer information about ourselves to strangers to learn more about them, so we can decide whether and how to continue the relationship. The second most important reason is impression formation. In other words, we often reveal information about ourselves to strangers to make ourselves look good. This information, of course, is usually positive—at least in the early stages of a friendship.

MISS PEACH   By Mell Lazarus

Guidelines for Self-Disclosure　　One fear we've had while writing this chapter is that a few overenthusiastic readers may throw down their books after reading this far and rush away to begin revealing every personal detail of their lives to whomever they can find. As you can imagine, this kind of behavior isn't an example of effective interpersonal communication.

Self-disclosure is a special kind of sharing that is not appropriate for every situation. Let's look at some guidelines that can help you recognize how to express yourself in a way that's rewarding for you and the others involved.

Letting people in is largely a matter of not expending energy to keep them out.

Hugh Prather

1. Is the other person important to you? There are several ways in which someone might be important. Perhaps you have an ongoing relationship deep enough so that sharing significant parts of yourself justifies keeping your present level of togetherness intact. Or perhaps the person to whom you're considering disclosing is someone with whom you've previously related on a less personal level. But now you see a chance to grow closer, and disclosure may be the path toward developing that personal relationship.

2. Is the risk of disclosing reasonable? Take a realistic look at the potential risks of self-disclosure. Even if the probable benefits are great, opening yourself up to almost certain rejection may be asking for trouble. For instance, it might be foolhardy to share your important feelings with someone you know is likely to betray your confidences or ridicule them. On the other hand, knowing that your partner is trustworthy and supportive makes the prospect of speaking out more reasonable. In anticipating risks, be sure that you are realistic. It's sometimes easy to indulge in catastrophic expectations in which you begin to imagine all sorts of disastrous consequences when in fact such horrors are quite unlikely to occur.

3. Are the amount and type of disclosure appropriate? It is usually a mistake to share too much information too soon. Research shows that in most relationships the process of disclosure is gradual.[13] At first most of the information that is exchanged is relatively nonintimate. As the parties move into the intensifying, integrating, and bonding stages of the relationship, the rate of disclosure begins to grow.

Even in relationships in which disclosure is an important feature, the amount of personal information is relatively small when compared to nonintimate information. Most long-term relationships aren't characterized by a constant exchange of intimate details. Rather, they are a mixture of much everyday, nonintimate information and less frequent but more personal messages.

Besides being moderate in amount, self-disclosure should consist of positive information as well as negative details. Hearing nothing but a string of dismal confessions or complaints can be discouraging. In fact, people who disclose an excess of negative information are often considered "negatively adjusted."[14]

Finally, when considering the appropriateness of disclosure in any relationship, timing is also important. If the other person is tired, preoccupied, or in a bad mood it may be best to postpone an important conversation.

4. Is the disclosure relevant to the situation at hand? Self-disclosure doesn't require long confessions about your past life or current thoughts unrelated to the present. On the contrary, it ought to be directly pertinent to your current conversation. It's ludicrous to picture the self-disclosing person as someone who blurts out intimate details of every past experience. Instead, our model is someone who, when the time is appropriate, trusts us enough to share the hidden parts of self that affect our relationship.

Usually, then, the subject of appropriate self-disclosure involves the present, the "here and now" as opposed to "there and then." "How am I feeling now?" "How are we doing now?" These are appropriate topics for sharing personal thoughts and feelings. There are certainly times when it's relevant to bring up the past, but only as it relates to what's going on in the present.

5. **Is the disclosure reciprocated?** There's nothing quite as disconcerting as talking your heart out to someone only to discover that the other person has yet to say anything to you that is half as revealing as what you've been saying. And you think to yourself, "What am I doing?" Unequal self-disclosure creates an imbalanced relationship, one doomed to fall apart.

There are few times when one-way disclosure is acceptable. Most of them involve formal, therapeutic relationships in which a client approaches a trained professional with the goal of resolving a problem. For instance, you wouldn't necessarily expect to hear about a physician's personal ailments during a visit to a medical office. Nonetheless, it's interesting to note that one frequently noted characteristic of effective psychotherapists, counselors, and teachers is a willingness to reveal their feelings about a relationship to their clients.

6. **Will the effect be constructive?** Self-disclosure can be a vicious tool if it's not used carefully. Psychologist George Bach suggests that every person has a psychological "beltline."[15] Below that beltline are areas about which the person is extremely sensitive. Bach says that jabbing at a "below-the-belt" area is a surefire way to disable another person, though usually at great cost to the relationship. It's important to consider the effects of your candor before opening up to others. Comments such as "I've always thought you were pretty unintelligent" or "Last year I made love to your best friend" *may* sometimes resolve old business and thus be constructive, but they also can be devastating—to the listener, to the relationship, and to your self-esteem.

7. **Is the self-disclosure clear and understandable?** When you are expressing yourself to others, it's important that you reveal yourself in a way that's intelligible. This means describing the sources of your message clearly. For instance, it's far better to describe another's behavior by saying, "When you don't answer my phone calls or drop by to visit anymore . . ." than to complain vaguely, "When you avoid me. . . ."

It's also vital to express your *thoughts* and *feelings* explicitly. "I feel worried because I'm afraid you don't care about me" is more understandable than "I don't like it. . . ."

More Readings on Relationships

Aaronson, Elliot. *The Social Animal,* 4th ed. New York: Freeman, 1984.
   Chapter 7 offers a clear and thorough survey of the factors influencing interpersonal attraction.

Altman, Irwin, and Dalmas Taylor. *Social Penetration: The Development of Interpersonal Relationships.* New York: Holt, Rinehart and Winston, 1973.
A detailed explanation of the theory of social penetration introduced in this chapter.

Berg, J. H., and R. L. Archer. "The Disclosure-Liking Relationship." *Human Communication Research* 10 (Winter 1983).
A review of research on the relationship between self-disclosure and interpersonal attraction.

Berscheid, Ellen, and Elaine Walster. *Interpersonal Attraction,* 2d ed. Reading, Mass.: Addison-Wesley, 1978.
A readable discussion of the theories of attraction introduced in this chapter, plus a look at that special relationship, love.

Bochner, Arthur P. "The Functions of Communicating in Interpersonal Bonding." In *Handbook of Rhetorical and Communication Theory.* Boston: Allyn and Bacon, 1984.
A thorough review of the research and theory focusing on the role of communication in forming and maintaining personal relationships. This essay is written for the serious scholar and student.

Knapp, Mark L. *Interpersonal Communication and Human Relationships.* Boston: Allyn and Bacon, 1984.
Knapp provides a thorough explanation of his theory of relational stages. An excellent source for readers interested in learning more about the rise and fall of interpersonal relationships.

Nierenberg, Gerald I., and Henry Colero. *Meta-Talk.* New York: Simon & Schuster, 1974.
A readable account of the relational messages that occur in everyday communication.

Parks, Malcolm R. "The Ideology of Intimacy." *Communication Yearbook 5.* New Brunswick, N.J.: Transaction Books, 1981.
Parks emphasizes the inaccuracy of assuming that total self-disclosure is desirable.

Rubin, Lilian. *Just Friends: The Role of Friendship in Our Lives.* New York: Harper & Row, 1985.
An examination of the ambiguous yet vital relationship we call friendship. Based on interviews with three hundred men and women, this book explores the many varieties of friendship: casual versus "best friends," same- and opposite sex friendships, marriage and friendship, and friendship and kinship.

Rubin, Zick. *Liking and Loving.* New York: Holt, Rinehart and Winston, 1973.
A thorough, readable treatment of the subject by a noted social psychologist.

Wilmot, William W. "Metacommunication: A Re-examination and Extension." In *Communication Yearbook 4.* New Brunswick, N.J.: Transaction Books, 1980.
A thorough explanation of how metacommunication functions in interpersonal relationships.

Chapter Nine

Improving Interpersonal Relationships

Chapter Eight introduced the basic characteristics of interpersonal relationships: What are they? Why do we form them? What stages do they follow? What role does self-disclosure play? Although this information is important, it doesn't offer much help with the biggest concern for most people: how to make relationships as satisfying as possible.

This chapter offers guidelines for building and maintaining healthy personal relationships. It explains what kinds of communication create positive and negative communication climates. It outlines the reasons why people act defensively and offers suggestions for minimizing defensiveness in yourself and others. It describes several ways of responding to the criticism of others without lashing out or retreating. Finally, it offers guidelines for promoting positive communication climates in your day-to-day affairs.

Communication Climate: The Key to Positive Relationships

How would you describe your most important relationships? Fair and warm? Stormy? Hot? Cold? Just as physical locations have characteristic weather patterns, interpersonal relationships have unique climates, too. You can't measure the interpersonal climate by looking at a thermometer or glancing at the sky, but it's there nonetheless. Every relationship has a feeling, a pervasive mood that colors the interactions of the participants.

The term **communication climate** refers to the emotional tone of a relationship. A climate doesn't involve specific activities as much as the way people feel about each other as they carry out those activities. Consider two interpersonal communication classes, for example. Both meet for the same length of time and follow the same syllabus. It's easy to imagine how one of these classes might be a friendly, comfortable place to learn, whereas the other could be cold and tense—even hostile. The same principle holds for families, co-workers, and other relationships: Communication climates are a function of the way people feel about one another, not so much the tasks they perform.

Confirming and Disconfirming Climates

What makes some climates positive and others negative? A short but accurate answer is that the *communication climate is determined by the degree to which people see themselves as valued.* When we believe others view us as important, we are likely to feel good about our relationship. On the other hand, the relational climate suffers when we think others don't appreciate or care about us.

Messages that show you are valued have been called **confirming responses**.[1] Some kinds of communication are obviously confirming. Sincere *praise* or *compliments* show that you value the recipient. So does *agreeing* with others' opinions. But it isn't necessary to express praise or agreement to send confirming messages. In many cases simply *acknowledging* the other person can be a confirmation. Stopping to exchange small talk with an acquaintance says, "you're important." So does smiling or waving when you see the other person from a distance. (If you don't believe this, recall how you felt when you were ignored.)

The worst sin towards our fellow creatures is not to hate them, but to be indifferent to them; that's the essence of inhumanity.

George Bernard Shaw

On a more personal level, *listening* attentively to the other person sends a confirming message. Listening is even confirming when you disagree with the speaker. For example, asking sincere questions and using the paraphrasing skills described in Chapter Seven show that you care enough about the other person to listen. When compared to the responses that characterize nonlistening (stage-hogging, ambushing, pseudolistening, and so on), it's clear that sincerely trying to understand a conversational partner is a sign of respect.

In contrast to confirming communication, messages that deny the value of others have been labeled **disconfirming responses.**[2] These show a lack of regard for the other person, either by disputing or ignoring some important part of that person's message. Disagreement can certainly be disconfirming, especially if it goes beyond disputing the other person's ideas and attacks the speaker personally. It may be tough to hear someone say, "I don't think that's a good idea," but a personal attack like "You're crazy" is even more insulting. However, disagreement is not the most damaging kind of disconfirmation. Far worse are responses that ignore others' ideas—or even their existence. The list of disconfirming responses on page 307 shows several kinds of messages that convey a lack of appreciation. It's easy to see how these sorts of messages can create negative relational climates.

Disconfirming Messages

Disconfirming responses communicate a lack of respect or appreciation. Like their confirming counterparts, these messages can shape the climate of an entire relationship.

Impervious responses ignore the other person's attempt to communicate. Refusing to answer another person in a face-to-face conversation is the most obvious kind of impervious response, though not the most common. Failing to return a phone call or write back in answer to a letter are more common impervious responses. So is not responding to a smile or a wave.

Interrupting responses occur when one person begins to speak before the other has finished. They show a lack of concern about what the other person has to say.

A: I'm looking for an outfit I can wear to work and when I travel to...

B: I've got just the thing. It's part wool and part polyester, so it won't wrinkle at all.

A: Actually wrinkling isn't that important. I want something that will work as a business outfit and...

B: We have a terrific blazer that you can dress up or down, depending on the accessories you choose.

A: That's not what I was going to say. I want something that will work both here and down south. I have to go to a...

B: Say no more. I know just what you want.

A: Never mind. I think I'll look in some other stores.

Irrelevant responses are unrelated to what the other person has just said.

A: What a day! I thought it would never end. First the car overheated and I had to call a tow truck, and then the computer broke down at work.

B: Listen, we have to talk about a present for Ann's birthday. The party is on Saturday, and I only have tomorrow to shop for it.

A: I'm really beat. Could we talk about it in a few minutes? I've never seen a day like this one.

B: I just can't figure what would suit Ann. She's got everything...

Tangential responses are conversational "take aways." Instead of ignoring the speaker's remarks completely, they use them as a starting point for a shift to a different topic.

A: I'd like to know for sure whether you want to go skiing during vacation. If we don't decide whether to go soon, it'll be impossible to get reservations anywhere.

B: Yeah. And if I don't pass my botany class, I won't be in the mood to go anywhere. Could you give me some help with this homework?...

Impersonal responses are loaded with clichés and other statements that never truly respond to the speaker.

A: I've been having some personal problems lately, and I'd like to take off work early a couple of afternoons to clear them up.

B: Ah, yes. We all have personal problems. It seems to be a sign of the times.

Ambiguous responses contain messages with more than one meaning, leaving the other party unsure of the responder's position.

A: I'd like to get together with you soon. How about Tuesday?

B: Uh, maybe so.

A: Well, how about it. Can we talk Tuesday?

B: Oh, probably. See you later.

Incongruous responses contain two messages that seem to deny or contradict each other. Often at least one of these messages is nonverbal.

A: Darling, I love you.

B: I love you too. (giggles)

How Communication Climates Develop   As soon as two people start to communicate, a relational climate begins to develop. If the messages are confirming, the climate is likely to be a positive one. If they disconfirm one another, the relationship is likely to be hostile, cold, or defensive.

Verbal messages certainly contribute to the tone of a relationship, but many climate-shaping messages are nonverbal. The very act of approaching others is confirming, whereas avoiding them can be disconfirming. Smiles or frowns, the presence or absence of eye contact, tone of voice, the use of personal space . . . all these and other cues send messages about how the parties feel toward one another.

Once a climate is formed, it can take on a life of its own and grow in a self-perpetuating spiral. This sort of cycle is most obvious in regressive spirals, when a dispute gets out of hand:[3]

A: (mildly irritated) Where were you? I thought we agreed to meet here a half-hour ago.

B: (defensively) I'm sorry. I got hung up at the library. I don't have as much free time as you do, you know.

A: I wasn't *blaming* you, so don't get so touchy. I do resent what you just said, though. I'm plenty busy. And I've got lots of better things to do than wait around for you!

B: Who's getting touchy? I just made a simple comment. You've sure been defensive lately. What's the matter with you?

Fortunately, spirals can work in a progressive direction too. One confirming behavior leads to a similar response from the other person, which in turn leads to further confirmation by the first party.

Spirals—whether positive or negative—rarely go on indefinitely. When a negative spiral gets out of hand, the parties might agree to back off from their disconfirming behavior. "Hold on," one might say, "this is getting us nowhere." At this point there may be a cooling-off period, or the parties might work together more constructively to solve their problem. If the partners pass the "point of no return," the relationship may end. As you read in Chapter One, it's impossible to take back a message once it has been sent, and some exchanges are so lethal that the relationship can't survive them. Positive spirals also have their limit: Even the best relationships go through rocky periods, in which the climate suffers. The accumulated good will and communication skill of the partners, however, can make these times less frequent and intense. Therefore, most relationships pass through cycles of progression and regression.

Evaluating Communication Climates

You can probably recognize the communication climate in each of your relationships without much analysis. But answering the following questions will help explain *why* these climates exist. Following these steps may also suggest how to improve negative climates.

1. Identify the communication climate of an important interpersonal relationship. Using weather metaphors (sunny, gloomy, calm) may help.

2. List the confirming or disconfirming communication that created and now maintains this climate. Be sure to identify both verbal and nonverbal messages.

3. Describe what you can do either to maintain the existing climate (if positive) or to change it (if negative). Again, list both verbal and nonverbal behaviors.

© 1967 Jules Feiffer

Defensiveness: Causes and Remedies

Probably no type of communication pollutes an interpersonal climate more often than defensive spirals. One verbal attack leads to another, and soon the dispute mushrooms out of control, leaving an aftermath of hurt and bitterness that is difficult—sometimes even impossible—to repair.

Causes of Defensiveness   The word *defensiveness* suggests protecting oneself from attack, but what kind of attack? Surely, few if any of the times you become defensive involve a physical threat. If you're not threatened by bodily injury, what *are* you guarding against? To answer this question we need to talk more about the "presenting self" introduced in Chapter Two.

Recall that the presenting self is made up of the physical traits, personality characteristics, attitudes, aptitudes, and all the other parts of the image you want to present to the world.* Of course, not all parts of your presenting self are equally significant. Letting others know that you are right-handed or a Gemini is probably less important than convincing them you are honest or a loyal friend.

When others are willing to accept important parts of our presenting image there is no need to feel defensive. On the other hand, **defensiveness** occurs when we try to protect key parts of an image that we believe is being attacked. To see how this process operates, imagine what might happen if an important part of your presenting self was attacked. Suppose, for instance, that

- An instructor criticized you for making a stupid mistake.
- An acquaintance accused you of being selfish.
- An employer called you lazy.

It's no surprise that you would feel justified if these attacks were unfair. But your own experience will show that we often react defensively even when we know deep inside that the criticism is justified. For instance, you have probably responded defensively at times when you *did* make a mistake, act selfishly, or cut corners on your work. In fact, we often feel most defensive when criticism is right on target.

One reason for such defensiveness has to do with our need for approval. In response to the question "Why am I afraid to tell you who I am?" author John Powell quotes one actual response: "Because if I tell you who I am, you may not like who I am, and that is all I have."[4] So one reason we wear defensive masks is to appear to be the kind of person who will gain the approval of others.

Responding defensively to unpleasant but accurate criticism not only involves fooling others but also ourselves. We want to believe the act we're putting on, since it's uncomfortable to admit that we are not the person we would like to be. When faced with a situation where the truth might hurt, we are tempted to convince ourselves that we do fit the idealized picture we have constructed.

Types of Defensive Reactions   When a part of your presenting self is attacked by others and you aren't willing to accept their judgment, you are faced

---

* Actually, it is a mistake to talk about a single presenting self. In truth, we try to project different selves to different people. You might, for instance, try to impress a potential employer with your seriousness, while showing friends a more playful side.

> ## *It is a curious psychological fact that the man who seems to be "egotistic" is not suffering from too much ego, but from too little.*
>
> Sydney J. Harris

with what psychologists call **cognitive dissonance**—an inconsistency between two conflicting pieces of information, attitudes, or behavior.[5] Dissonance is an uncomfortable condition, and communicators strive to resolve it by seeking consistency. One way to eliminate the dissonance, of course, is to accept the critic's judgment and revise your presenting self accordingly. You could agree that you were stupid or mistaken, for example. Sometimes, however, you aren't willing to accept attacks. The accusations of your critic may be false. And even if they are true, you may be unwilling to admit their accuracy. It isn't pleasant to admit that you were lazy, unfair, or foolish. There are three broad ways to resolve dissonance without agreeing with a critic. Each of them is characterized by **defense mechanisms:** psychological devices that resolve dissonance by maintaining a positive presenting image.

> *There is something I don't*
>   *know that I am supposed to*
>   *know.*
> *I don't know what it is I don't*
>   *know, and yet am supposed*
>   *to know,*
> *and I feel I look stupid*
>   *if I seem both not to know*
>   *it and not know what it is I*
>   *don't know.*
>
> *Therefore I pretend I know it.*
>   *This is nerve-wracking*
>   *since I don't know what I*
>   *must pretend to know.*
> *Therefore I pretend to know*
>   *everything!*
>
> R. D. Laing, *Knots*

Attacking the Critic   Counterattacking follows the old maxim that the best defense is a good offense. Attacking defensive maneuvers can take several forms.

- *Verbal aggression.* Sometimes the recipient uses **verbal aggression** to assault the critic directly. "Where do you get off calling me sloppy?" you might storm to a roommate. "You're the one who leaves globs of toothpaste in the sink and dirty clothes all over the bedroom!" This sort of response shifts the blame onto the critic, without acknowledging that the original judgment might be true. Other attacks on the critic are completely off the subject: "You're in no position to complain about my sloppiness. At least I pay my share of the bills on time." Again, this response resolves the dissonance without ever addressing the validity of the criticism.
- *Sarcasm* Disguising the attack in a barbed, humorous message is a less direct form of aggression. "You think I ought to study more? Thanks for taking a break from watching soap operas and eating junk food to run my life." Sarcastic responses might score high on wit and quick thinking, but their hostile, disconfirming nature usually leads to a counterattack and a mutually destructive defensive spiral.

Distorting Critical Information   A second way of defending a perceived self under attack is to somehow distort the information in a manner that leaves the presenting self intact—at least in the eyes of the defender. There are a number of ways to distort dissonant information.

- *Rationalization.* **Rationalization** is the invention of logical but untrue explanations of undesirable behavior. "I would help you out, but I really have to study," you might say as a convenient way to avoid an unpleasant chore. "I'm not overeating," you might protest to another critic who you secretly admit is on target. "I have a busy day ahead, and I need to keep my strength up."
- *Compensation.* Those using **compensation** emphasize a strength in one area to cover up a weakness in another. A guilty parent might keep up the façade of being conscientious by protesting, "I may not be around much, but I give those kids the best things money can buy!" Likewise, you might try to convince yourself and others that you are a good friend by compensating: "Sorry I forgot

your birthday. Let me give you a hand with that job." There's nothing wrong with most acts of compensation in themselves. The harm comes when they are used not sincerely but to maintain a fictitious presenting image.

- *Regression.* Another way to avoid facing attack is to play helpless, claiming you *can't* do something when in truth you *don't want* to do it. "I'd like to have a relationship with you, but I just can't: I'm not ready." "I wish I could do the job better, but I just can't: I just don't understand it." The test for **regression** is to substitute the word *won't* for *can't*. In many cases it becomes clear that "It's not my fault" is a fiction.

Avoiding Dissonant Information   A third way to protect a threatened presenting image is to avoid information altogether. Avoidance can take several forms.

- *Physical avoidance.* Steering clear of people who attack a presenting self is an obvious way to avoid dissonance. Sometimes physical avoidance may be wise. There's little profit in being battered by hostile or abusive criticism. In other cases, however, the relationship may be important enough and the criticism valid enough that avoiding the situation only makes matters worse.

- *Repression.* Sometimes we mentally block out dissonant information. You might, for instance, know that you ought to discuss a problem with a friend, boss, or instructor, yet you put the idea out of your mind whenever it arises. It's even possible to repress a problem in the face of a critic. Changing the subject, acting as if you don't understand, and even pretending you don't hear the criticism all fall into the category of **repression.**

- *Apathy.* Another avoidance response, **apathy,** is to acknowledge unpleasant information but pretend you don't care about it. You might, for instance, sit calmly through a friend's criticism and act as if it didn't bother you. Similarly, you might respond to the loss of a job by acting indifferent: "Who cares? It was a dumb job anyhow."

- *Displacement.* **Displacement** occurs when we vent aggressive or hostile feelings against people or objects that are seen as less dangerous than the person or persons who threatened us originally. You may be mad at your boss, but rather than risk getting fired you could displace your aggression by yelling at the people you live with. Displacement almost always lets us preserve (at least to ourselves) the image that we're *potent*—that we're in control and can't be pushed around by forces beyond our control. The very act of displacing proves this a lie, of course—but one the displacer fails to recognize.

Defense Mechanism Inventory

List the three defense mechanisms you use most often, and describe three recent examples of each. You can arrive at your list both by thinking about your own behavior and by asking others to share their impressions of you.

Conclude your inventory by describing

1. The people with whom you become defensive most often.
2. The parts of your presenting self you frequently defend.
3. The usual consequences of using defense mechanisms.
4. Any more satisfying ways you could act in the future.

A CHILD'S GARDEN OF DEFENSE MECHANISMS

VERBAL AGGRESSION

I was with my boyfriend a few months ago when this man ran a red light and smashed into the side of our van. It was definitely his fault—there were cars stopped in the lane next to him.

Even though this guy must have known he was guilty, he jumped out of his car and began yelling at us. He called us "dirty punks" and "bums." He let out all that verbal aggression just to cover up the truth—that he was wrong.

RATIONALIZATION

A guy I know broke up with his girlfriend not too long ago, and the way he handled the thing really shows how rationalization can hurt communication. The reason he gave her for splitting up was that he'd be going away to Europe soon and he didn't want to break off suddenly when he left. But the truth was that he was just tired of her. She knew this, and I think his rationalization hurt her way more than if he'd been honest. I know he was only fooling himself because he wants to think he's a great guy who is thinking only of her welfare!

COMPENSATION

The other night I was at a party when the conversation turned to politics. I'm really turned off by that whole subject even though I know it's important. So when somebody brought up the election, I tried to change the subject to motorcycles, which I know a lot about. I do this a lot. When there's something I don't understand or don't like, I try to change the conversation to an area where I'm an authority.

REGRESSION

I use regression at home when I don't want to do chores. If a job sounds unpleasant I claim I "can't" do it: I "can't" prune the fruit trees the right way, strip off the old paint, wax the car, and so on. This way I get other members of my family to help without admitting I'm lazy. It probably doesn't fool them—and now that I'm aware of it, this kind of regression won't fool me either.

REPRESSION

My family is especially good at repressing our feelings about a serious problem. My brother is turning into an alcoholic, and I'm worried that it's going to hurt him and the family seriously soon. Despite the concern everyone feels, when we get together we pretend nothing's wrong. I think we hope that by acting like a happy, trouble-free family we'll become one.

APATHY

After learning about defense mechanisms I discovered that one of my "favorites" is apathy. When I'm criticized by my family, friends, or professors I pretend I don't care. I really <u>do</u> care a great deal, but it's hard to admit that I'm wrong. I guess being wrong isn't part of my presenting image. After thinking about it, I see that acting apathetic doesn't impress others, and it keeps me from changing for the better.

DISPLACEMENT

Yesterday at work I used the defense mechanism of displacement. My supervisor had given me a bunch of static about a problem that was really his fault. He's an unrealistic old S.O.B. to begin with, and there's no use arguing with him. So I guess because I was so mad, when one of the guys on my crew asked me if he could take off a little early that afternoon, I chewed him out for being a lazy so-and-so. But all it was was my anger at the boss being displaced. I was really sorry and apologized later, but it'll take a few days for the guy to let the chip melt off his shoulder.

Don't be fooled by me.
Don't be fooled by the face I wear
For I wear a mask. I wear a thousand masks,
     masks that I'm afraid to take off
     and none of them are me.

Pretending is an art that's second
     nature with me
But don't be fooled, for God's sake
     don't be fooled.
I give you the impression that I'm
     secure
That all is sunny and unruffled with
     me
     within as well as without,
     that confidence is my name
     and coolness my game.
     That the water's calm
     and I'm in command,
     and that I need no one.
But don't believe me. Please!

My surface may be smooth but my
     surface is my mask,
My ever-varying and ever-
     concealing mask.
Beneath lies no smugness, no
     complacence.
Beneath dwells the real me in
     confusion, in fear, in
     aloneness.
     But I hide this.
     I don't want anybody to know it.
     I panic at the thought of my
     weaknesses
     and fear exposing them.
That's why I frantically create my
     masks to hide behind.

They're nonchalant, sophisticated
     façades to help me pretend,
To shield me from the glance that
     knows.
But such a glance is precisely my
     salvation,
     my only salvation,
     and I know it.
That is, if it's followed by accep-
     tance, if it's followed by love.
It's the only thing that can liberate
     me from myself
     from my own self-built prison
     walls
     from the barriers that I so
     painstakingly erect.
That glance is the only thing that
     assures me
     of what I can't assure myself,
     that I'm really worth something.
But I don't tell you this.
     I don't dare.
     I'm afraid to.

I'm afraid you'll think less of me,
     that you'll laugh
     and your laugh would kill me.
I'm afraid that deep-down I'm
     nothing, that I'm just no good
     and you will see this
     and reject me.
So I play my game, my desperate,
     pretending game
With a façade of assurance without
And a trembling child within.
So begins the parade of masks
The glittering but empty parade of
     masks,
And my life becomes a front.
I idly chatter to you in suave tones
     of surface talk.
I tell you everything that's nothing
And nothing of what's everything, of
     what's crying within me.

So when I'm going through my
     routine
Do not be fooled by what I'm
     saying.
Please listen carefully and try to
     hear
     what I'm *not* saying.
Hear what I'd like to say
     but what I cannot say.

I dislike hiding.
     Honestly.
I dislike the superficial game I'm
     playing
     the superficial phony game.
I'd really like to be genuine and
     spontaneous
     and me.
But I need your help, your hand to
     hold
Even though my masks would tell
     you otherwise.
It will not be easy for you.
Long felt inadequacies make my
     defenses strong.
The nearer you approach me
The blinder I may strike back.
Despite what books say of men,
     I am irrational;
I fight against the very thing that
     I cry out for.

You wonder who I am?
You shouldn't
     For I am everyman
     And everywoman
     Who wears a mask.
Don't be fooled by me.
At least not by the face I wear.

Charles C. Finn

I Am a Rock

A winter's day
In a deep and dark December
I am alone
Gazing from my window
To the streets below
On a freshly fallen silent
   shroud of snow
I am a rock
I am an island.

I built walls
A fortress deep and mighty
That none may penetrate
I have no need of friendship
Friendship causes pain
Its laughter and its loving I
   disdain
I am a rock
I am an island.

Don't talk of love
Well, I've heard the word
   before
It's sleeping in my memory
I won't disturb the slumber
Of feelings that have died
If I'd never loved I never
   would have cried
I am a rock
I am an island.

I have my books
And my poetry to protect me.
I am shielded in armor
Hiding in my room
Safe within my womb
I touch no one and no one
   touches me
I am a rock
I am an island

And a rock feels no pain
And an island never cries.

Paul Simon and Art Garfunkel

RATIONALIZATION READER FOR STUDENTS

Situation	What to say
When the course is the lecture type:	We never get a chance to say anything.
When the course is the discussion type:	The professor just sits there. We don't know how to teach the course.
When all aspects of the course are covered in class:	All he does is follow the text.
When you're responsible for covering part of the course outside class:	He never covers half the things we're tested on.
When you're given objective tests:	They don't allow for any individuality in us.
When you're given essay tests:	They're too vague. We never know what's expected.
When the instructor gives no tests:	It isn't fair! He can't tell how much we really know.
When you have a lot of quizzes instead of a midterm and final:	We need major exams. Quizzes don't cover enough to really tell anything.
When you have only two exams for the whole course:	Too much rides on each one. You can just have a bad day.

Preventing Defensiveness in Others   Defensive reactions like the ones described in the preceding pages can pollute a communication climate. But what kinds of communication trigger a defensive reaction in the first place? We've already said that defensiveness is caused by messages that threaten the receiver's self-concept, but the research of Jack Gibb gives a more detailed picture of what kinds of communication trigger defensive reactions—and what kinds prevent them.[6]

After observing groups for several years, Gibb was able to isolate six types of defense-arousing communication and six contrasting behaviors that seemed to reduce the level of threat and defensiveness. The **Gibb categories** are listed in Table 9–1 on page 320. Using the supportive types of communication and avoiding the defensive ones will increase the odds of creating and maintaining positive communication climates in your relationships.

1. **Evaluation vs. description.** The first type of defense-provoking behavior Gibb noted was **evaluative communication**. Most people become irritated at judgmental statements, which they are likely to interpret as indicating a lack of regard. Evaluative language has often been described as **"you" language**

because most such statements contain an accusatory use of that word. For example,

You don't know what you're talking about.
You're not doing your best.
You smoke too much.

Gibb contrasts evaluative "you" language with **descriptive communication** or **"I" language.** Instead of putting the emphasis on judging another's behavior, the descriptive speaker simply explains the personal effect of the other's action. For instance, instead of saying, "You talk too much," a descriptive communicator would say, "When you don't give me a chance to say what's on my mind, I get frustrated." Notice that statements such as this include an account of the other person's behavior plus an explanation of its effect on the speaker and a description of the speaker's feelings.

2. **Control vs. problem orientation.** A second defense-provoking message involves some attempt to **control** another. A **controlling communication** occurs when a sender seems to be imposing a solution on the receiver with little regard for the receiver's needs or interests. The object of controls can range from where to eat dinner or what TV show to watch to whether to remain in a relationship or how to spend a large sum of money. Whatever the situation, people who act in controlling ways create a defensive climate. None of us likes to feel that our ideas are worthless and that nothing we say will change other people's determination to have their way—yet this is precisely the attitude a controller communicates. Whether done with words, gestures, tone of voice, or through some other channel; whether control is accomplished through status, insistence on obscure or irrelevant rules, or physical power, the controller generates hostility wherever he or she goes. The unspoken message such behavior communicates is "I know what's best for you, and if you do as I say, we'll get along."

In contrast, in **problem orientation** communicators focus on finding a solution that satisfies both their needs and those of the others involved. The goal here isn't to "win" at the expense of your partner but to work out some arrangement in which everybody feels like a winner. (Chapter Ten has a great deal to say about "win-win" problem solving as a way to find problem-oriented solutions.)

Table 9–1   The Gibb Categories of Defensive and Supportive Behaviors

Defensive behaviors	*Supportive behaviors*
1. evaluation	1. description
2. control	2. problem orientation
3. strategy	3. spontaneity
4. neutrality	4. empathy
5. superiority	5. equality
6. certainty	6. provisionalism

3. **Strategy vs. spontaneity.** The third communication behavior that Gibb identified as creating a poor communication climate involves the use of **strategy** or manipulation. One of the surest ways to make people defensive is to get caught trying to manipulate them into doing something for you. The fact that you tried to trick them instead of just asking for what you wanted is enough to build mistrust. Nobody likes to be a guinea pig or a sucker, and even well-meant manipulation can cause bad feelings.

Spontaneity is the behavior that contrasts with strategy. Spontaneity simply means expressing yourself honestly. Despite the misleading label Gibb chose for this kind of behavior, spontaneous communication needn't be blurted out as soon as an idea comes to you. You might want to plan the wording of your message carefully so that you can express yourself clearly. The important thing is to be honest. Often spontaneity won't get what you want, but in the long run it's usually better to be candid and perhaps miss out on some small goal than to say all the right things and be a fraud. More than once we've heard people say, "I didn't like what he said, but at least I know he was being honest."

Although it sounds paradoxical at first, spontaneity can be a strategy, too. Sometimes you'll see people using honesty in a calculating way, being just frank enough to win someone's trust or sympathy. This "leveling" is probably the most defense-arousing strategy of all because once we've learned someone is using frankness as a manipulation, there's almost no chance we'll ever trust that person again.

You may be getting the idea that using supportive behaviors such as description, problem orientation, empathy, and so on, is a good way to manipulate others. Before going any further, we want to say loudly and clearly

> In interpersonal relationships, I believe first person singular is most appropriate because it places responsibility clearly.
>
> If I say to another person, "I do not like what you did," then no contradiction is possible. No one can correct me because my perception and what I have decided to think about is mine alone. The other person may, however, suggest that I received only a portion of the information, or that I received it unclearly for one reason or another. In such a case, the meaning of the message may be tentative until it can be negotiated. It also is legitimate for me to perceive the message quite differently from the way the other person perceives it.
>
> On the other hand, if I say "You have made me angry," then you may very well contradict me by responding with something such as "No I didn't." In fact, I am eliciting a defensiveness and also inviting "you" to attempt a control of me by your helplessness, suffering, or anger.
>
> Only I am responsible for my behavior. Only I can change what I do. However, when I change my behavior, I may give the other person in the relationship the opportunity to evaluate his behavior and perhaps modify it.

John Narciso and David Burkett,
Declare Yourself

that if you ever act supportively without being sincere in what you're saying, you've misunderstood the idea behind this chapter, and you're running a risk of causing even more defensiveness than before. None of the ideas we present in this book can go into a "bag of tricks" that can be used to control others: If you ever find yourself using them in this way, beware!

4. **Neutrality vs. empathy.** Gibb used the term **neutrality** to describe a fourth behavior that arouses defensiveness. Probably a better descriptive word would be *indifference*. A neutral attitude is disconfirming because it communicates a lack of concern for the welfare of another and implies that the other person isn't very important to you. This perceived indifference is likely to promote defensiveness because people do not like to think of themselves as worthless, and they'll protect a self-concept that pictures themselves as worthwhile.

The small child who has urgent things to tell a parent but is met with indifference may be expected to become upset. The physician who seems clinical and detached to his patients may wonder why they look for another doctor.

The poor effects of neutrality become apparent when you consider the hostility that most people have for the large, impersonal organizations with which they have to deal: "They think of me as a number instead of a person"; "I felt as if I were being handled by computers and not human beings." These two common statements reflect reactions to being handled in an indifferent way. Gibb has found that **empathy** helps rid communication of the quality of indifference. When people show that they care for the feelings of another there's little chance that the person's self-concept will be threatened. Empathy means accepting another's feelings, putting yourself in another's place. This doesn't mean you need to agree with that person. By simply letting someone know about your care and respect, you'll be acting in a supportive way. Gibb noted the importance of nonverbal messages in communicating empathy. He found that facial and bodily expressions of concern are often more important to the receiver than the words used.

5. **Superiority vs. equality.** A fifth behavior creating a defensive climate involves superiority. How many interpersonal relationships have you dropped because you couldn't stand the superiority that the other person projected? An individual who communicates superiority arouses feelings of inadequacy in the recipients. We're not particular about the type of superiority presented to us; we just become defensive. Money, power, intellectual ability, physical appearance, and athletic prowess are all areas our culture stresses. Consequently, we often feel a need to express our superiority along these lines.

Individuals who act superior communicate that they don't want to relate on equal terms with others in the relationship. Furthermore, people like this seem to imply that they don't want feedback or need help because it would be coming from someone "inferior." The listener is put on guard because the senders are likely to attempt to reduce the receiver's worth, power, or status to maintain or advance their own superiority.

Perhaps you've had professors who continually reminded their class of their superior intellectual ability and position. Remember how delighted you were when you or a classmate caught one of these superior types in a mistake? Why do you suppose that was so satisfying? Some might argue that this is a good strategy to keep students awake, but in reality much of

We do not need confirmation for qualities of which we are certain, but we will be extremely touchy when false claims are questioned.

Karen Horney

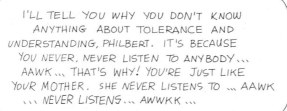

They defend their errors as if they were defending their inheritance.

Edmund Burke

the students' effort is then directed to defending self-worth rather than pursuing the objectives of the course.

When we detect people communicating superiority, we usually react defensively. We "turn them off," justify ourselves, or argue with them in our minds. Sometimes we choose to change the subject verbally or even walk away. Of course, there is always the counterattack, which includes an attempt to belittle the senders of the superiority message. We'll go to great lengths "to cut them down to size." All these defensive reactions to projected superiority are destructive to an interpersonal climate.

Many times in our lives we are in a relationship with individuals who possess talents greater than ours. But is it necessary for these people to project superiority? Your own experiences will tell you that it isn't. Gibb has found ample evidence that many who have superior skills and talents are capable of projecting feelings of **equality** rather than superiority. Such people communicate that although they may have greater talent in certain areas, they see others as having just as much worth as human beings.

6. **Certainty vs. provisionalism.** Have you ever run into people who are positive they're right, who know that theirs is the only or proper way of doing something, who insist that they have all the facts and need no additional information? If you have, you've met individuals who project the defense-arousing behavior Gibb calls **certainty.**

How do you react when you're the target of such certainty? Do you suddenly find your energy directed to proving the dogmatic individual wrong? If you do, you're reacting normally, if not very constructively.

Communicators who regard their own opinions with certainty while disregarding the ideas of others demonstrate a rather clear lack of regard for

"What do you mean 'Your guess is as good as mine'? My guess is a hell of a lot __better__ than your guess!"

Drawing by Ross; © 1983 The New Yorker Magazine, Inc.

the thoughts others hold to be important. It's likely the receiver will take the certainty as a personal affront, and react defensively.

In contrast to dogmatic communication is **provisionalism,** in which people may have strong opinions but are willing to acknowledge that they don't have a corner on the truth and will change their stand if another position seems more reasonable.

The need to be right—the sign of a vulgar mind.

Albert Camus

Defensiveness Feedback

1. Approach an important person in your life, and request some help in learning more about yourself. Inform the other person that your discussion will probably take at least an hour, so make sure both of you are prepared to invest the necessary amount of time.

2. Begin by explaining all twelve of the Gibb behaviors to your partner. Be sure to give enough examples so that each category is clearly understood.

3. When your explanation is complete and you've answered all your partner's questions, ask him to tell you which of the Gibb categories *you use.* Seek specific examples so that you are certain to understand the feedback fully. (Since you are requesting an evaluation, be prepared for a little defensiveness on your own part at this point.) Inform your partner that you are interested in discovering both the defense-arousing and the supportive behaviors you use and that you are sincerely interested in receiving a candid answer. (Note: if you don't want to hear the truth from your partner, don't try this exercise.)

4. As your partner speaks, record the categories he lists in sufficient detail for both of you to be sure that you have understood his comments.

5. When you have finished your list, show it to your partner. Listen to his reactions, and make any corrections that are necessary to reflect an accurate understanding of his comments. When your list is accurate, have your partner sign it to indicate that you have understood him clearly.

6. In a concluding statement note
   a. How you felt as your partner was describing you.
   b. Whether you agree with the evaluation.
   c. What effect your use of the various Gibbs categories has on your relationship with your partner.

Responding Nondefensively to Criticism   The world would be a happier place if everyone communicated supportively. But how can you respond nondefensively when others use evaluation, control, superiority, and all the other attacking behaviors Gibb identified? Despite your best intentions, it's difficult to be reasonable when you're faced with a torrent of criticism. Being attacked is hard enough when the critic is clearly being unfair, but it's often even more threatening when the judgments are on target. Despite the accuracy of your critic, the tendency is either to counterattack aggressively with a barrage of verbal aggression or to withdraw nonassertively.

Since neither of these responses is likely to resolve a dispute, we need alternative ways of behaving. There are two such methods. Despite their apparent simplicity, they have proved to be among the most valuable skills many communicators have learned.[7]

Seek More Information   The response of seeking more information makes good sense when you realize that it's foolish to respond to a critical attack until you understand what the other person has said. Even comments that on first consideration appear to be totally unjustified or foolish often prove to contain at least a grain of truth and sometimes much more.

Many readers object to the idea of asking for details when they are criticized. Their resistance grows from confusing the act of *listening open-mindedly* to a speaker's comments with *accepting* them. Once you realize that you can listen to, understand, and even acknowledge the most hostile comments without necessarily accepting them, it becomes much easier to hear another person out. If you disagree with a speaker's objections, you will be in a much better position to explain yourself once you understand the criticism. On the other hand, after carefully listening to the other's remarks, you might just see that they are valid, in which case you have learned some valuable information about yourself. In either case, you have everything to gain and nothing to lose by paying attention to the critic.

Of course, after one has spent years of instinctively resisting criticism, learning to listen to the other person will take some practice. To make matters clearer, here are several ways in which you can seek additional information from your critics.

1. **Ask for specifics.** Often the vague attack of a critic is virtually useless even if you sincerely want to change. Abstract accusations such as "You're being unfair" or "You never help out" can be difficult to understand. In such cases it is a good idea to request more specific information from the sender. "What do I *do* that's unfair?" is an important question to ask before you can judge whether the accusation is correct. "When haven't I helped out?" you might ask before agreeing with or disputing the accusation.

   If you already solicit specifics by using questions and are still accused of reacting defensively, the problem may be in the *way* you ask. Your tone of voice and facial expression, posture, or other nonverbal clues can give the same words radically different connotations. For example, think of how you could use the words "Exactly what are you talking about?" to communicate either a genuine desire to know or your belief that the speaker is crazy. It's important to request specific information only when you genuinely want to learn more from the speaker, for asking under any other circumstances will only make matters worse.

2. **Guess about specifics.** On some occasions even your sincere and well-phrased requests for specific details won't meet with success. Sometimes your critics won't be able to define precisely the behavior they find offensive. In these instances, you'll hear such comments as "I can't tell you exactly what's wrong with your sense of humor—all I can say is that I don't like it." In other cases, your critics may know the exact behaviors they don't like, but for some reason they seem to get a perverse satisfaction out of making you struggle to figure it out. At times like this, you hear such comments as "Well, if you don't know what you did to hurt my feelings, I'm certainly not going to tell you!"

Needless to say, failing to learn the details of another's criticism when you genuinely want to know them can be a frustrating experience. In instances like these, you can often learn more clearly what is bothering your critic by *guessing* at the specifics of a complaint. In a sense you become both detective and suspect, the goal being to figure out exactly what "crime" you have committed. Like the technique of asking for specifics, guessing must be done with goodwill if it's to produce satisfying results. You need to convey to the critic that for both of your sakes you're truly interested in finding out what is the matter. Once you have communicated this intention, the emotional climate generally becomes more comfortable because, in effect, both you and the critic are seeking the same goal.

Here are some typical questions you might hear from someone guessing about the details of another's criticism:

- "So you object to the language I used in writing the paper. Was my language too formal?"
- "OK, I understand that you think the outfit looks funny. What is it that's so bad? Is it the color? Does it have something to do with the fit? The fabric?"
- "When you say that I'm not doing my share around the house, do you mean that I haven't been helping enough with the cleaning?"

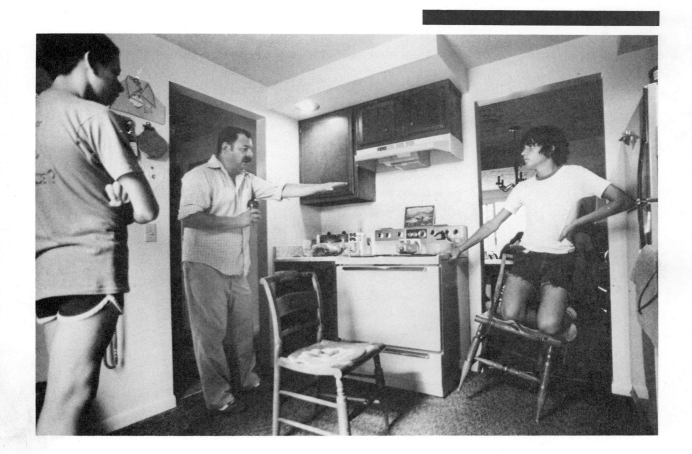

3. Paraphrase the speaker's ideas. Another strategy is to draw out confused or reluctant speakers by paraphrasing their thoughts and feelings and using the active listening skills described in Chapter Seven. Paraphrasing is especially good in helping others solve their problems; and since people generally criticize you because your behavior creates some problem for them, the method is especially appropriate at such times.

One advantage of paraphrasing is that you don't have to guess about the specifics of your behavior that might be offensive. By clarifying or amplifying what you understand critics to be saying, you'll learn more about their objections. A brief dialog between a disgruntled customer and an especially talented store manager using paraphrasing might sound like this:

Customer   The way you people run this store is disgusting! I just want to tell you that I'll never shop here again.

Manager   (reflecting the customer's feeling) It seems that you're quite upset. Can you tell me your problem?

Customer   It isn't *my* problem; it's the problem your salespeople have. They seem to think it's a great inconvenience to help a customer find anything around here.

Manager   So you didn't get enough help locating the items you were looking for, is that it?

Customer   Help? I spent twenty minutes looking around in here before I even talked to a clerk. All I can say is that it's a hell of a way to run a store.

Manager   So what you're saying is that the clerks seemed to be ignoring the customers?

Customer   No. They were all busy with other people. It just seems to me that you ought to have enough help around to handle the crowds that come in at this hour.

Manager   I understand now. What frustrated you the most was the fact that we didn't have enough staff to serve you promptly.

Customer   That's right. I have no complaint with the service I get once i'm waited on, and I've always thought you had a good selection here. It's just that I'm too busy to wait so long for help.

Manager   Well, I'm glad you brought this to my attention. We certainly don't want loyal customers going away mad. I'll try to see that it doesn't happen again.

This conversation illustrates two advantages of paraphrasing. First, the critic often reduces the intensity of the attack once he or she realizes that the complaint is being heard. Often criticism grows from the frustration of unmet needs—which in this case was partly a lack of attention. As soon as the manager genuinely demonstrated interest in the customer's plight, the customer began to feel better and was able to leave the store relatively calm. Of course this sort of active listening won't always mollify your critic, but even when it doesn't, there's still another benefit that makes the technique worthwhile. In the sample conversation, for instance, the manager learned some valuable information by taking time to understand the customer. The manager discovered that there were certain times when the number of employees was insufficient to help the crowd of shoppers and also that the delays at these times seriously annoyed at least some shoppers, thus threatening a loss in business. This knowledge is certainly important, and by reacting defensively to the customer's complaint, the manager would not have learned from it. As you read earlier, even apparently outlandish criticism often contains at least a grain of truth, and thus a person who is genuinely interested in improving would be wise to hear it out.

4. **Ask about the consequences of your behavior.** As a rule, people complain about your actions only when some need of theirs is not being met. One way to respond to this kind of criticism is to find out exactly what troublesome consequences your behavior has for them. You'll often find that actions that seem perfectly legitimate to you cause some difficulty for your critic; once you have understood this, comments that previously sounded foolish take on a new meaning.

   A: You say that I ought to have my cat neutered. Why is that important to you?

   B: Because at night he picks fights with my cat, and I'm tired of paying the vet's bills.

   C: Why do you care whether I'm late to work?

   D: Because when the boss asks where you are, I feel obligated to make up some story so you won't get in trouble, and I don't like to lie.

   E: Why does it bother you when I lose money at poker? You know I never gamble more than I can afford.

   F: It's not the cash itself. It's that when you lose, you're in a grumpy mood for two or three days, and that's no fun for me.

Sometimes soliciting more information from a critic isn't enough. What do you do, for instance, when you fully understand the other person's objections and still feel a defensive response on the tip of your tongue? You know that if you try to protect yourself, you'll wind up in an argument; on the other hand, you simply can't accept what the other person is saying about you. The solution to such a dilemma is outrageously simple and is discussed in the following section.

Agree with the Critic   But, you protest, how can you honestly agree with comments you don't believe are true? The following pages will answer this question by showing that there's virtually no situation in which you can't honestly accept the other person's point of view and still maintain your position. To see how this can be so, you need to realize that there are two different types of agreement, one of which you can use in almost any situation.

1. **Agree with the truth.** This is the easiest type of agreement to understand, though not always to practice. You agree with the truth when another person's criticism is factually correct:

   "You're right, I am angry."
   "I suppose I *was* being defensive."
   "Now that you mention it, I did get pretty sarcastic."

Love your enemies, for they tell you your faults.

Benjamin Franklin

Agreeing with the facts seems quite sensible when you realize that certain matters are indisputable. If you agree to be somewhere at 4:00 and don't show up until 5:00, you *are* late, no matter how good your explanation for tardiness is. If you've broken a borrowed object, run out of gas, or failed to finish a job you started, there's no point in denying it. In the same way, if you're honest, you will have to agree with many interpretations of your behavior even when they're not flattering. You do get angry, act foolishly, fail to listen, and behave inconsiderately. Once you rid yourself of the myth of perfection, it's much easier to acknowledge these truths.

But if it's so obvious that the descriptions others give of your behaviors are often accurate, why is it so difficult to accept them without being defensive? The answer to this question lies in a confusion between agreeing with the *facts* and accepting the *judgment* that so often accompanies them. Most critics don't merely describe the action that offends them; they also evaluate it, and it's this evaluation that we resist:

"It's silly to be angry."
"You have no reason for being defensive."
"You were wrong to be so sarcastic."

It's judgments like these that we resent. By realizing that you can agree with—and even learn from—the descriptive part of many criticisms and still not accept the accompanying evaluations, you'll often have a response that is both honest and nondefensive.

Of course, in order to reduce defensiveness, your agreements with the facts must be honest ones admitted without malice. It's humiliating to accept descriptions that aren't accurate, and maliciously pretending to agree with these only leads to trouble. You can imagine how unproductive the conversation given earlier would have been if the manager had spoken the same words in a sarcastic tone. Only agree with the facts when you can do so sincerely. Though this won't always be possible, you'll be surprised at how often you can use this simple response.

2. **Agree with the critic's perception.** What about occasions when there seems to be no basis whatsoever for agreeing with your critic? You've listened carefully and asked questions to make sure you understand the objections, but the more you listen, the more positive you are that the critic is totally out of line. Even in these cases there's a way of agreeing—this time not with the critics' conclusions but with their right to see things their way.

A: I don't believe you've been all the places you were just describing. You're probably just making all this up to impress us.

B: Well, I can see how you might think that. I've known people who lie to get approval.

C: I want to let you know right from the start that I was against hiring you for the job. I think the reason you got it was because you're a woman.

D: I can understand why you'd believe that with all the antidiscrimination laws on the books. I hope that after I've been here for a while, you'll change your mind.

E: I don't think you're being totally honest about your reasons for wanting to stay home. You say that it's because you have a headache, but I think you're avoiding Mary and Walt.

F: I can see why that would make sense to you because Mary and I got into an argument the last time we were together. All I can say is that I do have a headache.

Responses such as these tell critics that you're acknowledging the reasonableness of their perception even though you don't choose to accept it yourself or change your behavior. This coping style is a valuable one, for it lets you avoid the debates over who is right and who is wrong, which can turn an exchange of ideas into an argument. Note the difference in the following scenes between Amy and Bob.

Disputing the perception:

Amy: I don't see how you can stand to be around Josh. The guy is so crude that he gives me the creeps.

Bob: What do you mean, crude? He's a really nice guy. I think you're just touchy.

A: Touchy! If it's touchy to be offended by disgusting behavior, then I'm guilty.

B: You're not guilty about anything. It's just that you're too sensitive when people kid around.

A: Too sensitive, huh? I don't know what's happened to you. You used to have such good judgment about people. . . .

Agreeing with the perception:

A: I don't see how you can stand to be around Josh. The guy is so crude that he gives me the creeps.

B: Well, I enjoy being around him, but I guess I can see how his jokes would be offensive to some people.

A: You're damn right. I don't see how you can put up with him.

B: Yeah. I guess if you didn't appreciate his humor, you wouldn't want to have much to do with him.

Notice how in the second exchange Bob was able to maintain his own position without attacking Amy's in the least. This acceptance is the key ingredient for successfully agreeing with your critics' perceptions: You make it clear that in no way are you disputing their views of the matter. And since you have no intention of attacking your critics' views, they are less likely to be defensive.

Coping with Criticism

You can practice nondefensive responses to criticism by taking turns following these steps with a partner.

1. Choose a criticism from this list and brief your partner on how it might be directed at you:
    a. You're so selfish sometimes. You only think of yourself.
    b. Don't be so touchy!
    c. You say you understand me, but you don't really.
    d. I wish you'd do your share around here.
    e. You're so critical!

2. As your partner criticizes you, answer with the appropriate response from the preceding pages. As you do so, try to adopt an attitude of genuinely wanting to understand the criticism and finding parts you can sincerely agree with.

3. Ask your partner to evaluate your response. Does it follow the forms described in the previous pages? Does it sound sincere?

4. Replay the same scene, trying to improve your response.

More Readings on Improving Relationships

Duck, Steve, and Robin Gilmour, eds. *Personal Relationships*. New York: Academic Press, 1981.
This brief collection of research on effective interpersonal relationships is an excellent second step for readers interested in learning how professionals examine the subject.

Garner, Alan. *Conversationally Speaking: Tested Ways to Increase Your Personal and Social Effectiveness.* New York: McGraw-Hill, 1981.
> *A practical guide to the social skills that lead to confirming relationships. Topics include starting and maintaining conversations, handling criticism constructively, and reducing anxiety in social situations.*

Knapp, Mark L. *Interpersonal Communication and Human Relationships.* Boston: Allyn and Bacon, 1985.
> *Knapp provides a thorough, readable survey of the rise and fall of interpersonal relationships. Part V, "Toward More Effective Communication," is especially informative about what kinds of behavior is judged to be positive.*

Wells, Theodora. *Keeping Your Cool Under Fire: Communicating Non-Defensively.* New York: McGraw-Hill, 1980.
> *This is a lengthy but readable treatment of defensiveness. In addition to amplifying the material in this chapter, Wells discusses defensiveness in organizations and relates the subject to some of the principles of emotions you read about in Chapter 4 of this book.*

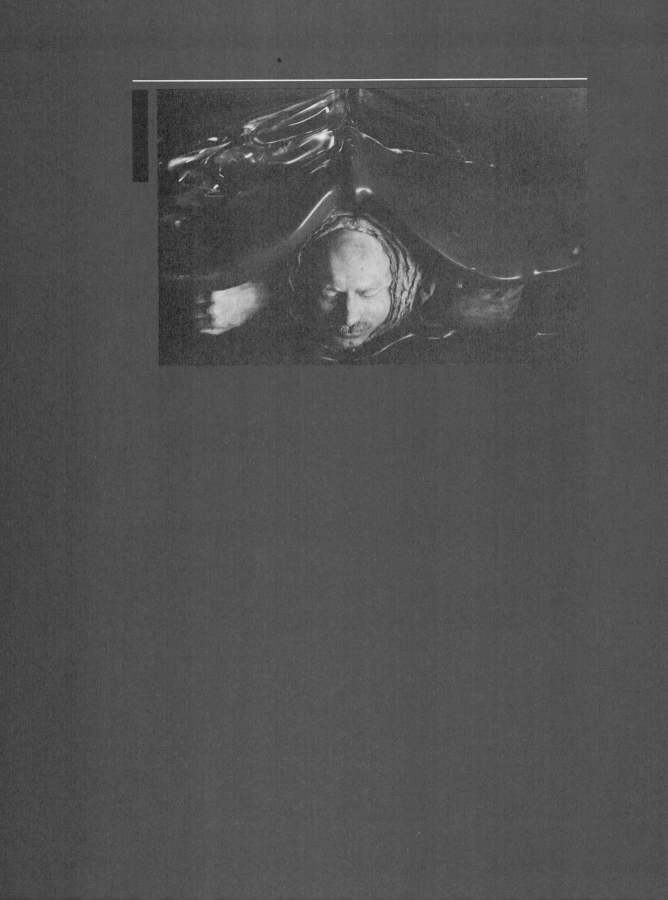

You've almost finished this first look at interpersonal communication. You've seen the major barriers that keep us from understanding each other, and you've practiced some ways to overcome them. If you've learned to use the skills presented in this book, you should now find that your relationships with others are everything you've ever wanted, free from any problems, right?

Wrong!

It's naive to expect to live a life free of conflicts. Problems are bound to arise any time two people get together for more than a short while. Some of these problems will be serious enough to threaten the relationship unless they are handled well.

Unfortunately there are no magic tricks to resolve all the conflicts in your life. On the other hand, there are ways to manage these conflicts constructively. If you follow these methods you will find that your relationships are actually stronger and more satisfying than before.

Not everything that is faced can be changed, but nothing can be changed until it is faced.

James Baldwin

The Nature of Conflict

Before focusing on how to solve interpersonal problems constructively we need to take a brief look at the nature of conflict. What is it? Why is it an inevitible part of life? How can it be beneficial?

Conflict Defined Before reading further, make a list of the interpersonal conflicts in your life. They probably involve many different people, revolve around very different subjects, and take many different forms. Some become loud, angry arguments. Others may be expressed in calm, rational discussions. Still others might simmer along most of the time with brief but bitter flareups.

Whatever form they may take, all interpersonal conflicts share certain characteristics. Joyce Hocker and William Wilmot provide a thorough definition when they define **conflict** as *an expressed struggle between at least two interdependent parties who perceive incompatible goals, scarce rewards, and interference from the other party in achieving their goals.*[1] A closer look at the key parts of this definition will help you recognize how conflict operates in your life.

Expressed Struggle   A conflict can exist only when both parties are aware of a disagreement. For instance, you may be upset for months because a neighbor's loud stereo keeps you awake at night, but no conflict exists between the two of you until the neighbor learns of your problem. Of course, the expressed struggle doesn't have to be verbal. You can show your displeasure with somebody without saying a word. A dirty look, the silent treatment, or avoiding the other person are all ways of expressing yourself. One way or another, both parties must know that a problem exists before they're in conflict.

Perceived Incompatible Goals   All conflicts look as if one party's gain would be another's loss. For instance, consider the neighbor whose stereo keeps you awake at night. Doesn't somebody have to lose? If the neighbor turns down the noise, he loses the enjoyment of hearing the music at full volume; but if the neighbor keeps the volume up, you're still awake and unhappy.

> *We struggled together, knowing. We prattled, pretended, fought bitterly, laughed, wept over sad books or old movies, nagged, supported, gave, took, demanded, forgave, resented—hating the ugliness of each other, yet cherishing that which we were. . . . Will I ever find someone to battle with as we battled, love as we loved, share with as we shared, challenge as we challenged, forgive as we forgave? You used to say that I saved up all of my feelings so that I could spew forth when I got home. The anger I experienced in school I could not vent there. How many times have I heard you chuckle as you remembered the day I would come home from school and share with you all of the feelings I had kept in. "If anyone had been listening they would have thought you were punishing me, striking out at me. I always survived and you always knew that I would still be with you when you were through." There was an honesty about our relationship that may never exist again.*

Vian Catrell

The goals in this situation really aren't completely incompatible—there are solutions that allow both parties to get what they want. For instance, you could achieve peace and quiet by closing your windows or getting the neighbor to close his. You might use a pair of earplugs, or perhaps the neighbor could get a set of earphones, allowing the music to be played at full volume without bothering anyone. If any of these solutions prove workable, the conflict disappears.

Unfortunately, people often fail to see mutually satisfying answers to their problems. As long as they *perceive* their goals to be mutually exclusive, a conflict exists.

Perceived Scarce Rewards   Conflicts also exist when people believe there isn't enough of something to go around. The most obvious example of a scarce resource is money—a cause of many conflicts. If a worker asks for a raise in pay and the boss would rather keep the money or use it to expand the business, the two parties are in conflict.

Time is another scarce commodity. As authors and family men, both of us constantly face struggles about how to use the limited time we have at home. Should we work on this book? Visit with our wives? Play with our children? Enjoy the luxury of being alone? With only twenty-four hours in a day, we're bound to wind up in conflicts with our families, editors, students, and friends—all of whom want more of our time than we have to give.

Interdependence   However antagonistic they might feel, the parties in conflict are usually dependent on each other. The welfare and satisfaction of one depends on the actions of another. If not, then even in the face of scarce resources and incompatible goals there would be no need for conflict. Interdependence exists between conflicting nations, social groups, organizations, friends, and lovers. In each case, if the two parties didn't need each other to solve the problem, they would go their separate ways. In fact, many conflicts go unresolved because the parties fail to understand their interdependence. One of the first steps toward resolving a conflict is to take the attitude that "we're all in this together."

CONFLICT BASIC AS HUNGER?

Psychologists often find themselves in the position of proving scientifically what people have always known implicitly.

So it is with new data on the value of conflict.

Conflict, a Canadian psychologist reported in *Scientific American*, 215:82, 1966, may be the same sort of driving force as hunger, thirst, sexual appetite and pain. If so, it can be placed among the ranks of those conditions which are most efficient in producing learning, with important implications for education.

All of the basic drives have in common the fact that they arouse the individual physically, sharpen his faculties, motivate him to act and enhance his learning capacity. . . .

SCIENCE NEWS

Conflict Is Natural   *Every* relationship of any depth at all has conflict. No matter how close, how understanding, how compatible you are, there will be times when your ideas or actions or needs or goals won't match those of others around you. You like rock music; but your companion prefers Beethoven; you want to date other people, but your partner wants to keep the relationship exclusive; you think a paper you've done is fine, but your instructor wants it changed; you like to sleep late on Sunday mornings, but your housemate likes to play the stereo—loudly! There's no end to the number and kinds of disagreements possible.

And just as conflict is a fact of life, so are the feelings that go along with it— hurt, anger, frustration, resentment, disappointment. Because these feelings are usually unpleasant, there is a temptation to avoid them or pretend they don't exist. But as sure as conflicts are bound to arise, so are the emotions that go with them.

At first this might seem depressing. If problems are inevitable in even the best relationships, does this mean that you're doomed to relive the same arguments, the same hurt feelings, over and over? Fortunately, the answer to this question is a definite no. Even though conflict is a part of a meaningful relationship, you can change the way you deal with it.

Conflict Can Be Beneficial   Most of us fear conflict because we have seen that serious disagreements can damage relationships. In truth, this sort of damage is preventable. In fact, effective handling of conflicts can actually keep good relationships strong. Research has demonstrated that people who use the constructive skills described in this chapter are more satisfied with their relationships[2] and with the outcomes of their conflicts.[3]

One nine-year study illustrated the value of constructive conflict resolution by revealing that happily married couples handled their disputes quite differently from unhappy ones.[4] The unhappy couples argued in ways that we have cataloged in this book as destructive. They were more concerned with defending themselves than with being problem oriented; they failed to listen carefully to one another, had little or no empathy for their partners, used evaluative "you" language, and ignored one another's nonverbal relational messages.

Are there genuinely nice, sweet people in this world? Yes, absolutely yes, and they get angry as often as you and I. They must—otherwise they would be full of vindictive feelings and slush, which would prevent genuine sweetness.

Theodore Isaac Rubin

Happy couples communicated far more effectively during their disagreements. While often arguing vigorously, partners used perception checking skills to find out what their partner was thinking, and they let one another know that they understood the other side of the dispute. They were willing to admit their defensiveness when it occurred, so that they could get back to solving the problem at hand. As you can see, the happy couples used many of the skills you have read about in earlier chapters of this book.

It is encouraging to know that these skills are learnable. The National Institute of Health funded a three-year program that has trained 150 engaged couples in communication skills, including how to argue constructively. In follow-up studies, couples who completed the training tended to remain happy together, whereas a control group of similar couples who did not receive the training grew significantly less satisfied with one another.

In the following pages, we will review communication skills that can make conflicts constructive, and we will introduce still more methods you can use to resolve the inevitable conflicts you face. Before doing so, however, we need to examine how individuals behave when faced with a dispute.

Personal Conflict Styles

There are four ways in which people can act when their needs aren't met (see Table 10–1). Each approach has very different characteristics, as we can show by describing a common problem. At one time or another almost everyone has been bothered by a neighbor's barking dog. You know the story: Every passing car, distant siren, pedestrian, and falling leaf seem to set off a fit of barking that makes you unable to sleep, socialize, or study. In a description of the possible ways of handling this kind of situation, the differences between nonassertive, directly aggressive, indirectly aggressive, and assertive behavior should become clear.

Nonassertive Behavior   Nonassertion is the inability to express one's thoughts or feelings when necessary because of a lack of confidence or skill or both. There are two ways in which nonasserters manage a conflict. Sometimes they ignore their needs. Faced with the dog, for instance, a nonassertive person would try to forget the barking by closing the windows and trying to concentrate even harder on something else. Another form of denial would be to claim that no problem exists—that a little barking never bothered anyone. To the degree that

© 1963 United Media, Inc.

it's possible to make problems disappear by ignoring them, such an approach is probably advisable. In many cases, however, it simply isn't realistic to claim that nothing is wrong. For instance, if your health is being jeopardized by the cigarette smoke from someone nearby, you are clearly punishing yourself by remaining silent. If you need more information from a supervisor before undertaking a project, you reduce the quality of your work by pretending to understand it at all. If you claim that an unsatisfactory repair job is acceptable, you are paying good money for nothing. In all these and many more cases, simply pretending that nothing is the matter when your needs are not met is clearly not the answer.

A second nonassertive course of action is to acknowledge that your needs are not being met but simply to accept the situation, hoping that it might clear up without any action on your part. You could, for instance, wait for the neighbor who owns the barking dog to move. You could wait for the dog to be run over by a passing car or to die of old age. You could hope that your neighbor will realize how noisy the dog is and do something to keep it quiet. Each of these occurrences is a possibility, of course, but it would be unrealistic to count on one of them to solve your problem. And even if by chance you were lucky enough for this to be solved without taking action, you couldn't expect to be so fortunate in other parts of your life.

In addition, while waiting for one of these eventualities, you would undoubtedly grow more and more angry at your neighbor, making a friendly relationship between the two of you impossible. You would also lose a degree of self-respect, for you would see yourself as the kind of person who can't cope with even a

Table 10–1   Styles of Conflict

	Nonassertive	*Directly Aggressive*	*Indirectly Aggressive*	*Assertive*
Approach to Others	I'm not OK, You're OK.	I'm OK, You're not OK.	I'm OK, You're not OK. (But I'll let you think you are.)	I'm OK, You're OK.
Decision Making	Let others choose.	Chooses for others. They know it.	Chooses for others. They don't know it.	Chooses for self.
Sulf-Sufficiency	Low.	High or low.	Looks high but usually low.	Usually high.
Behavior in Problem Situations	Flees, gives in.	Outright attack.	Concealed attack.	Direct confrontation.
Response of Others	Disrespect, guilt, anger, frustration.	Hurt, defensiveness, humiliation.	Confusion, frustration, feelings of manipulation.	Mutual respect.
Success Pattern	Succeeds by luck or charity of others.	Beats out others.	Wins by manipulation.	Attempts "no lose" solutions.

Adapted with permission from S. Phelps and N. Austin, *The Assertive Woman* (San Luis Obispo, Calif.: Impact, 1974), p. 11; and Gerald Piaget, *Training in Assertive Communication: A Practical Manual,* 3d ed. (Portola Valley, Calif.: IAHB, 1980).

common, everyday irritation. Clearly, nonassertion is not a very satisfying course of action—either in this case or in others.

Direct Aggression   In contrast to nonassertion, **direct aggression** occurs when a person overreacts. The usual consequences of aggressive behaviors are anger and defensiveness or hurt and humiliation. In either case, aggressive communicators build themselves up at the expense of others.

You could handle the dog problem with direct aggression by abusively confronting your neighbors, calling them names and threatening to call the dogcatcher the next time you saw their hound running loose. If the town in which you live has a leash law, you would be within your legal rights to do so and thus you would gain your goal of bringing peace and quiet to the neighborhood. Unfortunately, your direct aggression would have other, less productive consequences. Your neighbors and you would probably cease to be on speaking terms, and you could expect a complaint from them the first time you violated even the most inconsequential of city ordinances. If you live in the neighborhood for any time at all, this state of hostilities isn't very appealing.

Indirect Aggression   As its name suggests, **indirect aggression** occurs when a communicator expresses hostility in an obscure way. In several of his works, psychologist George Bach describes behavior that he terms "crazy-making."[5] **Crazymaking** occurs when people have feelings of resentment, anger, or rage that they are unable or unwilling to express directly. Instead of keeping these feelings to themselves, the crazymakers send these aggressive messages in subtle, indirect ways, thus maintaining the front of kindness. This amiable façade eventually crumbles, however, leaving the crazymaker's victim confused and angry at having been fooled. The targets of the crazymaker can either react with aggressive behavior of their own or retreat to nurse their hurt feelings. In either case indirect aggression seldom has anything but harmful effects on a relationship.

Behold the turtle who makes progress only when he sticks his neck out.

Cecil Parker

You could respond to your neighbors and their dog in several crazymaking, indirectly aggressive ways. One strategy would be to complain anonymously to the city pound and then, after the dog has been hauled away, express your sympathy. Or you could complain to everyone else in the neighborhood, hoping that their hostility would force the offending neighbors to quiet the dog or face being a social outcast. A third possibility would be to strike up a friendly conversation with one of the owners and casually remark about the terrible neighborhood you had just left, in which noisy dogs roamed the streets, uncontrolled by their thoughtless owners. (Or perhaps you could be more subtle and talk about noisy children instead!)

There are a number of shortcomings to such approaches as these, each of which illustrate the risks of indirect aggression. First, there is the chance that the crazymaking won't work: The neighbors might simply miss the point of your veiled attacks and continue to ignore the barking. On the other hand, they might get your message clearly, but either because of your lack of sincerity or out of sheer stubborness, they might simply refuse to do anything about it. In either case, it's likely that in this and other instances indirect aggression won't satisfy your unmet need.

Even when indirect aggression proves successful in the short run, a second shortcoming lies in its consequences over the longer range. You might manage to intimidate your neighbors into shutting up their mutt, for instance, but in winning that battle you could lose what would become a war. As a means of revenge, they could wage their own campaign of crazymaking by such tactics as badmouthing things like your sloppy gardening to other neighbors or by phoning in false complaints about your allegedly loud parties. It's obvious that feuds such as this one are counterproductive and outweigh the apparent advantages of indirect aggression.

In addition to these unpleasant possibilities, a third shortcoming of indirect aggression is that it denies the people involved a chance of building any kind of honest relationship with each other. As long as you treat your neighbors as if they were an obstacle to be removed from your path, there's little likelihood that you'll get to know them as people. Though this thought may not bother you, the principle that indirect aggression prevents intimacy holds true in other important areas of life. To the degree that you try to manipulate friends, they won't know the real you. The fewer of your needs you reveal directly to your co-workers, the less chance you have of becoming true friends and colleagues. The same principle holds for those people you hope to meet in the future. Indirect aggression denies closeness.

Assertion   Assertion occurs when a message expresses the speaker's needs, thoughts, and feelings clearly and directly but without judging or dictating to others. Most assertive messages follow the format described later in this chapter on pages 348–355.

Behaving assertively doesn't guarantee that you will always get what you want, but it often offers the chance of reaching your goal. In addition, this style of communicating maintains the self-respect of both you and those with whom you interact. People involved in an assertive exchange usually feel good about themselves and others afterward—quite a change from the outcomes of nonassertiveness and aggression.

An assertive course of action in the case of the barking dog would be to wait a few days to make sure the noise is not just a fluke. If the barking continues, you could introduce yourself to your neighbors and explain your problem. You could tell them that although they might not notice it, the dog often plays in the street and keeps barking at passing cars. You could tell them why this behavior bothers you. It keeps you awake at night and makes it hard for you to do your work. You could point out that you don't want to be a grouch and call the pound. Rather than behaving in these ways, you could tell them that you've come to see what kind of solution you can find that will satisfy both of you. This approach may not work, and you might then have to decide whether it is more important to avoid bad feelings or to have peace and quiet. But the chances for a happy ending are best with this assertive approach. And no matter what happens, you can keep your self-respect by behaving directly and honestly.

Your Conflict Style

1. Think back over your recent history, and recall five conflicts you've had. The more current they are, the better, and they should be ones that occurred with people who are important to you, people with whom your relationship matters.

2. Turn an 8½-by-11-inch sheet of paper horizontally, and copy the following chart. To give yourself plenty of room you might extend your chart onto a second page.

I The Conflict	II How I Managed It	III The Results
(Describe whom it was with; what it was about.)	(What did you say? How did you act?)	(How did you feel? How did the others involved feel? Are you happy with the results?)

3. For each of the conflicts, fill in the appropriate spaces on your chart.

4. Based on what you've written here, answer the following questions:
   a. Are you happy with the way you've handled your conflicts? Do you come away from them feeling better or worse than before?
   b. Have your conflicts made your relationships stronger or weaker?
   c. Do you recognize any patterns in your conflict style? For example, do you hold your angry feelings inside, are you sarcastic, do you lose your temper easily?
   d. If you could, would you like to change the way you deal with your conflicts?

CRAZYMAKERS: INDIRECT AGGRESSION

What's your conflict style? To give you a better idea of some unproductive ways you may be handling your conflicts, we'll describe some typical behaviors that can weaken relationships. In our survey we'll follow the fascinating work of George Bach, a leading authority on conflict and communication.

Bach explains that there are two types of aggression—clean fighting and dirty fighting. Either because they can't or won't express their feelings openly and constructively, dirty fighters sometimes resort to "crazymaking" techniques to vent their resentments. Instead of openly and caringly expressing their emotions, crazymakers (often unconsciously) use a variety of indirect tricks to get at their opponent. Because these "sneak attacks" don't usually get to the root of the problem and because of their power to create a great deal of hurt, crazymakers can destroy communication. Let's take a look at some of them.

The Avoider

The avoider refuses to fight. When a conflict arises, he'll leave, fall asleep, pretend to be busy at work, or keep from facing the problem in some other way. This behavior makes it very difficult for the partner to express his feelings of anger, hurt, and so on, because the avoider won't fight back. Arguing with an avoider is like trying to box with a person who won't even put up his gloves.

The Pseudoaccommodator

The pseudoaccommodator refuses to face up to a conflict either by giving in or by pretending that there's nothing at all wrong. This really drives the partner, who definitely feels there's a problem, crazy and causes him to feel both guilt and resentment toward the accommodator.

The Guiltmaker

Instead of saying straight out that she doesn't want or approve of something, the guiltmaker tries to change her partner's behavior by making him feel responsible for causing pain. The guiltmaker's favorite line is "it's OK; don't worry about me . . ." accompanied by a big sigh.

The Subject Changer

Really a type of avoider, the subject changer escapes facing up to aggression by shifting the conversation whenever it approaches an area of conflict. Because of his tactics, the subject changer and his partner never have the chance to explore their problem and do something about it.

The Distracter

Rather than come out and express his feelings about the object of his dissatisfaction, the distracter attacks other parts of his partner's life. Thus, he never has to share what's really on his mind and can avoid dealing with painful parts of his relationships.

The Mind Reader

Instead of allowing her partner to express his feelings honestly, the mind reader goes into character analysis, explaining what the other person really means or what's wrong with the other person. By behaving this way the mind reader refuses to handle her own feelings and leaves no room for her partner to express himself.

The Trapper

The trapper plays an especially dirty trick by setting up a desired behavior for her partner and then when it's met, attacking the very thing she requested. An example of this technique is for the trapper to say, "Let's be totally honest with each other," and then when the partner shares his feelings, he finds himself being attacked for having feelings that the trapper doesn't want to accept.

The Crisis Tickler

The crisis tickler almost brings what's bothering him to the surface, but he never quite comes out and expresses himself. Instead of admitting his concern about the finances, he innocently asks, "Gee, how much did that cost?" dropping a rather obvious hint but never really dealing with the crisis.

The Gunnysacker

This person doesn't respond immediately when she's angry. Instead, she puts her resentment into her gunnysack, which after a while begins to bulge with large and small gripes. Then, when the sack is about to burst, the gunnysacker pours out all her pent-up aggressions on the overwhelmed and unsuspecting victim.

The Trivial Tyrannizer

Instead of honestly sharing his resentments, the trivial tyrannizer does things he knows will get his partner's goat—leaving dirty dishes in the sink, clipping his fingernails in bed, belching out loud, turning up the television too loud, and so on.

The Beltliner

Everyone has a psychological "beltline," and below it are subjects too sensitive to be approached without damaging the relationship. Beltlines may have to do with physical characteristics, intelligence, past behavior, or deeply ingrained personality traits a person is trying to overcome. In an attempt to "get even" or hurt his partner the beltliner will use his intimate knowledge to hit below the belt, where he knows it will hurt.

The Joker

Because she's afraid to face conflicts squarely, the joker kids around when her partner wants to be serious, thus blocking the expression of important feelings.

The Blamer

The blamer is more interested in finding fault than in solving a conflict. Needless to say, she usually doesn't blame herself. Blaming behavior almost never solves a conflict and is an almost surefire way to make the receiver defensive.

The Contract Tyrannizer

The contract tyrannizer will not allow his relationship to change from the way it once was. Whatever the agreements the partners had for roles and responsibilities at one time, they'll remain unchanged. "It's your job to . . . feed the baby, wash the dishes, discipline the kids. . . ."

The Kitchen Sink Fighter

This person is so named because in an argument he brings up things that are totally off the subject ("everything but the kitchen sink"): the way his partner behaved last New Year's Eve, the unbalanced checkbook, bad breath—anything.

The Withholder

Instead of expressing her anger honestly and directly, the withholder punishes her partner by keeping back something—courtesy, affection, good cooking, humor, sex. As you can imagine, this is likely to build up even greater resentments in the relationship.

The Benedict Arnold

This character gets back at his partner by sabotage, by failing to defend him from attackers, and even by encouraging ridicule or disregard from outside the relationship.

Your Crazymakers

1. Pick the three crazymakers you use most often, and give three recent examples of each.

2. For each example, describe
   a. the situation in which you used the crazymaker.
   b. the consequences of using it, including the other person's behavior and your feelings.
   c. your level of satisfaction with having used it.
   d. any alternate style of expressing your problem which might have been more satisfying.

Which Style Is Best?   After reading this far, you might think that assertive communication is clearly superior to other styles. It allows you to express yourself honestly and seems to have the greatest chance of success. Actually, it's an oversimplification to say that any communication style is always best. A competent, successful communicator will choose the most effective style for a given situation.

How can you decide which style will be most effective? There are several factors to consider.

The Situation   When someone else clearly has more power than you, nonassertion may be the best approach. If the boss tells you to fill that order "*now!*" you probably ought to do it without comment. The more assertive response ("When you use that tone of voice, I feel defensive . . . ") might be more clear, but it also could cost you your job. Likewise, there are some situations when an aggressive message is most appropriate. Even the most mild-mannered parents will testify that sooner or later every child needs to be yelled at: "I've told you three times not to torture the cat. Now *stop it,* or you'll be sorry!"

The Receiver   Although assertiveness has the best chance of success with most people, some receivers respond better to other approaches. One businessman illustrated this point when he described how his normally even-tempered boss used shouting in a phone conversation with a particularly difficult person:

> I've never heard him so angry. He was enraged. His face was red, and the veins were bulging on his neck. I tried to get his attention to calm him down, but he waved me away impatiently. As soon as the call was over, he turned to me and smiled. "There," he said. "That ought to do it." If I were the guy he'd been shouting at, let me tell you, that would have done it, too. But it was all a put on.[6]

Your Goals   When you want to solve a problem, assertiveness is probably the best approach. But there are other reasons for communicating in a conflict. Sometimes your overriding concern is to calm down an enraged or upset person. Tolerating an outburst from your crotchety and sick neighbor, for example, is probably better than standing up for yourself and triggering a stroke. Likewise, you might choose to sit quietly through the nagging of a family member rather than ruin Thanksgiving dinner. In other cases, your moral principles might compel an aggressive statement even though it might not get you what you originally sought: "I've had enough of your racist jokes. I've tried to explain why they're so offensive, but you obviously haven't listened. I'm leaving!"

Assertion Without Aggression: The Clear Message Format

Knowing *when* to behave assertively isn't the same as knowing *how* to assert yourself. The next few pages will describe a method for communicating assertively. It works for a variety of messages: your hopes, problems, complaints, and appreciations.[7] Besides giving you a way to express yourself directly, this clear message format also makes it easy for others to understand you. Finally, since assertive messages are phrased in the kind of descriptive "I" language you learned in Chapter Nine, they are less likely than aggressive attacks to cause a defensive reaction that will start a needless fight or shut down discussion altogether.

A complete assertive message has five parts. We'll examine each of these parts one by one and then discuss how to combine them in your everyday communication.

Sensing   A **sensing statement** describes the raw material to which you react. Sense data include the things you see, hear, touch, smell, and feel with your skin. For instance, a camera records visual sense data and an audio tape recorder picks up and stores sounds.

For our purpose the important thing to recognize is that a sensing statement should be *objective.* A record of pure sensory information would simply describe an event without interpreting it.

Two examples of purely sensory records of events might look like this.

Example 1
"One week ago John promised me that he would ask my permission before smoking in the same room with me. Just a moment ago he lit up a cigarette without asking for my OK."

Example 2
"Chris has acted differently over the last week. I can't remember her laughing once since the holiday weekend. She hasn't dropped by my place like she usually does, hasn't suggested we play tennis, and hasn't returned my phone calls."

Notice that in both cases the descriptive statements record only data that are available through the senses. The observer has not attached any meaning to the behaviors so far. This is the essence of sensing.

Interpretation   Interpretation is the process of attaching meaning to sense data. The important thing to realize about interpretations is that they are *subjective.* That is, there is more than one interpretation that we can attach to any set of sense data. For example, look at these two different interpretations of each of the preceding descriptions:

Example 1
Interpretation A   "John must have forgotten about our agreement that he wouldn't smoke without asking me first. I'm sure he's too considerate to go back on his word on something he knows I feel strongly about."

Interpretation B   "John is a rude, inconsiderate person. After promising not to smoke around me without asking, he's just deliberately done so. This shows that he only cares about himself. In fact, I bet he's deliberately doing this to drive me crazy!"

Example 2

Interpretation A "Something must be bothering Chris. It's probably her family. She'll probably just feel worse if I keep pestering her."

Interpretation B "Chris is probably mad at me. It's probably because I kidded her about losing so often at tennis. I'd better leave her alone until she cools off."

These examples show that interpretations are based on more than simple sense data. They grow out of many factors, including

1. **Your past experience** "John has always (never) kept his promises in the past" or "When I'm preoccupied with personal problems I draw away from my friends."
2. **Your assumptions** "An unkept promise is a sign of uncaring (forgetfulness)" or "Lack of communication with friends is a sign that something is wrong."
3. **Your expectations** "John probably wants (doesn't want) to fight" or "I thought the family visit (or kidding about tennis) would upset her."
4. **Your knowledge** "Long-time, habitual cigarette smokers aren't even aware of lighting up" or "I know Chris's dad has been sick lately."
5. **Your current mood** "I feel good about John and about life in general" or "I've been awfully sarcastic lately. I went too far when I kidded Chris about her tennis game."

Once you become aware of the difference between sense data and interpretation, some of the reasons for communication breakdowns become clear. Many problems occur when a sender fails to share the sense data on which an interpretation is based. For instance, imagine the difference between hearing a friend say

"You are a tightwad!" (*no sense data*)

and explaining

"When you never offer to pay me back for the coffee and snacks I often buy you, I think you're a tightwad." (*sense data plus interpretation*)

The first speaker's failure to specify sense data would probably confuse the receiver, who has no way of knowing what prompted the sender's remarks. This failure to describe sense data also reduces any chance that the receiver will change the offensive behavior, which, after all, is unknown to that person.

Just as important as specifying sense data is the need to label an interpretation as such instead of presenting it as a matter of fact. Consider the difference between saying

"It's obvious that if you cared for me you'd write more often." (*interpretation presented as fact*)

and

"When you didn't write, I thought that you didn't care for me." (*interpretation made clear*)

As you learned in Chapter Nine, your comments are much less likely to arouse defensiveness in others when you present them in a tentative, provisional manner.

Have you ever seen a pound of anger, a quart of hate, or an ounce of joy? Of course, the question is ridiculous, yet we talk about emotions as if they were real "things." Rage, grief, ecstasy, joy, sadness, boredom —we use these terms so freely it is easy to forget that emotions are often inferred from the actions of others, they cannot be directly observed. A person staring off into space might be bored, depressed, in love, or stoned (the last, by the way, is not an emotion).

Dennis Coon,
Introduction to Psychology

A third important rule is to avoid making statements that appear to report sense data but are in fact interpretations. For instance, don't mistake these kinds of statements as objective descriptions:

"I see you're tired." (*Tired* is an interpretation. Your sense data might have been "I see your eyes closing and your head nodding.")

"I see you're in a hurry." (*Hurry* is an interpretation. The sense data could have been "I see you gathering up your books and looking at the clock.")

"I hear that you're hungry." (*Hungry* is an interpretation. The sense datum you heard was the sound of your friend's stomach growling.)

"You look anxious to get started." (*Anxious* is an interpretation. What could the sense data be in this case? The short time it took your friend to answer the doorbell? The outside clothing in which the person was already dressed?)

There's nothing wrong with making these interpretations. In fact, this is a necessary step because only by interpreting sense data do we arrive at a meaning. However, we often make inaccurate interpretations, and when we don't separate sense data from our interpretations, we fool ourselves into believing that our interpretations are reality—that is, what we *think* is what exists.

Sensing and Interpreting

1. Tell two other group members several interpretations you have recently made about other people in your life. For each interpretation, describe the sense data on which you based your remarks.

2. With your partners' help, consider some alternate interpretations of your sense data that might be as plausible as your original one.

3. After considering the alternate interpretations, decide
   a. Which one was most reasonable.
   b. How you might share that interpretation (along with the sense data) with the other person involved in a tentative, nondogmatic way.

Feeling   Reporting sense data and sharing your interpretations are important, but **feeling statements** add a new dimension to a message. For example, consider the difference between saying

"When you kiss me and nibble on my ear while we're watching television [sense data], I think you probably want to make love [interpretation], and *I feel excited.*"

and

"When you kiss me and nibble on my ear while we're watching television, I think you probably want to make love, and *I feel disgusted.*"

Notice how the expression of different feelings can change the meaning of another message.

"When you laugh at me [sense data], I think you find my comments foolish [interpretation], and *I feel embarrassed.*"

"When you laugh at me, I think you find my comments foolish, and *I feel angry.*"

No doubt you can supply other examples in which different feelings can radically affect a speaker's meaning. Recognizing this, we find it logical to say that we should identify our feelings in our conversations with others. Yet if we pay attention to the everyday acts of communication, we see that no such disclosure occurs.

It's important to recognize that some statements *seem* as if they're expressing feelings but are really interpretations or statements of intention. For instance, it's incorrect to say "I feel like leaving" (really an intention) or "I feel you're wrong" (an interpretation). Statements like these obscure the true expression of feelings and should be avoided.

What prevents people from sharing their feelings? Certainly one cause is that making such statements can bring on a great deal of anxiety. It's often frightening to come right out and say, "I'm angry," "I feel embarrassed," or "I love you," and often we aren't willing to take the risks that come with such clear-cut assertions.

A second reason why people fail to express their feelings clearly is simply because they don't recognize them. We aren't always aware that we're angry, confused, impatient, or sad. Asking yourself, "How do I feel?" can often uncover important information that needs to be communicated to your partner.

Name the Feeling

Add a feeling you would be likely to have to each of the following messages:

1. I felt _____ when I found out you didn't invite me on the camping trip. You said you thought I wouldn't want to go, but I have a hard time accepting that.

2. I felt _____ when you offered to help me move. I know how busy you are.

3. When you tell me you still want to be a friend but you want to "lighten up a little," I get the idea you're tired of me and I feel _____.

4. You told me you wanted my honest opinion about your paintings, and then when I tell you what I think, you say I don't understand them. I'm _____.

How would the impact of each message be different if it didn't include a feeling statement?

Consequence   A consequence statement explains what happens as a result of the sense data you have described, your interpretation, the ensuing feeling, or all three. There are three types of consequences:

1. What happens to you, the speaker

"When you forgot to give me the phone message yesterday [*sense data*], *I didn't know that my doctor's appointment was delayed and I wound up sitting in the office for an hour when I could have been studying or working* [*consequences*]. It seems to me that you don't care enough about how busy I am to even write a simple note [*interpretation*], and that really makes me mad [*feeling*]."

"I appreciate [*feeling*] the help you've given me on my term paper [*sense data*]. It tells me you think I'm on the right track [*interpretation*], and *this gives me a boost to keep working on the idea* [*consequences*]."

2. What happens to the person you're addressing

"When you have four or five drinks at a party after I've warned you to slow down [*sense data*], *you start to act strange: You make crude jokes that offend everybody, and on the way home you drive poorly* [*consequences*]. *For instance, last night you almost hit a phone pole* while you were backing out of the driveway [*more sense data*]. I don't think you realize how differently you act [*interpretation*], and I'm worried [*feeling*] about what will happen if you don't drink less."

3. What happens to others

"You probably don't know because you couldn't hear her cry [*interpretation*], but when you rehearse your lines for the play without closing the doors [*sense data*], *the baby can't sleep* [*consequence*]. I'm especially concerned [*feeling*] about her because she's had a cold lately."

"I thought you'd want to know [*interpretation*] that when you kid Bob about his height [*sense data*], he gets embarrassed [*feeling*] and *usually quiets down or leaves* [*consequences*]."

Consequence statements are valuable for two reasons. First, they help you understand more clearly why you are bothered or pleased by another's behavior. Just as important, telling others about the consequences of their actions can clarify for them the results of their behavior. As with interpretations, we often think others *should* be aware of consequences without being told; but the fact is that they often aren't. By explicitly stating consequences, you can be sure that you or your message leaves nothing to the listener's imagination.

When you are stating consequences, it's important simply to describe what happens without moralizing. For instance, it's one thing to say, "When you didn't call to say you'd be late, I stayed up worrying," and another to rant on "How can I ever trust you? You're going to drive me crazy!" Remember, it's perfectly legitimate to express your thoughts and feelings, but it's important to label them as such. And when you want to request change from someone, you can use intention statements, which we'll now describe.

It's easy to confuse some interpretation, feeling, or intention statements with consequences. For example, you might say, "As a consequence of your turning down my invitation, I got the idea [*interpretation*] you're mad at me. I'm worried [*feeling*], and I want to know what you're thinking [*intention*]." To say that these are not consequences as we're using the term is more than semantic hairsplitting. Confusing interpretations, feelings, and intentions with consequences might prevent you from mentioning the true consequence—what has happened as a result of this event. In our example, a real consequence statement might be ". . . and that's why I've been so quiet lately." As you'll read on page 355, sometimes a consequence is combined with another message element. The important point to remember is that you somehow need to explain the consequences of an incident if the other person is to understand your concern completely.

If I am not for myself, who will be?
If I am only for myself, what am I?

Rabbi Hillel

Intention   Intention statements are the final element of the assertive format. They can communicate three kinds of messages:

1. Where you stand on an issue

> "When you call us 'girls' after I've told you we want to be called 'women' [*sense data*], I get the idea you don't appreciate how important the difference is to us [*interpretation*] and how demeaning it feels [*feeling*]. Now I'm in an awkward spot: Either I have to keep bringing the subject up, or else drop it and feel bad [*consequence*]. *I want you to know how much this bothers me* [*intention*]."

> "I'm really grateful [*feeling*] to you for speaking up for me in front of the boss yesterday [*sense data*]. That must have taken a lot of courage [*interpretation*]. Knowing that you're behind me gives me a lot of confidence [*consequence*], and *I want you to know how much I appreciate your support* [*intention*]."

2. Requests of others

> "When you didn't call last night [*sense data*] I thought you were mad at me [*interpretation*]. I've been thinking about it ever since [*consequence*], and I'm still worried [*feeling*]. *I'd like to know whether you are angry* [*intention*]."

> "I really enjoyed [*feeling*] your visit [*sense data*], and I'm glad you had a good time, too [*interpretation*]. *I hope you'll come again* [*intention*]."

3. Descriptions of how you plan to act in the future

"I've asked you to repay the twenty-five dollars I loaned you three times now [*sense data*]. I'm getting the idea that you've been avoiding me [*interpretation*], and I'm pretty angry about it [*feeling*]. I want you to know that unless we clear this up now, *you shouldn't expect me ever to loan you anything again* [*intention*]."

"I'm glad [*feeling*] you liked [*interpretation*] the paper I wrote. *I'm thinking about taking your advanced writing class next term* [*intention*]."

Why is it so important to make your intentions clear? Because failing to do so often makes it hard for others to know what you want from them or how to act. Consider how confusing the following statements are because they lack a clear statement of intention.

"Wow! A frozen Snickers. I haven't had one of those in years." (Does the speaker want a bite or is she just making an innocent remark?)

"Thanks for the invitation, but I really should study Saturday night." (Does the speaker want to be asked out again, or is he indirectly suggesting that he doesn't ever want to go out with you?)

"To tell you the truth, I was asleep when you came by, but I should have been up anyway." (Is the speaker saying that it's OK to come by in the future, or is she hinting that she doesn't appreciate unannounced visitors?)

You can see from these examples that it's often hard to make a clear interpretation of another person's ideas without a direct statement of intention. Notice how much more direct statements become when the speakers make their position clear.

"Wow! A frozen Snickers. I haven't had one of those in years. *If I hadn't already eaten, I'd sure ask for a bite.*"

"Thanks for the invitation, but I really should study Saturday night. *I hope you'll ask me again soon.*"

"To tell you the truth, I was asleep when you came by, but I should have been up anyway. *Maybe the next time you should phone before dropping in so I'll be sure to be awake.*"

As in the preceding cases, we are often motivated by one single intention. Sometimes, however, we act from a combination of intentions, which may even be in conflict with each other. When this happens, our conflicting wants often make it difficult for us to reach decisions.

"I want to be truthful with you, but I don't want to violate my friend's privacy."

"I want to continue to enjoy your friendship and company, but I don't want to get too attached right now."

"I want to have time to study and get good grades, but I also want to have a job with some money coming in, too."

Although revealing your conflicting intentions guaranteed to clear up confusion, sometimes an outright statement, such as the preceding, can help you come to a decision. Even when you remain mixed up, expressing your contrary wants has the benefit of letting others know where you stand.

Using the Clear Message Format   Before you try to deliver messages by using the sense-interpret-feel-consequences-intention format, there are a few points you should remember. First, it isn't necessary or even wise always to put the elements in the order described here. As you can see from reviewing the examples on the preceding pages, it's sometimes best to begin by stating your feelings. In other cases you can start by sharing your intentions or interpretations or by describing consequences.

You also ought to word your message in a way that suits your style of speaking. Instead of saying, "I interpret your behavior to mean," you might choose to say, "I think . . ." or "it seems to me . . ." or perhaps "I get the idea. . . ." In the same way you can express your intentions by saying "I hope you'll understand (or do) . . ." or perhaps "I wish you would. . . ." It's important that you get your message across, but you should do it in a way that sounds and feels genuine to you.

Realize that there are some cases in which you can combine two elements in a single phrase. For instance, the statement ". . . and ever since then I've been wanting to talk to you" expresses both a consequence and an intention. In the same way saying, ". . . and after you said that, I felt confused" expresses a consequence and a feeling. Whether you combine elements or state them separately, the important point is to be sure that each one is present in your statement.

Finally, you need to realize that it isn't always possible to deliver messages such as the ones here all at one time, wrapped up in neat paragraphs. It will often be necessary to repeat or restate one part many times before your receiver truly understands what you're saying. As you've already read, there are many types of psychological and physical noise that make it difficult for us to understand each other. Just remember: You haven't communicated successfully until the receiver of your message understands everything you've said. In communication, as in many other activities, patience and persistence are essential.

Now try your hand at combining all these elements in this exercise.

Putting Your Message Together

1. Join with two other class members. Each person in turn should share a message he or she might want to send to another person, being sure to include sensing, interpreting, feeling, consequence, and intention statements in the remarks.

2. The others in the group should help the speaker by offering feedback about how the remarks could be made clearer if there is any question about the meaning.

3. Once the speaker has composed a satisfactory message he or she should practice actually delivering it by having another group member play the role of the intended receiver. Continue this practice until the speaker is confident that he or she can deliver the message effectively.

4. Repeat this process until each group member has had a chance to practice delivering a message.

I was angry with my friend.
I told my wrath, my wrath did end.
I was angry with my foe:
I told it not, my wrath did grow.

And I watered it in fears,
Night and morning with my tears;
And I sunned it with smiles,
And with soft deceitful wiles.

And it grew both day and night,
Till it bore an apple bright;
And my foe beheld it shine,
And he knew that it was mine,

And into my garden stole
When the night had veiled the pole:
In the morning glad I see
My foe outstretched beneath the tree.

William Blake

Styles of Conflict Resolution

So far we have discussed how individuals behave when faced with communication challenges. But since communication is transactional, the outcome of a conflict depends on the interaction of the participants' individual communication styles. In the following pages we will look at the various approaches people take to resolve conflicts.

When faced with a disagreement, the parties have three choices:

—They can accept the status quo: "I don't like some of your friends, and you aren't crazy about mine, but there isn't much we can do about it. I suppose we'll just have to live with them."

—They can use force—physical, social, or economic—to impose a settlement: "Either we spend the vacation backpacking or I'm staying home."

—They can reach an agreement by negotiating. **Negotiation** occurs when two or more parties discuss specific proposals in order to find a mutually acceptable agreement. Negotiation isn't foolproof: When poorly handled, it can leave a problem still unsolved or even worse than before. On the other hand, skillful negotiating can produce solutions that improve the situation for both parties.

We'll now examine the types of outcomes that can result from these approaches. By looking at each of them, you can decide which ones you'll seek when you find yourself facing an interpersonal conflict.

Win-Lose   In **win-lose problem solving,** one party gets what he or she wants whereas the other comes up short. People resort to this method of resolving disputes when they perceive a situation as being an "either-or" one: Either I get what I want or you get your way. The most clear-cut examples of win-lose situations are certain games such as baseball or poker, in which the rules require a winner and a loser. Some interpersonal issues seem to fit into this win-lose framework: two co-workers seeking a promotion to the same job or a couple who disagree on how to spend their limited money.

Power is the distinguishing characteristic in win-lose problem solving, for it is necessary to defeat an opponent to get what one wants. The most obvious kind of power is physical. Some parents threaten their children with warnings such as "Stop misbehaving or I'll send you to your room." Adults who use physical power to deal with each other usually aren't so blunt, but the legal system is the implied threat: "Follow the rules or we'll lock you up."

Real or implied force isn't the only kind of power used in conflicts. People who rely on authority of many types engage in win-lose methods without ever threatening physical coercion. In most jobs, supervisors have the authority to assign working hours, job promotions, and desirable or undesirable tasks, and of course, to fire an unsatisfactory employee. Teachers can use the power of grades to coerce students to act in desired ways.

Intellectual or mental power can also be a tool for conquering an opponent. Everyone is familiar with stories of how a seemingly weak hero defeats a stronger enemy through cleverness, showing that brains are more important than brawn. In a less admirable way, indirectly aggressive crazymakers such as you've read about earlier in this chapter can defeat their partners by inducing guilt, avoiding issues, withholding desired behaviors, pseudoaccommodating, and so on.

Even the usually admired democratic principle of majority rule is a win-lose method of resolving conflicts. However fair it may be, with this system one group gets its way and another is unsatisfied.

There are some circumstances in which the win-lose method may be necessary, as when there are truly scarce resources and only one party can achieve satisfaction. For instance, if two suitors want to marry the same person, only one can succeed. And to return to an earlier example, it's often true that only one applicant can be hired for a job. But don't be too willing to assume that your conflicts are necessarily win-lose: As you'll soon read, many situations that seem to require a loser can be resolved to everyone's satisfaction.

There is a second kind of situation when win-lose is the best method. Even when cooperation is possible, if the other person insists on trying to defeat you, the most logical response might be to defend yourself by fighting back. "It takes two to tango," the old cliché goes, and it also takes two to cooperate.

A final and much less frequent justification for trying to defeat another person occurs when the other party is clearly behaving in a wrong manner and where defeating that person is the only way to stop the wrongful behavior. Few people would deny the importance of restraining a person who is deliberately harming others even if the aggressor's freedom is sacrificed in the process. The danger of forcing wrongdoers to behave themselves is the wide difference in opinion between people about who is wrong and who is right. Given this difference, it would only seem justifiable to coerce others into behaving as we think they should in the most extreme circumstances.

Lose-Lose   In **lose-lose problem solving,** neither side is satisfied with the outcome. Although the name of this approach is so discouraging that it's hard to imagine how anyone could willingly use it, in truth lose-lose is a fairly common way to handle conflicts.

Compromise is the most respectable form of lose-lose conflict resolution. All the parties are willing to settle for less than they want because they believe that partial satisfaction is the best result they can hope for.

In his valuable book on conflict resolution, Albert Filley points out an interesting observation about our attitudes toward this method.[8] Why is it, he asks, that if someone says, "I will compromise my values," we view the action unfavorably, yet we talk admiringly about parties in a conflict who compromise to reach a solution? Although compromises may be the best obtainable result in some conflicts, it's important to realize that both people in a dispute can often work together to find much better solutions. In such cases *compromise* is a negative word.

Most of us are surrounded by the results of bad compromises. Consider a common example, the conflict between one person's desire to smoke cigarettes and another's need for clean air. The win-lose outcomes on this issue are obvious: Either the smoker abstains or the nonsmoker gets polluted lungs—neither very satisfying. But a compromise in which the smoker gets to enjoy only a rare cigarette or must retreat outdoors and in which the nonsmoker still must inhale some fumes or feel like an ogre is hardly better. Both sides have lost a considerable amount of both comfort and goodwill. Of course, the costs involved in other compromises are even greater. For example, if a divorced couple compromise on child care by haggling over custody and then finally grudgingly agree to split the time with their children, it's hard to say that anybody has won.

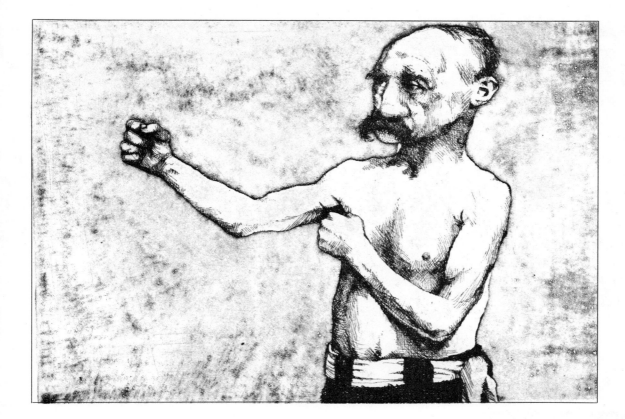

Compromises aren't the only lose-lose solutions or even the worst ones. In many instances the parties will both strive to be winners, but as a result of the struggle, both wind up losers. On the international scene many wars illustrate this sad point. A nation that gains military victory at the cost of thousands of lives, large amounts of resources, and a damaged national consciousness hasn't truly won much. On an interpersonal level the same principle holds true. Most of us have seen battles of pride in which both parties strike out and both suffer. It seems as if there should be a better alternative, and fortunately there often is.

Win-Win   In **win-win problem solving,** the goal is to find a solution that satisfies the needs of everyone involved. Not only do the partners avoid trying to win at the other's expense, but they also believe that by working together it's possible to find a solution in which all those involved reach their goals without needing to compromise.

One way to understand how win-win problem solving works is to look at a few examples.

Gordon was a stamp collector; his wife, Elaine, loved to raise and show championship beagles. Their income didn't leave enough money for both to practice their hobbies, and splitting the cash they did have wouldn't have left enough for either. Solution: Put all the first year's money into the puppies, and then after they were grown, use the income from their litters and show prizes to pay for Gordon's stamps.

Hug O'War

I will not play at
*   tug o'war.*
I'd rather play at
*   hug o'war,*
Where everyone hugs
Instead of tugs,
Where everyone giggles
And rolls on the rug,
Where everyone kisses,
And everyone grins,
And everyone cuddles,
And everyone wins.

Shel Silverstein

Mac loved to spend his evenings talking to people all over the world on his ham radio set, but his wife, Marilyn, felt cheated out of the few hours of each day they could spend together. Mac didn't want to give up his hobby, and Marilyn wasn't willing to sacrifice the time she needed alone with her husband. Solution: Three or four nights each week Mac stayed up late and talked on his radio after spending the evening with Marilyn. On the following mornings she drove him to work instead of having him take the bus, which allowed him to sleep later.

Wendy and Kathy were roommates who had different studying habits. Wendy liked to do her work in the evenings, which left her days free for other things, but Kathy felt that night time was party time. Solution: Monday through Wednesday evenings Wendy studied at her boyfriend's place while Kathy did anything she wanted. Thursday and Sunday Kathy agreed to keep things quiet around the house, and Friday and Saturday they both partied together.

The point here isn't that these solutions are the correct ones for everybody with similar problems: The win-win approach doesn't work that way. Different people might have found other solutions that suited them better. What the win-win method does is give you an approach—a way of creatively finding just the right answer for your unique problem. By using it you can tailor-make a way of resolving your conflicts that everyone can live with comfortably.

You should understand that the win-win approach doesn't call for compromises in which the participants give up something they really want or need. Sometimes a compromise is the only alternative, but in the method we're talking about you find a solution that satisfies everyone—one in which nobody had to lose.

A Positive Development in the Philosophy of Divorce

Lawyer Believes His Role Should Be a Peacemaker

Positive divorce. Marital dissolution that is not the equivalent of emotional Pac-Man. Steered by attorneys who refuse to use the legal system to hobble, harass or otherwise obliterate the other side.

Divorce lawyers who see themselves not as adversaries but . . . peacemakers. And then expect a client not just to survive a breakup but to be in better shape because of it.

Are we dreaming?

As farfetched as all that may appear to some, such situations are increasingly becoming the result of California divorce proceedings.

One law practice where such outcomes can virtually be counted on is that of Michael Kelly, a Santa Monica-based attorney and pro-tem judge who has become something of a crusader on the subject. After creating positive marital dissolutions for the last six of his 15 years in law, Kelly has been lecturing on this alternative for about a year-and-a-half.

As Kelly sees it, the legal system itself—the time-honored adversary system—is better designed to produce a confrontation than a mutually acceptable termination of a marriage. He defines the adversary proceedings as a struggle in which "each side puts out their version of the facts as strongly as possible and tries to destroy and eliminate the other side's version of the same story. And supposedly, somewhere within that wreckage, the truth is going to come out."

Precise Process

To avoid the demolition, Kelly has created a precise, step-by-step process that has resulted in about 80% of his clients settling their divorce disputes completely out of court and the remaining 20% with some litigation but no full trials. (His last complete trial occurred about 10 years ago.)

Predictably, however, a frequent reaction to the suggestion of positive divorce (with attorneys involved) often sounds something like this: "Great, honey, if we get divorced, you get this guy to represent you and I'll get the toughest rat in town."

"We hear that all the time," Kelly responds. "What that's saying is, 'I'm gonna get a bigger stick and beat you to death for leaving me.' I cannot, obviously, and will not stand idly by with a complete peace branch if I am dealing with one of the lawyers who simply litigates a case, period, no matter what happens. This is not a process that can be done unilaterally. It requires cooperation and intention (to settle rather than litigate). I cannot produce that result when the other party will not do it."

But Kelly does exercise considerable control of his clients and has been known to fire them for demanding that he "get" spouses. And he provides clients the same freedom to waltz out by signing a substitution of attorney agreement.

"Very often spouses forget that the person who's on the other side of litigation is the person they've been living with and sleeping with for the last 5 or 10 or 15 years and to the extent that you hurt that person, very often you mortally wound your own self," Kelly says. "You cannot have an emotional experience with somebody for that long and then damage that person or cheat that person as the last thing you do to them and ultimately be satisfied with that or feel good about it. People forget they're holding the other end of the stick of dynamite that they're trying to hand their spouse. What they will get out of that is a big bill and no satisfaction.

Both Sides Pay

"Clients sometimes have the mistaken notion that the other guy's going to pay for it. Well, in the rare instance that the husband is very wealthy and the wife has no income and they've been married 20 years, the husband may be made to pay it all. But more and more, judges are ordering the house sold and both sides are made to pay a share of the legal fees."

Kelly further notes that while people are consumed with anger and vengeance, they may also find it tricky to be productive in their work and impossible to create a fulfilling new relationship while they're "stuck" in the old one.

Lloyd Zeiderman, a business manager for entertainers, concurs. He refers many of his clients to Kelly for divorce representation. "My experience has been that a divorcing person in an extended litigation can probably lose 50% of his or her income during that year, in addition to the other costs of divorce. They're preoccupied with antagonism.

"I use Mike in every case that I can that does not include a belligerent opposition," Zeiderman says. "He has a method where he comes up with settlements that are fair to both sides without the antagonism most attorneys are known for. With the high-income, high-net-worth clients I represent, there is a tendency by the opposing attorneys to generate tremendously high legal fees that cause both parties an unnecessary cost. Mike's methods seem to create a very compassionate situation for the husband, wife and children."

Useless Confrontation

Reasons Kelly, "If you start out your conversation with another lawyer saying, 'What can we do to handle this problem between our clients?' as opposed to 'My client just told me your client (cheated) him or was a liar,' you start steering him toward a mutually acceptable termination as opposed to a useless confrontation."

Beyond that, Kelly works to isolate the matters both sides agree on and shuffle them out of the way so that areas of disagreement may (a) appear minimal by comparison and (b) be examined without the added confusion of the other matters. Through all this friendliness, Kelly insists that he invites opposing lawyers to meet him with no less than the same vigor, concentration and thoroughness they apply to other proceedings. He favors speed but cautions that haste can create its own set of difficulties.

Sometimes, though, all that still doesn't work. Kelly admits to having arrived at the end of seemingly flawless settlements only to find a land mine exploding in the form of one final item, say an antique dining table both parties want. His solution is to encourage his client to just give it up, let it go and get the whole odious event over with.

Clients' Gratitude

The benefits of this approach are evident not only in the percentage of cases Kelly settles out of court but also in gratitude from his clients for ongoing ease in relationships with their ex-wives or ex-husbands.

Hollywood talent consultant Ashley Rothschild, for instance, retained Kelly to represent her in what looked to be a bitter custody battle for her son. She had lost custody of another son to her first husband, and after the breakup of her second marriage, both spouses were prepared to fight for full custody of their son.

"When my husband said, 'I want full custody,' I said, 'Over my dead body. I'll use every trick I can to get you,' " Rothschild recalls. "We would hang up screaming on the phone just to get each other. I was going to use every bit of ammunition that I could to get my child."

Kelly convinced her that joint custody might be more appropriate for all parties, especially the son.

"It's thanks to Michael Kelly's commitment that divorce doesn't have to be ugly, that my husband and I are friends now," Rothschild said.

There is no way to know precisely how typical the Rothschild case is of Kelly's practice. But one observer who's repeatedly watched Kelly operate suggests it may be a regular occurrence.

"I'm speaking only for myself, not for the court, but I'm favorably impressed," says commissioner John Alexander of the Los Angeles Superior Court, Santa Monica District.

"Is that a good idea? Of course it is," Alexander says. "A contested dissolution is an expensive thing and it's hard on the emotions. Kelly looks to me like the kind of person who would resign from the case rather than present an unreasonable demand. He's his own man. He won't let a client ask for the moon, the sun and the whole solar system."

Even opposing counsel have been impressed with Kelly's approach. One attorney, John Dunne, found his divorce methodology so "refreshing" that he invited Kelly and his partner, Michael Cogan, to move into his luxurious suite of offices overlooking the Pacific Ocean in Santa Monica (which they did).

"Kelly's an unusual lawyer," Dunne says. "His approach was so novel. He writes me this letter and wants to come over and sit down and brings all the facts and all the information that normally takes us a year to get and we settled a substantial case in, I think, four weeks. I'm always surprised when I get something like that from a lawyer. Usually it's something you get from a parish priest."

Beth Ann Krier,
Los Angeles Times

Win-Win Communication Skills

Win-win problem solving is clearly superior to the win-lose and lose-lose approaches. Why, then, is it so rarely used? There are three reasons. The first is lack of awareness. Some people are so used to competition that they mistakenly think winning requires them to defeat their "opponent."

Even when they know better, another reason prevents many people from seeking win-win solutions. Conflicts are often emotional affairs, in which people react combatively without stopping to think of better alternatives. Because this kind of emotional reflex prevents constructive solutions, it's often necessary to stop yourself from speaking out aggressively in a conflict and starting an escalating spiral of defensiveness. The time-honored advice of "counting to ten" applies here. Once you've thought about the matter, you'll be able to *act* constructively instead of *reacting* in a way that's likely to produce a lose-lose outcome.

A third reason win-win solutions are rare is that they require the other person's cooperation. It's difficult to negotiate constructively with someone who insists on trying to defeat you. When faced with this sort of person, you'll need to use your best persuasive skills to explain that by working together you can find a solution that satisfies both of you.

In spite of these challenges, it is definitely possible to become better at resolving conflicts. In the following pages we will outline a method to increase your chances of being able to handle your conflicts in a win-win manner, so that both you and others meet your needs. As you learn to use this approach, you should find that more and more of your conflicts wind up with win-win solutions. And even when total satisfaction isn't possible, this method can help by showing you how to solve problems in the most satisfying way possible and also by preventing individual conflict from spoiling your future interactions with the person involved.

Before introducing this method, there are a few ideas you should keep in mind. This technique is highly structured. Although you're learning how to use it, it's important that you follow all the stages carefully. Each step is essential to the success of your encounter, and skipping one or more can lead to misunderstandings that might threaten your meeting and even cause a "dirty fight." After you've practiced the method a number of times and are familiar with it, this style of conflict will become almost second nature to you. You'll then be able to approach your conflicts without having to follow the step-by-step approach. But for the time being try to be patient, and trust the value of the following pattern.

As you read the following steps, try to imagine yourself applying them to a problem that's bothering you now.

Step 1—Identify Your Problem and Unmet Needs   Before you
speak out, it's important to realize that the problem that is causing conflict is yours. Whether you want to return an unsatisfactory piece of merchandise, complain to a noisy neighbor because your sleep is being disturbed, or request a change in working conditions from your employer, the problem is yours. Why? Because in each case *you* are the person who is dissatisfied. You are the one who has paid for the defective article; the merchant who sold it to you has the use of your good money. You are the one who is losing sleep as a result of your

A quarrel between friends, when made up, adds a new tie to friendship, as experience shows that the callosity formed round a broken bone makes it stronger than before.

St. Francis De Sales

neighbors' activities; they are content to go on as before. You are the one who is unhappy with your working conditions, not your boss.*

Realizing that the problem is yours will make a big difference when the time comes to approach your partner. Instead of feeling and acting in an evaluative way, you'll be more likely to state your problem in a descriptive way, which will not only be more accurate but also reduce the chance of a defensive reaction.

Once you realize that the problem is yours, the next step is to identify the unmet needs that make you dissatisfied. For instance, in the barking dog incident, your need may be to get some sleep or to study without interruptions. In the case of a friend who teases you in public, your need would probably be to avoid embarrassment.

Sometimes the task of identifying your needs isn't as simple as it first seems. Behind the apparent content of an issue is often a relational need. Consider these examples:

> A friend hasn't returned some money you loaned long ago. Your apparent need in this situation might be to get the cash back. But a little thought will probably show that this isn't the only, or even the main, thing you want. Even if you were rolling in money, you'd probably want the loan repaid because of your most important need: *to avoid feeling victimized by your friend's taking advantage of you.*

> Someone you care about who lives in a distant city has failed to respond to several letters. Your apparent need may be to get answers to the questions you've written about, but it's likely that there's another, more fundamental need: *the reassurance that you're still important enough to deserve a response.*

As you'll soon see, the ability to identify your real needs plays a key role in solving interpersonal problems. For now, the point to remember is that before you voice your problem to your partner, you ought to be clear about which of your needs aren't being met.

Step 2—Make a Date

Destructive fights often start because the initiator confronts a partner who isn't ready. There are many times when a person isn't in the right frame of mind to face a conflict, perhaps owing to fatigue, being in too much of a hurry to take the necessary time, being upset over another problem, or not feeling well. At times like these it's unfair to "jump" a person without notice and expect to get full attention for your problem. If you do persist, you'll probably have an ugly fight on your hands.

After you have a clear idea of the problem, approach your partner with a request to try to solve it, for example, "Something's been bothering me. Can we talk about it?" If the answer is yes, you're ready to go further. If it isn't the right time to confront your partner, find a time that's agreeable to both of you.

Step 3—Describe Your Problem and Needs

Your partner can't possibly meet your needs without knowing why you're upset and what you want. Therefore, it's up to you to describe your problem as specifically as possible. The

---

* Of course, others involved in the conflict may have problems of their own. For instance, the shopkeeper, the noisy neighbor, and your boss may all be bothered by your requests. But the fact still remains that the reason you are speaking up about these matters is because *you* are dissatisfied. Thus, the problem is at least initially yours.

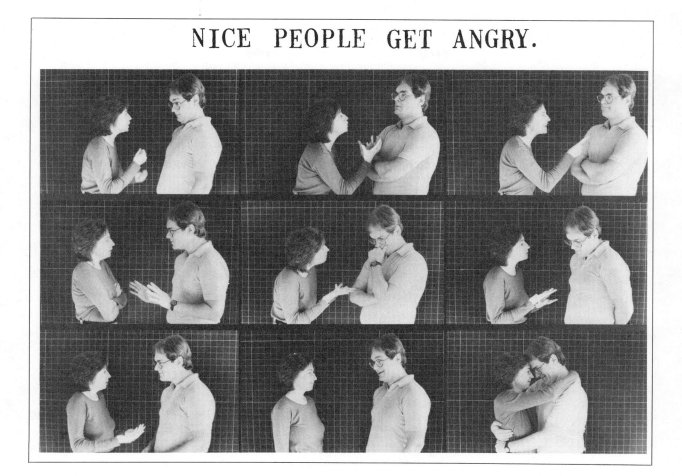

NICE PEOPLE GET ANGRY.

best way to deliver a complete, accurate message is to use the assertive sense-interpret-feel-consequence-intend format. Notice how well this approach works in the following examples:

Example 1

"I have a problem. It's about your leaving dirty clothes around the house after I've told you how much it bothers me [*sense*]. It's a problem because I have to run around like crazy and pick things up whenever guests come, which is no fun at all [*consequence*]. I'm starting to think that either you're not paying attention to my requests or you're trying to drive me crazy [*thoughts*], and either way I'm getting more and more resentful [*feeling*]. I'd like to find some way to have a neat place without my having to be a maid or a nag."

Example 2

"I have a problem. When you drop by without calling ahead and I'm studying [*sense*], I don't know whether to visit or ask you to leave [*thought*]. Either way, I get uncomfortable [*feeling*], and it seems like whatever I do, I lose: Either I have to put you off or get behind in my work [*consequences*]. I'd like to find a way to get my studying done and still socialize with you [*intention*]."

Example 3

"Something is bothering me. When you tell me you love me and yet spend almost all your free time with your other friends [*sense*], I wonder whether you mean it [*thought*]. I get insecure [*feeling*], and then I start acting moody [*consequence*]. I need some way of finding out for sure how you feel about me [*intention*]."

By expressing yourself in this way, you're opening up yourself to your partner, explaining just what's going on inside you and how important it is to you. It's surprising how often people argue without ever telling each other the extent of their feelings and thoughts.

One of the most important parts of this step is to describe your needs clearly in the intention phase of your message. The biggest danger here is to confuse your true needs, which we can call *ends,* with one or more means that might satisfy these ends. This distinction requires some definitions.

Ends are the goals you are seeking, and not having them met is what leads you to feel that a problem exists in the first place. In the examples you just read the desired ends were as follows:

Example 1: A house free of dirty clothes. No need to nag or do more than your own share of housekeeping.

Example 2: The chance to study without sending away friends who drop by.

Example 3: A definite reassurance of love (or a definite statement of nonlove).

Means are ways of achieving ends. For instance, if your goal were to become rich, some possible means might include investing in the stock market, robbing banks, gambling for high stakes, or marrying a wealthy person with a short time to live.

We can go back to our previous examples and see that there are many possible means that could achieve the ends we identified.

Example 1

End: House free of dirty clothes. No need to nag or do more than own share of housework.
Means: a.   Partner agrees to clean up without being reminded.
            b.   Hire a housekeeper.
            c.   You pick up clothes in exchange for partner's doing a share of your work.

Example 2

End: A chance to study without sending away friends who drop by.
Means: a.   You do all your studying at school.
            b.   Study at home when friends aren't likely to drop by (for example, late at night).
            c.   Ask friends to phone before dropping by.

Example 3

End: A definite reassurance of love (or definite statement of nonlove).
Means: a.   Companion regularly schedules time to see you.
            b.   You learn to accept loving messages, which your partner has been sending already.
            c.   You ask friend for reassurance whenever feeling insecure.

You might have found some of these means personally unacceptable, and you probably could think of others to add to the list. That's fine! For now, the important point to remember is that you should approach your partner in a conflict by describing your ends rather than focusing on one or more means. When people mistakenly identify means as ends, they usually increase the level of hostility and resistance. Insisting on specific means is a perfect example of defense-arousing controlling behavior, such as you read about in Chapter Nine; and concentrating on working with your partner to achieve a mutually satisfactory end constitutes the more supportive attitude of problem orientation.

Our marriage used to suffer from arguments that were too short. Now we argue long enough to find out what the argument is about.

Hugh Prather,
Notes to Myself

Step 4—Confirm Your Partner's Understanding

After you've stated your problem and described what you need, it's important to make sure your partner has understood what you've said. As you can remember from our discussion of listening in Chapter Seven, there's a good chance—especially in a stressful conflict—that your words will be misinterpreted.

It's usually unrealistic to insist that your partner paraphrase your statement, and fortunately there are more tactful and subtle ways to make sure you've been understood. For instance, you might try saying, "I'm not sure I expressed myself very well just now—maybe you should tell what you heard me say so I can be sure I got it right." In any case, be absolutely sure that your partner understands your whole message before going any further. Legitimate agreements are tough enough, but there's no point in getting upset about a conflict that doesn't even exist.

Step 5—Solicit Your Partner's Needs

Now that you've made your position clear, it's time to find out what your partner needs to feel satisfied about this issue. There are two reasons why it's important to discover your partner's needs. First, it's fair. The other person has just as much right as you to feel satisfied, and if you expect help in meeting your needs, it's reasonable that you behave in the same way. But in addition to decency, there's another, practical reason for concerning yourself with what the other person wants. Just as an unhappy partner will make it hard for you to become satisfied, a happy one will be more likely to cooperate in letting you reach your goals. Thus, it's in your own self-interest to discover and meet your partner's needs.

You can learn about your partner's needs simply by asking about them: "Now I've told you what I want and why. Tell me what you need to feel OK about this." Once your partner begins to talk, your job is to use the listening skills discussed earlier in this book to make sure you understand.

Not having studied interpersonal communication, your partner might state intentions in terms of means rather than ends, for instance, saying things like "I want you to be around when I call" instead of "I need to know where you are when I need you." In such cases, it's a good idea to rephrase the statements in terms of ends, thus making it clear to both yourself and your partner what he or she really needs to feel satisfied.

Step 6—Check Your Understanding of Partner's Needs

Reverse the procedure in step 4 by paraphrasing your partner's needs until you're certain you understand them. The surest way to accomplish this step is to use the active listening skills you learned in Chapter Seven.

Step 7—Negotiate a Solution   Now that you and your partner understand each other's needs, the goal becomes finding a way to meet them. This is
done by trying to develop as many potential solutions as possible and then
evaluating them to decide which one best meets everyone's needs. Perhaps you
can best appreciate how the win-win method works by looking at one example.

Some time ago Ron and his wife, Sherri, used the win-win approach to solve
a problem that had been causing friction between them. To understand the
problem, you have to know that Ron is basically a tightwad, whereas Sherri isn't
nearly as concerned with finances and doesn't worry as much as Ron does
about budgets, savings accounts, or balanced checkbooks. This difference
led to their problem: Every month Sherri would come home from shopping
expeditions with antiques, new clothes, and other goodies. It wasn't that these
things were very expensive, but it bothered Ron that Sherri seemed to think there
was something wrong with coming home empty-handed.

It got so that Ron dreaded the times Sherri would walk into the house carrying
a shopping bag, and of course, Ron's constant worrying about money bothered
Sherri too. After what seemed like an endless number of "discussions" about the
problem, they didn't seem to be getting anywhere. This was one area in which
their needs came into conflict.

Eventually, both Ron and Sherri realized that they had to find a solution that
both could live with. So one evening they sat down and wrote all the alternatives
they could think of:

1. Ron learns not to worry about money.
2. Sherri stops being a compulsive shopper.
3. Sherri and Ron discuss each purchase before it's made.
4. Sherri waits a day after first seeing something before buying it.

None of these ideas seemed workable. Since neither Ron nor Sherri could
change their personalities overnight, solutions 1 and 2 were out. They had tried 3
once or twice before and found it caused just as many disagreements as the
original problem. The fourth alternative made sense, but it didn't sound like
much fun, nor would it always be practical. Fortunately after some more
brainstorming they came up with another alternative:

5. Each month they would set aside a certain amount of money for Sherri to
   spend any way she wanted.

This sounded good to both Ron and Sherri, and after figuring the best
amount for this "discretionary fund," things worked well. Now Sherri can buy
most of the things she wants, and Ron can enjoy Sherri's shopping sprees
without worrying about the budget.

Probably the best description of the win-win approach has been written by
Thomas Gordon in his book *Parent Effectiveness Training*.[9] The following steps
are a modification of this approach.

A. Identify and define the conflict   We've discussed identifying and defining the
conflict in the preceding pages. It consists of discovering each person's problem
and needs, setting the stage for meeting all of them.

B. Generate a number of possible solutions   In step B, the partners work together to think of as many means as possible to reach their stated ends. The key
word here is *quantity:* It's important to generate as many ideas as you can think

of without worrying about which ones are good or bad. Write down every thought that comes up, no matter how unworkable: Sometimes a farfetched idea will lead to a more workable one.

C. Evaluate the alternative solutions   This is the time to talk about which solutions will work and which ones won't. It's important for everyone to be honest about their willingness to accept an idea. If a solution is going to work, everyone involved has to support it.

D. Decide on the best solution   Now that you've looked at all the alternatives, pick the one that looks best to everyone. It's important to be sure everybody understands the solution and is willing to try it out. Remember that your decision doesn't have to be final, but it should look potentially successful.

Step 8—Follow Up the Solution   You can't be sure the solution will work until you try it. After you've tested it for a while, it's a good idea to set aside some time to talk over its progress. You may find that you need to make some changes or even rethink the whole problem. The idea is to keep on top of the problem, to keep using creativity to solve it.

   Win-win solutions aren't always possible. There will be times when even the best intentioned people simply won't be able to find a way of meeting all their needs. In cases like this, the process of negotiation has to include some compromises. But even then the preceding steps haven't been wasted. The genuine desire to learn what the other person wants and to try to satisfy those desires will build a climate of goodwill that can help you find the best solution to the present problem and also improve your relationship in the future.

Win-Win Solutions and You

1. Make a list of the situations in your life in which a conflict of needs is creating tension between you and someone else.

2. Analyze what you're doing at present to resolve such conflicts, and describe whether your behavior is meeting with any success.

3. Pick at least one of the problems you just listed, and together with the other people involved, try to develop a win-win solution by following the steps listed in the preceding pages.

4. After working through steps 1 to 7, disclose the results of your conference to the class. After you've had time to test your solution, report the progress you've made and discuss the follow-up conference described in step 8.

Constructive Conflict: Questions and Answers

After learning about win-win negotiating, people often express doubts about how well it can work. "It sounds like a good idea," they say, but. . . . " Three questions arise more than any others, and they deserve an answer.

Isn't the Win-Win Approach Too Good to Be True?   Research shows that seeking mutual benefit is not only desirable—it works. In fact, the win-win approach produces better results than a win-lose negotiating style.

In a series of experiments, Robert Axelrod presented subjects with a bargaining situation called "prisoner's dilemma," in which they could choose either to cooperate or betray a confederate.[10] There are three types of outcome in prisoner's dilemma: One partner can win big by betraying a confederate, both can win by cooperating, or both can lose by betraying one another.

Although cynics might assume that the most effective strategy is to betray a partner (a win-lose approach), Axelrod demonstrated that cooperation is actually the best hard-nosed choice. He staged a tournament in which participants played against a computer that was programmed to represent several negotiating strategies. The winning strategy was one called "Tit-for-Tat." It starts out by cooperating and continues to cooperate until the other party betrays it. After that, the program always does what the other player did on the previous move. It never punishes an opponent more than once for a betrayal, and it will always cooperate if the other player does.

A win-win Tit-for-Tat strategy succeeds for several reasons.[11] First, it isn't a patsy. It responds quickly to betrayal, discouraging others from taking unfair advantage. At the same time, it is quick to forgive. It doesn't hold a grudge: As soon as the other party cooperates, it does too. Finally, it isn't too sneaky. By making its behavior obvious and predictable, Tit-for-Tat creates an atmosphere of trust.

There are certainly some conflicts that can't be resolved with win-win outcomes. Only one suitor can marry the prince or princess, and only one person can be hired for the advertised job. Furthermore, it's impossible to reach a win-win solution when your partner refuses to cooperate. Most of the time, however, good intentions and creative thinking can lead to outcomes that satisfy everyone's needs.

Is It Possible to Change Others?   Readers often agree that win-win problem solving would be terrific—if everyone had read *Looking Out/Looking In* and understood the method. "How can I get the other person to cooperate?" the question goes.

Though you won't always be able to gain your partner's cooperation, a good job of selling can do the trick most of the time. The key lies in showing that it's in the other person's self-interest to work together: "Look, if we can't settle this, we'll both feel miserable. But if we can find an answer, think how much better off we'll be." Notice that this sort of explanation projects both the favorable consequences of cooperating and the costs of competing.

You can also boost the odds of getting your partner's cooperation by modeling the communication skills described in this book. You've read that defense-arousing behavior is reciprocal, but so is supportive communication. If you can listen sincerely, avoid evaluative attacks, and empathize with your partner's concerns, for example, there's a good chance you'll get the same kind of behavior in return. And even if your cooperative attitude doesn't succeed, you'll gain self-respect from knowing that at least you behaved honorably and constructively.

Isn't Win-Win Negotiating *Too* Rational?   Frustrated readers often complain that the win-win approach is so sensible that only a saint could use it successfully. "Sometimes I'm so angry that I don't care about being supportive or empathetic or anything else," they say. "I just want to blow my top!"

When you feel like this, it's almost impossible to be rational. At times like these probably the most therapeutic thing to do is to get your feelings off your chest in what George Bach calls a "Vesuvius"—an uncontrolled, spontaneous explosion. A Vesuvius can be a terrific way of blowing off steam, and after you do so, it's often much easier to figure out a rational solution to your problem.

So we encourage you to have a Vesuvius, with the following qualifications: Be sure your partner understands what you're doing and realizes that whatever you say doesn't call for a response. Your partner should let you rant and rave for as long as you want without getting defensive or "tying in." Then when your eruption subsides, you can take steps to work through whatever still troubles you.

There you have it—probably some new and different ways of looking at conflict. We've tried to show you how disagreements are a natural part of life and how handling them well can turn what used to be frustrating experiences into encounters that can make your relationships stronger than they were before.

Of course, the ideas we've presented here are only a beginning for you; you'll have to tailor them to suit your own personality. But we do believe that the general approach we've showed here works; it has for us and many people we know, and we hope it will for you.

More Readings on Conflict Resolution

Axelrod, Robert. *The Evolution of Cooperation.* New York: Basic Books, 1984.
    A detailed study of how cooperation is possible in a world run by self-interest. Axelrod is a political scientist, but his work also applies to interpersonal conflicts. Especially useful are chapters on "How to Promote Cooperation," "The Social Structure of Cooperation," and "The Robustness of Reciprocity."

Bach, George R., and Peter Wyden. *The Intimate Enemy.* New York: Avon, 1968.
    In this very readable best seller, Bach and Wyden detail the destructive styles of dealing with conflict most marriage partners use. They then present the "fair fight" as an alternative. They present many examples of how couples have learned to deal constructively and successfully with conflicts.

Fisher, Roger, and William Ury. *Getting to Yes: Negotiating Agreement Without Giving In.* Boston: Houghton Mifflin, 1981.
    This is perhaps the best of the expanding collection of books on the subject of negotiating. Fisher and Ury show that you needn't choose between being an aggressive, demanding negotiator and a pushover. Their discussion of principled negotiation shows how to seek win-win solutions whenever possible and what to do when you face a partner who seems interested only in winning at your expense.

Hocker, Joyce L., and William W. Wilmot. *Interpersonal Conflict,* 2d ed. Dubuque, Iowa: W. C. Brown, 1985.
    A thorough survey of the nature of interpersonal conflict and how it can be resolved. This is an ideal second step for readers who want to explore the subject in further detail.

Jandt, Fred E., and Paul Gillette. *Win-Win Negotiating: Turning Conflict Into Agreement.* New York: Wiley, 1985.
    A readable description of the differences between win-lose and win-win problem solving. The book offers examples from both business and personal situations.

Endnotes

Chapter One

1. J. B. Ross and M. M. McLaughlin, eds., *A Portable Medieval Reader* (New York: Viking, 1949).

2. S. Schachter, *The Psychology of Affiliation* (Stanford, Calif.: Stanford University Press, 1959), pp. 9–10.

3. UPI, *Wisconsin State Journal,* September 7, 1978.

4. R. Narem, "Try a Little TLC," research reported in *Science* 80:1 (1980): 15.

5. J. Lynch, *The Broken Heart: The Medical Consequences of Loneliness* (New York: Basic Books, 1977), pp. 239–242.

6. Ibid.

7. E. A. Liljefors and R. H. Rahe, "Psychosocial Characteristics of Subjects with Myocardial Infarction in Stockholm," in *Life Stress Illness,* ed. E. K. Gunderson and R. H. Rahe (Springfield, Ill.: Charles C. Thomas, 1974), pp. 90–104.

8. W. D. Rees and S. G. Lutkins, "Mortality of Bereavement," *British Medical Journal* 4 (1967): 13.

9. R. Shattuck, *The Forbidden Experiment: The Story of the Wild Boy of Aveyron* (New York: Farrar, Straus & Giroux, 1980), p. 37.

10. W. Schutz, *The Interpersonal Underworld* (Palo Alto, Calif.: Science and Behavior Books, 1966).

11. A. H. Maslow, *Toward a Psychology of Being* (New York: Van Nostrand, Reinhold, 1968).

12. E. M. Rogers and D. L. Kincaid, *Communication Networks: Toward a New Paradigm for Research* (New York: Free Press, 1981), pp. 43–48, 63–66.

13. J. Stewart and G. D'Angelo, *Together: Communicating Interpersonally,* 2d ed. (Reading, Mass.: Addison-Wesley, 1980), pp. 75–78. See also J. Stewart, "Foundations of Dialogic Communication," *Quarterly Journal of Speech* 45 (April 1978): 183–201.

14. Adapted from J. McCroskey and L. Wheeless, *Introduction to Human Communication* (Boston: Allyn and Bacon, 1976), pp. 3–10.

15. Ibid., p. 5.

16. For a review of research on communication competence see B. H. Spitzberg and W. M. Cupach, *Interpersonal Communication Competence* (Beverly Hills, Calif.: Sage, 1984).

17. J. M. Wiemann and P. M. Backlund, "Current Theory and Research in Communication Competence," *Review of Educational Research* 50 (1980): 185–199. See also M. V. Redmond, "The Relationship Between Perceived Communication Competence and Perceived Empathy," *Communication Monographs* 52 (December 1985): 377–382.

18. D. B. Wackman, S. Miller, and E. W. Nunnally, *Student Workbook: Increasing Awareness and Communication Skills* (Minneapolis: Interpersonal Communication Programs, 1976), p. 6.

19. Adapted from the work of R. P. Hart as reported by M. L. Knapp in *Interpersonal Communication and Human Relationships* (Boston: Allyn and Bacon, 1984), pp. 342–344. See also R. P. Hart and D. M. Burks, "Rhetorical Sensitivity and Social Interaction," *Speech Monographs* 39 (1972): 75–91; and R. P. Hart, R. E. Carlson, and W. F. Eadie, "Attitudes Toward Communication and the Assessment of Rhetorical Sensitivity," *Communication Monographs* 47 (1980): 1–22.

Chapter Two

1. J. Kagan, *The Nature of the Child* (New York: Basic Books, 1984).

2. J. McCroskey and V. Richmond, *The Quiet Ones: Communication Apprehension and Shyness* (Dubuque, Iowa: Gorsuch Scarisbrick, 1980).

3. C. H. Cooley, *Human Nature and the Social Order* (New York: Scribner's, 1912). For a brief but comprehensive description of reflected appraisal and social comparison, see Morris Rosenberg, *Conceiving the Self* (New York: Basic Books, 1979).

4. Adapted from J. W. Krinch, "A Formalized Theory of the Self-Concept," in *Symbolic Interaction,* 2d ed., ed. J. Manis and B. N. Meltzer (Boston: Allyn and Bacon, 1972), pp. 245–252.

5. Reported in D. E. Hamachek, *Encounters with Others: Interpersonal Relationships and You* (New York: Holt, Rinehart and Winston, 1982), pp. 3–5.

6. R. Rosenthal and L. Jacobson, *Pygmalion in the Classroom* (New York: Holt, Rinehart and Winston, 1968).

7. Ibid., pp. 5–6.

Chapter Three

1. P. Watzlawick, J. Beavin, and D. D. Jackson, *Pragmatics of Human Communication* (New York: Norton, 1967), p. 56.

2. L. Bartoshuk, "Separate Worlds of Taste," *Psychology Today* 14 (September 1980): 48–56, 63.

3. R. W. Moncrieff, *Odour Preferences* (London: Leonard Hill, 1966).

4. J. Piaget, *The Origins of Intelligence in Children* (New York: International Universities Press, 1952).

5. G. G. Luce, *Body Time* (New York: Pantheon Books, 1971).

6. E. Ramey, "Men's Cycles," *Ms.* 1 (Spring 1972): 10–14.

7. R. Armao, "Worst Blunders: Firms Laugh Through Tears," *American Business* (January 1981): 11.

8. R. Harrison, "Nonverbal Behavior: An Approach to Human

Communication," in *Approaches to Human Communication,* ed. R. Budd and B. Ruben (New York: Spartan Books, 1972).

9. E. T. Hall, *The Hidden Dimension* (New York: Doubleday Anchor, 1969), p. 160.

10. J. Horn, "Conversation Breakdowns: As Different as Black and White," *Psychology Today* 8 (May 1974): 30.

11. P. G. Zimbardo, C. Haney, and W. C. Banks, "A Pirandellian Prison," *New York Times Magazine,* April 8, 1973.

12. See, for example, P. Baron, "Self-Esteem, Ingratiation, and Evaluation of Unknown Others," *Journal of Personality and Social Psychology* 30 (1974): 104–109.

13. D. E. Hamachek, *Encounters with Others: Interpersonal Relationships and You* (New York: Holt, Rinehart and Winston, 1982), p. 3.

14. B. Sypher and H. E. Sypher, "Seeing Ourselves as Others See Us, *Communication Research* 11 (January 1984): 97–115.

15. Reported by D. Myers, "The Inflated Self," *Psychology Today* 14 (May 1980): 16.

16. Hamachek, op. cit., pp. 23–30.

17. R. G. King, *Fundamentals of Human Communication* (New York: Macmillan, 1979), p. 152.

18. D. T. Regan and J. Totten, "Empathy and Attribution: Turning Observers into Actors," *Journal of Personality and Social Psychology* 35 (1975): 850–856.

19. Hamachek, op. cit., pp. 23–24.

20. G. Cronkhite, *Communication and Awareness* (Menlo Park, Calif.: Cummings, 1976), p. 82.

Chapter Four

1. P. Ekman, R. W. Levenson, and W. V. Friesen, "Autonomic Nervous System Activity Distinguishes Among Emotions," *Science* 221 (September 16, 1983): 1,208–1,210.

2. S. Valins, "Cognitive Effects of False Heart-Rate Feedback," *Journal of Personality and Social Psychology* 4 (1966): 400–408.

3. P. Zimbardo, *Shyness: What It Is, What to Do About It* (Reading, Mass.: Addison-Wesley, 1977), p. 53.

4. Ibid., p. 54.

5. R. Plutchik, "A Language for the Emotions," *Psychology Today* 14 (February 1980): 68–78. For a more detailed explanation, see R. Plutchik, *Emotion: A Psychoevolutionary Synthesis* (New York: Harper & Row, 1980).

6. Plutchik, "A Language for the Emotions."

7. S. B. Shimanoff, "Commonly Named Emotions in Everyday Conversations," *Perceptual and Motor Skills* 58 (1984): 514. See also J. M. Gottmann, "Emotional Responsiveness in Marital Conversations," *Journal of Communication* 32 (1982): 108–120.

8. S. B. Shimanoff, "Linguistic References to Emotive States in Naturally Occurring Conversations," *Journal of Communication.* Forthcoming.

9. L. B. Rosenfeld, "Self-Disclosure and Avoidance: Why Am I Afraid to Tell You Who I Am?" *Communication Monographs* 46 (1979): 63–74.

10. A. Beck, *Cognitive Therapy and the Emotional Disorders* (New York: International Universities Press, 1976).

11. A. Ellis and R. Harper, *A New Guide to Rational Living* (North Hollywood, Calif.: Wilshire Books, 1977).

Chapter Five

1. J. Davidson, "How to Translate English," in *The Language of Man,* Vol. 4, ed. Joseph Fletcher Littell (Evanston, Ill.: McDougal Littell, 1971), p. 33.

2. S. I. Hayakawa, *Language in Thought and Action* (New York: Harcourt Brace Jovanovich, 1964), pp. 176–179.

3. J. B. Carroll, ed., *Language, Thought, and Reality: Selected Writings of Benjamin Lee Whorf* (Cambridge, Mass.: MIT Press, 1966).

4. C. Miller and K. Swift, "One Small Step for Genkind," *New York Times Magazine,* April 16, 1972. Reprinted in *Language: Concepts and Processes,* ed. J. DeVito (Englewood Cliffs, N.J.: Prentice-Hall, 1973), pp. 171–182.

5. Summarized in M. G. Marcus, "The Power of a Name," *Psychology Today* 10 (October 1976): 75–77, 108.

6. See, for example, B. Erickson, E. A. Lind, B. C. Johnson, and W. M. O'Barr, "Speech Style and Impression Formation in a Court Setting: The Effects of Powerful and Powerless Speech," *Journal of Experimental Social Psychology* 14 (1978): 266–279.

7. P. Watzlawick, J. H. Beavin, and D. D. Jackson, *Pragmatics of Human Communication* (New York: Norton, 1967).

8. B. A. Fisher and G. R. Drecksel, "A Cyclical Model of Developing Relationships: A Study of Relational Control Interaction," *Communication Monographs* 50 (1983): 66–78.

9. J. Bradac and A. Mulac, "Attributional Consequences of Powerful and Powerless Speech Styles in a Crisis-Intervention Context," *Journal of Language and Social Psychology* 3 (1984): 1–19.

10. M. Wiener and A. Mehrabian, *A Language Within Language: Immediacy: A Channel in Verbal Communication* (New York: Appleton-Century-Crofts, 1968).

Chapter Six

1. A. Mehrabian and M. Wiener, "Decoding of Inconsistent Communications," *Journal of Personality and Social Psychology* 6 (1967): 109–114; also, A. Mehrabian and S. Ferris, "Inference of Attitudes from Nonverbal Communication in Two Channels," *Journal of Consulting Psychology* 31 (1967): 248–252.

2. R. Birdwhistell, *Kinesics and Context* (Philadelphia: University of Pennsylvania Press, 1970).

3. P. Ekman, W. V. Friesen, and J. Baer, "The International Language of Gestures," *Psychology Today* 18 (May 1984): 64–69.

4. E. Hall, *The Hidden Dimension* (Garden City, N.Y.: Anchor Books, 1969).

5. C. R. Kleinke, "Compliance to Requests Made by Gazing and Touching Experimenters in Field Settings," *Journal of Experimental Social Psychology* 13 (1977): 218–233.

6. M. LaFrance and C. Mayo, "Racial Differences in Gaze Behavior During Conversations: Two Systematic Observational Studies," *Journal of Personality and Social Psychology* 33 (1976): 547–552.

7. See P. Ekman, "Communication Through Nonverbal Behavior: A Source of Information About an Interpersonal Relationship," in *Affect, Cognition, and Personality,* ed. S. Tomkins and C. E. Izard (New York: Springer, 1965).

8. P. Ekman and W. V. Friesen, "The Repertoire of Nonverbal Behavior: Categories, Origins, Usage, and Coding, *Semiotica* 1 (1969): 49–98.

9. Summarized in M. L. Hickson III and D. W. Stacks, *NVC: Nonverbal Communication: Studies and Applications* (Dubuque, Iowa: W. C. Brown, 1985), pp. 117–118.

10. For a detailed discussion of nonverbal deception, see P. Ekman, *Telling Lies: Clues to Deceit in the Marketplace, Politics, and Marriage* (New York: Norton, 1985).

11. M. L. Knapp, *Nonverbal Communication in Human Interaction* (New York: Holt, Rinehart and Winston, 1978).

12. J. A. Hall, "Gender, Gender Roles, and Nonverbal Communication Skills," in *Skill in Nonverbal Communication: Individual Differences,* ed. R. Rosenthal (Cambridge, Mass.: Oelgeschlager, Gunn, and Hain, 1979), pp. 32–67.

13. A. Mehrabian, *Silent Messages,* 2d ed. (Belmont, Calif.: Wadsworth, 1981), pp. 47–48, 61–62.

14. M. B. Myers, D. Templer, and R. Brown, "Coping Ability of Women Who Become Victims of Rape," *Journal of Consulting and Clinical Psychology* 52 (1984): 73–78. See also C. Rubenstein, "Body Language That Speaks to Muggers," *Psychology Today* 20 (August 1980): 20; and J. Meer, "Profile of a Victim," *Psychology Today* 24 (May 1984): 76.

15. A. E. Scheflen, "Quasi-Courting Behavior in Psychotherapy," *Psychiatry* 228 (1965): 245–257.

16. Ekman, *Telling Lies,* pp. 109–110.

17. P. Ekman and W. V. Friesen, "Nonverbal Behavior and Psychopathology," in *The Psychology of Depression: Contemporary Theory and Research,* ed. R. J. Friedman and M. N. Katz (Washington, D.C.: J. Winston, 1974).

18. Ekman, *Telling Lies,* p. 107.

19. P. Ekman and W. V. Friesen, *Unmasking the Face: A Guide to Recognizing Emotions from Facial Clues* (Englewood Cliffs, N.J.: Prentice-Hall, 1975).

20. Ibid., p. 150.

21. E. H. Hess and J. M. Polt, "Pupil Size as Related to Interest Value of Visual Stimuli," *Science* 132 (1960): 349–350.

22. E. T. Hall, *The Silent Language* (New York: Fawcett, 1959).

23. *Newsweek,* October 5, 1970, p. 106.

24. J. A. Starkweather, "Vocal Communication of Personality and Human Feeling," *Journal of Communication* 11 (1961): 69; and K. R. Scherer, J. Koiwunaki, and R. Rosenthal, "Minimal Cues in the Vocal Communication of Affect: Judging Emotions from Content-Masked Speech," *Journal of Psycholinguistic Speech* 1 (1972): 269–285.

25. Mehrabian and Wiener, op. cit.; Mehrabian and Ferris, op. cit.

26. Ekman, *Telling Lies,* p. 93.

27. H. Bakwin, "Emotional Deprivation in Infants," *Journal of Pediatrics* 35 (1949): 512–521.

28. A. Montagu, *Touching: The Human Significance of the Skin* (New York: Harper & Row, 1971).

29. L. J. Yarrow, "Research in Dimension of Early Maternal Care," *Merrill-Palmer Quarterly* 9 (1963): 101–122.

30. B. Gunther, *Sense Relaxation: Below Your Mind* (New York: Macmillan, 1968).

31. R. Heslin and T. Alper, "Touch: A Bonding Gesture," in *Nonverbal Interaction,* ed. J. M. Wiemann and R. P. Harrison (Beverly Hills, Calif.: Sage, 1983), pp. 47–75.

32. Ibid.

33. Ibid.

34. W. Thourlby, *You Are What You Wear* (New York: New American Library, 1978), p. 1.

35. J. H. Fortenberry, J. Maclean, P. Morris, and M. O'Connell, "Mode of Dress as a Perceptual Cue to Deference," *The Journal of Social Psychology* 104 (1978).

36. L. Bickman, "Social Roles and Uniforms: Clothes Make the Person," *Psychology Today* 7 (April 1974): 48–51.

37. M. Lefkowitz, R. R. Blake, and J. S. Mouton, "Status of Actors in Pedestrian Violation of Traffic Signals," *Journal of Abnormal and Social Psychology* 51 (1955): 704–706.

38. T. F. Hoult, "Experimental Measurement of Clothing as a Factor in Some Social Ratings of Selected American Men," *American Sociological Review* 19 (1954): 326–327.

39. E. T. Hall, *The Hidden Dimension.*

40. A. Maslow and N. Mintz, "Effects of Aesthetic Surroundings: Initial Effects of Those Aesthetic Surroundings Upon Perceiving 'Energy' and 'Well-Being' in Faces," *Journal of Psychology* 41 (1956): 247–254.

41. R. Sommer, *Personal Space: The Behavioral Basis of Design* (Englewood Cliffs, N.J.: Prentice-Hall, 1978).

Chapter Seven

1. L. Barker, R. Edwards, C. Gaines, K. Gladney, and F. Holley, "An Investigation of Proportional Time Spent in Various Communication Activities by College Students," *Journal of Applied Communication Research* 8 (1981): 101–109.

2. B. E. Bradley, *Fundamentals of Speech Communication,* 3d ed. (Dubuque, Iowa: W. C. Brown, 1981), pp. 205–206.

3. R. Nichols, "Listening Is a Ten-Part Skill," in *Readings in Interpersonal and Organizational Communication,* eds. R. C. Huseman et al. (Boston: Holbrook Press, 1969), p. 476.

4. M. Davidowitz and D. D. Myrick, "Responding to the Bereaved: An Analysis of 'Helping' Statements," *Death Education* 8 (1984): 1–10.

5. T. Gordon, *Parent Effectiveness Training* (New York: Wyden, 1970), pp. 49–94.

6. G. Egan, *Interpersonal Living: A Skills/Contract Approach to Human-Relations Training in Groups* (Monterey, Calif.: Brooks-Cole, 1976), pp. 108–111.

Chapter Eight

1. See P. Watzlawick, J. H. Beavin, D. D. Jackson, *Pragmatics of Human Communication* (New York: Norton, 1967); and W. J. Lederer and D. D. Jackson, *The Mirages of Marriage* (New York: Norton, 1968).

2. Ibid.

3. See C. M. Rossiter, Jr., "Instruction in Metacommunication," *Central States Speech Journal* 25 (1974): 36–42; and W. W. Wilmot, "Metacommunication: A Re-examination and Extension," in *Communication Yearbook 4* (New Brunswick, N.J.: Transaction Books, 1980).

4. These theories are summarized in D. E. Hamachek, *Encounters with Others: Interpersonal Relationships and You* (New York: Holt, Rinehart and Winston, 1982), pp. 52–69; and E. Berscheid and E. H. Walster, *Interpersonal Attraction,* 2d ed. (Reading, Mass.: Addison-Wesley, 1978).

5. M. L. Knapp, *Interpersonal Communication and Human Relationships* (Boston: Allyn and Bacon, 1984), pp. 32–54.

6. Ibid., p. 36.

7. I. Altman and D. A. Taylor, *Social Penetration: The Development of Interpersonal Relationships* (New York: Holt, Rinehart and Winston, 1973).

8. Adapted from J. Powell, *Why Am I Afraid to Tell You Who I Am?* (Chicago: Argus Communications, 1969), pp. 50–62.

9. J. Luft, *Of Human Interaction* (Palo Alto, Calif.: National Press, 1969).

10. Adapted from V. J. Derlega and J. Grezlak, "Appropriateness of Self-Disclosure," in *Self-Disclosure,* ed. G. J. Chelune (San Francisco: Josey-Bass, 1979).

11. See V. J. Derlega and A. L. Chaikin, *Sharing Intimacy: What We Reveal to Others and Why* (Englewood Cliffs, N.J.: Prentice-Hall, 1975).

12. L. B. Rosenfeld and W. L. Kendrick, "Choosing to Be Open: Subjective Reasons for Self-Disclosing," *Western Journal of Speech Communication* 48 (Fall 1984): 326–343.

13. T. E. Runge and R. L. Archer, "Reactions to the Disclosure of Public and Private Self-Information," *Social Psychology Quarterly* 44 (December 1981): 357–362.

14. C. L. Kleinke, "Effects of Personal Evaluations," in *Self-Disclosure* (San Francisco: Josey-Bass, 1979).

15. G. Bach and Y. Bernhard, *Aggression Lab: The Fair Fight Training Manual* (Dubuque, Iowa: Kendall-Hunt, 1971).

Chapter Nine

1. E. Sieburg, "Confirming and Disconfirming Communication in an Organizational Setting," in *Communication in Organiza-* *tions,* ed. J. Owen, P. Page, and G. Zimmerman (St. Paul, Minn.: West, 1976), pp. 129–149.

2. Ibid.

3. W. Wilmot, *Dyadic Communication* (Reading, Mass.: Addison-Wesley, 1979), p. 123.

4. J. Powell, *Why Am I Afraid to Tell You Who I Am?* (Chicago: Argus Communications, 1969), p. 12.

5. L. Festinger, *A Theory of Cognitive Dissonance* (Stanford, Calif.: Stanford University Press, 1957).

6. J. Gibb, "Defensive Communication," *Journal of Communication* 11 (September 1961): 141–148. See also W. F. Eadie, "Defensive Communication Revisited: A Critical Examination of Gibb's Theory," *Southern Speech Communication Journal* 47 (1982): 163–177.

7. Adapted from M. Smith, *When I Say No, I Feel Guilty* (New York: Dial Press, 1975), pp. 93–110.

Chapter Ten

1. J. L. Hocker and W. W. Wilmot, *Interpersonal Conflict,* 2d ed. (Dubuque, Iowa: W. C. Brown, 1985), pp. 22–29.

2. J. M. Gottman, "Emotional Responsiveness in Marital Conversations," *Journal of Communication* 32 (1982): 108–120. See also W. R. Cupah, "Communication Satisfaction and Interpersonal Solidarity as Outcomes of Conflict Message Strategy Use," paper presented at the International Communication Association Conference, Boston, May 1982.

3. P. Koren, K. Carlton, and D. Shaw, "Marital Conflict: Relations Among Behaviors, Outcomes, and Distress," *Journal of Consulting and Clinical Psychology* 48 (1980): 460–468.

4. G. Mettetal and J. M. Gottman, "Affective Responsiveness in Spouses: Investigating the Relationship Between Communication Behavior and Marital Satisfaction," paper presented at the Speech Communication Association, New York, November 1980. See also J. M. Gottman, *Marital Interaction: Experimental Investigations* (New York: Academic Press, 1979); and A. Brandt, "Avoiding Couple Karate," *Psychology Today* 16 (October 1982): 39–43.

5. See, for example, G. Bach, *Aggression Lab: The Fair Fight Manual* (Dubuque, Iowa: Kendall-Hunt, 1971), pp. 193–200.

6. C. Tarvis, "Anger Defused," *Psychology Today* 16 (November 1982): 34.

7. Adapted from S. Miller, E. W. Nunnally, and D. B. Wackman, *Alive and Aware: How to Improve Your Relationships Through Better Communication* (Minneapolis, Minn.: International Communication Programs, 1975).

8. A. C. Filley, *Interpersonal Conflict Resolution* (Glenview, Ill.: Scott Foresman, 1975), p. 23.

9. T. Gordon, *Parent Effectiveness Training* (New York: Wyden, 1970), pp. 236–264.

10. R. Axelrod, *The Evolution of Cooperation* (New York: Basic Books, 1984).

11. M. Kinsley, "It Pays to Be Nice," *Science* 222 (1984): 162.

Glossary

Abstraction ladder   A range of more-to-less abstract terms describing an event or object.

Active listening   The act in which a receiver paraphrases the speaker's message.

Advising response   A helping response in which the receiver offers suggestions about how the speaker should deal with a problem.

Affection   The social need to care for others and to be cared for by them.

Ambiguous response   A disconfirming response with more than one meaning, leaving the other party unsure of the responder's position.

Ambushing   A style in which the receiver listens carefully to gather information to use in an attack on the speaker.

Analyzing statement   A helping style in which the listener offers an interpretation of a speaker's message.

Androgynous   Possessing both masculine and feminine traits.

Apathy   A defense mechanism in which a person avoids admitting emotional pain by pretending not to care about an event. *See also* Emotional insulation.

Assertion   A direct expression of the sender's needs, thoughts, or feelings, delivered in a way that does not attack the receiver's dignity.

Attribution theory   An explanation that suggests emotions are a function of the interpretation a person gives physiological responses to an activating event.

Behavioral description   An account that refers only to observable phenomena.

Bypassing   A misunderstanding that occurs when two people use the same term in two different ways or use different words to represent the same thing.

Certainty   Messages that dogmatically imply that the speaker's position is correct and that the other person's ideas are not worth considering. Likely to generate a defensive response.

Channel   The medium through which a message passes from sender to receiver.

Cognitive dissonance   An inconsistency between two conflicting pieces of information, attitudes, or behavior. Communicators strive to reduce dissonance, often through defense mechanisms that maintain an idealized presenting image.

Communication   A continuous, irreversible, transactive process involving communicators who occupy different but overlapping environments and are simultaneously senders and receivers of messages, many of which are distorted by physical and psychological noise.

Communication climate   The emotional tone of a relationship between two or more individuals.

Compensation   A defense mechanism in which a person stresses a strength in one area to camouflage a shortcoming in some other area.

Complementary relationship   One in which the distribution of power is unequal, with one party occupying a "one-up" and the other a "one-down" position.

Confirming response   A message that expresses caring or respect for another person.

Conflict   An expressed struggle between at least two interdependent parties who perceive incompatible goals, scarce rewards, and interference from the other party in achieving their goals.

Congruency   The matching of verbal and nonverbal messages sent by a communicator.

Connotation   The emotional associations of a term.

Consequence statement   An explanation of the results that follow from either the behavior of the person to whom the message is addressed or from the speaker's interpretation of the addressee's behavior. Consequence statements can describe what happens to the speaker, the addressee, or others.

Content message   A message that communicates information about the subject being discussed. *See also* Relational message.

Control   The social need to influence others.

Controlling communication   Messages in which the sender tries to impose some sort of outcome on the receiver, usually resulting in a defensive reaction.

Crazymaking   An indirect expression of aggression, delivered in a way that allows the sender to maintain a façade of kindness.

Debilitative emotions   Emotions that prevent a person from functioning effectively.

Decoding   The process in which a receiver attaches meaning to a message. Synonymous with *interpreting*.

Defense mechanism   A psychological device used to maintain a presenting self-image that an individual believes is threatened.

Defensive listening   A response style in which the receiver perceives a speaker's comments as an attack.

Defensiveness   The attempt to protect a presenting image a person believes is being attacked.

Denotation   The objective, emotion-free meaning of a term. *See also* Connotation.

Descriptive communication Messages that describe the speaker's position without evaluating others. Synonymous with "I" language.

Desired self The person we would like to be. It may be identical to or different from the perceived and presenting selves.

Direct aggression An expression of the sender's thoughts and/or feelings that attacks the position and dignity of the receiver.

Disconfirming response A message that expresses a lack of caring or respect for another person.

Disfluency A nonlinguistic verbalization, for example, *um, er, ah.*

Displacement A defense mechanism in which a person vents hostile or aggressive feelings on a target that cannot strike back instead of on the true target.

Double message Contradiction between a verbal message and one or more nonverbal cues.

Emblems Deliberate nonverbal behaviors with precise meanings, known to virtually all members of a cultural group.

Emotive language Language that conveys the sender's attitude rather than simply offering an objective description.

Empathy The ability to project oneself into another person's point of view, so as to experience the other's thoughts and feelings.

Encoding The process of putting thoughts into symbols, most commonly words.

Ends The ultimate goal a person is seeking. Ends are often confused with means, resulting in unproductive conflicts. *See also* Means.

Environment Both the physical setting in which communication occurs and the personal perspectives of the parties involved.

Equality A type of supportive communication described by Gibb, suggesting that the sender regards the receiver as worthy of respect.

Equivocal words Words that have more than one dictionary definition.

Evaluative communication Messages in which the sender judges the receiver in some way, usually resulting in a defensive response.

Exchange theory The theory that people seek relationships in which the benefits they gain equal or exceed the costs they incur.

External noise Factors outside the receiver that interfere with the accurate reception of a message.

Facilitative emotions Emotions that contribute to effective functioning.

Factual statement A statement based on direct observation of sense data.

Fallacy of approval The irrational belief that it is vital to win the approval of virtually every person a communicator deals with.

Fallacy of catastrophic expectations The irrational belief that the worst possible outcome will probably occur.

Fallacy of causation The irrational belief that emotions are caused by others and not by the person who has them.

Fallacy of helplessness The irrational belief that satisfaction in life is determined by forces beyond one's control.

Fallacy of overgeneralization Irrational beliefs in which (1) conclusions (usually negative) are based on limited evidence or (2) communicators exaggerate their shortcomings.

Fallacy of perfection The irrational belief that a worthwhile communicator should be able to handle every situation with complete confidence and skill.

Fallacy of shoulds The irrational belief that people should behave in the most desirable way.

Feedback The discernible response of a receiver to a sender's message.

Feeling statement An expression of the sender's emotions that result from interpretation of sense data.

Gibb categories Six sets of contrasting styles of verbal and nonverbal behavior. Each set describes a communication style that is likely to arouse defensiveness and a contrasting style that is likely to prevent or reduce it. Developed by Jack Gibb.

"I" language Language that describes the speaker's position without evaluating others. Synonymous with *description.*

Illustrators Nonverbal behaviors that accompany and support verbal messages.

Impersonal communication Behavior that treats others as objects rather than individuals. *See* Interpersonal communication.

Impersonal response A disconfirming response that is superficial or trite.

Impervious response A disconfirming response that ignores another person's attempt to communicate.

Inclusion The social need to feel a sense of belonging in some relationship with others.

Incongruous response A disconfirming response in which two messages, one of which is usually nonverbal, contradict one another.

Indirect aggression A concealed attack on another person. *See* Crazymaking.

Inferential statement A statement based on interpretation of sense data.

Influence *See* Control.

Insensitive listening Failure to recognize the thoughts or feelings that are not directly expressed by a speaker, instead accepting the speaker's words at face value.

Insulated listening A style in which the receiver ignores undesirable information.

Intention statement A description of where the speaker

stands on an issue, what he or she wants, or how he or she plans to act in the future.

Interactive communication model   A characterization of communication as a two-way event in which sender and receiver exchange messages in response to one another.

Interpersonal communication   Communication in which the parties consider one another as unique individuals rather than as objects. It is characterized by minimal use of stereotyped labels; unique, idiosyncratic social rules; and a high degree of information exchange.

Interpersonal relationship   An association in which the parties meet each other's social needs to a greater or lesser degree.

Interpretation   The process of attaching meaning to sense data. Synonymous with *Decoding.*

Interpretative reflection   An active listening response in which the receiver goes beyond the speaker's explicit statement, paraphrasing in a tentative way the themes the speaker seems to have been expressing.

Interrupting response   A disconfirming response in which one communicator interrupts another.

Intimate distance   One of Hall's four distance zones, ranging from skin contact to eighteen inches.

Irrelevant response   A disconfirming response in which one communicator's comments bear no relationship to the previous speaker's ideas.

Johari Window   A model that describes the relationship between self-disclosure and self-awareness.

Judging response   A reaction in which the receiver evaluates the sender's message either favorably or unfavorably.

Kinesics   The study of body motion.

Linear communication model   A characterization of communication as a one-way event in which a message flows from sender to receiver.

Lose-lose problem solving   An approach to conflict resolution in which neither party achieves its goals. Sometimes lose-lose outcomes result from both parties' seeking a win-lose victory over one another. In other cases, the parties settle for a lose-lose outcome (for example, compromise) because they cannot find any better alternative.

Manipulators   Movements in which one part of the body grooms, massages, rubs, holds, fidgets, pinches, picks, or otherwise manipulates another part.

Means   Ways of achieving one's ends. There are usually several means to an end. Unproductive conflicts often occur when people argue over a limited number of means rather than focusing on finding the best ones to achieve their ends.

Message   Information sent from a sender to a receiver.

Metacommunication   Messages (usually relational) that refer to other messages: Communication about communication.

Microexpressions   Brief facial expressions.

Mixed emotions   Emotions that are combinations of primary emotions. Some mixed emotions can be expressed in single words (that is, *awe, remorse*) whereas others require more than one term (that is, *embarrassed and angry, relieved and grateful*).

Negotiation   A process in which two or more parties discuss specific proposals in order to find a mutually acceptable agreement.

Neutrality   A defense-arousing behavior described by Gibb in which the sender expresses indifference toward a receiver.

Noise   External, physiological, and psychological distractions that interfere with the accurate transmission and reception of a message.

Nonassertion   The inability to express one's thoughts or feelings when necessary. Nonassertion may be due to a lack of confidence or communication skill or both.

Nonverbal communication   Messages expressed by other than linguistic means.

One-way communication   Communication in which a receiver provides no feedback to a sender.

Operational definition   A definition that refers to observable referents rather than using other words with no apparent concrete meanings.

Paralanguage   Nonlinguistic means of vocal expression: rate, pitch, tone, and so on.

Parallel relationship   One in which the balance of power shifts from one party to the other, according to the situation.

Passive listening   *See* One-way communication.

Perceived self   The person we believe ourselves to be in moments of candor. It may be identical with or different from the presenting and desired selves.

Perception checking   A three-part method for verifying the accuracy of interpretations, including a description of the sense data, two possible interpretations, and a request for confirmation of the interpretations.

Personal distance   One of Hall's four distance zones, ranging from eighteen inches to four feet.

Physiological noise   Biological factors in the receiver that interfere with accurate reception of a message.

Pillow method   A method for understanding an issue from several perspectives rather than with an egocentric "I'm right and you're wrong" attitude.

Presenting self   The image a person presents to others. It may be identical with or different from the perceived and desired selves.

Primary emotions   Basic emotions. Some researchers have identified eight primary emotions: joy, acceptance, fear, surprise, sadness, disgust, anger, and anticipation.

Problem orientation   A supportive style of communication described by Gibb in which the communicators focus on working together to solve their problems instead of trying to impose their own solutions on one another.

Proprioceptive stimuli   Sensations activated by movement of internal tissues (for example, upset stomach, pounding heart).

Provisionalism   A supportive style of communication described by Gibb in which the sender expresses a willingness to consider the other person's position.

Proxemics   The study of how people and animals use space.

Pseudolistening   An imitation of true listening in which the receiver's mind is elsewhere.

Psychological noise   Forces within a communicator that interfere with the ability to express or understand a message accurately.

Public distance   One of Hall's four distance zones, extending outward from twelve feet.

Questioning response   A style of helping in which the receiver seeks additional information from the sender. Some questioning responses are really disguised advice.

Rationalization   A defense mechanism in which logical but untrue explanations maintain an unrealistic desired or presenting self-image.

Receiver   One who notices and attends to a message.

Reference groups   Groups against which we compare ourselves, thereby influencing our self-concept and self-esteem.

Reflected appraisal   The theory that a person's self-concept matches the way the person believes others regard him or her.

Regression   A defense mechanism in which a person avoids assuming responsibility by pretending that he or she is unable to do something instead of admitting to being simply unwilling.

Relational message   A message that expresses the social relationship between two or more individuals.

Relationship   *See* Interpersonal relationship.

Relative words   Words that gain their meaning by comparison.

Repression   A defense mechanism in which a person avoids facing an unpleasant situation or fact by denying its existence.

Respect   The social need to be held in esteem by others.

Selective listening   A listening style in which the receiver responds only to messages that interest him or her.

Self-actualization   One of five of Maslow's needs. The desire to reach one's maximum potential.

Self-concept   The relatively stable set of perceptions each individual holds of himself or herself.

Self-disclosure   The process of deliberately revealing information about oneself that is significant and that would not normally be known by others.

Self-esteem   The degree of regard a person holds for himself or herself.

Self-fulfilling prophecy   A prediction or expectation of an event that makes the outcome more likely to occur than would otherwise have been the case.

Semantic rules   Rules that govern the meaning of language, as opposed to its structure. *See also* Syntactic rules.

Sender   The creator of a message.

Sensing statement   A description of the observable data on which the receiver's interpretation is based.

Significant other   A person whose opinion is important enough to affect one's self-concept strongly.

Simple reflection   An active listening response in which the receiver paraphrases the message the sender has explicitly stated.

Social comparison   Evaluating oneself in terms of or by comparison to others.

Social distance   One of Hall's distance zones, ranging from four to twelve feet.

Social penetration   A model that describes relationships in terms of their breadth and depth.

Spontaneity   A supportive communication behavior described by Gibb in which the sender expresses a message without any attempt to manipulate the receiver.

Stage-hogging   A listening style in which the receiver is more concerned with making his or her own point than in understanding the speaker.

Strategy   A defense-arousing style of communication described by Gibb in which the sender tries to manipulate or deceive a receiver.

Superiority   A defense-arousing style of communication described by Gibb in which the sender states or implies that the receiver is not worthy of respect.

Supporting response   A response style in which the receiver reassures, comforts, or distracts the person seeking help.

Symmetrical relationship   One in which the parties strive to share power equally in all situations.

Syntactic rules   Rules that govern the ways symbols can be arranged, as opposed to the meanings of those symbols. *See also* Semantic rules.

Tangential response   A disconfirming response that uses the speaker's remark as a starting point for a shift to a new topic.

Transactional communication model   A characterization of communication as the simultaneous sending and receiving of messages in an ongoing, irreversible process.

Two-way communication   An exchange of information in which the receiver deliberately provides feedback to a sender.

Verbal Aggression   A defense mechanism in which a person avoids facing unpleasant information by verbally attacking the confronting source.

Whorf-Sapir hypothesis   The theory that the structure of a language shapes the world view of its users.

Win-lose problem solving   An approach to conflict resolution in which one party reaches its goal at the expense of the other.

Win-win problem solving   An approach to conflict resolution in which the parties work together to satisfy all their goals.

"You" language   Language that judges another person, increasing the likelihood of a defensive reaction. *See also* Evaluative communication.

Index

A

Abernathy, Bob, 224
abstraction in language, 161–167
abstraction ladder, 161–162
abstractions, problems with, 162–165
active listening, 243–245, 252–262
   advantages of, 244–245, 255
   defined, 243–244, 252–253
   types of, 254–255
   when to use, 260–262
Active Listening, 245
Adler, Ron, vii, 39
Adventures of Sherlock Holmes, The,
   187
advising response, 247–248
affection, 10
affinity of interpersonal relationships,
   271
Alda, Alan, 281
Altman, Irwin, 286–287
ambiguous response, 307
ambushing nonlistening, 235
Analyzing Interpersonal Attraction,
   282
analyzing statement, 248–249
androgyny, 84
apathy, 313
assertion, 343–344
"At a Lecture—Only 12% Listen," 235
Attitude Survey, 153–154
attribution theory, 114–115
Auden, W.H., 219, 236
Austin, N., 341
avoider, 345
avoiding in relationships, 286

B

Bach, George, 345
Baldwin, James, 337
Barker, Larry, 199
Beck, Aaron, 125
behavioral description, 165–167
beltliner, 346
Benchley, Robert, 129
Benedict Arnold, 346
"Beware of a Crocodile Bag," 82
Berne, Eric, 51

Bierce, Ambrose, 234
Birdwhistell, Ray, 188
Blake, William, 356
blamer, 346
Bleiberg, Aaron, 47
body orientation, 197–200
bonding in relationships, 285
Branden, Nathaniel, 48
Brilliant, Ashleigh, 165
Bruning, James, 177
Buchanan, Barbara, 177
Buchwald, Art, 45
Building a Johari Window, 294
Burke, Edmund, 324
Burkett, David, 322
bypassing, 164

C

Camus, Albert, 325
Carroll, Lewis, 53, 146, 149, 164, 177
Cattrell, Vian, 338
certainty (a Gibb category), 324–325
channels, 11
Chase Stuart, 163
Check Your Competence, 24–25
"Children Learn What They Live," 43
"Child's Garden of Defense
   Mechanisms, A," 314–315
"Cipher in the Snow," 41–42
circumscribing in relationships, 285
Classifying Your Relationship, 18
clear message format, 348–355
   using the, 355
"Close to the Vest," 205–206
clothing, 216–217
cognitive dissonance, 311
communication
   climate, 305
   climates develop, 308–309
   confirming, 305
   defensive and supportive, 319–325
   defined, 15
   disconfirming, 305
   misconceptions, 20–21
   model of, 11–15
   and physical health, 7–8
   principles, 18–20

   process of, 11–15
   reasons for, 6–11
   supportive, defensive and, 319–325
compensation, 312
complementary relationship, 178–179,
   273, 278
confirming response, 305
conflict
   nature of, 337–340
   personal styles of, 340–344
   styles of resolution, 357–360
"Conflict Basic As Hunger," 339
congruency, 194, 225 (*see also* double
   message)
Conjugating "Irregular Verbs," 160
connotative meaning, 158
consequence statement, 352–353
content message 19, 274–275, (*see
   also* relational message)
context of relationships, 269–270
contract tyrannizer, 346
control, 9, 272–273
control (a Gibb category), 320
Cooley, Charles, 35
Coon, Dennis, 70, 349
Coping with Criticism, 332
Coughlin, William J., 151–152
Crane, Stephen, 131
crazymakers (crazymaking), 345–346
Crichton, Michael, M.D., 223
crisis tickler, 345
criticism
   responding nondefensively to,
      325–332
Cummings, E. E., 30

D

"Danny," 257–258
debilitative emotions, 125
decoding, 12
defense mechanism, 311
Defense Mechanism Inventory, 313
defensive listening, 235
defensiveness
   causes and remedies, 310–332
   definition, 310
   in listening, 235

Chapter 3

75 Drawing by M. C. Escher. Used by permission © M. C. Escher Heirs in c/o Cordon Art–Baarn–Holland. **77** From *Crazy Talk, Stupid Talk* by Neil Postman. Copyright © 1976 Dell Publishing Co., Inc. Used by permission. **77** Drawing by Jerry Marcus. Reprinted by permission of Jerry Marcus. **79** Excerpt by Estelle Ramey from *Ms.* magazine. Reprinted by permission of Estelle Ramey. **81** Drawing by Davall from *What's Funny About That?* by the Editors of *This Week*, copyright 1954 by E. P. Dutton & Co., Inc. Reproduced with their permission. **82** "Beware of a Crocodile Bag" by Peter Mayne from *Punch* November 2,1960, pp. 638–639. © 1960 Punch/Rothco. **83** Drawing by John Jonik. Reprinted from *Psychology Today*. Permission granted by cartoonist, John Jonik. **84** "Coming and Going" from *The Deserted Rooster* by Ric Masten. Reprinted by permission of Publisher, Sunflower Ink, Palo Colorado Road, Carmel, CA 93923. **87–88** "Field Experiment: Preparation for the Changing Police Role" by Fred Ferguson. Reprinted by permission of the author. **88** "23 Judges Shaken by Night in Nevada Prison" reprinted by permission of United Press International. **99–100** "Pillow Education in Rural Japan" from *Square Sun, Square Moon* by Paul Reps. Reprinted by permission of Charles E. Tuttle Co., Inc.

Chapter 4

113 Drawing by Weber from *The New Yorker* © 1981 The New Yorker Magazine, Inc. **118** "Cathy" by Cathy Guisewite. Copyright © 1982 Universal Press Syndicate. All Rights Reserved. Reprinted by Permission. **122** "I Remember" from *Love View* by Bernard Gunther. Copyright © 1969 by Bernard Gunther. Reprinted by permission of International Creative Management. **124** "There Are, I Know, Cats" by Lenni Shender Goldstein. Used by permission of the poet. **129** Abridged from p. 127 in *Benchley Beside Himself* by Robert Benchley. Copyright 1925 by Harper & Row, Publishers, Inc. Reprinted by permission of the publisher. **131** "Peanuts" by Charles Schulz © 1963 United Media. Used by permission.

133 "Ziggy" by Tom Wilson. Copyright © 1974. Universal Press Syndicate. Used by permission.

Chapter 5

148 Drawing by Malcolm Hancock. Reproduced by special permission of *Playboy* Magazine: Copyright © 1972 by *Playboy* Magazine. **149** "'Shooting' Report Creates a Stir" from the *Santa Barbara News-Press*, September 9, 1981. Used by permission. **151–152** "The Great Mokusatsu Mistake" by William J. Coughlin. Copyright © 1953 by *Harper's Magazine*. All rights reserved. Reprinted from the March issue by special permission. **154** Reprinted from *Glimpse* No. 29 by permission of the International Society for General Semantics. **157** Excerpt from *Conversation and Communication* by J. A. M. Meerloo. © International University Press. Used by permission. **158** Drawing by Gahan Wilson. © Gahan Wilson. Used by permission. **164** "Cathy" by Cathy Guisewite. Copyright © 1983 Universal Press Syndicate. All Rights Reserved. Reprinted by Permission. **165** From *Pot Shots* by Ashleigh Brilliant. © Copyright Ashleigh Brilliant. Used by permission of Ashleigh Brilliant 117 N. Valerio St., Santa Barbara, CA 93101. **169** "Is Is What Was Was?" by Tom Hicks. Reprinted from *Et Cetera* Vol. XXVIII, No. 3, by permission of the International Society for General Semantics. **171** "The Husbands in My Life" by Mary Grahm Lund. Reprinted from *Et Cetera* Vol. XVII, No. 1, by permission of the International Society for General Semantics. **173** "The Better Half" by Barnes. Used by permission of King Features. All rights reserved. **175–176** "De-Sexing the English Language" by Casey Miller and Kate Swift. Copyright © 1971 by Casey Miller and Kate Swift. Used by permission of the authors. **178** Drawing by Saul Steinberg. Reprinted by permission of Julian Bach Literary Agency, Inc. Copyright © 1965 by Saul Steinberg, from *The Catalogue*. **180** Drawing by Lorenz; © 1985 The New Yorker Magazine, Inc. Used by permission. **181** Excerpt from *I and Thou: Here and Now: Contributions of Gestalt Therapy* by Claudio Naranjo. Used by permission of the author.

Chapter 6

187 From "A Scandal in Bohemia" from *The Adventures of Sherlock Holmes* by Sir Arthur Conan Doyle. Reprinted by permission. **193** "Peanuts" by Charles Schulz. © 1963 United Media. Used by Permission. **195** "Flags" from *Even As We Speak* by Ric Masten. Reprinted by permission of Publisher, Sunflower Ink, Palo Colorado Road, Carmel, CA 93923. **196** "Nothing" from *Love Poems for the Very Married* by Lois Wyse. Copyright © 1967 by Lois Wyse. (World Publishing Company). Reprinted by permission of Harper & Row, Publishers, Inc. **199** "The Look of a Victim" from *Introduction to Nonverbal Communication* by Loretta Malandro and Larry L. Barker. Copyright © 1982 Random House. Used by permission. **200** "I Don't Want to Disgrace You" from *City, Uncity* by Gerald Huckaby. Copyright © 1969 by Gerald Huckaby. Reprinted by permission of Doubleday & Co., Inc. **202** Excerpt from *Zorba the Greek* by Nikos Kazantzakis. Copyright © 1953, 1981 by Simon & Schuster, Inc. Reprinted by permission of Simon & Schuster, Inc. **205–206** "Close to the Vest" from Chapter IV of *Oswald Jacoby on Poker* by Oswald Jacoby. Copyright 1940, 1947 © 1981 by Doubleday & Co., Inc. Reprinted by permission of the publisher. **208** Excerpt from *Sophie's Choice* by William Styron. Copyright © 1979 by Random House, Inc. Used by permission. **208** "Peanuts" by Charles Schulz. © 1976 by United Media. Used by Permission. **213–215** "Touch Sparks Love" by Phyllis Spangler. From August 1971 *Good Housekeeping Magazine* © 1971 by Hearst Corporation. Reprinted by permission. **217** "The Groomer" from *Time* Magazine. Copyright 1972 Time Inc. All rights reserved. Reprinted by permission from *Time*. **219** Postscript of "Prologue: The Birth of Architecture" from *Collected Poems* by W. H. Auden, edited by Edward Mendelson. Copyright © 1965 by W. H. Auden. Reprinted by permission of Random House, Inc. **225** Thurber drawing, "Home," Copyright © 1943 James Thurber. Copyright © 1971 Helen W. Thurber and Rosemary Thurber Sauers. From *Men, Women, and Dogs,* published by Harcourt Brace Jovanovich.

Chapter 7

230 "Conversation" from *Dragonflies, Codfish & Frogs* by Ric Masten. Reprinted by permission of Publisher, Sunflower Ink, Palo Colorado Road, Carmel, CA 93923. **232** From "Everybody's Talkin'" by Fred Neil. Copyright © 1967 Third Story Music. Used by permission. **233** Excerpt from *Time Lurches On* by Ralph Schoenstein. Copyright © 1961, 1962, 1963, 1964, 1965 by Ralph Schoenstein. Reprinted by permission of Doubleday & Co., Inc. **233** Drawing by Saul Steinberg. Reprinted by permission of Julian Bach Literary Agency, Inc. Copyright © 1965 by Saul Steinberg, from *The New World*. **234** "Peanuts" by Charles Schulz. © 1985 United Media. Used by Permission. **235** "At a Lecture—Only 12% Listen" from the *San Francisco Sunday Examiner and Chronicle*. Reprinted by permission. **236** "At a Party" from *Collected Poems* by W. H. Auden, edited by Edward Mendelson. Copyright © 1965 by W. H. Auden. Reprinted by permission of Random House, Inc. **238** "Duet" by Lenni Shender Goldstein. Used with permission of the poet. **239** "Momma" by Mell Lazarus. Used by permission of Mell Lazarus and News America Syndicate. **240** Drawing by Joseph Farris. © 1982. Reprinted by permission of *New Woman* and Joseph Farris. **242** Drawing from *Communication: The Transfer of Meaning* by Don Fabun. Reprinted with permission of Glencoe Publishing Co., Inc. Copyright © 1968, Kaiser Aluminum & Chemical Corporation. **247** "B.C." by Johnny Hart. Used by permission of Johnny Hart and News America Syndicate. **251** "So Penseroso" from *Bed Riddance* by Ogden Nash. Copyright 1935 by Ogden Nash. Reprinted by permission of Little, Brown and Co. **253** Drawing of Chinese character by Angie Av from *Simple Gifts* by Joseph Marchi. Copyright © 1979 by Innographics, 2040 Pioneer Court, San Mateo, CA 94403. Used by permission of the author. **257–258** Excerpt from Thomas Gordon's *Parent Effectiveness Training*. New York: New American Library, 1975. Used with permission. **259** "They Learn to Aid Customers by Becoming Good Listeners" from *The San Diego Union*. Reprinted by permission. **260** "Peanuts" by Charles Schulz. Copyright © 1978 United Media. Used by permission. **262** "The Superactive Listener"

from an article by Kristin Sheridan Libbee and Michael Libbee in *Personnel and Guidance Journal,* Vol. 58, No. 1. Copyright 1979 American Personnel and Guidance Association. Reprinted with permission.

Chapter 8

270 Excerpt from *Notes on Love and Courage* by Hugh Prather. Copyright © 1977 by Hugh Prather. Reprinted by permission of Doubleday & Company, Inc. **270** Drawing by Richter; © 1970 The New Yorker Magazine, Inc. Used by permission. **277** Excerpt from Mark L. Knapp, *Social Intercourse: From Greeting to Goodbye.* Copyright © 1978 by Allyn and Bacon, Inc. Reprinted with permission. **280** Drawing by Dana Freden; © 1979 The New Yorker Magazine, Inc. Used by permission. **281** Remarks made by Alan Alda on TV. Reprinted by permission of *The San Diego Union.* Copyright 1981. **283** Excerpt from Mark L. Knapp's *Interpersonal Communication and Human Relationships*. Boston: Allyn and Bacon. 1984. Reprinted with permission. **287** Model of Social Penetration from *Social Penetration: The Development of Interpersonal Relationships* by Altman & Taylor. © 1973. Used by permission of authors. **289** Drawing by Drucker; © 1981 The New Yorker Magazine, Inc. Used by permission. **290** "B.C." by Johnny Hart. Used by permission of Johnny Hart and News America Syndicate. **292–294** Johari Window Model from *Group Processes: An Introduction to Group Dynamics* by Joseph Luft. Copyright 1963, 1970 by Joseph Luft. Used by permission. **295** From *The Poetry of Robert Frost* edited by Edward Connery Lathem. Copyright 1930, 1939, © 1969 by Holt, Rinehart and Winston. Copyright © 1958 by Robert Frost. Copyright © 1967 by Lesley Frost Ballantine. Reprinted by permission of Henry Holt and Company. **296** "Looking Out, Looking In" from *Stark Naked* by Ric Masten. Reprinted by permission of Publisher, Sunflower Ink, Palo Colorado Road, Carmel, CA 93923. **297** Drawing by Stan Hunt; © 1982 The New Yorker Magazine, Inc. Used by permission. **298** "Miss Peach" by Mell Lazarus. Used by permission of Mell Lazarus and News America Syndicate.

Chapter 9

308 "Peanuts" by Charles Schulz. © 1965 United Media. Used by permission. **309** Drawing by Jules Feiffer. Copyright 1967. Used by permission. **312** Poem from *Knots* by R. D. Laing. Copyright © 1970 Pantheon Books, a Division of Random House, Inc. New York. **317** "Please Hear What I'm Not Saying" by Charles C. Finn. Used courtesy of the poet. **318** "I Am a Rock" by Paul Simon and Art Garfunkel © 1965 Paul Simon. Used by permission. **320** Chart of "The Gibb Categories of Defensive and Supportive Behaviors" from "Defensive Communication" by Jack R. Gibb published in the *Journal of Communication,* Vol. 11:3 (1961), pp. 141–148. Reprinted courtesy of *Journal of Communication* and the author. **324** Drawing by Ross; © 1983 The New Yorker Magazine, Inc. Used by permission.

Chapter 10

339 "Conflict Basic as Hunger" from *Science News.* Copyright 1966 by Science Service, Inc. Reprinted with permission from *Science News,* the weekly news magazine of science. **340** "Peanuts" by Charles Schulz. © 1963 United Media. Used by Permission. **341** From *The Assertive Woman* © 1975 by Stanlee Phelps and Nancy Austin. Reproduced for Holt, Rinehart and Winston with permission from Impact Publishers, Inc., P.O. Box 1094, San Luis Obispo, CA 93406. Further reproduction is prohibited. **360** "Hug O'War" from *Where the Sidewalk Ends: The Poems and Drawings of Shel Silverstein,* Copyright © 1974 by Shel Silverstein. By permission of Harper & Row, Publishers, Inc. **361–362** "A Positive Development in the Philosophy of Divorce" by Beth Ann Krier. Copyright, 1982, Los Angeles Times. Reprinted by permission.

Photo Credits

vii Anthony Rosenwald. *1* © Roger Malloch, Magnum. *4* © Betty Lane, Photo Researchers. *7* © Abigail Heyman, Archive Pictures. *9* © Martin Rotker, Taurus. *9* © Robert V. Eckert, Stock, Boston. *10* © Jean Claude Lejeune, EKM-Nepenthe. *17* © Kent Reno, Jeroboam. *19* © James Carroll, Archive Pictures. *26—27* © Michael O'Brian, Archive Pictures. *28* © Elliott Erwitt, Magnum. *35* © Michael O'Brian, Archive Pictures. *36* © Ferdinando Scianna, Magnum. *40* © Joan Liftin, Archive Pictures. *43* © Jane Kramer, EKM-Nepenthe. *44* © Constantine Manos, Magnum. *49* © Rick Smolan, Stock, Boston. *50* © Maje Waldo, Stock, Boston. *54* © Richard Kalvar, Magnum. *62* © Christopher Brown, Stock, Boston. *66—67* © Ian Berry, Magnum. *70* © Kent and Donna Dannen, Photo Researchers. *76* Drawing by Andre Francois. Reproduced by permission of the artist and John Locke. *80* © Richard Reinhold, EKM-Nepenthe. *85* © Elliott Erwitt, Magnum. *86* © Patricia Hollander Gross, Stock, Boston. *93* © Henri Cartier-Bresson, Magnum. *96* © Betsy Cole, Stock, Boston. *98* © H. W. Silvester, Photo Researchers. *108—109* © Charles Harbutt, Archive Pictures. *110* © Charles Harbutt, Archive Pictures. *112* © John Arms, Jeroboam. *120* © Jeffry W. Myers, Stock, Boston. *121* (top) © Betsy Cole, Stock, Boston; (bottom) © Michael Hayman, Stock, Boston. *122* © Eugene

Richards, Magnum. *128* © Joan Liftin, Archive Pictures. *130* © Sylvia Placy, Archive Pictures. *142—143* © Ira Kirshenbaum, Stock, Boston. *144* The Bettmann Archive. *147* © Christopher S. Johnson, Stock, Boston. *150* © Contact Press Images, Woodfin Camp. *154* © Bohdan Hrynewych, Stock, Boston. *156* EKM-Nepenthe. *170* © Laimute Druskis, Taurus. *174* EKM-Nepenthe. *184—185* © Owen Franken, Stock, Boston. *190* © Charles Harbutt, Archive Pictures. *191* © Owen Franken, Stock, Boston. *192* © Bohdan Hrynewych, Stock, Boston. *195* © Eric Jacquier, Stock, Boston. *198* The Bettmann Archive. *199* © Charles Harbutt, Archive Pictures. *201* © Paul Fusco, Magnum. *203* © John Benton-Harris, Archive Pictures. *204* © The Bettmann Archive. *210* © Eve Arnold, Magnum. *212* © Clif Garboden, Stock, Boston. *217* © The Bettmann Archive. *219* © Elliott Erwitt, Magnum. *222* © Rene Burri, Magnum. *228—229* © Jim Ritscher, Stock, Boston. *232* © Mike Mazzaschi, Stock, Boston. *236* © Jim Anderson, Stock, Boston. *224* © Michael O'Brian, Archive Pictures. *247* © Robert Pacheco, EKM-Nepenthe. *255* © Bruce Roberts, Photo Researchers. *256* © Eve Arnold, Magnum. *259* © Robert Burroughs, Jeroboam. *261* © Charles Harbutt, Archive Pictures. *266—267* © Josef Koudelka, Magnum. *268* © Allan Grant.

271 © Owen Franken, Stock, Boston. *272* © Charles Gatewood, Stock, Boston. *276* © Paul Fortin, Stock, Boston. *279* © Allan Grant. *284* © Bernard Pierrre Wolff, Magnum. *286* © Anthony Rosenwald. *296* © Mike Mazzaschi, Stock, Boston. *302—303* © Leonard Freed, Magnum. *304* © Jeff Albertson, Stock, Boston. *306* © Leonard Freed, Magnum. *311* © Leonard Freed, Magnum. *313* Paintings by Dick Sargeant. Reprinted by permission from *The Saturday Evening Post* © 1954, The Curtis Publishing Company. Photo courtesy Dr. Maurice Riseling, Tustin, California. *316* © Inge Morath, Magnum. *318* © Charles Harbutt, Archive Pictures. *321* © Jon Rawles, Stock, Boston. *327* © Michael O'Brian, Archive Pictures. *331* © Jim Harrison, Stock, Boston. *334—335* The Museum of Modern Art/Film Stills Archives. *336* © Robert V. Eckert, EKM-Nepenthe. *339* © Tom Cheek, Stock, Boston. *340* © The Bettmann Archive. *342* © Joe Kelly, Archive Pictures. *351* © Ian Berry, Magnum. *356* © Frank Siteman, Stock, Boston. *358* © Tim Jewett, EKM-Nepenthe. *359* © Charles Bragg. Reprinted by permission. *360* © Owen Franken, Stock, Boston. *365* © Hold the Mustard.